Introduction to Persuasion and Advocacy

Aspen Custom Publishing Series

Introduction to Persuasion and Advocacy

Compiled by Professors
Jennifer Sheppard
Sue Painter-Thorne
David Ritchie

Mercer University School of Law

Selected pages from

Legal Reasoning and Legal Writing: Structure, Strategy, and Style, 6th Edition
© 2009 by Richard K. Neumann, Jr.

A Practical Guide to Appellate Advocacy, 3rd Edition
© 2010 by Mary Beth Beazley

Legal Writing: Process, Analysis, and Organization, 5th Edition
© 2010 by Linda H. Edwards

Legal Writing, 2nd Edition
© 2011 by Richard K. Neumann, Jr. and Sheila Simon

Advanced Legal Writing: Theories and Strategies in Persuasive Writing, 2nd Edition
© 2008 by Michael R. Smith

Synthesis: Legal Reading, Reasoning, and Writing, 3rd Edition
© 2007 by Deborah A. Schmedemann and Christina L. Kunz

 Wolters Kluwer
Law & Business

CONTENTS

1

APPELLATE PRACTICE

2

PERSUASION GENERALLY

8

STATEMENTS OF THE CASE   75

9

SUMMARY OF THE ARGUMENT   111

10

ARGUMENT SECTION: CREAC ORGANIZATION   115

11

POINT HEADINGS   141

12

UMBRELLA SECTIONS   157

13

ARTICULATING PERSUASIVE RULES & RULE EXPLANATIONS   167

18

DEALING WITH ADVERSE AUTHORITY AND YOUR OPPONENT'S ARGUMENTS

19

FINAL STEPS

20

ORAL ARGUMENT   311

CHAPTER

1

Appellate Practice

A. INTRODUCTION TO APPEALS

A *judgment* (or, in equity, a decree) is the document a court makes to terminate a lawsuit and to record the court's final determination of the parties' rights. If either party has been awarded relief, the judgment may include an award of money or an injunction or a declaration of the parties' rights and so on.

An *order,* on the other hand, is a court's command during the lawsuit that something be done or not be done while the litigation is still in progress. Depending on the complexity of the case and how long it remains in litigation, many orders or only a few might be entered before judgment. Some orders may control the discovery process; others may manage the court's calendar or the trial itself; and still others may award parties provisional relief, such as preliminary injunctions.

The document you have learned to call an opinion or a decision is neither a judgment nor an order. You have by now read hundreds of opinions, most of them in the casebooks you study for other courses, but you might never have seen an order or a judgment. The order or judgment is a court's *action,* and the opinion records the *reasons* for that action.

Within the limitations described in Section 1.D, a party aggrieved by a trial court's judgment or order can appeal to a higher court, where a group of judges will decide whether the trial court's judgment or order was correct or erroneous. The appellate process performs three functions. The most obvious is the correction of errors made by trial courts. A second is to cause the law to be applied uniformly throughout the jurisdiction, to the extent that is practical. And the most intellectually challenging function is the making and clarification of the law itself through precedents that fill gaps in the common law and in statutory interpretation.

In those jurisdictions with two levels, or tiers, of appellate courts, the intermediate court tends to view its goal largely as error correction, although it must also necessarily cause some uniformity in application of the law and, to a lesser extent, engage in law formation and clarification. A court of last resort, on the other hand, generally believes that its task is primarily to make and clarify law. Such a court might be willing to perform the other two functions only where the intermediate court has not merely failed to do so, but failed badly. In the jurisdictions with only one appellate court, of course, that court is responsible for all three appellate functions equally.

Issues of state law can be appealed only once in a one-tiered state and no more than twice in a two-tiered state. In federal courts, there can be no more than two appeals because the federal courts are organized into a two-tiered appellate system. But where an issue of federal law arises in the courts of a state with two appellate tiers, three appeals are possible because the United States Supreme Court has jurisdiction to decide federal issues even if originally raised in a state court. Thus, if a defendant convicted in a California criminal trial believes that his conviction is defective because the trial court misinterpreted the state statute defining the crime (a state issue) and because the trial court erroneously admitted into evidence items seized in violation of the Fourth Amendment to the United States Constitution (a federal issue), the defendant can appeal both issues to the California Court of Appeal. If that court affirms, the defendant may be able to appeal both issues further to the California Supreme Court. If unsuccessful there, the defendant may be able to appeal to the United States Supreme Court, but only on the federal issue because the United States Supreme Court has no jurisdiction over issues of state law.

With some exceptions (explained in Section 1.D), the dissatisfied party generally has a right to seek review by the appellate court immediately above the trial court. That one appeal should be enough, in most instances, to perform the error-correcting function of the appellate process. In a state with a one-tiered appellate system, this appeal *as of right* will be to the state's supreme court, but in other states and in the federal system, it will be to an intermediate court of appeals.

An appeal to a still higher court will probably be *discretionary* because it will not happen unless a court permits it. Although every litigant should be entitled to one appeal for error-correction purposes, the other two functions of the appellate process are performed best if the higher appellate courts in two-tiered jurisdictions can concentrate their efforts on those issues where law needs to be made or clarified. Thus, the higher appellate courts in two-tiered systems tend to be invested with *discretionary appellate jurisdiction,* which means that they are empowered to choose the appeals they will hear and to turn others aside. A party unhappy with a judgment made by a United States District Court, for example, has a right to have that judgment reviewed by a United States Court of Appeal, but there can be no further appeal to the United States Supreme Court unless that court gives its permission by granting a would-be appellant[1] a writ of certiorari.

What kinds of issues are important enough to persuade a discretionary appellate court to exercise its jurisdiction? Generally, such a court may be inclined to grant leave to appeal or a writ of certiorari—the terminology differs from jurisdiction to jurisdiction—where the party seeking permission to appeal wants the court to fill a troubling gap in the jurisdiction's law. A gap might be troubling where lower courts have published decisions coming to opposite results on analogous facts or where a significant part of society needs clarification of the law. Some gaps are large, such as where a court is asked to recognize a cause of action

---

1. In this text, "appellant" refers to the party who commences an appeal, and "appellee" to refer to the opposite party. The terms "petitioner" and "respondent" are used in certain types of appeals in some courts. Before writing a brief, check the court's rules for the terms appropriate to your type of appeal. If you cannot find the answer that way, see how the parties are referred to in a reported case in the same court that *procedurally* resembles your own.

that some states have adopted and others have rejected. But even relatively small gaps can be troubling: a court that has recently recognized a particular cause of action, for example, may need to decide several further appeals until all the elements are clearly defined. If, however, local law is settled, clear, and consistently applied, a discretionary appellate court is likely to give permission to appeal only in two instances. The first is where the intermediate appellate court appears to have made an error that would represent an intolerable failure of the intermediate court's error-correction function. And the second is the unusual situation where the discretionary appellate court is receptive to changing the law.

In the Supreme Court of the United States and in the highest court of every state, all the judges meet together to hear and decide appeals. In some intermediate appellate courts, appeals are heard by panels, rather than by the full court. In the United States Courts of Appeals, for example, decisions are made by panels of three judges; only in rare cases can a party who has lost before a panel persuade the full court en banc to review the panel's decision. Ultimately, of course, the losing party can petition—usually unsuccessfully—for review by the United States Supreme Court.

B.   WHAT HAPPENS DURING AN APPEAL

Although practice varies from court to court, these are the significant events in an appeal:

First, the appellant *serves and files whatever document is required by law to commence the appeal.* If the appeal is as of right, the document is a notice of appeal, an uncomplicated paper that is usually no longer than a page and need not specify grounds for the appeal. If leave to appeal is required, the appellant must petition for it, specifying errors and arguing their importance. The notice of appeal is short and simple because it is a mere declaration that the appellant is doing what a losing party has a right to do. But the petition for discretionary review *asks* for something and is therefore far more complex. Because the denial of such a petition forecloses appeal, its contents are crucial and must be drafted persuasively. The notice or petition must be served and filed within the time required by law, and the time limits can vary from jurisdiction to jurisdiction. A notice of appeal is filed with the clerk of the court being appealed *from,* rather than the clerk of the court being appealed to, but the contrary is true of a petition for leave to appeal.

The second step in the appeal is the *transmittal of the record* from the court below to the court above. Although one might imagine this to be an easy matter of the clerk of one court locating a file and sending it to the clerk of another court, it happens that way only in cases where the record is very simple. A record can be simple, for example, where the appeal is from an order dismissing a complaint for failure to state a cause of action. There the record might not include much more than the complaint, the papers submitted by both parties in connection with the defendant's motion to dismiss, and the court's order.

Most appeals, however, arise only later in the litigation, and in those cases the preparation and transmittal of the record can delay matters for months and add thousands of dollars to the cost of the appeal. Wherever the trial court has held a hearing or trial, one or more court reporters will have to type up a transcript from stenographic notes, a time-consuming process that can produce literally volumes of material.

The third step—required in some jurisdictions and optional in others—is the assembling of an abbreviated version of the record called the *joint appendix* or the *record appendix.*[2] At the appealing party's expense, it is printed in sufficient quantity that a copy can be given to each judge who will hear the appeal. The appellate judges need the joint appendix because the full record can be gargantuan, and the appellate court will have only one copy of it. Even if all the judges hearing an appeal were to work in the same building, it would be impractical to ask them to share a single copy, which may be bound into several bulky volumes. Moreover, in many appellate courts the judges do not do all of their work in the same building: they have additional chambers near their homes, which may be scattered about a state, a district, or a circuit, and they gather only when scheduled to hear oral arguments and to deliberate. Whether chambers are scattered or located centrally, the judges can work most efficiently if each has a copy of the most important parts of the record, and if the full record is available in the clerk's office as a reserve.

Although rules vary from jurisdiction to jurisdiction, there are generally two methods of assembling the appendix. The parties can agree on a joint appendix, but that does not happen often. More frequently, the appellant designates those portions of the record that she or he wants in the appendix; the appellee counter-designates portions to be added; and the portions are combined and printed in the same sequence in which they appear in the full record.

The fourth step is the *drafting of briefs,* which each attorney files with the appellate court and serves on opposing counsel. For some lawyers, this is the most intellectually challenging part of litigation, and it is the subject of Chapters 32 [Richard K. Neumann, Jr., Legal Reasoning and Legal Writing: Structure, Strategy, and Style, 6th ed., (2009)]-4.

In a court without discretionary jurisdiction, the fifth step—and the first in which the appellate court becomes actively involved—is *screening.* Until relatively recently, most appeals were given a full adjudication that included oral argument and a formal opinion, whether or not published. Because of geometrically increasing appellate caseloads, that time is gone forever. Now, in most appellate courts, the appellant must struggle to get a full adjudication, and a wise appellee fights to prevent it. If the appeal is not given full treatment, it is shunted onto a summary adjudication track, where there may be no oral argument or formal opinion, where the judges might not even meet to discuss the appeal. The result of that is usually affirmance. Courts that do not have discretionary jurisdiction use screening to ensure that their error-correction function is performed economically while they concentrate on the most important appeals, which are still given full adjudicatory treatment. The factors that motivate a court without discretionary jurisdiction to give an appeal full adjudicatory treatment are not very different from the factors that would cause a discretionary court to accept an appeal that it is not obligated to decide. Screening is done by one or more specially assigned judges, who may be assisted by attorneys employed by the court to study the briefs and the record. In some courts, every appeal is screened, while in others screening occurs only when a party—usually the appellee—requests

2. The joint appendix is not the Statement of the Case. Nor is it the type of appendix that you might add to the brief to set out in full those statutes that a court might be asked to construe. The Statement of the Case and a statutory appendix are each only a few pages long, and both are part of the brief. The joint appendix is often larger than the brief, and it is bound separately.

it. Some courts require the attorneys to meet with a judge in a pre-briefing or pre-argument conference, which is used partly for screening, partly to clarify and limit the issues, and partly to encourage negotiation between the parties. A few courts without discretionary jurisdiction—most notably the United States Court of Appeals for the Second Circuit—refuse to screen (except perhaps in preargument conferences) and require oral argument in every case on the theory that the screening consumes as much judicial effort as it saves.

In virtually all appeals in a discretionary court and in fully adjudicated appeals in a court without discretionary jurisdiction, the next step is *oral argument*. Each attorney is allotted a predetermined period, such as fifteen minutes, to speak in open court with the judges, who might ask many questions or only a few. Oral argument is particularly satisfying work because it is the attorney's only chance to speak directly with the judges about the problems and issues raised by the appeal. Where the judges and the attorneys are perceptive and well-prepared, oral argument can be the most scholarly type of conversation known to the practice of law,[3] and it is the subject of Chapter 34 [Richard K. Neumann, Jr., Legal Reasoning and Legal Writing: Structure, Strategy, and Style, 6th ed., (2009)].

After oral argument, the judges confer and discuss the merits of the appeal. In some courts, this conference occurs on the same day as argument; in others, it may happen several days later. One judge is selected to write the court's opinion. In some courts, the assignment is made by chance rotation, but in others it is made by the presiding judge. In the United States Supreme Court, the assignment is made by the most senior judge among the majority. The assigned judge drafts an opinion and circulates it to the other judges, who might suggest changes or might draft and circulate concurring or dissenting opinions of their own. In routine appeals, the draft majority opinion is often quickly approved, and concurrences and dissents may be held to a minimum. But in more complex and troubling cases, views can change, and an opinion originally written as a dissent might be transformed into the court's opinion, while the original majority draft is demoted into a dissent.

If the losing party can appeal further, the whole process may begin again, with a new notice of appeal or petition for some sort of leave to appeal—more likely the latter, as one moves up the appellate ladder.

C.   THE ROLES OF THE BRIEF AND OF ORAL ARGUMENT

To understand the different roles of the brief and oral argument, you must be able to visualize the effect of increasingly crowded dockets on the work of appellate judges.

---

3. "I can see the Chief Justice as he looked at that moment. [B]efore counsel began to argue, the Chief Justice would nib his pen; and then, when everything was ready, pulling up the sleeves of his gown, he would nod to the counsel who was to address him, as much as to say 'I am ready; now you may go on.' I think I never experienced more intellectual pleasure than in arguing that novel question to a great man who could appreciate it, and take it in; and he did take it in, as a baby takes in its mother's milk." This is how Daniel Webster recalled his oral argument to the Supreme Court, led by Chief Justice John Marshall, in *Gibbons v. Ogden*, 22 U.S. (9 Wheat.) 1 (1824), one of the leading Constitutional cases of the nineteenth century. (The quote is from 1 Charles Warren, *The Supreme Court in United States History* 603 (Little, Brown & Co. 1935).) Although pens have not been "nibbed" since they were made from feathers, modern appellate litigators know every other sensation Webster described.

Depending on the court, an appellate judge might in a month hear oral arguments and confer with colleagues on several dozen appeals, and in many courts substantially more than a hundred. For each appeal, the judge will have to read at least two briefs and in multiparty cases or public-interest cases[4] a half-dozen briefs or more, together with portions of the record. The judge will have to write majority opinions in a proportion of the appeals not summarily disposed of; on a five-judge court, for example, each judge is assigned one-fifth of the majority opinions. In addition, the judge may feel obligated to write several concurring or dissenting opinions. The judge will also have to read opinions drafted by other judges and at times will write memoranda to colleagues suggesting changes in those opinions. The judge will spend a fair amount of time reading some of the cases and statutes cited to in all these briefs and draft opinions. And the judge may have screening and other administrative responsibilities. With all this work, the typical appellate judge would find it a luxury to spend as much as an hour reading the average brief, and the time available is often no more than half an hour per brief. That is why briefs, although large, must be carefully crafted to reveal their logic while demanding the least possible time and effort from the reader. Judges spend more time, of course, on briefs where the appeal raises deeply troubling issues than on briefs in more routine cases. And a judge who writes an opinion might read the briefs more thoroughly than one who does not.

In a work environment like this, the brief and oral argument are asked to perform different functions. Each is critical, but in a different way.

The brief can best lay out the theory of the appeal by explaining in persuasive detail the authorities and evidence on which a favorable decision should be based. A successful brief not only persuades the judge that your client should win, but it can also be used as a manual explaining to the judge exactly how to make the decision and how to justify it in an opinion. A judge may use the brief for initial screening, to prepare for oral argument, to prepare for the conference with other judges, and while writing the opinion.

The oral argument, on the other hand, can do two things better than the brief can. First, in oral argument the attorney can more immediately motivate the court by focusing on the most important ideas—the few facts, rules, and policies—that most make the attorney's theory of the appeal compelling. Although the brief should show both the forest and the trees, the oral argument can be a bit more powerful at illuminating the forest. (Conversely it is a horrible medium through which to examine the trees.) Second, in oral argument the attorney can try to discover, through the bench's questions, each judge's doubts, and the attorney can on the spot explain exactly why those doubts should not prevent a ruling in the attorney's favor. Oral argument, in fact, is the attorney's only opportunity to learn directly from the judges the precise problems they have with the attorney's theory. Oral argument's greater efficiency at these two things is not a reason to skimp on trying to accomplish them through the brief as well. Oral argument lasts only a few minutes, and memories of it can fade. The brief, on the other hand, has permanence: it is always among the judge's working materials, and it "speaks from the time it is filed and continues through oral argument, conference, and opinion writing."[5]

---

4. In cases that would affect groups that are not parties, the court may grant permission for non-parties to file briefs as amicus curiae (friends of the court).

5. Herbert Funk Goodrich, *A Case on Appeal—A Judge's View*, in *A Case on Appeal* 10-1 (ALI-ABA 1967).

Briefs and oral argument have assumed these roles more through evolution than by design, as courts have gradually realized how different kinds of information can most efficiently be conveyed. Detail is communicated best in writing, which can be studied. Conversation, on the other hand, both encourages spontaneous dialogue and lends itself to the broad sweep of underlying ideas.

D.   LIMITATIONS ON APPELLATE REVIEW

You have already learned of one limitation on the scope of appeals: many courts have *discretionary appellate jurisdiction* and use it to avoid deciding large numbers of cases.[6]

In addition, appellate courts will disturb an order or judgment only if it is based on *reversible error.* An appellate court will affirm unless the appellant can point to a specific error by the trial court that the law considers ground for reversal. Be careful of two kinds of situations, neither of which will lead to a reversal. In the first, the result below seems unfortunate, but no error by the court below can be identified. In the absence of reversible error, an appellate court must affirm what the trial court did. That is because an appeal is only a review for the kind of mistake the law categorizes as error. In the second situation, error can be identified, but it did not cause the order or judgment appealed from. Even if the result below was unfortunate, and even if the court below committed error, an appellate court will reverse only if the result below is traceable to the error. Error that affected the result below is called *material* or *prejudicial.* Error without such an effect is called *harmless.*

To identify error, and to figure out whether it was material or harmless, start with the procedural posture in the trial court. For example, assume that the plaintiff has requested a particular jury instruction; that the trial court denied the request and instead gave another instruction; that the jury returned a verdict for the defendant; and that, on the basis of the verdict, the trial judge entered a judgment for the defendant. The issue on appeal cannot be whether the plaintiff should have won below; rather, it is whether the trial court so erroneously instructed the jury that the entire case should be tried again to a jury properly instructed. If the instruction was error, but if the record shows that the error was not so material as to lead the jury astray, the error was harmless and will not be reversed. The error would be harmless, for example, if the evidence in support of the verdict was so overwhelming that a properly instructed jury would have returned the same verdict.

Appellate review is mostly (but not entirely) limited to *issues of law.* A jury's verdict is a purely factual determination and thus not generally reviewable on appeal. Where a case is tried to a judge without a jury, the judge makes findings of fact that correspond to a jury's verdict. Are judicial findings of fact reviewable on appeal? In some appellate courts, they are not. In the appellate opinions you have read for other courses, you may have noticed the stock phrasing used in such courts to introduce a factual finding over which an appellant is unhappy: "The trial court found as a fact, not reviewable by us on appeal, that . . . " In other appellate courts, judicial fact finding is reversible—but only

6. See Section 1.B.

if it is "clearly erroneous."[7] This standard is harder on appellants than that applied to a trial judge's conclusions of law, which can be reversed if merely "erroneous."

Appellate review is further limited to *issues preserved below*. An issue is preserved below only if the appellant raised it and only if the court below decided it. Because an appeal is a review for error, an appellate court will not concern itself with matters the lower court did not decide. An issue is waived unless the appellant raises the issue below and seeks a decision there. There are two exceptions to the requirement that error be preserved. The more rigid exception concerns subject matter jurisdiction, defects in which can never be waived because a court should on its own motion refuse to adjudicate a case outside its authority. The more flexible exception concerns "plain error," which is error so fundamental to the process of justice that it cries out to be corrected even if the appellant seemed unconcerned about it when it happened. Be careful: "plain error" cannot be invoked whenever an appellant has been careless below. Only in the rarest of circumstances is an appellate court so shocked that it will save an appellant who, in the court below, did not even try to save himself.

What happens where, in the trial court, a party advanced several different grounds, all in support of the same relief, and where the court granted the relief on one ground and ignored the others? The ignored grounds are not waived: it would have been pointless to press for a decision on them. In fact, if an appellate court rejects the ground adopted by the lower court, the appellate court can still affirm, if it chooses to do so, on one of the grounds ignored by the lower court. A correct result is affirmable even if the lower court accomplished it for the wrong reason.

Appellate review is still further limited to issues that are actually *raised on appeal*. An appellate court does not survey the record below looking for error: in the adversary system, that is the job of the appellant's attorney. If the appellate court has discretionary appellate jurisdiction, an issue is waived unless raised in the petition seeking leave to appeal. In any appellate court, an issue is waived unless raised in the brief. Only very rarely does an appellate court overlook this limitation and itself raise an issue not asserted by a party. This happens most strikingly when the appellant's attorney has not realized that some of the judges are interested in changing rules of law that the parties have taken for granted.

Appellate courts will review only *final* orders and judgments. Although finality generally occurs when the court below has nothing left to adjudicate, in many jurisdictions the law hedges the concept often. One reason is that finality itself is not always easy to recognize. Sometimes an order may plainly be one that does not terminate litigation on a particular issue, but it may so alter the positions of the parties that the practical effect would be final if not reviewed. Another reason is that it is hard to accomplish the purpose of the final order rule—economizing everyone's effort and speeding the real end of a lawsuit by reviewing on appeal only the trial court's finished product—without at the same time precluding review of some types of interlocutory orders that ought not be immune from appellate scrutiny. As a result, most jurisdictions have developed, through statutes and case law, a number of exceptions to the final order rule.[8]

7. *See, e.g.,* Rule 52(a) of the Federal Rules of Civil Procedure. This is explained more fully in Section 4.A.
8. For example, under 28 U.S.C. §§1291 and 1292, federal appellate courts are authorized to review a variety of interlocutory orders, including orders granting or denying preliminary

Appellate courts generally refuse to consider facts that do not appear in the trial court's record (also called the *record below*). You can determine whether a fact is in the record by focusing on the procedural posture in the trial court. If the order appealed from is one dismissing a complaint for failure to state a cause of action, a fact is in the record if it is alleged in the complaint. That is because, for the purpose of deciding a motion to dismiss a complaint, all facts properly pleaded are treated as though they could be proven. (And, of course, on such a motion the only factual record before the trial court is the complaint itself.) But the situation is different where the motion in the trial court challenged a party's evidence rather than allegations (see §§24.2.1 and 24.2.3). For example, assume that the appeal is from a summary judgment. If a fact appears as an allegation in a pleading but does not appear in any evidentiary form, it is not "a fact in the record" because the motion below tested evidence and not allegations. (If you are confused about the difference between facts, allegations, and evidence, see §17.1 [Richard K. Neumann, Jr., Legal Reasoning and Legal Writing: Structure, Strategy, and Style, 6th ed., (2009)].)

There are two exceptions to the rule against considering facts outside the record. One involves the doctrine of judicial notice, through which a court—trial or appellate—will, without evidence, accept as proven certain facts that are beyond dispute. Do not make more of this than it really is. The following are examples of the kinds of indisputable facts of which courts will take judicial notice: A meter equals 39.37 inches. Cleveland is in Cuyahoga County, Ohio. March 15, 2001, was a Thursday.

The other exception is for what are called "legislative facts," which are generalized social, economic, or scientific information that guides a court in the development of law—as opposed to the "case facts" or "adjudicatory facts," which are the specific events that transpired between the parties. Legislative facts can include empirical data on the detrimental effects of racial segregation, or on the national deterioration of groundwater quality, or on the ways consumers use videocassette recorders—all useful in determining public policy. Although the adversary system is not very efficient at collecting legislative facts,[9] appellate courts need them when making or changing law. And although legislative facts can be placed in the trial record, an attorney called in to handle an appeal sometimes needs to put before the appellate court legislative facts not developed in the record below. The appellate attorney might include in the brief published empirical research that complements but does not crowd out the legal analysis that is the core of argument.[10] Empirical material added on appeal is not set out in the Statement of the Case, because it is not part of the record below. Rather, it appears, with citations, in the Argument, most often in support of policy contentions.

The law presumes an order or judgment to be correct unless an appellant demonstrates that the appropriate *standard of review* has been violated. The standard of review will vary from one kind of appeal to another. Think of it as a

---

injunctions. And the Supreme Court has developed a collateral order doctrine "whose reach is limited to trial court orders affecting rights that will be irretrievably lost in the absence of an immediate appeal." *Richardson-Merrell, Inc. v. Koller,* 472 U.S. 424, 430-31 (1985).

9. Legislatures are far more efficient at using the knowledge of experts, collecting and studying empirical research, and weighing conflicting scientific analyses. Courts must rely on individual attorneys, who are rarely able to match the resources of legislative staffs.

10. A brief that uses a fair amount of empirical material is called a "Brandeis brief," after the successful one submitted by Louis D. Brandeis in *Muller v. Oregon,* 208 U.S. 412 (1908).

formula of deference. Depending on the type of decision made below, the appellate court may defer—to a specified degree—to the decision of the trial court judge. Some types of decisions, for example, will be reversed if "erroneous"; others only if "clearly erroneous"; and yet others only if "an abuse of discretion." (Standards of review are explained in detail in Section 4.A.)

Finally, appellate courts are temperamentally "affirmance-prone." Unless deeply troubled by what happened below, an appellate judge will be inclined to affirm for several reasons. The trial judge handled the problem first-hand and might know more than distant appellate judges reading a cold transcript of the testimony. Because many trial decisions must be made instantly "in the heat of battle," it is unrealistic to expect perfection from a trial judge. Every reversal disturbs the status quo, and circumspect people like judges are not comfortable disturbing the status quo unless it is truly necessary. And reversals impose tangible costs, which can be large, such as retrials.

E. APPELLATE JURISDICTION AND STANDARDS OF REVIEW

Understanding some basic principles about the various courts and their powers will help you to make decisions as you prepare your written and oral arguments. Your arguments will be different if you are writing a brief to a trial court as opposed to an appellate court. In the appellate system, you may argue differently to an intermediate court of appeals as opposed to a court of last resort. On the one hand, intermediate courts of appeals must hear every appeal (with few exceptions)[11] and must follow the decisions of the courts above them. Courts of last resort, on the other hand, usually have some authority to decide which cases they will hear[12] and the authority to make new law.

This chapter briefly explains principles of appellate jurisdiction before discussing how writers can use the appropriate standards of review in both appellate briefs and motion briefs.

1. Jurisdiction in Courts of Last Resort

A "court of last resort" is the highest court in a particular legal system. It is the last court to which litigants can resort when seeking resolution of a legal issue. In the federal system, the United States Supreme Court is the court of last resort, and the majority of its cases come from the United States Courts of Appeals of the various circuits. In state systems, the highest court of appeals—often called the Supreme Court—is the court of last resort, and it generally hears cases from that state's intermediate appellate courts. The United States Supreme Court can hear appeals from state courts of last resort, but only if the issue is a matter of federal law. For example, the Court may hear an appeal in order to determine whether a state court has interpreted a law in a way that may have conflicted with the United States Constitution.

---

11. *See, e.g.,* Tenn. R. App. P. 3; Fed. R. App. P. 3.
12. *See, e.g.,* Ohio Sup. Ct. Prac. R. II, §1(A) (listing "appeals of right," "claimed appeals of right," "discretionary appeals," and "certified conflict cases"). *See also* U.S. Sup. Ct. R. 10.

Most courts of last resort are not merely courts of error; that is, they do not take cases simply because one party claims that there was an error of law in a lower court decision. For example, Rule 10 of the Rules of the Supreme Court of the United States explicitly says that "[a] petition for a writ of certiorari [the main method for gaining access to the Court] is rarely granted when the asserted error consists of erroneous factual findings or the misapplication of a properly stated rule of law." Instead, a court of last resort takes cases in order to resolve pressing issues, and it may refuse to take cases unless or until it believes that its intervention is necessary.[13] Two factors make it more likely that the United States Supreme Court, for instance, will grant a petition for a writ of certiorari. First, the Court frequently grants certiorari if it believes that a state court or a lower federal court of appeals is misinterpreting or misapplying the Court's jurisprudence. Second, and more commonly, the Court will grant certiorari when two or more courts are in conflict over an interpretation of the federal Constitution, or when courts are in conflict over a question of federal law.[14]

Interestingly, the Court does not always grant certiorari immediately when either of these factors is present. It is not uncommon for the Court to let a conflict simmer for a few years, with different lower courts writing decisions either way. The Court may use this method purposefully, to benefit from the analysis and reasoning of several different lower courts. By allowing several opinions to be written on a subject, the Court can assess several different resolutions and analyses of the same issue.

Perhaps for these reasons, the Court attaches no precedential value to the denial of a petition for a writ of certiorari. That is, a denial of certiorari does *not* indicate that the Court approves of the decision below. Rather, it means only that the Court did not believe, for whatever reason, that it was an issue that was worthy of its review *at that time*.

2. *Jurisdiction in Intermediate Courts of Appeals*

The rules are somewhat different in intermediate courts of appeals. Generally, state and federal intermediate courts of appeals will hear any appeal of a final order if the appellant has met specified procedural guidelines.[15] The United States Courts of Appeals have jurisdiction over appeals from all final decisions of the United States District Courts.[16] The courts of appeals also have jurisdiction to hear appeals from a variety of other judicial and quasi-judicial bodies, including, for example, appeals to enforce or challenge orders of the National Labor Relations Board.[17]

13. The Ohio Supreme Court, for example, distinguishes between "claimed appeals of right" and "discretionary appeals." Ohio Sup. Ct. Prac. R. II, §1. It then decides whether to grant each type of appeal, depending on whether the appeal meets the court's standards, e.g., whether the appeal involves any "substantial constitutional question" (one standard for claimed appeals of right) or asserts a "question of public or great general interest" (one standard for discretionary appeals). Ohio Sup. Ct. Prac. R. II, §1(A)(2), (A)(3).

14. *See generally* U.S. Sup. Ct. R. 10.

15. *See, e.g.*, Ohio R. App. P. tit. II, R. 3; Fed. R. App. P. 3. Appeals of certain criminal appeals may have to meet different standards. In most situations, federal courts of appeals have discretion whether to hear interlocutory appeals according to the guidelines in 28 U.S.C. §1292. *See also Mohawk Indus. v. Carpenter*, 130 S. Ct. 599, 603 (2009) (interlocutory decisions adverse to attorney-client privilege do not qualify for immediate appeal); *Coopers & Lybrand v. Livesay*, 437 U.S. 463, 475 (1978) (describing court discretion).

16. 28 U.S.C. §1291.

17. 29 U.S.C. §160(e), (f).

Federal intermediate courts of appeals may decide cases without oral argument. Although, according to the rules, oral argument is presumed, a three-judge panel can vote unanimously that oral argument is unnecessary in a given case for any of the following three reasons:

1. The appeal is frivolous.
2. The dispositive issue or issues have been authoritatively decided.
3. The facts and legal arguments are adequately presented in the briefs and record, and the decisional process would not be significantly aided by oral argument.[18]

What this rule means in practice is that a large percentage of cases are assigned to the so-called summary docket, and many of those are decided based on memoranda submitted by law clerks and staff attorneys who have reviewed the party briefs. The courts' statistics indicate that in 2008, a typical year, more than 65 percent of the appeals terminated on the merits were decided without oral argument.[19] When cases are on the summary docket, some judges make their decisions based on staff memoranda alone; they may not read the briefs in full at all. The practical brief-writer will presume that oral argument will not be granted, and will write a brief that can persuade a law clerk as well as a judge.

18. Fed. R. App. P. 34(a)(2).
19. Federal Judicial Center, *U.S. Courts of Appeals: Appeals Commenced, Terminated, and Pending (Excludes Federal Circuit)*, http://www.uscourts.gov/judicialfactsfigures/2008/Table202.pdf (last visited Mar. 30, 2010). *See also* Patricia M. Wald, *19 Tips from 19 Years on the Appellate Bench*, 1 J. App. Prac. & Proc. 7, 9 (1999) (estimating that 60 percent of cases nationwide are decided without oral argument).

CHAPTER

2

Persuasion Generally

1. *Compelling Arguments Persuade*

Arguments provide the logical reasons to accept the theory. They're based on the interpretation of statutes and judicial precedent as well as public policy. In all your courses, you've been immersed in arguments since you started law school.

2. *How Arguments and Stories Work Together*

Suppose you're being asked to believe the last sentence in the paragraph below:

> Almost 80% of the people of India live on less than $2 a day, according to the World Bank, and a typical work day might be 12 or 15 hours long. Millions of Indians are self-employed as farmers or other small producers or as sellers or resellers. *A self-employed Indian in these circumstances can earn dramatically more income and reduce work hours substantially simply by owning a cell phone.*

Assume that you're a government official with a budget. You're besieged by people and organizations asking you to spend money on projects they consider important. For every request you agree to, you will have to turn down a hundred more. You're asked to spend a million dollars in a seed program to get cell phones into the hands of Indian farmers, fishermen, sellers, and resellers. A logical argument in support of this plan appears in the left column below. Read it and ask yourself whether it persuades you and, if so, how *deeply* you are persuaded ("this might work," "it probably will work," or "absolutely will it work!"). Then read the story in the right column.[1]

---

1. The details in both columns come from Kevin Sullivan, *Dialing Up a Sea of Change*, Wash. Post, Oct. 15, 2006, at A01, and Kevin Sullivan, *Cell Phone Turns Out To Be Grocer's Best Buy*, Wash. Post, Oct. 14, 2006.

A Logical Argument

In economics, a market is any system in which buyers and sellers can transact business with each other. In an *efficient* market, all information is available to everybody so that each buyer or seller can make rational decisions. If all information is available to everybody, each person gets the most value out of the market, and waste is minimized. Developing countries are plagued by inefficient markets, where people don't have access to the information they need, and where buyers and sellers have a hard time even finding each other.

The smallest and cheapest medium for transmitting information instantly is a cell phone. It is cheaper than a Blackberry or a laptop and does not require telephone wires or a wifi infrastructure. All it requires is cellular transmitting towers, which are being built anyway throughout the world to satisfy the wealthy. A cell phone also does not require any education. A person who does not know how to read or write can operate a cell phone. Although the U.S. cost of buying a cell phone and paying the monthly service charges would consume most of an average Indian worker's income, costs in India are lower than in the United States. Cell phone air time in India costs less than one U.S. cent per minute.

Cell phone subscribers in India have grown from 1.6 million in 2000 to 125 million in 2006 (when cell phones in India outnumbered land lines by three to one).

"One element of poverty is the lack of information," according to C.K. Prahalad, a professor in the business school at the University of Michigan, who has studied how cell phones can help people escape poverty. "The cell phone gives poor people as

A Story

Devi Datt Joshi sells fruit and vegetables on the street in New Dehli. He has no store and no refrigerator. He has only a three-wheeled cart and a regular spot on the street where his customers know to find him.

Well before dawn, he goes to a fruit and vegetable wholesale market and buys as much produce as he thinks he can sell that day. That pre-dawn decision of how much to purchase—based on his prediction of how much his customers will want to buy by afternoon—is crucial to whether he will make any money at all that day and how hard he will have to work to make it. Without refrigeration in a hot climate, if he buys more than he can sell, he will have to throw away most of the excess because it will not be fresh the following day. If he buys too little, he loses sales and risks also losing frustrated customers to some other produce seller.

Making this kind of gamble, he used to earn an average of $3 a day for more than 12 hours of work. Once his morning customers had bought what they wanted, he would have to wander through the streets looking for buyers for the produce that was left.

Everything changed when he got a cell phone.

Customers call him the night before to place their orders. He knows how much to buy, and they can depend on him to supply what they need. He buys a little extra for customers who do not call ahead, and he sells that, too—without having to wander in the streets.

"The mobile phone has more than doubled my profits," he told an American newspaper reporter. He now earns $8 a day for about eight hours of work. He still gets up before dawn but his work day ends before lunch. He has been able to hire an

A Logical Argument	*A Story*
much information as the middleman."	assistant and put his children into better schools.
Therefore, if small businesses in India start using cell phones, their owners, employees, and customers will all be better off.	And the food he buys rarely goes to waste.

Again, you're the government official with a budget. Suppose you hear the story above without the logical argument. The story makes you interested, even excited, about the idea, but you don't yet have confidence that this is a good use of development money. Now you hear the logical argument, which gives you the confidence you didn't have before. The story provided motivation, and the logical argument finished the job by justifying with logic.

The story and the logical argument work together. Neither alone would be sufficient. The story touches us and motivates us to act. The logical argument explains why the story is valid and provides a justification a decision-maker can rely on to explain the decision to someone else. Persuading thus requires telling a good story *and* making an argument that *work together*.

3. Overcoming Your Weaknesses Persuades

Which cases and statutes favor your adversary? Which facts work to your adversary's advantage? What are your adversary's strongest arguments? And what will your adversary say to fight against your arguments? The answers to these questions identify your weaknesses.

Hiding from these problems will not make them slink away in the night. You have to confront and defeat them. "Be truthful in exposing . . . the difficulties in your case," an appellate judge has written. "Tell us what they are and how you expect to deal with them."[2] If you fail to mention your weaknesses, and if you fail to explain why they do not undermine your case, the court probably will hold them against you.

Acknowledging your challenges can preserve your reader's trust in you. Tell the reader the bad news with your spin on it. Think of inviting a friend to your apartment for an impromptu study session. If the apartment is a mess, you might explain—sheepishly and before you bring the guest in—that your place is usually cleaner. Then your guest could still think well of you, despite your mountains of dirty laundry.

4. Solving Judges' Problems Persuades

Make it easy for the judge to rule in your favor.

Imagine an office with a desk, a side table, and book shelves. On the desk and side table, many files are piled up. Each file is very thick and represents a motion or appeal the judge must decide. The judge behind the desk has a huge docket of cases. To decide each of them, the judge must read what the lawyers

---

2. Roger J. Miner, *Twenty-five "Dos" for Appellate Brief Writers*, 3 Scribes J. Leg. Writing 19, 24 (1992).

have submitted—page after page after page of reading—and for most judges there are too few hours in the day to read all that.

Most writing seen by judges has a high word-to-meaning ratio: Many words are used to express a given amount of meaning. If your writing has a low word-to-meaning ratio—no wasted words, every word carrying weight—your work will be more persuasive simply because for the judge it solves a problem instead of creating one. You may have spent days writing a motion memo or brief, but the judge needs to be able to read it—and *completely understand it*—in minutes. To persuade, you will spend more time writing so the judge can spend less time reading.

Think about the other problems a judge might have with your memo or brief, and solve them, too, so that judges find your writing a pleasure. For example, the font should be easy to read, and the headings should look like genuine headings (and not like part of the text). A visually inviting document is more likely to be read with care. See Appendix H [Richard K. Neumann, Jr. and Sheila Simon, Legal Writing, 2nd ed., (2011)].

5. *Professionalism Persuades*

Professionalism generates trust. Judges respect lawyers who hold themselves to high professional standards. One mark of professionalism is to produce memos and briefs that are sharply focused on the issue, carefully reasoned, thoroughly researched, precisely written, and diligently proofread, with careful attention to details.

A. EXPLOITING POSITIONS OF EMPHASIS

Within the brief itself, the practical advocate exploits physical positions of emphasis. Your words will have more impact if you place them in certain physical locations within the brief. Scientists called psycholinguists have learned that readers pay more attention to certain physical positions in a document. Any time there is extra white space in a document—at the beginning or ending of a paragraph, for example, or more importantly, at the beginning or ending of a document element such as a point heading section, a statement of the case, or a summary of the argument—readers subconsciously pay more attention.[3] Just as Scrabble players angle to put certain letters or words in certain positions on the game board, you should angle to put your strongest arguments and statements in certain positions in your brief.

A reader's attention peaks to varying degrees when reading all titles and headings, as well as when reading the first and last paragraphs in document segments (e.g., the statement of the case, the argument), the first and last paragraphs in point heading sections, and even the first and last sentences in paragraphs. To a lesser degree, information at the beginning or ending of a sentence is also in a position of emphasis,[4] as is a short sentence, particularly

3. *See generally* Robert P. Charrow & Veda R. Charrow, *Making Legal Language Understandable: A Psycholinguistic Study of Jury Instructions*, 79 Colum. L. Rev. 1306 (1979).
4. *See, e.g.,* Joseph M. Williams & Gregory G. Colomb, *Style: Lessons in Clarity and Grace* 82-86, 91-94 (10th ed., Longman 2010). *See also* Laurel Currie Oates & Anne M. Enquist, *The Legal Writing Handbook* §§17.5.3, 18.12.5, and 24.6.3 (4th ed., Aspen 2006).

when it is placed within a group of longer sentences. Finally, within a sentence itself, the reader pays more attention to the information expressed in the sub-ject-verb combination, with particular emphasis on the verb.[5]

Positions of deemphasis are positions that are away from white space, away from the natural breaks that the reader takes while reading. In other words, "middles": the middle of a point heading section, a paragraph, a document. A series of long sentences slows down comprehension by making the reader work harder to assemble the information in the sentences. Within a sentence, moving information from a verb to a noun, or removing an actor (that is, the person or thing that "verbed") by using passive voice, also deemphasizes information.

Thus, to make your brief more persuasive, focus your attention. Decide (a) what information you want to emphasize and (b) what information you want to deemphasize. Exploit the positions of emphasis by making sure that you fill them with the information that is most important to the case and/or the reader. Lessen the impact of negative information by placing it in positions of deemphasis. The various positions of emphasis present many opportunities for persuasion in your brief.

1.   *Persuading with Large-Scale Organization*

To exploit the reader's peak attention at the beginning of the argument sec-tion, begin with your best point rather than starting with a weak point and lead-ing up to a strong point. Judge Coleman advises you to "[p]resent your strongest points first to try to capture votes early."[6] When you start your argu-ment with a weak point, your reader may think, "Is this the best they can do?" That bad impression can taint the rest of the argument. On the other hand, when you start your argument with a strong point, the reader's first thought is "This is a good argument," and that impression can carry over to the rest of the points that you make.

One exception to this guideline is a case that could be governed by a thresh-old issue. If you are arguing a standing or jurisdictional issue in addition to a substantive issue, for example, logic dictates that you should place the substan-tive issue second. It could be ludicrous to argue for several pages about a legal error as to one of the case's issues, and then move to the point that the court should not be hearing the case at all.

Particularly in a lengthy brief, your last argument is also in a position of emphasis. For example, if you have decided that you must include a despera-tion argument in your brief, you may *not* want it to be the last thing the court reads. Just as you want to start with a good impression, you also want to leave the court with a good taste in its mouth. Whenever possible, move that weak argument to the second-to-the-last position to help keep your image as a credi-ble, responsible advocate.

---

5. This point is now a staple for most legal writing teachers. It was famously articulated by Richard Wydick in a law review article that later became a book: Richard C. Wydick, *Plain English for Lawyers* chs. 3-4 (5th ed., Carolina Academic Press 2005). *See also* Williams & Colomb, *supra* n. 14, at Lesson 3. See Section 11.4.4(a) below for specific examples.

6. James H. Coleman, Jr., *Appellate Advocacy and Decisionmaking in State Appellate Courts in the Twenty-First Century*, 28 Seton Hall L. Rev. 1081, 1083 (1998).

2. *Persuading Within Each Issue*

Exploit natural positions of emphasis within each unit of discourse as well. Make sure that the first paragraph in the section articulates the point you are proving in that section. The CREXAC formula recommends using the first paragraph in the section to state your conclusion as to the issue addressed in that section. Similarly, end the section by using the connection-conclusion to restate your main assertion and connect it to your argument. In this way, your point is driven home in the precise locations where the reader is likely to be paying the most attention.

In general, state your conclusion as if it is the truth, not as if it is one of many possible ways for the court to rule. Do not begin any section of your argument by stating the issue as a question that must be resolved:

Bad Example

The next issue turns on whether an officer issuing a citation in lieu of arrest should have the same authority to search as an officer who is placing a suspect under arrest.

Instead, articulate the issue as an assertion:

Good Example

Officers who issue citations in lieu of arrest and officers who actually arrest should have the same authority to search for weapons that might be used against them.

Similarly, do not label your arguments as your arguments. The petitioner should avoid statements like "The Petitioner argues. . . . " If you do this with any argument, you might as well start every argument with that statement, for each argument in the brief is one of the petitioner's arguments. The entire document is labeled as "Brief for the Petitioner," so the court knows that it will be made up of petitioner's arguments. Do not remind the court of your partisan slant by labeling individual arguments within the brief.

Finally, if practical or ethical requirements require you to discuss cases or arguments that do not support your client's case, you may decide to deemphasize them by including them in the middle of a point heading section rather than highlighting them in a separate section. For example, in the example below, the writer of a respondent's brief in *Minnesota v. Carter*, 525 U.S. 83 (1998), is trying to emphasize connections to cases in which the Court found that a privacy right existed and to deemphasize cases in which the privacy right was found not to exist. Notice how the topic sentence (the first sentence in the paragraph) states the rule in a way that is favorable to her clients before the paragraph discusses a case in which the Court found no expectation of privacy:

> Indeed, this Court has consistently found that legitimate expectations of privacy exist outside the home, as long as the circumstances are those in which most people would normally expect to enjoy a feeling of privacy. <u>Olson</u>, 496 U.S. at 96-97. Accordingly, this Court has found that defendants did not have a legitimate expectation of privacy in the contents of a car in which they were merely passengers, and where they had expressed no expectation of privacy in the areas of the car searched. <u>Rakas v. Illinois</u>, 439 U.S. 128, 148-49 (1978). The <u>Rakas</u> Court specifically refused to make a finding as to whether guests in houses or apartments would be treated similarly, noting that "cars are not to be treated identically with houses or apartments for Fourth Amendment purposes." <u>Id</u>. at 148 (citations omitted).

Of course, "hiding" a contrary authority in the middle of a paragraph or section will not turn a losing case into a winner. You must also show why the substance of your argument is more effective. Using positions of emphasis and deemphasis simply makes it easier for the reader to see and understand the validity of your points. In the example above, the writer takes care to emphasize the Court's distinction between cars and houses, and ends her paragraph on that point, rather than on the negative point about the passengers' expectations of privacy.

3. *Persuasive Paragraph Structure*

Within the argument, review the topic sentences to make sure that you are not wasting the first sentence in a paragraph on a case citation or a description of authority case facts. Instead, exploit these positions of emphasis by using them to state rules or make favorable assertions about the result you want the court to reach. If you must deal with a negative authority, you may wish to sandwich it between positive assertions. (See Chapter Ten [Mary Beth Beazley, A Practical Guide to Appellate Advocacy, 3rd ed., (2010)] for more information about writing effective topic sentences.)

In addition to considering structure within paragraphs, you can use a short paragraph to create a position of emphasis. Although conventional wisdom frowns on one-sentence paragraphs, on rare occasions, one- or two-sentence paragraphs can effectively draw attention to a statement. Conversely, you can bury a negative point in a long paragraph to lessen its impact. Take care when using this tactic, however; if the paragraph is so long that it distracts or annoys your reader, you will cancel out any benefit from the persuasive technique.

In this example, the writer applies the law to the facts in one long paragraph that provides the details to establish that respondents did not manifest a subjective expectation of privacy:

Bad Example

In the case at bar, both Respondents' behavior and their location within the apartment indicate that they had no actual, subjective expectation of privacy.

Respondents manifested at most a hope that no one would observe their unlawful pursuits inside Thompson's apartment. Unlike the defendant in <u>Katz</u>, Respondents introduced no evidence of conduct that demonstrated an intent to keep their activity private. Nothing in the record indicates Respondents took any action to preserve their privacy. Though the blinds were drawn, there is no indication that Respondents drew them. <u>See</u> Record at E-2, E-10. On the night in question, Respondents were present in a first-floor apartment that had several windows at ground level. Record G-26. The windows faced a public area that apartment residents and nonresidents frequented. Record G-69, G-70. As darkness fell in early evening, Respondents sat illuminated under a chandelier light at a table directly in front of one of these windows. Record G-13. Only a pane of glass and a set of blinds that featured a series of laths, Record G-50, separated Respondents from the adjacent common area. On the night in question, the blinds, though drawn, had a gap in them large enough for a citizen who passed by and an officer who stood a foot or more from the window to view easily the entire illuminated interior scene. Record G-13.

The only difference in the following example is that the writer has provided paragraph breaks to draw attention to the fact that respondents did not take action to preserve their privacy. The white space creates a position of emphasis that highlights not only the one-sentence paragraph, but also the paragraphs around it, particularly the paragraph after the one-sentence paragraph.

Good Example

In the case at bar, both Respondents' behavior and their location within the apartment indicate that they had no actual, subjective expectation of privacy. Respondents manifested at most a hope that no one would observe their unlawful pursuits inside Thompson's apartment. Unlike the defendant in <u>Katz</u>, Respondents introduced no evidence of conduct that demonstrated an intent to keep their activity private.

Nothing in the record indicates Respondents took any action to preserve their privacy.

Though the blinds were drawn, there is no indication that Respondents drew them. <u>See</u> Record at E-2, E-10. On the night in question, Respondents were present in a first-floor apartment that had several windows at ground level. Record G-26. The windows faced a public area that apartment residents and nonresidents frequented. Record G-69, G-70. As darkness fell in early evening, Respondents sat illuminated under a chandelier light at a table directly in front of one of these windows. Record G-13. Only a pane of glass and a set of blinds that featured a series of laths, Record G-50, separated Respondents from the adjacent common area. On the night in question, the blinds, though drawn, had a gap in them large enough for a citizen who passed by and an officer who stood a foot or more from the window to view easily the entire illuminated interior scene. Record G-13.

As you might imagine, you should use this method sparingly. A one sentence paragraph is a dramatic technique; if overused, it will lose its drama and annoy the reader.

4.   *Persuading with Sentence Structure*

There are many ways that sentence structure can create positions of emphasis; this chapter will address three that most legal writers can conquer. First, by using active voice and strong verbs rather than passive voice and nominalizations, you can focus the reader's attention on subjects and verbs that emphasize actors and actions that support your argument. Second, you can alternate independent and dependent clauses in sentences to emphasize the information in the independent clauses and deemphasize the information in the dependent clauses. Finally, using short sentences in the middle of a series of long sentences can pique the reader's interest.

a.   **Subject-Verb Combinations**

Just as readers pay more attention to information at beginnings and endings of documents and sections, they place subconscious emphasis on the information in the verb position of a sentence. They also subconsciously look for the verb's actor—that is, the noun that is "doing" the action of the verb. You can control what information is in the subject position and the verb position, and where (or whether) you include information about the verb's actor.[7] How you arrange that information will affect how your reader comprehends your message. To take a simple example:

> The dog bit the child.
> The child was bitten by the dog.
> The child was the victim of a dog bite.
> A dog bite occurred.
> A bite occurred.

Most of these sentences convey essentially the same information. You have a dog, you have a child, and the child gets bitten. In some of the sentences, however, the reader has to work harder to get that information; in others, even when working hard, the reader can get only a vague idea of what has happened.

Thus, the way you arrange the information within a sentence can have a big impact on how quickly the reader understands the message. Information arrangement can sometimes have an impact on how the reader feels about the message as well. Take a look at these two versions of a sentence that might appear in a letter from a law school to its students:

> We are increasing your tuition by $5,000 per year.
> A tuition increase of $5,000 will occur.

The first sentence is more likely to make the student angry at the law school faculty and administration. Through their use of subjects and verbs, they have taken direct responsibility for the tuition increase. The reader instantly understands the message, and its clarity may intensify the reader's reaction. The second sentence is a more typical example of how to deliver bad news. No one takes responsibility for the dramatic tuition increase; it seems to come from the

---

7. *See, e.g.,* Williams, *supra* note 14, at Lesson 3.

outside. Thus, the clarity that is helpful when easy understanding is beneficial ("the dog bit the child") has quite a different impact on those rare occasions when the writer wants to blunt the impact of the message ("we are increasing your tuition").

Writers can learn a wide variety of techniques to control the clarity of a sentence. Two of the most important are (1) using or avoiding nominalizations, and (2) using or avoiding passive voice.

i. Nominalizations

A nominalization is, quite simply, a verb that has been turned into a noun. Turning a verb into a noun does not violate any rules of grammar, but it does slow down the reader's comprehension of the information in that word. For example, the word *decision* is a nominalization of the verb *decide.* When you move the word *decide* from the verb position into the noun position, you lessen the impact of that verb:

> We decided to raise your tuition.
> We made a decision that a tuition increase is necessary.

Look at these two different questions presented that describe the actions of a police officer looking into the windows of a basement apartment from a distance of 12 to 14 inches. Notice how nominalizations in one illustration and concrete verbs and other language in the other may change the perception of what the officer did:

> Under the Fourth Amendment, does an officer's sight observation into a home, made while standing a foot or more from the apartment and peering through gaps in the covered window of the apartment, constitute an unlawful invasion of curtilage?
> Under the Fourth Amendment, does an officer invade the curtilage of an apartment house when he stands within inches of the building and looks through a gap in the blinds of a basement apartment?

Neither sentence is wrong; they are just different ways of conveying the same information, depending on what the writer wants to emphasize.

You can often find nominalizations by looking for words that end in *-ence,* *-ment,* or *-ion.* In the alternative, review your sentences (particularly overlong sentences) and circle just the verbs. When you find sentences in which all of the verbs are weak words without a lot of concrete meaning—e.g., *was, is* (or other *to be* verbs), *had, made, occurred, existed,* etc.—look for verbs that are "hidden" in nominalizations in that sentence.

When deciding whether or how to change nominalizations back into verbs, ask yourself whether you want to put more emphasis on the information that you nominalized. The answer may not always be yes. Sometimes, as in the tuition letter example above, you may want to deemphasize certain negative information. Unless that is the case, however, identify your hidden verbs, find the actor that is "verbing" (i.e., doing the action of that verb), and create a stronger, more easily comprehensible sentence.

When looking for nominalizations, you might find a sentence like this:

> This case is a recognition of the coercion that may happen during an arrest.

If you circled the verbs in this sentence, you would identify the rather weak verbs *is* and *may happen*. Once you identify the hidden verbs *recognize, coerce,* and *arrest,* you can work on making the sentence more clear:

> In this case, [someone] recognized that [someone] may coerce [someone] when [someone] arrests [someone].

Revising to avoid nominalizations provides a hidden benefit: You may realize when information is missing from the sentence. Thus, your next step might be to include some of the missing information. On the other hand, you may decide to leave some of the nominalizations as is:

> In this case, the Court recognized that police officers may coerce citizens during an arrest.

Knowing how nominalizations can affect your writing can help you to make your points more explicitly when clarity is your goal and to blunt your message when it is appropriate to do so.

ii.   *Active and Passive Voice*

Most writers know about "tense" as it relates to verbs; they consciously decide, for example, whether to write in present tense or past tense. Many, however, are unfamiliar with the concept of "voice." No matter what its tense, a verb can be cast in active or passive voice. Voice relates not to the tense of the verb, but to whether the verb's actor is in the subject position of the sentence or clause. If the verb's actor is in the subject position, the verb is said to be cast in "active voice"; if the verb's actor is not in the subject position, the verb is said to be cast in "passive voice." In almost every case in which the verb is cast in passive voice, the subject of the sentence is receiving the action of the verb rather than doing the action of the verb. Thus, in most cases, the subject of an active voice sentence or clause is "verbing"; the subject of a passive voice sentence or clause is "being verbed." Think of the subject passively receiving the action of the verb to help you remember the meaning of "passive voice":

> The court decided the case. (Active voice; the subject [court] is verbing [deciding].)
> The case was decided by the court. (Passive voice; the subject [case] is being verbed [being decided].)

Passive and active voice verbs, like nominalizations, are grammatically correct. Because active voice verbs can be understood more quickly, however, you should use active voice unless you have a specific reason to use passive voice. Passive voice is preferred on occasion:

1. if you don't know who the actor is or you want to hide or deemphasize the actor ("a decision was made to raise your tuition" hides the decision maker);
2. when you want to emphasize the object of the verb rather than the subject ("she was hit by a car" emphasizes the victim of the accident); or
3. when your sentence just works better with the object of the verb in the subject position (e.g., when the subject is unusually long or when the object is a more familiar person or concept than the subject).[8]

Look at these examples of similar information included in passive voice and active voice sentences. Try to decide which sentence might be better given various rhetorical situations:

> The statute was designed to limit the number of aliens who can bypass INS-mandated citizenship procedures.
> Congress designed the statute to limit the number of aliens who can bypass INS-mandated citizenship procedures.
> The evidence in question was obtained by observations made by a police officer looking into the window of an apartment.
> A police officer obtained the information for the warrant when he looked into the window of the apartment.
> A person's home, the place where he lives, has been recognized by this Court as the most important place in which to invoke Fourth Amendment protection.
> This Court has recognized that a person's home, the place where he lives, is the most important place in which to invoke Fourth Amendment protection.

As at least two of these illustrations show, using active voice results in shorter, more direct sentences. The point of this section, however, is not to say that you must eliminate all nominalizations and all uses of passive voice; rather, the point is that you should use nominalizations and passive voice only when you have a good reason to do so. When there is no reason to use them, use more direct, easier-to-understand subjects and verbs.

b. Independent and Dependent Clauses

The second way that a writer can use sentence structure to persuade is by using dependent clauses to "hide" information that the writer wants to deemphasize. In grammatical terms, an independent clause is a clause that can stand on its own as a sentence, while a dependent clause cannot. Readers subconsciously put more emphasis on information in independent clauses and less emphasis on information in dependent clauses. It may help to think of information in a dependent clause as being in parentheses: The reader often sees it as a less important part of the sentence. Notice how switching information between the dependent and the independent clauses subtly changes the impression that the sentence gives the reader:

---

8. *See* Mary Barnard Ray & Jill J. Ramsfield, *Legal Writing: Getting It Right and Getting It Written* 279-81 (4th ed., Thomson/West 2005).

First, although the area where the officer stood is close to Thompson's apartment, the communal nature of the grounds makes the claim of curtilage less valid.

First, even though the officer stood in a communal area, the place where he stood was so close to Thompson's apartment that it increases the validity of the curtilage claim.

Though the blinds were drawn at the time of the alleged search, there is no indication that Respondents drew them.

Although there was no testimony at the trial about who closed the window blinds, the fact remains that at the time of the search the blinds were drawn.

On the night in question, the blinds, though drawn, had a gap in them large enough for a citizen who passed by and an officer who stood a foot or more from the window to view easily the entire illuminated interior scene.

On the night in question, the blinds had been drawn to cover the entire window, even though a small gap remained.

Again, all of these sentences are grammatically correct. The sentence you choose to write will depend on which information you want to emphasize and deemphasize.

c.   Using Short Sentences for Emphasis

One guideline for sentence structure and length is the same for legal writing as for any kind of expository writing: Sentence variety is good. One short sentence can be effective. More than two short sentences are not. Compare the two examples below, and notice the impact of a short sentence and concrete language as compared to a long sentence and more abstract language:

Thus, society will be prepared to recognize Respondents' expectation of privacy in Thompson's apartment as reasonable only if they were present on the premises for a purpose society deems permissible and valuable. Respondents, who introduced no evidence that they were anything other than temporary, transient visitors on the premises for the sole purpose of conducting illegal business, simply do not belong to the class of individuals who have an expectation of privacy that society is prepared to recognize as reasonable.

Thus, society will be prepared to recognize Respondents' expectation of privacy in Thompson's apartment as reasonable only if they were present on the premises for a purpose society deems permissible and valuable. Respondents were there to bag cocaine. They simply do not belong to the class of individuals who have an expectation of privacy that society is prepared to recognize as reasonable.

To make the point even more emphatic, put the short sentence in a position of emphasis at the end of a paragraph:

Thus, society will be prepared to recognize Respondents' expectation of privacy in Thompson's apartment as reasonable only if they were present on the premises for a purpose society deems permissible and valuable. Respondents were there to bag cocaine.

Use this persuasive technique with care. If you use too many short sentences in your document, they will lose their dramatic effect.

5. *Effective Word Choice*

When it comes to word choice, the effective advocate must make decisions carefully. Certainly, it makes sense to choose words that have connotations that are more positive for your client's side. Think in terms of "claimed" instead of "stated," "admitted" instead of "said." Once again, however, you must take care. It is easy to push this method into ridiculousness:

Bad Example

The officer was able to peer into the private window of the apartment because he abandoned the sidewalk, marched across the grass, and wedged himself behind bushes placed 24 to 48 inches away from the window. Record G-43.

Good Example

The officer was able to approach a window belonging to the apartment by leaving the sidewalk leading up to the building, walking onto the grass and behind bushes located two to four feet away from the window. Record G-43.

Most writers know enough not to use exclamation points to emphasize points or to write in all capital letters to draw attention to a point. Yet many writers try to intensify their arguments with words that are just as ineffective as these techniques. *Clearly, obviously, of course,* and *it is evident that* have been so overused that they go beyond having no meaning to having a negative meaning. Many writers refer to them as "negative intensifiers."

Instead of using a negative intensifier, identify and use "positive intensifiers." Positive intensifiers include *precisely, exactly, specifically, significantly,* and *explicitly.* These words are positive intensifiers because they signal that the writer will be giving the reader concrete information about what happened to parties before the court or in a case, about what a rule says, or about how a rule relates to the client's facts. Note the differences between the two examples below:

Bad Example

Second, the drawn blinds on the window of the apartment through which the police officer peered clearly indicated that the apartment was not open to public observation.

Good Example

The blinds were drawn in the apartment precisely because the occupants did not want the apartment to be open to public observation. Whoever drew the blinds, that person was taking steps to prevent members of the public—and the police—from looking through the windows.

Of course, if you use a positive intensifier, you have to follow it up with the specifics that it promises, lest it become a negative intensifier:

Good Example

The court specifically noted that its holding was not predicated on antiquated notions about the relative abilities of men and women; rather, the holding was predicated on the objectively verifiable fact that women could not serve in combat roles in the United States armed forces.

Whenever you use a positive intensifier, ask yourself how the law or the facts show that this information is *precisely, specifically,* or *significantly* true, and then include those details in your writing.

6.   *Persuasive Punctuation*

Writers use punctuation marks to organize sentences and the words within sentences. They also use punctuation to show relationships between and among phrases and clauses within sentences. Legal writers can use punctuation marks to emphasize information and to imply relationships when argument is inappropriate. Three types of punctuation marks are particularly helpful: the semicolon, the dash, and the colon.

a.   **The Semicolon**

Semicolons are used in two circumstances. First, semicolons punctuate a list when items in the list contain internal commas. In legal writing, this situation occurs most frequently when writers cite multiple cases in support of a proposition. Second, semicolons separate two independent clauses. This technique is frequently used to highlight some sort of relationship between the two clauses, as in the following examples:

Good Example

Section 1409(a) does more than legislate on the basis of this stereotype beyond infancy; it applies this stereotype *forever.*

Good Example

The Supreme Court has allowed a warrantless search when a custodial arrest is performed largely because the suspect already will be subject to substantial interference with individual liberties; similar intrusions exist when a citation is issued in lieu of an arrest.

Semicolons can also be used to juxtapose information in a way that leads the reader to draw a conclusion. In *Minnesota v. Carter,* for example, the petitioner might want the reader to draw the conclusion that the respondents did not have a legitimate expectation of privacy in the apartment in which they were bagging cocaine. This conclusion could be supported by the lack of a connection between the respondents and Thompson, who lived in the apartment. In the statement of facts, it is inappropriate to argue, but the writer could use a semicolon to juxtapose two facts that might lead the reader to the desired conclusion:

Good Example

Nothing in the record indicates any personal or social relationship between Thompson and the Respondents; none of Respondents' personal effects were found in the apartment, and they did not present any evidence that they were overnight guests. See Record E-4, E-7, and G-2.

Because you can state conclusions rather than imply them within the argument, this method is used to greatest effect in the statement of the case. But you can always use semicolons to make clear a close relationship between two ideas. In any case, it is a good idea to be able to write sentences in a variety of ways. Proper use of semicolons separates sophisticated writers from unsophisticated ones; it's a good idea to learn to use them properly.

b. The Dash

Mary Barnard Ray and Jill Ramsfield refer to the dash as "the gigolo of the punctuation world,"[9] and too many dashes may give your writing an inappropriately casual tone. The dash is used effectively, however, to highlight information in the middle of a sentence. Proper use of the dash consists of a space, two hyphens, and another space (at which point many word processing systems properly convert the two hyphens to a connected line called an *em dash*). When you use a dash on either side of an interrupting phrase, it creates white space on either side of the phrase and thus creates a position of emphasis within the sentence. Notice how the writer of a *Miller v. Albright* brief uses the dash to

9. Ray & Ramsfield, *supra* n. 18, at 109.

highlight a comparison between how the law treats the foreign-born children of United States citizens in different relationships:

Good Example

Children in the first two groups—those who are "legitimate" and those who have a United States citizen mother—are United States citizens by birthright. See 8 U.S.C. §1401(g) (1994). Children in the last group, however—those "illegitimate" children with United States citizen fathers—may receive their fathers' citizenship only after clearing several hurdles.

To avoid making your writing sound too casual, don't overuse the dash, and use it only to set off an interrupting phrase in the middle of a sentence rather than as a means to add an afterthought at the end of a sentence.

c.   The Colon

The colon is my favorite way to use punctuation for emphasis. Most writers use it only to introduce a long quotation or list, and it is properly used for that purpose. But it is very effectively used within sentences both to highlight information and to explain or elaborate on the information that came before the colon, as in these examples:

Good Examples:

Through gaps in the drawn horizontal mini-blinds on the window, Officer Thielen observed the same scene the informant had described to him: two males and one female sitting at a kitchen table handling a white powdery substance. Record E-2.

In Chimel, this Court examined the search-incident-to-an-arrest exception to the warrant requirement and made note of the two major policy justifications for the search: preserving officer safety and preventing the destruction of evidence by the suspect. 395 U.S. at 763.

The cases in which no substantial relation was found have one common element: They reject gender stereotypes that are little more than vestiges of past discrimination.

The information that comes after the colon elaborates on or explains the information that comes before the colon. In a sense, the colon prompts the reader to ask a "who, what, when, where, why, or how" question that the information after the colon answers. In the last example above, for example, the colon prompts the reader to ask "what is the common element?" The information after the colon answers this question.

The shorter the phrase or sentence after the colon, the more emphatic the use of the colon is. Note the differences among these examples: As the phrases get shorter, the sentences get more emphatic.

Good Examples

As illustrated by the plight of Lorelyn and Charlie Miller, these burdens can become insurmountable: Section 1409(a) will prevent Mr. Miller and Ms. Miller from ever legally proving that they have a close family relationship unless this court refuses to accept the irrebuttable gender stereotype in Section 1409(a).
The government argued that the observation was analogous to looking through a knothole or an opening in a fence: "If there is an opening, the police may look."
The record indicates that Respondents engaged in only one activity while inside Thompson's apartment: bagging cocaine.

Grammatically, the information that precedes the colon should be a complete sentence. The information that comes after need not be. Do not capitalize the first word after a colon unless the information after the colon could be a separate sentence; even then, you may choose to leave it uncapitalized. If, like me, you fall in love with the colon, you should still avoid overusing it.

CHAPTER

3

Appellate Briefs

A. AN OVERVIEW OF THE BRIEF

Although it might seem that a brief, being a court document, would have a more standardized format than would an internal document like an office memo, a comparison of sample briefs will quickly dispel this notion. Trial-level briefs differ from appellate-level briefs; state court briefs of each level differ from federal court briefs of each level; briefs filed in one jurisdiction differ from briefs filed in another; briefs originating from one firm differ from briefs originating from another; and response and reply briefs differ from opening briefs. It might seem that the most one can say about the components of all briefs is that they all have an Argument!

This variety is no cause for concern, however. The following sections describe each component you might see or be asked to include in your brief. Simply include those required by the applicable court rule,[1] by local or firm custom, or by the particular circumstances and legal issues of the case. The trial- and appellate-level briefs in Appendices D, E, and F [Linda H. Edwards, Legal Writing: Process, Analysis, and Organization, 5th ed., (2010)] can serve as examples of customary formats. When in doubt about whether to include a particular section, consult the court rules or ask your teacher or the attorney for whom you are writing the brief. If no instructions are available, here are guidelines for which components to include and the order in which to place them.

Component	Trial-Level Brief	Appellate Brief
Caption	Yes	Yes
Table of Contents	Yes, if the brief is long and complex	Yes
Table of Authorities	Only if the brief cites many sources	Yes
Statutes Involved		

---

1. *See, e.g.*, Fed. R. App. P. 28.

Component	Trial-Level Brief	Appellate Brief
	Yes, if providing the text would help the reader	Yes, if feasible; otherwise provide statute's text as an Appendix
Opinion Below	No	Optional
Jurisdiction	No	Optional unless court rules require
Standard of Review	Only if the trial court is reviewing a matter decided in another forum	Yes[2]
Preliminary Statement[3]	Optional	Optional
Questions Presented[4]	Yes, if the brief covers several issues	Yes
Statement of Facts[5]	Yes	Yes
Summary of Argument	Only if the brief is long and complex	Yes
Argument	Yes	Yes
Conclusion	Yes	Yes
Certificate of Service	Yes	Yes

1. Caption. The function of the Caption is simply to identify the case and the document. For examples of customary formatting on the page, refer to the captions and titles for the briefs in Appendices D [Linda H. Edwards, Legal Writing: Process, Analysis, and Organization, 5th ed., (2010)], E, and F [Linda H. Edwards, Legal Writing: Process, Analysis, and Organization, 5th ed., (2010)]. In cases with multiple parties, the brief's caption need list only the first plaintiff and the first defendant followed by "et al."[6] The caption must include the case number assigned by the court.[7] Court rules may require additional information such as the name and address of the attorney or the name of the assigned judge. The caption also must include the title of the document, for example, "Brief in Support of Defendant's Motion to Dismiss." For an appellate brief, the caption will appear on a cover sheet of the color prescribed by the

---

2. Some court rules require the Standard of Review to constitute its own section. If the court rules are silent as to placement, the writer can cover the Standard of Review early in the Argument section rather than in a separate section.

3. Sometimes called "Introduction."

4. Sometimes called "Statement of Issues." Some court rules require the Questions Presented to appear as the first item after the Caption.

5. Sometimes called "Statement of the Case."

6. *Et al.* is an abbreviation for *et alii,* meaning literally "and others." *See* Fed. R. Civ. P. 10(a).

7. *See* Fed. R. Civ. P. 10(a).

court rules. For a trial-level brief, the caption can appear on a cover sheet (as shown in the sample trial-level brief in Appendix D [Linda H. Edwards, Legal Writing: Process, Analysis, and Organization, 5th ed., (2010)]) or simply at the top of the first page of the brief.

2. Table of Contents.   The Table of Contents should include each component that follows the Table of Contents and should designate the number of the page on which that component begins. For the Argument section, include each point heading and subheading, using the same style of print (all caps or initial caps only) as used for that heading in the body of the argument.

3. Table of Authorities.   List the authorities cited in the brief and the page(s) on which each is cited. If the authority is cited so frequently throughout the brief that listing individual page numbers would be unwieldy, use the term *passim* (meaning "throughout") instead. List the authorities in separate categories, such as cases, statutes, treatises, articles, and miscellaneous. If the brief cites many cases, consider organizing the cases by issuing court, starting with the highest level and going to the lowest level. Within each list of cases, order the entries alphabetically.

4. Statutes Involved.   This section sets out the text of the relevant part(s) of any statutes at issue. It allows the reader to refer conveniently to the statutory language. If the relevant language is short enough, place it in a section entitled "Statutes Involved." If its length would make placement within the brief unwieldy, consider placing it in an Appendix and referring the reader to the Appendix on your first mention of the statute.

5. Opinion Below.   This section of an appellate brief tells the reader where to find the opinion from the court below. Provide the page numbers within the court record and, for a reported opinion, the citation.

6. Jurisdiction.   This section provides the citation to the statute conferring on the court the jurisdiction to hear this type of case.

7. Standard of Review.   Set out the appropriate standard for the court's review of the legal issue(s) raised by the brief. Include citations to relevant authority establishing the standard.[8] If the brief addresses more than one issue, remember that the standard of review might be different for each.

8. Preliminary Statement (or Introduction).   The Preliminary Statement summarizes the procedural history that has led to the occasion for the brief, that is, the pending motion or appeal.

9. Question(s) Presented (or Statement of Issues).   The Question(s) Presented section states the legal issues addressed by the brief and the factual context in which they have arisen. Articulating Questions Presented offers an important opportunity for advocacy, requiring skill and care. Chapter 15 explains the drafting of Questions Presented in more detail.

---

8. *See* section III of Chapter 19 [Linda H. Edwards, Legal Writing: Process, Analysis, and Organization, 5th ed., (2010)] for a discussion of standards of review.

10. Statement of Facts (or Statement of the Case).   This section sets out the facts relevant to the legal issues addressed by the brief, as well as the context necessary for understanding those facts. Like the Questions Presented, the Statement of the Case is an important opportunity for advocacy, requiring skillful and careful drafting. Chapter 22 [Linda H. Edwards, Legal Writing: Process, Analysis, and Organization, 5th ed., (2010)] explains drafting a Statement of Facts in more detail.

11. Summary of Argument.   The Summary of the Argument is exactly that— a concise statement of the nub of your argument on each issue. It is often the first place a reader looks to answer the question, "OK, so what is this case about?" Consequently, it should be drafted to make the strongest, most effective presentation of the core of your argument(s). The Summary must not simply repeat the argument headings. For each issue, it should set out, more fully than a point heading can, the application of the relevant rule to the most compelling facts. Usually one paragraph covers each issue.

12. Argument.   The Argument contains the fully articulated argument on the legal issues. Just as your working draft became the Discussion section of the office memo, your working draft will become the Argument section of the brief. Chapters 18 [Linda H. Edwards, Legal Writing: Process, Analysis, and Organization, 5th ed., (2010)] through 15 will cover the process of creating the Argument section of the brief.

13. Conclusion.   Two schools of thought exist on Conclusions. The more traditional approach is a *pro forma* statement of the precise relief sought.

> For the foregoing reasons, the Court should reverse the trial court's opinion and remand this case for trial.

For appellate briefs, use this more traditional form of conclusion.

However, for trial-level briefs, if court rules and local customs permit, consider a Conclusion that gives you one last opportunity for advocacy. This sort of Conclusion should still be short—no more than half a double-spaced page— but it could gather together the most compelling arguments on each issue in support of its assertion of the correctness of the result you seek.

> Therefore, as this brief has demonstrated, the circumstances of this case render the covenant's terms unreasonable. The covenant would protect Carrolton to a degree far greater than necessary, while devastating both Ms. Watson's fledgling business and her personal finances. Further, it would significantly infringe upon the public's interest in reasonably priced health care equipment, merchandise vital to the community's well-being. For these reasons, Carrolton's Motion for Summary Judgment should be denied.

14. Certificate of Service.   Ethical rules prohibit *ex parte* contact with the judge about the merits of a legal matter.[9] Court rules require copies of all filings to be served upon all parties, via their attorneys.[10] Also, ethical rules prohibit contact with a party represented by an attorney except through the party's

---

9. Model R. Prof. Conduct 3.5(b).
10. *See, e.g.,* Fed. R. Civ. P. 5(a) (2001).

attorney.[11] Therefore, the copy of the brief must be served on the party's attorney rather than directly on the party. The Certificate of Service demonstrates
compliance with these rules. The Certificate is placed on a separate page at the
end of the brief. It certifies that copies of the brief have been mailed or delivered to all parties via their attorneys.

———————

This chapter has described the ethical responsibilities of a brief-writer[12] and
the general characteristics of judges as readers. It has provided an overview of
the components of trial-level and appellate briefs. Now you are ready to begin
work on the brief you have been assigned.

B.   THE PROCESS OF WRITING A BRIEF

Before you begin to write, digest the record, do a significant amount—but
not all—of the research, and develop the basic shape of your theory.

Digesting the record is more than merely reading it: study the record to identify potential reversible error by the trial court and to find every fact that could
be used either to prove error or to defend what the trial court did. Look for
both kinds of facts—regardless of whom you represent. Facts favorable to your
position will, of course, become ammunition. But your theory must also show
the appellate court why and how the facts that run against you should not
become determinative.

Before starting to write, do enough research to have all the ingredients for
your theory. That includes all the major authorities on each issue, as well as
enough of the lesser authorities for you to have a good handle on relevant policy, on the procedural posture that governed the decision below, and on the
standard of review in the appellate court (explained in Section 4.A). But you do
not need to find everything in the library on your issue before you begin to
write. In fact, if you try to do that, your brief will probably suffer. Remember the
inseparability of writing and thinking: when you begin to write, you will understand more about the kinds of details from authorities that you will need to fill
out the Argument (see §14.7).

Just as a judge does not read a brief from beginning to end, neither does a
lawyer write it that way. The Table of Contents and Table of Authorities are
always done last, after the rest of the brief has already been typed (see §32.1
[Richard K. Neumann, Jr., Legal Reasoning and Legal Writing: Structure, Strategy, and Style, 6th ed., (2009)]). The order in which the other parts are written
differs from lawyer to lawyer and from appeal to appeal because one lawyer's
work habits are not necessarily effective for someone else and because an effective lawyer adapts to the individual task at hand. Eventually, you will settle into a
range of work habits that are effective for you, and your first brief is an opportunity to begin to define yourself in that way.

To help you start, consider two very different methods of writing a brief.

11. Model R. Prof. Conduct 4.2.
12. For exercises and discussion questions about the material in this chapter, see the exercises
at the end of Chapter 18 [Linda H. Edwards, Legal Writing: Process, Analysis, and Organization,
5th ed., (2010)].

Order in Which a First Draft Might Be Written	
Model I	*Model II*
1. point headings	1. Questions Presented
2. Argument	2. Statement of the Case
3. Statement of the Case	3. point headings
4. Questions Presented	4. Argument
5. rest of brief	5. rest of brief

A lawyer who uses Model I outlines the Argument by composing the point headings and sub-headings and by listing under each heading the material to be covered there when the Argument is written. The logical next step is drafting the Argument itself. This lawyer might draft the Statement of the Case after the Argument on the ground that the value of specific facts is not fully understood until after the Argument is written. The Questions Presented would be written afterward because the lawyer identifies the most determinative facts—the ones recited in the Questions—while working out the Argument and the Statement of the Case.

Conversely, a lawyer using Model II would begin the first draft by writing the Questions Presented on the theory that the other parts of the brief will be more focused if the issues are first precisely defined. A lawyer who uses this model writes the Statement of the Case next, using it to work out the details of the theory of the appeal (which the Model I lawyer does while writing the Argument). Both lawyers draft the point headings before the Argument because the Argument is easier to write in segments (which the headings create).

A lawyer with flexible work habits might use Model I in an appeal where the authority and issues are difficult and complex and Model II in a more fact-sensitive appeal. Some lawyers write the Question Presented and the Statement of the Case (and sometimes even the Argument) simultaneously, moving back and forth from one pad to another (or from one word processing disk file to another).

Start making practice oral arguments while you are writing the brief. It might seem logical to finish writing the brief and then work on the oral argument. After all, in court you submit the brief long before making the oral argument. But when we talk about a complicated subject, often we find ourselves saying surprisingly interesting and perceptive things. The act of talking can help us understand the subject better. That is because many people learn not just by reading and listening, but also by talking and doing. Some lawyers find it useful to begin work on the oral argument before completing the brief. They find that planning the oral argument sharply focuses their attention on the central problems in the appeal. And when they make practice oral arguments to colleagues, they find themselves unexpectedly saying things that would work well in the brief. So you may be able to write a better brief if you start practicing oral argument while you are still writing.

Before writing each subsequent draft, work on something else for a while or take a break to put the brief out of your thoughts. Come back to it in a frame of mind that enables you to put yourself in the judge's position: If you were a skeptical judge, would you be persuaded? Is the brief clear and easy to read? Does it teach you the appeal and show you how to make the decision? Reverting to your role as writer, have you organized the Argument around some variation of the paradigm formula explained in Chapters 10-13 [Richard K. Neumann, Jr., Legal Reasoning and Legal Writing: Structure, Strategy, and Style, 6th ed., (2009)] and in §26.3 [Richard K. Neumann, Jr., Legal Reasoning and Legal Writing: Structure, Strategy, and Style, 6th ed., (2009)]? Or do you begin applying a rule to the facts before you have finished proving it (a sure sign that your organization is out of control)? At the other extreme, have you invested so much energy in proving a rule that you have forgotten to show the court how the rule governs the facts of your appeal? (When reviewing the Argument in general, see the checklist on organization in Section 10.G.2.) If a particular rule is not clearly expressed in the authorities, have you stated it yourself and then proved it with a synthesis? Where a gap in the law must be filled, have you defined the gap and explained the extent of local law before you begin to rely on persuasive authority? Have you used argument techniques (Section 14.A.3) and fact description tactics (§29.2 [Richard K. Neumann, Jr., Legal Reasoning and Legal Writing: Structure, Strategy, and Style, 6th ed., (2009)])? Do your Point Headings and Questions Presented satisfy the criteria in §§28.2 and 30.2 [Richard K. Neumann, Jr., Legal Reasoning and Legal Writing: Structure, Strategy, and Style, 6th ed., (2009)]? Throughout the brief, ask yourself the questions in the paragraphing, style, and quotation checklists in Chapters 18 [Richard K. Neumann, Jr., Legal Reasoning and Legal Writing: Structure, Strategy, and Style, 6th ed., (2009)], 19, and 20 [Richard K. Neumann, Jr., Legal Reasoning and Legal Writing: Structure, Strategy, and Style, 6th ed., (2009)].

It is a good idea—even before you begin research—to set up a schedule with a series of deadlines. Start from the date on which the brief is due, and figure out how many days it will take to have the final draft typed, proofread, and photocopied. Then set a deadline on which those tasks will begin and all rewriting must stop. Figure out how long it will take to turn a second or third draft into a final draft and so on, working your way backward in time to deadlines where each draft must be finished and, for the first draft, where each component must be done. Writing a brief is a big job, and writing it in the time available requires self-discipline from you.

C.   CREATING AN ABSTRACT OF THE RECORD

The first thing you should do as you prepare to write a brief is to get to know the case to which you have been assigned. If you are preparing a motion brief, it is likely that you were with the case from its inception. If you are preparing an appellate brief, you may also have worked on the case from the initial pleadings onward. Sometimes, however, both in law school and in practice you may arrive on the scene a little later. When that happens, your job is to get to know the facts and the procedure as if they had happened to you. Thus, you should carefully study the "record" of the case. The record can consist of many different elements, depending on the stage of litigation and on the case itself. If you are filing a motion to dismiss, for example, the only "record" you may have is the complaint. If you are filing a motion for summary judgment, the record may include not only pleadings, but also affidavits, depositions, answers to interrogatories, and written admissions or stipulations of fact. If you are writing an appellate brief, the record will also include the decision(s) below, and it may include transcripts of trial testimony, reproductions of exhibits or other evidence offered at trial, and other items.

Because appellate records can be so voluminous, many appellate courts either require or allow what is often called a *joint appendix*, prepared by the petitioner and perhaps supplemented by the respondent. The joint appendix is a printed document that includes record elements that one or both of the parties would like the appellate court to have before it while the court is making its decision. Technically, the joint appendix does not take the place of the *record*; the court may always refer to the complete record if it wishes. As a practical matter, however, it is reasonable to think that judges would prefer not to have to consult the full record when reviewing decisions below. Thus, you should certainly plan the joint appendix and, later, write the brief, as if the joint appendix is the entire universe of factual information to which the judges will refer.

The joint appendix always contains certain procedural information; it also contains information that one or both of the parties believe is relevant to the appeal. United States Supreme Court Rule 26.2 specifies how the parties should collaborate to compile the joint appendix. Rule 26.1 describes the categories of material that should be included in the joint appendix:

> The joint appendix shall contain: (1) the relevant docket entries in all the courts below; (2) any relevant pleadings, jury instructions, findings, conclusions, or opinions; (3) the judgment, order, or decision under review; and (4) any other parts of the record that the parties wish to bring to the Court's attention.

Rule 26.1 also provides that "[a]ny of the foregoing items already reproduced in a petition for a writ of certiorari . . . need not be reproduced again in the joint appendix." As a practical matter, the joint appendix is often relatively short because the appendix to the petition for the writ of certiorari contained much or all of the needed information. Combined, these appendixes usually contain the complete text of any decisions below and may contain excerpts of trial testimony, excerpts of other documents submitted into evidence (e.g., depositions), or reproductions of exhibits used in the case. The selected materials provide the court access to sufficient knowledge about the case without forcing the judges to wade through an enormous record.[13]

When filing an appeal in a court other than the United States Supreme Court, you should consult the relevant rules of procedure and local rules to see what requirements exist regarding the "record on appeal," as it is often

13. Although the joint appendix is usually not the complete record, courts may use the term *record* to refer to information from the joint appendix or from the appendix to the petition for the writ of certiorari. *E.g.*, *Horne v. Flores*, 129 S. Ct. 2579, 2606 (2009) ("The record contains no factual findings or evidence that any school district other than Nogales failed (much less continues to fail) to provide equal educational opportunities to ELL students. See App. to Pet. for Cert. in No. 08-294, pp. 177a-178a."); *Herring v. United States*, 129 S. Ct. 695, 708 (2009) ("[T]he record indicates that there is no electronic connection between the warrant database of the Dale County Sheriff's Department and that of the County Circuit Clerk's office, which is located in the basement of the same building. App. 39-40, 43, 45").

known.[14] If you are at the intermediate level, you may be assembling the record on appeal as you work on the brief. If you are arguing to a court of last resort, you may be able to start from an excerpted record that was created for the intermediate court.

Whether the record is a joint appendix, a "raw" record and opinions below, or just pleadings and affidavits, your job at this early stage of the writing process is to identify the important facts of the case. One of the best ways to organize this process is to create an abstract of the record. An *abstract* in this sense is a referenced summary of the information contained in the record. The purpose of an abstract is to help the lawyer—or whoever is working on the case—to easily find important information from the record throughout the writing process.

Reading the record materials carefully a few times and creating a good abstract will enable you to learn more about your case now and to find important record information later, while you are conducting legal research or writing the brief.

Like conducting legal research, preparing an abstract is often a recursive process. It is difficult to understand the significance of the case's facts until you know what law applies to the case, but it's difficult to identify the relevant law until you know the facts. Therefore, as preparation for creating an abstract, read over the lower court opinions or the pleadings first to familiarize yourself with the major issues that the case presents. Then, read through any other materials two or three times. You may wish to abstract information as you go through it each time, or you may wish to wait until you have read the documents through once before you begin to abstract the details that you think are important.

Your method may differ if you are working on an appellate brief as opposed to a motion brief. If you are working on an appellate brief, be sure to abstract the information and arguments contained in the decisions below. When reviewing an appellate record, note that you may need to distinguish between the court's findings of fact and the information that was merely offered into evidence in the trial court. Consider precisely what decisions of the court are being appealed and be sure to record significant information about each one. If you are working on a motion to dismiss or a motion for summary judgment, consider the standard of review. If you are writing a brief in opposition to a motion for summary judgment, for example, you may be arguing that you have provided evidence sufficient to establish your claim as to one of your causes of action. In that situation, when reviewing the record, you would consider your client's burden of proof as to the relevant issues and be sure to review carefully any information in the record relevant to those issues.

To create the actual abstract, make a chart—either on paper or on a word processor—and summarize the important information found in each part of the record or joint appendix as you read through it. Here are some things to look for and to record:

1.   Page cites for positive facts, testimony, and other evidence
2.   Page cites for negative facts, testimony, and other evidence

---

14. *E.g.*, Fed. R. App. Proc. R. 10 (describing requirements for the "Record on Appeal"); Mo. Sup. Ct. R. 81.12 (describing the "legal file" and "transcript" that should be included in the "Record on Appeal"); Mo. Sup. Ct. R. 30.04 (same).

3. Page cites for segments of the appendix (e.g., each separate pleading or other type of document) (if a formal joint appendix has been created, this information may appear in its table of contents)

4. Page cites for evidence that establishes needed elements of the crime or cause of action

5. Page cites for findings of fact in the opinions below

6. Page cites for legal findings in the opinions below

7. Page cites for major arguments that each side has made below

8. Page cites for concessions that either side has made below (e.g., in pleadings or in stipulations)

9. Page cites for information that may support any policy arguments you plan to make

10. Page cites for any information you think is important, even if you are not yet sure why it is important[15]

A section of an abstract of the joint appendix in the case of *Adolph Coors Co. v. Bentsen* (later decided as *Rubin v. Coors Brewing Co.*, 514 U.S. 476 (1995)) might look like the example that follows. In that case, counsel for Coors was arguing that the First Amendment allowed beer manufacturers to print on beer labels the percentage of alcohol in the beer and that therefore the prohibition-era regulation that forbade this information was unconstitutional. The joint appendix was over 350 pages long, and it contained excerpts of various depositions as well as photographic reproductions of several trial exhibits.

In the excerpts below (from two different parts of the abstract), the attorney has recorded the page number from the joint appendix in the left-hand column. In the right-hand column, the attorney has described the information that can be found on that page. The comments in brackets are what an attorney for Coors might write as a way of using the abstract to think about potential arguments in the case. When the attorney is actually writing the brief, he or she could scan through the abstract to find references to information that might be helpful; the attorney could then quickly find the appropriate page in the joint appendix or opinion below and find specific language, citations, or other information to include in the brief itself.

Excerpts from Abstract

PAGE #	INFORMATION
135	First page of deposition of Timothy Ambler, alcohol mktg. expert from England
139-40	Testimony re: mandatory disclosure of alcohol on beer labels in Britain and the European Community [Any precedent for following international precedent?]
* * *	* * *
284	5wPlaintiff's Exh. 3A—Chart showing alcohol % by weight of various beers [Use to show low range of variation among most beers?]

15. *See* Michael R. Fontham, Michael Vitiello, and David W. Miller, *Persuasive Written and Oral Advocacy in Trial and Appellate Courts* §§11.6, 11.7 (2d ed. Aspen 2007).

PAGE #	INFORMATION
289	U.S. Dept. of HHS, Inspector General's Survey on Youth and Alcohol: "Do they know what they're drinking?"
294	Survey findings: "2/3 students can't distinguish alcoholic beverages from nonalcoholic beverages" [Use to show public benefit of putting alcohol percentage on the label?].

In these days of digital recordkeeping, you may find that some or all of the record materials are available in digital form. In that situation, it may be wise to create links to the full text of the record while creating the abstract. But be sure that you still take the time to include relevant quotations and paraphrases in the abstract itself. Do not let the ease of switching to full text make you skip the important step of reading and re-reading the complete record and creating a careful summary of the information.

Creating an abstract may be time-consuming, but it can actually save time in the long run. The process of creating an abstract helps you get to know the realities of your case and lets you rely on recorded information instead of memory. During brief-writing, a good abstract makes it easier for you to support your fact statement and your arguments with vital citations to the record. When you prepare for oral argument, you can use your abstract to study the crucial facts, so that you can refer the court to specific record pages as needed.

D.   THE LAST STEP: CREATING THE TABLE OF CONTENTS AND THE TABLE OF AUTHORITIES

Why you should create the Tables last: For pagination purposes, a brief is broken down into two parts. The two Tables (sometimes called the "front matter") are paginated together in lowercase roman numerals ("i," "ii," "iii," and so on). The rest of the brief (the "body") is paginated separately in arabic numbers, beginning with "1," on the first page immediately following the Tables.

This might seem odd. But it has a very practical purpose. Because the Tables must include page references to the body, *any* change in the body—even a change of only a few words—can alter the page breaks and require changes in the Tables. And because you cannot know how many pages the Tables will occupy until you are ready to print them, the body must begin on page 1. The only efficient solution is to use two separate paginations: lowercase roman numbers for the Tables and arabic numbers for the body. (The same thing is done for the same reasons in your textbooks, including this one.)

What the Table of Authorities should look like: Although the Table of Contents is easy to visualize and put together, the Table of Authorities is more complicated. In the Table of Authorities, list a complete cite for every authority, with an asterisk to the left of those authorities that form the core of your theory. In a footnote, identify those citations as "authorities chiefly relied on" or similar words to the same effect.

The Table of Authorities is broken down into at least three sections headed "Cases," "Statutes," and "Other Authorities." List cases in alphabetical order. If constitutional provisions, court rules, administrative regulations, or legislative histories are cited in the brief, you can add one or more extra sections for them. Regulations, court rules, and legislative histories might be grouped under one heading. Sometimes legislative histories are included with statutes instead. Some lawyers include constitutional provisions with statutes. Others put them in a separate section. The heading should reflect where they are. "Other Authorities" is reserved for secondary authorities, such as restatements, treatises, and law review articles (which are listed there in that order).

CHAPTER

4

Standards of Review

A. HANDLING THE STANDARD OF REVIEW AND THE PROCEDURAL POSTURE BELOW

(Before reading this section, you might review Chapter 26 [Richard K. Neumann, Jr., Legal Reasoning and Legal Writing: Structure, Strategy, and Style, 6th ed., (2009)] on procedural postures.)

On appeal the question is not whether the appellant should have won in the trial court, but instead whether the relevant standard of review was violated in the particular ruling appealed from. For that reason, judges become quite annoyed with attorneys who write and speak as though there were no standards of review. In fact, the appellant's goal is to show that the standard of review has been violated, and the appellee's goal is to show that it has not.

How much error does it take to cause reversal? That depends on the appellate court and the procedural posture below. The appellate court matters because standards of review differ somewhat from one court to another. The procedural posture matters because different standards are applied to different rulings by the court below.

Many rulings of law—such as orders dismissing pleadings, summary judgments, directed verdicts, jury instructions, and judgments notwithstanding the verdict—are evaluated on appeal "de novo."[1] For appeals from these rulings, the appellate court does not use a standard that defers in any way to the trial court. Instead, the appellate court measures error simply by asking itself whether it would have done what the trial court did. The appellate court can do that because all of these rulings present pure questions *of law*. They do not require the trial judge to determine facts or exercise discretion.

Most law school appellate advocacy assignments involve de novo standards of review. If that is true of your assignment, you probably will not have much difficulty arguing within the standard properly. A de novo standard is neutral, like a pane of clear glass through which light passes without distortion. As you will see in a moment, the other standards are like filters and lenses that modify the image.

If the jurisdiction permits a judge's findings *of fact* to be challenged on appeal,[2] the appellate court will apply a higher standard, one which grants a

---

1. "De novo" is the term used in federal courts for this type of standard. Many states use other but synonymous phrases, such as "independent and nondeferential review."
2. See Section 1.D.

certain amount of deference to what the trial court has done. In federal appeals, for example, a judge's fact-finding will be reversed only if it is "clearly erroneous."[3]

And on an issue where the lower court has *discretion,* the result below will be reversed only for an "abuse of discretion," which, again, represents a degree of deference to the trial court. A trial court has a wide range of discretion on issues of equity and on issues concerning management of the progress of the litigation, such as rulings on discovery motions and on the conduct of the trial.

The diagram below illustrates how standards of review work and how they are related to procedural tests in trial courts. (Read the diagram *from the bottom up.*)

4

APPELLATE COURT

Because the granting or denial of a preliminary injunction is a discretionary decision in a trial court, the appellate court will reverse only if the trial court abused its discretion. (*This is the standard of review.*)

↑

3

Plaintiff wins the motion, and defendant appeals.

↑

1

TRIAL COURT

Plaintiff moves for a preliminary injunction in the trial court. ⟶

2

The trial court will grant a preliminary injunction only if the plaintiff is threatened with irreparable harm, is likely to succeed on the merits, will suffer more if the injunction is denied than the defendant would if the motion were granted, and seeks relief not adverse to the public interest. (*This is the procedural test in the trial court.*)

---

3. *See, e.g.,* Rule 52(a) of the Federal Rules of Civil Procedure.

The only way to find out which standard controls a given appellate issue is to research local law in the same manner that you would research rules governing the procedural posture in a trial court.[4] Look for authority that tells you not only what the standard is, but also what it means and how it works. Where a court mentions the standard of review in a decision, it usually does so immediately after reciting the facts and immediately before beginning the legal analysis. This is an example of the type of language you will find:

> A dismissal for failure to state a claim pursuant to Fed. R. Civ. P. 12 is a ruling on a question of law and as such is reviewed de novo. [Citation omitted.] Review is limited to the contents of the complaint.[5]

Here we learn what the standard is ("de novo"), and we learn a little—but certainly not everything—about how the standard operates ("Review is limited to the contents of the complaint"). Occasionally, a court will tell you much more about how the standard is used:

> "In reviewing the [National Labor Relations] Board's decision, we must scrutinize the entire record, 'including the evidence opposed to the Board's view from which conflicting inferences reasonably could be drawn.'" [Citation omitted.] Nevertheless, this court will defer to the Board's judgment and the Board's factual findings shall be conclusive if supported by substantial evidence on the record considered as a whole. [Citation omitted.] This "court may not substitute its judgment for that of the Board when the choice is 'between two fairly conflicting views, even though the court would justifiably have made a different choice had the matter been before it *de novo*.'" [Citation omitted.] We shall also defer to the Board's inferences in areas where the Board is considered to have "specialized evidence and expertise." [Citation omitted.][6]

And the court might explain at the same time both the standard of review and the rules governing the procedural posture in the trial court:

> The grant or denial of a motion for preliminary injunction is a decision within the discretion of the trial court. [Citation omitted.] Appellate review . . . is very narrow. [Citation omitted.] Accordingly, a district court's decision will be reversed only where there is a clear abuse of discretion. [Citation omitted.] That discretion is guided by four requirements for preliminary injunctive relief: (1) a substantial likelihood that the movants will ultimately prevail on the merits; (2) that they will suffer irreparable injury if the injunction is not issued; (3) that the threatened injury to the movants outweighs the potential harm to the opposing party and (4) that the injunction, if issued, will not be adverse to the public interest. [Citation omitted.][7]

---

4. See §26.4 [Richard K. Neumann, Jr., Legal Reasoning and Legal Writing: Structure, Strategy, and Style, 6th ed., (2009)]. You can add the term "standard of review" (or "standard review") to a computer inquiry that you have already used to find substantive cases. But do this only after you have found the substantive cases you need. If you look for substantive cases and standards of review in the same search, the standard of review term in your inquiry might exclude valuable substantive cases.

5. *Kruso v. International Tel. & Tel. Corp.*, 872 F.2d 1416, 1421 (9th Cir. 1989).

6. *NLRB v. Emsing's Supermarket, Inc.*, 872 F.2d 1279, 1283-84 (7th Cir. 1989).

7. *Haitian Refugee Center, Inc. v. Nelson*, 872 F.2d 1555, 1561-62 (11th Cir. 1989).

Occasionally, you will come across an issue that is subject to a bifurcated or even (as in the example below) a trifurcated standard of review. Each portion of this test for laches has a different standard of review:

> Our standard of review on the laches issue has various components. We review factual findings such as length of delay and prejudice under the clearly erroneous standard; we review the district court's balancing of the equities for abuse of discretion; and our review of legal precepts applied by the district court in determining that the delay was excusable is plenary. [Citation omitted.][8]

How do you handle the standard of review in a brief? Do three things:

First, set out the relevant standard of review at or near the beginning of the Argument section of the brief (or, if you have more than one point, each point's standard of review can be set out shortly after the point heading).[9] While doing so, identify the procedural posture below and invoke the procedural test that governs it. And—if it can be done succinctly—tell the court how the standard was violated (if you are the appellant) or how it was not (if you are the appellee). For example, from an appellant's brief:

> This is an appeal from a summary judgment, which is reviewed de novo in this court. [Citation omitted.] Summary judgment should occur only where there is no genuine issue as to any material fact and the movant is entitled to judgment as a matter of law. [Citation omitted.] In this case, the movant was not entitled to judgment as a matter of law.

This passage tells us that the standard is de novo, and that the appellant's theory of error is that the second element of the test for summary judgment was not satisfied. (The writer does not say that there was a genuine dispute as to a material fact, which means that only one element of the summary judgment test is at issue.)

An appellee might write the paragraph above differently. In the second sentence, an appellee might write "is appropriate where" instead of "should occur only where." (Why?) And in place of the last sentence, an appellee might write "Here, the appellant concedes that there was no issue as to a material fact, and the record below amply demonstrates that the appellee was entitled to judgment as a matter of law."

A good place to put this material is between a point heading and the first subheading. Cite to local authority to prove the procedural rule that governed the trial court and the standard of review on appeal. Unless the law is unclear, a conclusory proof is usually sufficient because these rules are the type with which an appellate court would be routinely familiar. (Notice how this is handled in the Appendix G and H [Richard K. Neumann, Jr., Legal Reasoning and Legal Writing: Structure, Strategy, and Style, 6th ed., (2009)] briefs.)

Second, argue *through* the standard of review. If, for example, you are appealing from a decision committed to a trial court's discretion, show throughout rule application (see Chapter 10 [Richard K. Neumann, Jr., Legal Reasoning and Legal Writing: Structure, Strategy, and Style, 6th ed., (2009)]) that the trial court

---

8. *Bermuda Express, N.V. v. M/V Litsa*, 872 F.2d 554, 557 (3d Cir. 1989).
9. This is required in federal appeals and in several states. For example, see Fed. R. App. P. 28(a)(9)(B) (The appellant's argument "must contain . . . for each issue a concise statement of the applicable standard of review (which may appear in the discussion of the issue or under a separate heading placed before the discussion of the issues)."). Rule 28(b) permits the appellee to omit this statement "unless the appellee is dissatisfied with the statement of the appellant."

abused its discretion. If you are the appellee in such a case, show the opposite. It is not enough merely to state the standard of review at the beginning and then ignore it for the rest of the Argument. Instead, use it and corollary rules wherever they are relevant, weaving the substantive and procedural law together to show either error (if you seek reversal) or the absence of it (if you urge affirmance).

But a de novo standard need not be referred to throughout the Argument unless the very neutrality of the de novo standard helps your case. Because the de novo standard grants no deference at all to the trial court, arguments can be based entirely on the substantive law once the court has been told that a de novo standard is in effect.

Third, throughout the brief (and in oral argument), describe the facts just as they were in the procedural posture in the trial court. (That is because the standard of review is geared to the procedural posture below.) If the appeal is from the dismissal of a complaint, for example, describe the facts as allegations ("the complaint alleges that the defendant struck the plaintiff"). Describe them as evidence ("Smith testified that the defendant struck the plaintiff") if the appeal is from a judgment resulting from a motion challenging the quality of evidence (see §26.2.3 [Richard K. Neumann, Jr., Legal Reasoning and Legal Writing: Structure, Strategy, and Style, 6th ed., (2009)]) or from an order resulting from a case management motion (see §26.2.4 [Richard K. Neumann, Jr., Legal Reasoning and Legal Writing: Structure, Strategy, and Style, 6th ed., (2009)]). But if the facts are undisputed, describe the facts as truth ("the defendant struck the plaintiff").

If you are unsure of how to do any of these things, take a look at several opinions in which the court for which you are writing has used the same standard of review in appeals from the same procedural posture involved in your case. Chances are that you will see them invoked near the beginning of the opinion and used at logically appropriate spots thereafter. Look for a definition of the standard, and try to learn its relationship to other procedural rules and get a feel for the court's expectations about how the standard should be used.

B.   HANDLING STANDARDS OF REVIEW

Appellate judges cannot reverse merely because they don't like what the lower court did. Instead, they can reverse only when the relevant standard of review lets them do so. The standard of review controls the appellate court's decision. For that reason, appellate judges become annoyed when lawyers write and speak as though standards of review don't exist.

1.   The Three Main Standards of Review

The type of ruling made by a trial court determines the standard of review. The three main standards of review are

1.   *de novo* review for issues of law
2.   *clear error* review for issues of fact
3.   *abuse of discretion* review for discretionary issues

Other standards of review exist, but these are the most important ones.

Issues of Law—de novo review: A trial court decides an issue of law when it interprets the law or decides what the law is. For example, when a trial judge instructs the jury at the end of a trial, the judge explains to the jury the elements of the legal rules the jury must follow in reaching a verdict. When deciding what to say to the jury, the judge decides a pure issue of law. If the jury instruction accurately states the law, the trial judge has not committed error. But if the instruction is wrong, the judge has erroneously decided an issue of law and could be reversed on appeal.

In reviewing a trial court's ruling on an issue of law, an appellate court measures error simply by asking whether it would have interpreted the law in the same way the trial court did. *De novo* is the term used in federal courts for this standard of review. In Latin, it means to do "from the beginning" or "as though new." Some states use other phrases, such as "independent and nondeferential review." They mean the same thing. If the trial court interpreted the law incorrectly, an appellate court can reverse.

When you're assigned to write an appellate brief, look first for the type of decision the trial court made. If it is one of the following, you have an issue of law:

- an order dismissing a plaintiff's complaint or other pleading
- a summary judgment
- a directed verdict or, in federal court, judgment as a matter of law
- a jury instruction
- a judgment notwithstanding the verdict or, in federal court, judgment as a matter of law
- a decision denying a motion or request for any of the above

Many other trial court decisions resolve issues of law, but these are the big ones.

Most, but not all, law school appellate brief assignments involve de novo standards of review. If that's true of your assignment, you probably won't have much difficulty arguing within the standard. A de novo standard is neutral, like a pane of glass through which light passes without distortion. The other standards (explained below) are like filters and lenses that modify the image because they defer to the trial court, which a de novo standard does not.

With a question of law there's no reason to defer in any way to the trial court. An appellate court can decide an issue of law at least as well as a trial court can, and the appellate court might do a better job because an appeal is decided by several judges as opposed to a single judge in the trial court.

Issues of fact—review for clear error: An issue of fact is a question about what happened factually between the parties. For example, was the defendant's gun loaded or unloaded at the time of the crime? Which witness should be believed: the one who testified that the defendant loaded the gun with bullets just before the crime, or the one who testified that the defendant instead emptied the gun of bullets?

Although these fact issues and many others would typically be decided by a jury, some fact issues are decided by a trial court judge. When a law school appellate brief assignment includes a fact issue, it usually involves a bench trial or a pretrial motion. A bench trial is one where a judge decides the facts without a jury.

A pretrial motion asks the judge to make a procedural decision before the trial begins. For example, if a criminal defendant moves to suppress his confession, the defendant is asking the judge to exclude the confession from the evidence admitted at trial. If the defendant claims that he confessed only because a police officer threatened to beat him up, the judge would decide whether the police really did that—which is a fact issue.

Don't confuse a fact issue with a law issue. Suppose the defendant claims that the police officer bragged that he is an amateur boxer who is so good at punching opponents that he almost qualified for the U.S. boxing team at the last Olympics.

fact issue:	Did the police officer brag in the defendant's presence?
law issue:	Does that kind of bragging violate the defendant's Fifth Amendment right against forced confessions?

When a trial judge's findings of fact are challenged on appeal, the appellate court will reverse only if the trial judge's decision was "clearly erroneous."[10] It's not enough that the trial court was wrong. A deeper level of error is required for reversal.

Typically, courts say that they will reverse only if they "are left with a definite and firm conviction that a mistake has been made."[11] The Seventh Circuit has put it more bluntly: "To be clearly erroneous, a decision must strike us as more than just maybe or probably wrong; it must . . . strike us as wrong with the force of a five-week-old, unrefrigerated, dead fish."[12] Other courts use less vivid language to express the same idea.

However you express it, this is a very difficult standard for an appellant to satisfy. Appellate courts defer to the trial court's factual determinations because the trial judge saw and heard the witnesses testify while appellate courts can only read the trial court's transcript, which appellate judges describe as a "cold record."

Discretionary issues—review for abuse of discretion: Many procedural issues permit a trial judge to exercise discretion. Here is a typical appellate court formulation of what that means:

> When we say that . . . a district court has discretion to grant or deny a motion, we do not mean that the district court may do whatever pleases it. The phrase means instead that *the court has a range of choice, and that its decision will not be disturbed as long as it stays within that range.* . . . An abuse of discretion, on the other hand, can occur . . . when a relevant factor that should have been given significant weight is not considered; when an irrelevant or improper factor is considered and given significant weight; and when all proper factors, and no improper ones, are considered, but the court, in weighing those factors, commits a clear error of judgment.[13]

The most important words here are "the court has a range of choice, and . . . its decision will not be disturbed as long as it stays within that range." How do you know what that range is? You have to read your jurisdiction's case law, where you'll find general definitions that might (or might not) resemble the one above.

---

10. See, *e.g.*, Rule 52(a) of the Federal Rules of Civil Procedure.
11. *United States v. Brown*, 156 F.3d 813, 816 (8th Cir. 1998).
12. *Parts & Electric Motors, Inc. v. Sterling Electric, Inc.*, 866 F.2d 228, 233 (7th Cir. 1988).
13. *Kern v. TXO Prod. Corp.*, 738 F.2d 968, 970 (8th Cir. 1984) (emphasis added).

The abuse-of-discretion standard—like the clear-error standard for fact decisions—reflects appellate deference to the trial court. Appellate courts reason that the trial judge is closer to the problem and might have a better view of how to solve it. As long as the trial judge chooses a decision within the permissible range, that decision will be affirmed.

Some decisions involve a combination of discretionary and other types of issues. For example, suppose a plaintiff moves for a preliminary injunction alleging that the defendant is infringing the plaintiff's trademark by selling a product called a Hyper Blob Blaster. (A preliminary injunction is a court's command to a party to do or not do certain things before trial.)

Some appellate courts will divide up the issues like this:

fact issue:	Is the defendant selling a product called a Hyper Blob Blaster?
law issue:	What rules of trademark law govern this dispute?
discretionary issue:	Is a preliminary injunction an appropriate remedy in this situation?

With this view of the issues, an appellate court will reverse for clear error in fact-finding, or for an erroneous interpretation of the law (de novo), or for abuse of discretion in choosing or rejecting a preliminary injunction as a remedy.

Mixed issues of law and fact: Sometimes a fact issue can't be separated from a law issue. For example,

fact issue:	What factually happened between the parties?
law issue:	What's the governing legal test?
mixed issue:	How does the legal test apply to these facts?

It's hard to generalize about how appellate courts handle mixed issues of law and fact. If you have a mixed issue, find the case law on issues like the one in your assignment and read carefully to see how the courts in your jurisdiction analyze the issue.

2. How to Determine Which Standards of Review Govern Your Issues

Look at what the appellate court is being asked to decide. Suppose the trial court determined what the facts are, decided what the law is, and chose a discretionary remedy. Suppose also that the losing party appeals only on the ground that the trial court misinterpreted the law.

In this example only the trial court's law decision has been appealed. The fact and discretion issues have been left behind and are not before the appellate court. (Most, but not all, law school assignments are pure issues of law.)

Law issues usually don't have labels on them that say "Law Issue Right Here." Instead, you might be told something like "The appellant contends that the trial court misinterpreted §1331." That's an issue of law, which can be resolved entirely by deciding what the law is and how it should be applied to the facts.

Look also at how the analogous case law discusses your issue. Standards of review are usually found in case law, although they might partially be addressed in court rules. Look for cases that tell you not only what the standard is, but also what it means and how it works. When a court mentions the standard of review in a decision, it usually does so right after reciting the facts and just before beginning the legal analysis. Here's an example of the type of language you will find:

> We review *de novo* the district court's dismissal of a complaint for failure to state a claim under Rule 12(b)(6). In reviewing such a motion, we accept all material allegations of fact as true and construe the complaint in a light most favorable to the non-moving party. We have consistently emphasized, however, that "conclusory allegations of law and unwarranted inferences" will not defeat an otherwise proper motion to dismiss. Dismissal for failure to state a claim is appropriate only "if it appears beyond doubt that the non-moving party can prove no set of facts in support of his claim which would entitle him to relief."[14]

Here we learn what the standard of review is (de novo). The court explains how the standard works by describing how the lower court should have made its decision ("Dismissal for failure to state a claim is appropriate only . . . ").

Occasionally, you'll come across an issue that is subject to more than one standard of review. Each portion of this test for laches has a different standard of review:

> Our standard of review on the laches issue has various components. We review factual findings such as length of delay and prejudice under the clearly erroneous standard; we review the district court's balancing of the equities for abuse of discretion; and our review of legal precepts applied by the district court in determining that the delay was excusable is plenary [meaning de novo].[15]

3.   How to Use Standards of Review in a Brief

In federal appeals, the appellant's argument "must contain . . . for each issue a concise statement of the applicable standard of review (which may appear in the discussion of each issue or under a separate heading placed before the discussion of the issues)."[16] The appellee can omit this statement "unless the appellee is dissatisfied with the statement of the appellant."[17]

When you tell the court the standard of review, it often helps to explain, at the same time, the procedural posture below and the procedural test that governs it. And—if it can be done succinctly—tell the court how the standard justifies reversal (if you're the appellant) or how it doesn't (if you're the appellee). For example, from an appellant's brief:

> The plaintiff appeals from a summary judgment, which is reviewed de novo in this court. [Citation omitted.] Summary judgment should be granted only where there is no genuine issue as to any material fact and the movant is entitled to judgment as a matter of law. [Citation omitted.] In this case, the defendant should not have been granted summary judgment because he was not entitled to judgment as a matter of law.

This passage tells us that the standard is de novo, and that appellant will argue that the second element of the test for summary judgment was not satisfied.

---

14. *Vasquez v. Los Angeles County*, 487 F.3d 1246, 1249 (9th Cir. 2007) (citations omitted).
15. *Bermuda Express, N.V. v. M/V Litsa*, 872 F.2d 554, 557 (3d Cir. 1989) (citation omitted).
16. Fed. R. App. P. 28(a)(9)(B).
17. Fed. R. App. P. 28(b).

In the paragraphs that follow, the writer will have to explain thoroughly why the appellee was not entitled to judgment as a matter of law.

Set out the relevant standard of review at or near the beginning of the Argument section of the brief. Or, if you have more than one point, each with a different standard of review, a point's standard can be set out shortly after the point heading. Cite to authority to prove the standard of review. A conclusory rule explanation (Chapter 17 [Richard K. Neumann, Jr. and Sheila Simon, Legal Writing, 2nd ed., (2011)]) is usually sufficient because appellate courts are generally familiar with the applicable standards of view.

If the standard is de novo, you can state it at the beginning and ignore it afterward because it's a neutral standard. But if the standard is one of the deferential ones—clear error or abuse of discretion—you have to argue in terms of the standard. For example, if you're appealing from a decision committed to a trial court's discretion, show exactly how the trial court abused its discretion. If you're the appellee in such a case, show the opposite. With a deferential standard, weave it into your argument.

If you're unsure of how to do any of these things, take a look at several opinions in which the court to which you're writing has handled the same standard of review in appeals involving the same procedural posture as in your case. Look for a definition of the standard. Try to learn its relationship to other procedural rules. And get a feel for the court's expectations about how the standard should be used.

CHAPTER

5

Developing a Theory

A.   WHAT PERSUADES A COURT?

What could you write to persuade a judge to give you what you're asking for? What persuades?

1.   A Compelling Theory and Theme Persuade

A *theory* is a way of looking at the controversy that makes your client the winner. A *theme* is a sentence or two or even just a phrase that summarizes the theory. You're already familiar with theories and themes in a commercial sense. Think of the businesses or products to which you are loyal. Each of them has been marketed with a theory and theme—sometimes implied rather than stated openly—that has persuaded you to spend money. Here are a few examples:

> iPod and iTouch—so much inside; take it anywhere with all your tunes
> jetBlue—fly on an airline that's fun
> Amazon—stop driving to stores: just click, and it's delivered to you

In law, a persuasive theory is a view of the facts and law—intertwined together—that *justifies* a decision in your favor and that *motivates* a court to render that decision. A persuasive theory

1.   relies on the supportive facts;
2.   explains why the adverse facts should not prevent a decision in your favor;
3.   has a solid basis in law and overcomes your adversary's interpretation of the law;
4.   appeals to a judge's sense of fairness and good policy; and
5.   can be summarized in one or two easily remembered sentences or a vivid image (the theme).

Unfocused writing can make a judge feel as though she's drowning in detail without a clear idea of how all the detail adds up to a coherent view of the case. Judges complain about lawyers who write that way. *A judge needs a clearly stated theory and a memo or brief sharply focused on proving that theory.*

B. DEVELOPING A PERSUASIVE THEORY

1. Introduction

Persuasive writing aims to convince judges to do what your client wants. Whether you are writing a motion memorandum or an appellate brief, the ability to persuade centers on three skills: developing a persuasive theory (explained in this chapter), developing persuasive arguments (see Chapter 14), and working within a procedural posture (see Chapter 26 [Richard K. Neumann, Jr., *Legal Reasoning and Legal Writing: Structure, Strategy, and Style,* 6th ed., (2009)]).

2. Theories: Of the Case, of the Motion, of the Appeal

To make their decisions, judges need more than raw information about the law and the facts. They make decisions by *choosing between theories,* and you will lose if your adversary's theory is more attractive than yours is.

Think back to the last major decision you had to make—perhaps the choice of a career, the selection of a law school, a decision about where to live, or the purchase of a car or an appliance. If your decision-making was conscious and deliberative—as judges hope their decisions are—you can probably recall an idea—or a small number of related ideas—that caused you to choose one career over another, one law school over another, and so forth. And if your decision-making was conscious and deliberative, there was probably a moment when you first identified and appreciated this idea (or small group of ideas). At that moment, you probably also realized that one of the alternatives had become inevitable. Some people who specialize in sales work call this moment the "selling point" because the decision to buy becomes inevitable once the selling idea is fully appreciated by the buyer.

Persuading is selling, and judges have accurately been described as "professional buyers of ideas."[1] Judges have their selling points, and both lawyers and judges use the word *theory* to refer to the collection of ideas that, in a given case, a lawyer offers for purchase. At trial, each lawyer propounds a *theory of the case.* Where the court is to decide a motion or an appeal, the phrases *theory of the motion* or *theory of the appeal* might be used instead. Each lawyer proposes a theory, and the court chooses between them, or—if neither theory is satisfactory—the court may fashion one of its own, often causing unhappiness to both sides.

A theory, then, is an idea on which a decision can be based. A persuasive theory is a view of the facts and law—intertwined together—that justifies a decision in the client's favor and motivates a court to make that decision. A persuasive theory "explains not only *what* happened but also *why*" through a compelling story that "has both rational and psychological appeal" and thus is "persuasive both to the mind and to the heart."[2]

For example, if Welty is prosecuted for burglarizing Lutz's apartment (see pages 80-81 [Richard K. Neumann, Jr., *Legal Reasoning and Legal Writing:*

---

1. Girvan Peck, *Strategy of the Brief,* Litigation, Winter 1984, at 26, 27.
2. David Binder & Paul Bergman, *Fact Investigation: From Hypothesis to Proof* 140, 184 (West 1984).

Structure, Strategy, and Style, 6th ed., (2009)]), the prosecution's theory of burglary might be that Lutz's conduct did not imply permission to break the threshold and enter the apartment, and that Welty's actions show beyond a reasonable doubt that—when she stepped into the apartment—she had already formed an intent to assault Lutz.[3] To prove the element of a breaking, for example, the prosecutor might point to four facts: (1) Lutz opened the door only six inches, (2) he never told Welty she could enter, (3) his only reason for stepping away from the door was to turn down the volume on his stereo so that he could hear what Welty was already saying while she was outside the apartment, and (4) as soon as Lutz discovered that Welty had entered the apartment, he ordered her to leave. To prove the element of "intent to commit a felony therein," the prosecutor might focus—in a way you have already explored in Chapter 9 [Richard K. Neumann, Jr., Legal Reasoning and Legal Writing: Structure, Strategy, and Style, 6th ed., (2009)]—on Welty's anger at the time she entered the apartment.

On the other hand, Welty's attorney might develop the theory that the evidence creates reasonable doubt about whether she broke through a threshold to get into Lutz's apartment and about whether, at the instant she walked through the door, she intended to strike him. To substantiate this theory, Welty's attorney might argue that there was nothing to break once the door was open; that Lutz's actions could reasonably have been understood by Welty to have implied permission to enter and continue the conversation inside the apartment; and that Welty's actions before she was ordered to leave are consistent with an innocent intent to persuade Lutz to behave in a more neighborly fashion. If believed, this theory should cause an acquittal on the charge of burglary.[4]

You might see something of how hard adjudicating is by putting yourself in the position of the judge and jury in this case, and by considering the consequences if you make a mistake: either an innocent person could be punished or a person could go free despite evidence of guilt beyond a reasonable doubt. You might also understand some of the difficulties of advocacy by putting yourself in the position of each of the lawyers and asking yourself how you would go about persuading the decision-makers both to adopt your theory *and to reject your adversary's theory.*

3.   *Characteristics of a Persuasive Theory*

A theory is worth arguing if it stands a significant chance of being adopted by the judge or jury who must adjudicate the dispute. The more a theory satisfies the following criteria, the greater its chances of adoption.

1. Does the theory "[a]ccount for or explain all of . . . the undeniable facts"?[5] When a judge or jury first looks at the case, if your theory is inconsistent with an undeniable fact, one of the two will be considered wrong—and it will not be the undeniable fact. Beyond that point, ambiguous evidence and debatable

3. The other elements of common law burglary would not be hard to prove: Welty did, in the nighttime, enter the dwelling of another. See §8.1 [Richard K. Neumann, Jr., Legal Reasoning and Legal Writing: Structure, Strategy, and Style, 6th ed., (2009)].

4. For the separate charge of assault, the lawyer might have to ask some questions to develop a further theory: for example, if Welty struck Lutz because she thought he had become so angry that he might strike her, she might—to the charge of assault (but not burglary)—argue self-defense.

5. David M. Malone & Peter T. Hoffman, *The Effective Deposition* 53 (2d ed., NITA 1996).

inferences are usually resolved in whatever way is most consistent with the evidence that cannot be questioned. When the time for decision arrives, the adjudicator's natural tendency is to say, "Let's start with what we *do* know."

2. Does the theory "explain away in a plausible manner as many unfavorable facts as it can"?[6] It is not enough to build on the evidence you like. Your theory should also explain why the evidence you *dislike* should not prevent a decision in your favor. Is it overcome by other evidence in your favor? Does it prove facts that are not as important under the law as other facts that your evidence has proved?

3. Does the theory "[e]xplain why people acted in the way they did"?[7] If your theory does not do that, some significant part of the case will still seem mysterious to the judge or jury. As long as that mystery remains, a judge or jury will feel that your theory hasn't "solved" the controversy. If a theory assumes that the actors behaved differently from the way people normally do in similar circumstances, the theory is not persuasive unless it includes a compelling reason for the difference. Theories that impute deceit to disinterested witnesses, for example, are less attractive than those that suggest honest but faulty abilities to observe and remember. Innocent misunderstandings are much more common in life than lying or stealing.

4. Is the theory "supported by the details"?[8] "Detail . . . on contested key facts enhances the believability of the story"[9] at the heart of your theory. If the case turns on whether a certain car was green or yellow and your star witness testifies that it was green but says nothing about whether it was a station wagon or a sedan, whether the driver was male or female, or whether the day was sunny or rainy, a judge or jury can naturally conclude that the witness has an unreliable memory.

5. Does the theory have a solid basis in law? Are your interpretations of the statutes and cases reasonable? When a court examines your legal arguments using the tools and skills explained in Chapters 14, 15, 16 [Richard K. Neumann, Jr., Legal Reasoning and Legal Writing: Structure, Strategy, and Style, 6th ed., (2009)], and 14, will the court be persuaded?

6. Is the theory "consistent with common sense and . . . plausible"?[10] All other things being equal, a simple theory is more down-to-earth than a complex one, although even a simple theory must address all the facts. A theory has a commonsense appeal if its internal logic is consistent, if it is realistic, if its explanations are compatible with the judge or jury's experiences in life, and if it reflects their values and the values of the community to which they feel responsible. The most easily sold theories are those that are based on easily believable interpretations of the evidence and the authorities; that would lead to reasonable results; that do not ask a judge or jury to believe that people have behaved in improbable ways; and that ask for narrow decisions rather than earth-shaking ones.

Like any other kind of consumer, a judge buys only when struck with a feeling of confidence that the purchase will turn out well, without causing injustice or embarrassment on appeal or before the public. Like most people who have had

6. George Vetter, *Successful Civil Litigation* 30-31 (Prentice-Hall 1977).
7. David M. Malone & Peter T. Hoffman, *The Effective Deposition* 53 (2d ed., NITA 1996).
8. *Id.*
9. *Id.*
10. *Id.*

substantial opportunity to observe human nature, judges can be astute at surmising how various kinds of people would behave under given circumstances. And like most people with substantial responsibilities, judges see the world as a place that works well when people are reasonable, rather than extreme. Judges feel safer when they can make narrow decisions, rather than earth-shaking ones, because narrow decisions are less likely to create new problems and controversies. (A judge would much rather find that your client is not guilty on the facts than hold that the statute defining the crime is unconstitutional.)

A theory that sells in an appellate court has a flavor different from one that seems attractive to a trial court. That is because trial judges and appellate judges do not see their work in precisely the same way. A trial court is a place of routine, and trial judges want to make decisions the way they are usually made and not in ways that would greatly disturb the world. Although trial judges sometimes try to avoid the full impact of appellate authority, the rulings of the courts to which a trial judge's decision could be appealed are like orders from a superior, and the trial judge needs and wants to know—through those rulings—what the supervising courts expect. In contrast, appellate judges are conscious of their responsibility to see the bigger picture and to keep the law as a whole fair and reasonable, even if that requires modifying the common law now and then to fit changes in society. Judicial circumspection and the doctrine of stare decisis keep these changes in direction to a minimum, however, and appellate courts generally presume the decision below to be correct, reversing only if deeply troubled by what happened in the lower court. Generally, theories presented to high appellate courts are more policy-oriented than theories presented to trial courts.

4.   Developing a Theory

Luck is the residue of design.

—Branch Rickey

Before the memorandum in Appendix C [Richard K. Neumann, Jr., Legal Reasoning and Legal Writing: Structure, Strategy, and Style, 6th ed., (2009)] was written, Goslin undoubtedly showed his lawyer a deed that, on its surface, seemed to give the nephew every right to have Goslin and his belongings removed. A lawyer who lacks the skill of theory design might say something like this to such a client: "Well, Mr. Goslin, you made a mistake. In future, don't give a deed without securing some rights for yourself, either by making a collateral contract or by taking payment for your equity. In the meantime, I think you'll have to move out."

Another—and better—lawyer might look under the surface for possibilities: at the time of the deed, did Goslin believe he was giving up all his property rights? Did he think he was going to continue to live in the house? Had the nephew said or done anything that would show that the nephew thought Goslin was making a gift or was going to move out? Is there anything in the history of this uncle and this nephew on which some sort of reliance theory might be based? Since people do not usually negotiate with their relatives at arm's-length or with written contracts, and since people can turn on each other even in family relationships, might some part of the law go so far as to enforce understandings between relatives, even if those understandings have never been spoken or written down? Notice the technique: first, open doors to factual possibilities; then find out how the law treats those possibilities and discover whether there is evidence to prove them.

A theory will not spring forth in final form from your mind. Instead, a germ first occurs and then grows as new information is learned and more law researched. Although research guides the growth of the theory, the theory also guides the course of the research, each filling in the gaps of the other. Sometimes, there is rapid progress; at other times, it may be painfully slow. More than at any other time in legal writing, this is when you depend on the creative process described in §24.3.

How do you develop a theory?

First, narrow your focus to the issues. What will really matter to the court? Every case has some aspects that have distressed the client or the attorney but will be greeted in court with profound boredom. Certain kinds of suffering—for good reasons or bad—have no effect whatever on the typical judge. Some suffering can be dismissed on the ground that it is too small to merit judicial intervention, or that it is as much the client's own fault as anybody else's, or that it represents problems courts cannot solve. Conversely, every case has some aspects that both client and attorney would like to forget but will nevertheless strongly influence a judge. The client might have suffered a wrong, for example, but only while doing something that judges find grossly unacceptable. Or the other side might enjoy one of the traditional advantages in court: it might, for instance, be engaged in one of those industries that courts like to protect. Every theory has to take these kinds of things into account. Identifying them corresponds very roughly to the problem-identification stage of professional creativity mentioned in §24.3.

Second, list your case's strengths and weaknesses and the other side's strengths and weaknesses. What are your best facts? Conversely, what facts make you worry? What are your best and worst authorities and rules of law? And the human equities of the situation? Be realistic about the people in the courthouse and the way they are likely to deal with your case. This is part of the gathering and evaluating information and raw materials stage of professional creativity described in §24.3.

Third, think of a way of looking at the case that, if believed, would make your client the winner. This is solution-generation from §24.3.

Fourth, compare your theory to the criteria for effectiveness explained in Section 5.B.3. To the extent your theory falls short of effectiveness, can you fix it? This is solution-evaluation from §24.3. If your theory is ineffective and cannot be fixed, go back to solution-generation and develop another one.

Finally, once you have an effective theory, write the memo or brief that will present it. This combines the decision and action stages from §24.3.

It can help to develop contradictory theories together—to develop, in other words, your adversary's most likely theory while creating your own. If you look at the case as your adversary will see it and if you hypothetically work up a theory for your adversary to argue, you will be able to identify the weaknesses in your theory. Otherwise, you will look at the controversy one-sidedly, and your theories will reflect wishful thinking and be too one-dimensional to withstand attack.

5. *Imagery and Story-Telling*

> *A picture held us captive.*
>
>   — *Wittgenstein*

Imagery has a powerful effect in theory development. Thinking in images—in other words, focused daydreaming—helps to find new ways of looking at things that would otherwise be iron-bound givens.

A truck runs off the highway, through a farmer's fence, and over the farmer's cow. The truck driver's insurance company wants to pay as little as possible for this cow, and the farmer, of course, wants more.

The insurance company's lawyer wants to treat the cow as "a unit of livestock" or "a farm asset." The insurance company is better off litigating this as a question about how much money the farmer is entitled to for the replacement of a machine-like object that consumes grass as fuel to produce milk and an occasional calf. The farmer's books can be gone over to determine the productivity of this object, its acquisition costs, depreciation, useful life remaining at the time of its destruction, etc.

The farmer's lawyer, on the other hand, wants to know if the cow had any other value. The lawyer asks the farmer some questions. "That wasn't just any cow," replies the farmer.

> That was Bessie! She was the only Guernsey cow left in this county. She didn't give that thin milk you get out of a Holstein that people buy in the grocery store. She gave the thickest, most flavorful milk you ever tasted. We didn't sell it to the dairy. We drank it ourselves and made the best butter and cheese out of it. And Guernseys are smaller cows. They're friendly, like pets, and Bessie was like part of our family.

The persuasive weight of each of these theories is in the imagery of what we *see*. The farmer's lawyer wants us to see a big pair of Guernsey eyes in a head that is nudging the farmer with affection—a loss to the farmer's family that includes but is greater than the loss of a grass-to-milk machine. The insurance company's lawyer wants us to see the farmer's balance sheet, where a certain item of livestock is carried as an asset valued at a certain number of dollars. In any writing that grows out of this controversy, the farmer's lawyer probably will not mention Bessie's head nudging the farmer, and the insurance company's lawyer probably will not mention the balance sheet—because those things are not, strictly speaking, relevant to the legal controversy. But if they are good writers, these lawyers will include enough relevant detail so that we will see these scenes anyway because they are implied.

If you develop an eye for revealing detail, your theories will much more quickly come to life as vivid, compelling stories. Vividness not only helps the reader remember the story (and the theory it embodies), but it makes the story and the theory more believable. Imagery makes a theory real.

C. DEVELOPING A THEORY OF THE APPEAL

In Chapter 5, you learned that a theory is attractive only if it is solidly built on the record and the law, explains away unfavorable facts, is framed in terms of basic fairness to the parties, and appeals to logic and common sense. An effective appellate theory, however, has some additional qualities.

First, a persuasive theory of the appeal is grounded on the procedural posture below and the standard of review in ways described in Section 4.A. For the attorney urging reversal, the theory is one of *error*, while for the attorney defending the result below, the theory is one of *the absence of error*. And neither error nor its absence can be explained without taking into account the procedural posture below and the standard of review.

Second, a persuasive appellate theory does not ignore any of the limitations on appellate review described in Section 1.D. An appellate court will reject a theory that would violate restrictions on the court's own power to act.

Third, a persuasive appellate theory goes beyond a technical analysis and addresses the judges' concern about a fair and just result. An appellant must show both error and injustice: "If you can convince the appellate judges that the court below is wrong as an intellectual matter, but leave them with the impression that no worthwhile damage was done, the prior result will be affirmed."[11] Although an appellee might succeed by showing either an absence of error or an absence of harm, the wiser strategy is to try to show both, if that can credibly be argued.

Fourth, a persuasive appellate theory is soundly grounded in public policy. Judges engaged in law formation or clarification are understandably concerned about the wider consequences of what they do. How would the precedent the court will create in your case affect others in the future?

Fifth, a persuasive appellate theory asks the court to make no more law than is necessary to the attorney's goal. Most judges do not believe that their purpose on the bench is to change society in fundamental ways, and you will have a better chance to win if your theory asks only for those changes that are truly necessary to the result you want.

Finally, a persuasive appellant's theory raises no more than two, three, or at the very most four claims of error. A theory is damaged, not strengthened, by adding additional but weaker grounds to the two or three best ones available. The weaker grounds by their mere assertion cheapen the stronger ones and take up room in the brief that is better used to more fully develop the grounds most likely to cause reversal. Good theory development requires the good judgment to choose the strongest grounds, the self-discipline to focus the court's attention on them alone, and the courage to ignore other grounds that may seem tempting but, in the end, are unlikely to persuade.

11. Edward J. Lampron, *Observations on Appellate Advocacy,* 14 N.H. B.J. (No. 3) at 105, 106 (Winter 1973).

CHAPTER

6

Table of Contents & Table of Authorities

A. EFFECTIVE TABLES

Because judges and clerks who read briefs often consult the tables of contents and authorities, it is important that these tables look good as well as contain accurate information. One of the four basic principles of design is alignment, and effective alignment is crucial in making tables look good. Page numbers and document elements should be aligned consistently, so that readers can easily find the information that they need.

In this excerpt from a table of contents, note how none of the elements are aligned; the reader's eye bounces all over the page to look for information:

Bad Example

In the next example, note how the writer uses alignment to make obvious the relationships between and among point headings. This method allows the user to find headings he or she cares about more easily or to choose which level of headings to review.

Good Example

> Respondents may not claim a legitimate expectation of privacy, because by engaging in criminal acts in a well-lit room, directly in front of a window facing a widely used common area, they exhibited no subjective expectation of privacy ....

You may believe that you need not worry about design because in practice you will have an administrative assistant who will type and print the document. You should not presume, however, that your assistant will know or care about document design. You must take responsibility for what your document says and for how it looks because you will have to face the consequences for the impression it makes.

CHAPTER
7

Statement of the Issue, aka Questions Presented

A.   GENERALLY

How you frame the issues before the court is of the utmost importance when persuading a legal audience to take action in favor of your client. In fact, according to Bryan A. Garner, framing the issues is the "most important analytical step" in both the litigation and appellate process.[1] In an appellate or motion brief, just as in an office memorandum, we frame the issue in the question presented.

The function of a question presented is twofold in an appellate or motion brief. First, just as in an office memorandum, a question presented indentifies the legal issue or issues to be decided by the court. However, while a question presented in an office memorandum articulates the legal issue in an objective or neutral fashion, a question presented in an appellate or motion brief begins to persuade the court to resolve the legal issue in your client's favor.

What does it take to draft a good question presented? A good question presented generally does three things. First, a question presented states the legal issue the court has to answer. Second, a question presented identifies the legal concept that will govern the result. Third, a question presented includes the most important key facts that the court will rely on in deciding the question. Also, a good question presented should be written so that a reader can understand it in one reading and include enough information that a reader can understand it independent of the Statement of the Case. This requires that you balance the facts carefully. You should include only those facts that are essential to the court's decision and eliminate all unnecessary detail. Finally, legal writing convention generally requires that a question presented be written as a single sentence.

---

1. Bryan A. Garner, "The Language of Appellate Advocacy" in Appellate Practice Manual 188, 189 (Priscilla A. Schwab ed., 1992).

B.　FORMAT

1.　*Traditional Format*

a.　**Generally**

A traditional question presented is one sentence that begins with a verb and ends with a question mark. It states the legal issue before the court, identifies the governing legal concept or test, and identifies the most important key facts the court will rely on in deciding the issue. And it does each of those things in that order. Thus, a template for a traditional question presented would resemble that shown below:

Template

State the legal issue the court has to answer;
Identify the legal concept that will govern the result; and
Include the most important key facts

Thus, if you draft an abstract question of law that includes the statement of the legal issue ("Is a doctor liable to a patient?") and identifies the governing law but fails to include the key facts, you have not drafted a question presented. Remember that the legal issue before the court is shaped by the concrete facts of the case. Consequently, if the facts before the court are different, then the issue before the court is different.

When stating the legal issue before the court, you should begin with a verb. The statement of the legal issue may begin with "is," "can," "did," "does," "was," or whatever verb is most appropriate.

Did the Government violate . . . ?
Is a surgeon liable . . . ?

In practice you may read some briefs with questions presented that begin with "whether." Such questions might state "Whether the Government violated . . . ." or "Whether a surgeon is liable. . . ." Unless required by local court rules to use it, you should avoid using this "whether" construction. Questions presented that are drafted using the "whether" construction are more difficult to read than questions that begin with a verb. This is likely because they are not a grammatically correct sentence and they do not end in a question mark. What sort of question doesn't end in a question mark? Such questions presented may also seem artificial and, truthfully, are just weird.

Once you have stated the legal issue and alluded to the law governing the issue, you should identify the most important key facts before the court. The key facts are those that the court will rely on in making its decision. They are limited to those facts that are determinative of the outcome; they do not include contextual facts or coincidental facts. Nor do the key facts include factual inferences that you have made or legal conclusions. A legal conclusion assumes the answer to a legal question that the court must decide, whether it is the ultimate question or some smaller question concerning an element, factor, or prong of the test. Rather than stating a legal conclusion, let the facts speak for themselves— replace the legal conclusion with the facts that you based that conclusion on.

When drafting a question presented, you may be able to weave some of the key facts into your articulation of the legal issue and legal concept. Those facts that you cannot naturally weave into your articulation of the legal issue and legal concept should follow the question in clauses beginning with "when." The key facts are located at the end of the question because the reader will not understand their relevance until you've articulated the legal issue and identified the governing legal concept. The legal issue and legal concept provide context for the key facts.

b. Sample Question Presented

Was there sufficient evidence to convict a mother of child neglect in the death of her daughter from anorexia when the mother closely monitored her daughter's weight, encouraged her daughter to eat, but was unaware of her daughter's drastic diet reduction or that the daughter was actively hiding her weight loss?

2. Alternative Formats

The requirement that a question presented be written so that a reader can understand it in one reading and the legal writing convention that a question presented be written as one sentence can sometimes be incompatible. This occurs when the key facts in a case are so complicated that they cannot be boiled down to a short list. When the facts are complicated, a question presented may seem to meander, drowning the reader in facts and causing the reader to have to read the sentence several times before understanding it. If you find that your question presented seems too lengthy or that a reader would be overwhelmed by the sheer number of "when" clauses needed to understand the issue, you should experiment with the alternative formats discussed below.

The first alternate format reorganizes the presentation of the materials into a fact-statement-plus-question form. The second alternate format presents the question presented as a syllogism. Each of these formats breaks the question presented into more than one sentence to improve readability. They improve readability by providing information in smaller chunks (e.g., shorter sentences), keeping the subject of the sentence and the verb together, telling a "story in miniature,"[2] and articulating the question that emerges from that story at the end of the question presented.

a. Fact-Statement-Plus-Question Format

i. Generally

This alternate format places the key facts in an introductory paragraph that precedes the questions presented. This format is useful in a couple different

---

2. Bryan A. Garner, Dictionary of Modern Legal Usage 473 (2d ed. 1995).

scenarios: 1) when you have several issues, and 2) when you have complicated facts. Consequently, you may use this format when you have only one legal issue, but you have a complicated set of facts.

Recall that a question presented states the legal issue before the court, identifies the legal concept that governs the dispute, and includes the most important key facts that the court will rely on in making its decision. While this alternate format includes each of these things, this format organizes them differently than the traditional format. Instead of locating the key facts at the end of the inquiry as does the traditional format, this format moves most of the key facts to the beginning, in an introductory paragraph that precedes the questions presented. When you have only one legal issue, all the key facts will appear in the introductory paragraph. Similarly, when you have multiple legal issues, this introductory paragraph will include all the key facts common to most or all of the issues. However, if you have a fact that relates to only one of the legal issues, you should include that fact in the question presented for that issue rather than in the introductory paragraph.

The questions presented will follow this introductory paragraph. Each question presented will state the legal issue before the court and identify the legal concept that governs the dispute. Generally, the questions presented will be devoid of facts because you have included the relevant facts in the introductory paragraph. However, as stated in the previous paragraph, if you have a fact that relates to only one legal issue, you should include that fact in the question presented for that issue. Thus, a template for this alternate format would resemble that shown below:

Template

Introductory paragraph identifying the key facts common to most or all of the legal issues

1.   Question Presented—statement of the legal issue, identification of the governing legal concept or test, and articulation of any key facts relevant only to this issue
2.   Question Presented—statement of a different legal issue, identification of the governing legal concept or test, and articulation of any key facts relevant only to this issue
3.   Question Presented—statement of a different legal issue, identification of the governing legal concept or test, and articulation of any key facts relevant only to this issue

While this alternate format can be used when you have a complicated fact pattern, you should not just default to this format in that situation. Make certain that you have reduced the list of key facts to only those that are truly essential and that you have stated each fact as concisely as possible. Only when you have made these efforts and you feel that a reader would be overwhelmed by the facts should you consider using this format.

---

ii.   Sample Question Presented

Fourteen-year-old Macy Vanderhoff, a talented gymnast, was coached by her father, who had coached five Olympic gymnasts. Coach Vanderhoff set Macy's training schedule and her strict diet. He was very critical of his gymnasts' weight. Though she weighed only eighty pounds when she was thirteen, Macy became obsessed with her weight and, unbeknownst to her parents, reduced her food intake. Noticing her weight loss, Coach Vanderhoff praised her efforts, while Ms. Vanderhoff closely monitored it. When Macy did not perform as expected at the Summer Olympic trials, her father suggested she lose weight despite her weighing only sixty-five pounds. A doctor later diagnosed Macy with serious health problems and told her to eat more. Her father disagreed. Later, Macy secretly cut her diet to just an apple slice a day, which caused her to begin fainting during practice. On September 20, 2012, Macy did not wake up. Upon arrival at the hospital, she weighed only fifty-two pounds. On October 1, 2012, Macy died of multiple organ failure and cardiac arrest, the most common cause of death for anorexics.

1.   Should Ms. Vanderhoff's conviction for negligence resulting in her daughter's death be reversed for insufficient evidence because she constantly monitored Macy's weight and told her she could eat any food in the house; she did not realize the full extent of her daughter's weight loss as she was putting rocks in her pants and leaning into the wall to appear heavier; and Ms. Vanderhoff was not aware that her daughter had drastically reduced her diet?
2.   Should Ms. Vanderhoff's conviction for murder by denying her daughter necessities be reversed for insufficient evidence that she knowingly allowed her husband to maliciously and intentionally deny food to their daughter because his goal was to help Macy become an Olympic gymnast, not kill her, and Ms. Vanderhoff trusted his professional judgment given his previous success in training several other Olympic gymnasts?

b.   The Question Presented as a Syllogism

i.   Generally

This alternate format for a question presented mirrors a syllogism, which is the basis for all logical thought. In a syllogism you have a major premise, a minor premise, and a conclusion. A major premise is a general statement that applies to many cases. A minor premise is a particular statement of fact that ties into that general statement. The conclusion is drawn when we apply the major premise to the minor premise. For example,

Major Premise:	All men are mortal.
Minor Premise:	Socrates is a man.
Conclusion:	Therefore, Socrates is mortal.

Syllogisms are effective in persuading an audience because "[w]hen presented with the properly framed major and minor premises of a syllogism, the human mind seems to produce the conclusion without any additional prompting.

Moreover, the mind recognizes the conclusion to be of such compelling force that the conclusion simply cannot be denied."[3]

In a question presented that mirrors a syllogism, the governing legal rule is the major premises, the particular facts of the case before the court that are relevant to the governing legal rule are the minor premise, and the conclusion is articulated as a question. To draft an effective question presented, the elements must appear in this order. The governing legal rule (major premise) must be listed first to provide context for the particular facts from the case (minor premise). The question falls at the end of the question presented because it should appear to flow naturally from the minor premise and suggest an answer that is favorable to your client. The template for this alternate format would resemble that below:

Template

Major premise, or governing legal rule;
Minor premise, or the particular facts of the case before the court that are relevant to the governing legal rule; and
Question

While your major premise should explicitly articulate the governing legal rule, you should not include citations for that rule. Including the governing legal rule in the major premise usually clutters the issue statement and muddles the reader's understanding of the issue. Instead, just identify the governing jurisdiction and articulate the relevant legal principle that governs the dispute. For example:

Under Utah law, to recover for fraud a plaintiff must prove detrimental reliance on a deliberate misrepresentation.
The U.S. Supreme Court has mandated that lower courts must not "accept as true a legal conclusion couched as a factual allegation in pleadings.
To decide a parent's request to modify child-support obligations, Virginia law requires a trial court to consider both parents' incomes.
The U.S. Supreme Court has held that Title VI of the Civil Rights Act of 1964 does not confer a private right of action under the statute or its implementing regulations.

The minor premise includes the particular facts of the case that are relevant to the governing legal rule, or the key facts that the court will rely on in making its decision. These facts should be specific and concrete. Additionally, the minor premise should not be conclusory—it should not include legal conclusions or factual inferences. Including legal conclusions or factual inferences will harm your credibility as the legal reader is extremely skeptical by nature and is not likely to just accept what you are saying. Rather than asking the reader to just trust you, you should include the facts on which your legal conclusion is based.

3. James A. Gardner, Legal Argument 6 (1993).

Further, the minor premise should tell "a story in miniature."[4] This story should relate the facts in chronological order. Additionally, this miniature story can be told in more than one sentence.

Follow this story in miniature with a short, direct question. This question will essentially be the statement of the legal issue that you would have included in a question presented drafted using the traditional format. The question presented may ask "Did the Government violate Mr. Dell's right to privacy?" or "Is Dr. Humphreys liable?" You should not include facts in the question, whether they are facts listed in the minor premise or new facts not mentioned there. Thus, using this alternate format, the question presented will not include "when" clauses.

ii. Sample Questions Presented

1. QUESTION PRESENTED A

Under Washington law, county commissioners may not appoint a civil servant for a term that is longer than the commissioners' own elective terms. The Skulalia County commissioners, who serve three-year terms, appointed Bartleby as county manager. In a tight labor market, Bartleby was able to negotiate a five-year employment contract. The commissioners accepted and signed the contract. Is Bartleby's contract enforceable?[5]

Consider this question presented in terms of the template identified above. What is the major premise? What is the minor premise? What is the question?

Major premise:	Under Washington law, county commissioners may not appoint a civil servant for a term that is longer than the commissioners' own elective terms.
Minor premise:	The Skulalia County commissioners, who serve three-year terms, appointed Bartleby as county manager. In a tight labor market, Bartleby was able to negotiate a five-year employment contract. The commissioners accepted and signed the contract.
Question:	Is Bartleby's contract enforceable?

2. QUESTION PRESENTED B

Florida rules allow deposition testimony to be used at trial only if the witness cannot be located after a good-faith attempt to serve a subpoena or if the witness is more than 100 miles from the court. Judge Hand, in Miami, barred the use of the deposition of Jack Throckmorton, an Orlando resident, because the proffering party did not show a good-faith attempt to serve a subpoena. Was Judge Hand's ruling erroneous?[6]

Consider this question presented in terms of the template identified above. What is the major premise? What is the minor premise? What is the question?

4. Bryan A. Garner, The Winning Brief 93.
5. This sample question presented is taken from Bryan A. Garner, The Winning Brief: 100 Tips for Persuasive Briefing in Trial and Appellate Courts 89 (2d ed. 2004).
6. Bryan A. Garner, The Winning Brief: 100 Tips for Persuasive Briefing in Trial and Appellate Courts 86 (2d ed. 2004).

Major premise:	Florida rules allow deposition testimony to be used at trial only if the witness cannot be located after a good-faith attempt to serve a subpoena or if the witness is more than 100 miles from the court.
Minor premise:	Judge Hand, in Miami, barred the use of the deposition of Jack Throckmorton, an Orlando resident, because the proffering party did not show a good-faith attempt to serve a subpoena.
Question:	Was Judge Hand's ruling erroneous?

3. QUESTION PRESENTED C

Under West Virginia criminal law, a parent is guilty of neglect resulting in her child's death when the parent fails to exercise a minimum degree of care by standing by passively and refusing to help her child when it is reasonably within the parent's power to do so and this unreasonable failure results in the child's death. Though Mr. Vanderhoff was highly critical of his daughter's weight and kept her on a strict diet, Ms. Vanderhoff constantly monitored her daughter's weight and encouraged her to eat. Ms. Vanderhoff was unaware of her daughter's drastic diet reduction or that the daughter was actively hiding her weight loss. Macy later died from cardiac arrest, the most common cause of death in anorexics. Should Ms. Vanderhoff's conviction for neglect resulting in her daughter's death be reversed for insufficient evidence?

Consider this question presented in terms of the template identified above. What is the major premise? What is the minor premise? What is the question?

C.   PERSUASION

The question presented is your first opportunity to persuade the court to decide the issue in favor of your client. However, when drafting a question presented, you should refrain from using over-the-top persuasive techniques or making your bias obvious. You will lose credibility if you are strident or overstated. Rather, you should *subtly* persuade the reader to decide the issue in favor of your client, much like you do when drafting a Statement of the Case.

How do you subtly persuade? One means of subtle persuasion is simply articulating the question presented as a question that ends with a question mark. According to Bryan A. Garner, "[A] bona fide question looks and sounds objective even when it's gently slanted. Rather than pushing your answer, you're putting a question on the table. You're also challenging your opponent to explain how the answer could be other than you're suggesting."[7]

Another means of subtle persuasion is articulating the question and the key facts in a way that opposing counsel cannot object to. That means that opposing counsel cannot say your description of the facts is inaccurate—that you included facts that are not in the record or that you misrepresented a fact. It also means that you cannot include legal argument in the question presented.

---

7. Bryan A. Garner, The Winning Brief: 100 Tips for Persuasive Briefing in Trial and Appellate Courts 86 (2d ed. 2004).

What techniques can be used to subtly persuade the reader? One technique is to draft the question presented so that it suggests an affirmative answer in favor of your client. Thus, if you represent an appellant, you might articulate a question presented in the follow ways:

Did the district court err when . . . ?
Did the Government violate Mr. Dell's Fourth Amendment right to privacy when it . . . ?
Was Ms. Aquilina's use of Major League Baseball's Chief Wahoo image a fair use when . . . ?

If you represent an appellee, you might articulate a question presented in the following ways:

Was the district court correct in deciding that . . . ?
Was the Government justified in searching Mr. Dell under the Fourth Amendment without violating his right to privacy when . . . ?
Did Aquilina violate Major League Baseball's copyright in the Chief Wahoo image when . . . ?

Another way to subtly persuade a reader is to include both positive and negative facts. Acknowledging facts that are harmful to your client adds to your credibility with the reader. While you should include facts that are not necessarily favorable to your client, don't let them harm your client. Juxtapose those negative facts with positive facts that neutralize their harmful impact. While this technique is used when drafting the Statement of the Case, it is used much more concisely when drafting a question presented!

Another technique that you can use to subtly persuade a reader is word choice. If you represent a party who was allegedly wronged, you should use strong verbs and vivid nouns—words that illicit a reaction from the reader. On the other hand, if you represent a party who is the supposed wrongdoer, you should use weak verbs and bland nouns.

Exercise 1[8]

Consider the following three drafts of a question presented for an appellant challenging his conviction for the offense of intentional assault with a dangerous instrument on the sole ground that he did not use a dangerous instrument. The evidence at trial showed only that appellant, a patron at a crowded bar, threw a small, thick "on-the-rocks" glass at a bartender, lacerating the bartender's cheek and eye when the glass struck her face and broke; no altercation or interaction of any sort between the appellant and the complainant preceded this incident.

Intentional assault with a dangerous instrument is committed when a person intends to cause physical injury (not death or serious physical injury) and causes such injury by means of a dangerous instrument. The law defines a

---

8. This exercise is adapted from a chapter in Elizabeth Fajans, Mary R. Falk, and Helene S. Shapo, Writing for Law Practice (Foundation Pr. 2010).

"dangerous instrument" as "any object which, under the circumstances in which it is used, is readily capable of causing death or serious physical injury."
Compare the following Questions Presented. Determine whether each Question Presented satisfies the requirements for a question presented, whether the Question Presented is persuasive, and if it does not satisfy either of the 2 previous questions, identify why it does not.

1. Whether the appellant's conviction for assault should be reversed because he did not use a dangerous instrument.
2. Did the appellant commit assault when he merely tossed the object in the bartender's direction to get her attention?
3. Should appellant's conviction for intentional assault with a dangerous instrument be reversed on the ground that the glass he threw at the complainant bartender was small and thick and, under the circumstances, unlikely to break?

CHAPTER

8

Statements of the Case

A. THE STATEMENT OF THE CASE IN A MOTION MEMO OR APPELLATE BRIEF

1. How a Statement of the Case Persuades

It may sound paradoxical, but most contentions of law are won or lost on the facts.

—Justice Robert H. Jackson

In a persuasive memorandum or brief, the judge learns about the facts in the Statement of the Case (also called a Statement of Facts or just Facts). In the Statement, you must include every fact that you mention elsewhere in your memo or brief. You must also include in the Statement all facts on which your adversary relies. This is the one place in the document where all the legally significant facts can be seen together in the context of your client's story. And you lose credibility if you omit unfavorable facts.

In the Statement, you are not allowed to argue, analyze law, draw factual inferences, or even characterize the facts. It is called a *Statement* of the Case because the facts are *stated* there and analyzed elsewhere. Inferences and characterizations of facts belong in the Argument. You are, however, allowed to report the inferences witnesses drew and the characterizations they made while testifying.

If you cannot argue in a Statement of the Case, how can you persuade there? Persuade by *telling the story in a way that emphasizes facts that support your theory while saying nothing that the adversary could reasonably claim to be inaccurate.* Consider the two examples below. Assume that the plaintiffs are suing a backcountry hiking guide for negligence after the guide led them into disaster. (Citations to the record have been deleted.)

On July 2, the plaintiffs asked in Stove Pipe Springs whether a backcountry guide might be available to lead them through certain parts of Death Valley. After some discussion, they hired the	The climate in Death Valley is one of the hottest and driest known. The highest temperature recorded each summer reaches at least 120° and in many years at least 125°. The highest temperature recorded in Death

defendant to take them on a full-day hike the next day.

When they started out, the defendant carried a compass and map. Each plaintiff carried sunglasses, a large-brim hat, and a quart of water.

A climatologist testified about the climate in Death Valley. Occasionally, winter temperatures fall below freezing, but there is no water to freeze. Spring and fall temperatures approximate summer temperatures elsewhere. July is the hottest month, with an average high of about 116° and an average low of about 87°. The highest temperature ever recorded in Death Valley was 134°. (The highest recorded on earth was 136°.) Average annual rainfall is about $1\frac{1}{2}$ inches, and the number of days on which precipitation falls in an average year is eight.

Valley—134°—is also the second highest recorded on earth. (The highest was only two degrees hotter and was recorded in the Sahara desert.) Rainfall is only $1\frac{1}{2}$ inches per year, the lowest in the Western Hemisphere, and in a few years no rain falls at all.

In the summer sun in Death Valley, a person can lose, on average, about four gallons of perspiration per day. After about two gallons are lost, that person can become delirious and, if the lost water is not quickly replaced, die of dehydration.

The defendant advertised himself as a professional and experienced back-country guide. Relying on that, the plaintiffs hired him. He then took them into Death Valley for a full-day hike in July with a quart of water each.

After reading the example on the right, you can believe that this hike was madness and that the guide was responsible for it. But in early drafts, many beginners instinctively produce a Statement like the one on the left, which tells the story, but not in a compelling way. How does the example on the right persuade?

First, in the example on the right the writer selected a very few facts that would illustrate the theory: You can lose four gallons of water a day in such a place. After losing two gallons, you can become delirious, and if the water is not replaced, lives will be in danger. This was a full-day hike. The plaintiffs had a quart of water each. The defendant claimed to be a professional and experienced guide. As each of these facts is added, the logic of the theory unfolds.

Second, the example on the right is free of factual clutter—marginal facts, such as the temperatures in other months, that can obscure critical information. It focuses instead on the facts crucial to the persuasive story.

Finally, the example on the right gives the kind of vivid details that make a theory come alive—the delirium, for example, and the comparison to the Sahara desert.

But the example on the right *appears* to be nothing more than a description of the relevant facts. An adversary cannot reasonably challenge anything in it as untrue. Each fact is objectively verifiable in the record. And—most importantly—the writer never expressed any inferences from the evidence. *You drew all the inferences yourself.*

Sometimes a reader can think, "I can't tell whether this Statement was written by the plaintiff's lawyer or by the defendant's." That confusion is a sure sign that the Statement fails to persuade. Is it true of either of the Death Valley excerpts? If so, which one?

2.   *The Record*

The record might include any or all of the following:

- the pleadings
- evidence in the form of testimony, affidavits, and exhibits
- prior court orders, judicial opinions in the same case, and, on appeal, the judgment below

A Statement of the Case can describe *only* facts that are before the court through the record. Other facts must be ignored, a process called *limiting the Statement to the record.* But you can point to the *absence* from the record of a particular allegation or piece of evidence—"no witness identified the defendant," for example—if the absence shows that the opposing party has failed to satisfy a relevant legal test.

In the Statement, describe the facts in terms of the type of record where they can be found. If the record includes testimony, explain what the witnesses testified to. But if the "facts" are allegations in a pleading,[1] don't describe those allegations as events that actually happened. Section 28.4.1 explains how to describe this kind of record and why.

For every fact you mention, courts require that you provide a cite to a specific page or paragraph in the record—not only when you recite the fact in the Statement of the Case, but also when you analyze it in the Argument.[2] This provides an easy method of checking what you say. Court rules aside, cites to the record have a persuasive effect of their own. Careful cites give the reader confidence that every fact on which you rely is fully supported in the record. Spotty or missing cites arouse a court's skepticism. Both the ALWD Citation Manual and the Bluebook explain how to cite to the record. In either book, look in the index for "record" or "records."

3.   *Fact Ethics*

It is unethical for a lawyer to "knowingly . . . make a false statement of fact . . . to a tribunal."[3] Even if it were not unethical, factual misrepresentation never fools a court and hurts only the misrepresenting lawyer and that lawyer's client. Misrepresentations are quickly spotted by opposing attorneys, and once a misrepresentation is pointed out to a court, the entire memorandum or brief will be treated with deep suspicion. And afterward the court will mistrust the misrepresenting lawyer.

B.   DEVELOPING A PERSUASIVE STORY

> *When I was an attorney . . . , I realized after much trial and error that in a courtroom whoever tells the best story wins.*
> —*John Quincy Adams (fictionally) in the movie* Amistad

---

1. Allegations are most often at issue when the pleading is challenged through a motion to dismiss for failure to state a claim. *See* Rule 12(b)(6) of the Federal Rules of Civil Procedure.
2. *See, e.g.,* Rules 28(a)(7) and (e) of the Federal Rules of Appellate Procedure.
3. ABA Model Rules of Professional Conduct, Rule 3.3(a)(1).

1.   The Power of Stories

Robert McKee[4] has taught many of the best screenwriters in Hollywood how to write stories. So many screenwriters are in his debt that he was actually portrayed in that role in the movie *Adaptation*. Nicholas Cage plays a screenwriter who consults McKee about writer's block.

McKee also teaches business people how to persuade by telling stories. In a typical business situation, a young start-up company has developed a valuable idea, such as a drug that will prevent heart attacks, and the company needs investment bankers to lend money or buy stock so the company can finish the job and put the drug on the market. This situation resembles the one lawyers face when asking a court for relief: A person who wants something (a lawyer or a company's executives) tries to persuade a decision-maker (a judge or an investment banker) who has very rational criteria for making the decision (legal rules or the math that would predict whether an investment will make a profit).

If the company's chief executive officer meets with the investment bankers and makes only a logical presentation with Powerpoint slides, based on statistics and sales projections, the "bankers would nod politely and stifle yawns while thinking of all the other companies better positioned" to bring this drug to market. But suppose the CEO tells a compelling story about how the company overcame obstacles to develop the drug, get it patented, and get regulatory approval, and now has to overcome one final hurdle—financing—to bring the drug to market. That causes "great suspense" and the possibility that "the story might not have a happy ending. The CEO has the bankers on the edges of their seats, and he says 'We won the race, we got the patent, we're poised to go public and save a quarter-million lives a year.' And the bankers just throw money at him."

Why? Nothing should be more rational than finance. If the numbers on the spreadsheets and Powerpoint slides show that this project will produce a profit without too much risk, the bankers should invest in it. But they won't unless they feel enthusiasm—unless they have been captured by the story. If you challenge McKee on this, he will say, "I know the storytelling method works, because after I consulted with a dozen corporations whose principals told exciting stories to Wall Street, they all got their money."

2.   How Stories Persuade

In a law school classroom, making the best logical argument is everything. That is as it should be. Legal argumentation is difficult to master, and legal education devotes a lot of effort to teaching students how to argue.

But in the real world, when you make purely logical arguments to decision-makers like judges, as Mckee points out, "they are arguing with you in their heads"—because logic and argument naturally arouse skepticism—and "if you do persuade them, you've done so only on an intellectual basis. That's not good enough because people are not inspired to act by reason alone." A story, he says, persuades "by uniting an idea with an emotion."

---

4. The quotes from McKee and the material about him are from *Storytelling that Moves People: A Conversation with Screenwriting Coach Robert McKee*, Harv. Bus. Rev., June 2003, at 51.

A story also persuades by letting the reader decide—on her own—to agree with you *before* you have asked her to agree. In an argument, you start by telling the reader what you want her to believe, and then you set out the steps of logic to prove that position. With a story, you tell what happened. If you develop a good story and if you tell it well, the reader's decision *comes from her* while reading the story, and she is therefore more committed to it. She's motivated to act for two reasons. First, she saw the point before you told her what it was. (If you tell her the point during the story, it isn't a story any more. It's an argument.) And second, stories move us in ways that logic can't.

Some litigation stories can be told only to juries. They have too much emotion, and if you were to tell those stories to judges, they would feel that you have insulted their sense of professionalism. A story told to a judge can succeed only by simultaneously addressing both the legal issues and the judge's basic human sense of right and wrong.

3.   Building the Story—Generally

In a Statement of the Case, the story should

1.   "ignite action"—motivate by making a judge care enough to act
2.   "communicate who you are"—actually, communicate who your side is by defining your client and supporting witnesses favorably
3.   communicate who the other side is by defining the opposing party or the harmful witnesses or some combination of them unfavorably
4.   "neutralize bad news" by explaining why facts that at first seem bad for your case should not be held against you (more about this in Chapter 8).[5]

These are the four goals in storytelling. Most stories have a simple, three-part structure:

1.   The story starts in a state of equilibrium.   Things might not be wonderful, but they are at least okay.

2.   Bad things happen to disrupt the equilibrium.   If you represent the plaintiff or the prosecution, the disruption is whatever the defendant did wrong. If you represent the defendant, the disruption is the lawsuit or prosecution itself, which puts the defendant under stress and at risk.

3.   The protagonist struggles to restore equilibrium.   Unless you're the prosecutor, the protagonist is probably your client. Because prosecutors have no client, they often cast the victim as a protagonist. If you represent a plaintiff, equilibrium could be restored by a judgment awarding your client an injunction or damages. If you represent the prosecution, equilibrium could be restored by convicting and sentencing the defendant. If you represent the defendant in either kind of case, equilibrium could be restored by dismissing the lawsuit or prosecution and freeing the defendant from the unjust burden of being an involuntary litigant in fear of losing.

---

5. The quotes are from Stephen Denning, *Squirrel Inc.* 44, 47 (2004). See also Stephen Denning, *The Springboard: How Storytelling Ignites Action in Knowledge-Era Organizations* (2001).

Next time you watch a movie, ask yourself whether the plot in the movie has this structure—equilibrium, disturbance, struggle to restore equilibrium. Most do. Sometimes you will tell your client's story in exactly this sequence, and sometimes you will tell it differently.

This structure also works when the issue isn't who should win in the end, but instead some smaller part of the litigation. For example, if you represent a party resisting discovery before trial in a civil case, the equilibrium is your client's possessing private information that your client reasonably wants to keep secret. Disruption is the other side's demand for this information through interrogatories or a deposition. The struggle to restore equilibrium is your attempt to persuade the judge to grant a protective order that would prevent discovery of this information.

The judge is a hidden character in the third phase of the story, the struggle to restore equilibrium. Will the plaintiff win an injunction? Will the defendant win a dismissal? Will the party resisting discovery win a protective order? That is all up to the judge. If you build a good story and tell it well, the judge should *want* to restore equilibrium.

Once you have determined the inner structure of the story, the most important components are characters and imagery.

4. Characters

Character cannot be described. You can't say, "My client is a really nice person, extremely conscientious and responsible." Nobody will believe you. You have to imply character by reciting things your client has or has not done. You'll do the same, if you can, with witnesses and with other parties.

> Take, for example, a rear-end collision that caused a lot of soft-tissue and nerve damage to the driver. At first glance, it seemed like a routine personal injury case. The at-fault driver was a business woman coming home from work who had been talking on her cell phone when the accident occurred. What really established her character was the fact that she continued talking during the accident and for another five minutes afterward [which defined her] as callous.[6]

5. Imagery

> *If you want to win a case, paint the Judge a* picture *and keep it simple.*
> *—John W. Davis*

Imagery has a powerful effect in stories.

A truck runs off the highway, through a farmer's fence, and into the farmer's cow. The truck driver's insurance company wants to pay as little as possible for this cow, and the farmer, of course, wants more.

The insurance company's lawyer will tell a story in which the cow is "a unit of livestock" or "a farm asset," as though the issue is how much money the farmer should get to replace a machine-like object that consumes grass as fuel to produce milk and an occasional calf. This story will focus on numbers from the farmer's books that show the productivity of this object, its acquisition costs, depreciation, useful life remaining at the time of its destruction, etc. The

6. Joel ben Izzy, *Character Development*, L.A. Daily J., Oct. 26, 1999, at 8.

insurance company's lawyer will use this story because the numbers show the cow to be an unexceptional object.

The farmer's lawyer looks for a different story to tell. "Tell me about the cow," she asks the farmer. "That wasn't just any cow," replies the farmer,

> That was Bessie! She was the only Guernsey cow left in this county. She didn't give that thin milk you get out of a Holstein that people buy in the grocery store. She gave the thickest, most flavorful milk you ever tasted. We didn't sell it to the dairy. They wouldn't pay a decent price for it anyway because dairies care about quantity, not quality. We drank it ourselves and made the best butter and cheese out of it. And Guernseys are smaller cows. They're friendly, like pets, and Bessie was part of our family.

Imagery you can "see" in your mind creates the persuasive weight of each of these stories. The farmer's lawyer wants us to see a big pair of eyes in a Guernsey head nudging the farmer with affection—a loss to the farmer's family that exceeds the loss of a grass-to-milk machine. The insurance company's lawyer, on the other hand, wants us to see the farmer's balance sheet, where a certain item of livestock is carried as an asset valued at a certain number of dollars.

If you develop an eye for revealing detail, your stories will much more quickly come to life as vivid and compelling. Vividness not only helps the reader remember the story, but it makes the story more believable. Imagery makes a story real.

Word choice is critical. The right words help the judge see the image.

6.   Finding the Story

Facts are not the story. They are the raw materials for the story.

A client sits in your office, describing in detail a problem that the client wants you to solve. The facts are these details. The client is not telling you a persuasive story. Clients usually don't know how to do that. They hire lawyers to do it for them. The client can tell you only facts—"I got this letter in the mail," "Smith told me the company was going bankrupt," "I can't pay my bills." In a law school writing assignment, you might get these details as part of your assignment.

Regardless of how you get the facts, they are not yet a story. The story is *hidden* in the facts. You have to find it there. Look for the equilibrium, the disturbance, and the struggle to restore equilibrium. Look for details that reveal character. Look for details that lend themselves to persuasive imagery. Assemble these into a story that fulfills the four purposes of storytelling—to motivate the judge to act, to communicate who your client and witnesses are, to communicate who the other side and their witnesses are, and to neutralize the unfavorable facts.

Try telling the story to a friend or relative whose intelligence and judgment you respect and who does not know the case you are working on. Telling the story orally helps you refine it and test it out before you start writing it. *Saying* it helps you understand it and how to improve it. Then ask how your friend or relative feels about the story. Does it motivate? Do the characters seem realistic? And so on.

7.   Two Last Questions

You've discovered the story. Now step back and ask yourself two questions.

First, can you summarize the essence of it persuasively in one or two sentences? If you can do that persuasively, those sentences are your theme (see

Section 5.A.1). If you can't, either the story is too complicated or you haven't identified the core facts. If the story is too complicated, your reader will get lost. If you don't know the core facts, you won't be able to focus on them when you tell the story. You will need to focus on them at the very beginning of the Statement of the Case. The Statement of the Case should begin with a paragraph that summarizes these very facts (see Chapter 31 [Richard K. Neumann, Jr. and Sheila Simon, Legal Writing, 2nd ed., (2011)]).

Second, will the judge care? If not, the story won't work because it doesn't motivate.

C.   TELLING THE STORY PERSUASIVELY

1.   Selecting Facts to Tell the Story

Here's how to select the facts for the Statement of the Case:

Step 1: Identify the facts that show how the relevant legal tests have or have not been satisfied. Make a list of the facts that show either how you have satisfied the governing legal tests or how your adversary has not. Some lawyers do this by making an elements-facts-witness/evidence chart. For example, you might make the chart on the next page if you represent the plaintiff and must show that you have satisfied the test for negligence concerning an auto accident witnessed by two pedestrians, Smith and Jones, both of whom corroborate the plaintiff's story (π = plaintiff; Δ = defendant).

The chart helps you see what the dispute is all about. The elements of duty, injury, and proximate causation are easily satisfied. The real issue is breach. Three witnesses say the defendant ran the stop sign, and one says the defendant did not. The chart helps you realize that your factual theory should be that the two disinterested witnesses (Smith and Jones), as well as the plaintiff, testified that the defendant ran the stop sign, and that only the defendant testified that he stopped before entering the intersection. Why is that a good theory? The plaintiff and defendant testified consistently with their own interests. But Smith and Jones are credible because they are disinterested.

Elements, Facts, Witnesses/Evidence Chart

Elements	Satisfied?	Facts	Witnesses/ Evidence
1. duty owed by Δ to π	yes	π driving on street that has no stoplight or stop sign—Δ driving on cross street with stop sign	testimony of π, Δ, Smith, and Jones

Elements	Satisfied?	Facts	Witnesses/ Evidence
2. Δ's breach of that duty	probably yes	Δ drove through stop sign without stopping	testimony of π, Smith, and Jones
			contradicted only by Δ
3. injury to π	yes	π's medical injuries	testimony of π, doctor, and paramedic; x-rays
		damage to π's car	testimony of π, mechanic, Smith and Jones; photos
4. proximately caused by Δ's breach	yes (if Δ breached)	the front of Δ's car hit the side of π's car	testimony of police officer, mechanic, π, Smith, and Jones; photos of damaged cars

When you write the Statement of the Case, include everything in the Facts column together with the supporting proof from the Witnesses/Evidence column. For example, find the duty element in the chart. Look at the facts that satisfy that element and the witnesses who testified to those facts. Now you know what to say in the Statement of the Case concerning that element:

> All the witnesses, including the defendant, testified that the intersection did not have a traffic light; that the plaintiff entered the intersection from the north on State Street, where there was no stop sign; and that the defendant entered from the east on Maple Lane, where a stop sign required him to stop.

In the Statement, you will *not* mention the duty element or say it was satisfied. That is legal analysis, which you will do in the Argument. In the Statement, you will only mention the substantiating facts and whatever proved them.

The defendant's lawyer might make her own version of this chart to identify the facts and proof she will need to mention in the Statement.

If several tests are involved, you might make a chart for each test. For example, suppose the defendant in the auto accident case has pleaded the affirmative defense of comparative negligence. Now two tests are in the case. The plaintiff must prove that the defendant was negligent. And the defendant must prove that the plaintiff was comparatively negligent. The facts relevant to each test can be identified by making a chart for that test.

Step 2: Identify additional facts that help tell your client's story persuasively. Include facts that accomplish the storytelling goals explained in §28.3 [Richard K. Neumann, Jr. and Sheila Simon, Legal Writing, 2nd ed., (2011)], such as facts that communicate who your client and witnesses are, as well as similar facts about the other side. Who is an innocent victim, who is predatory, who is careless, and so forth? Only by understanding what each fact *reveals* about people and events can you tell the client's story in a compelling way. Also include facts that a reader would need to understand the story, facts that hold the story together.

Step 3: Identify facts that hurt your case and facts on which your adversary will rely. If you do not include unfavorable facts, your Statement of the Case will lack credibility. Treat an unfavorable fact as an opportunity rather than a threat. If you include the unfavorable fact, you can try to neutralize it. The next section in this chapter explains how (see question 6 there). If you don't include the unfavorable fact in your Statement, you can't neutralize it—and it really will be a threat.

Step 4: Eliminate factual clutter. Too much information distracts from the story. Identify a witness by name only if the reader really needs to know. In the example above, the names of Smith and Jones are needed because they testify to so many different things, and because their testimony is crucial to the disputed element. But the doctor, paramedic, mechanic, and police officer can each be identified by their role instead ("the emergency room doctor who treated the plaintiff testified that . . . ").

Specify dates, times, and places only if they are essential to the story or your theory. Specifics about them can be seductively concrete while you are writing. But to a reader they can also obscure what really happened. It isn't necessary to say that the witnesses agree that the accident occurred at 1:25 p.m., that an ambulance arrived at 1:40, that at 1:53 the ambulance delivered the plaintiff to the emergency room at Highview Memorial Hospital, or that at 1:55 a doctor there began to treat the plaintiff. Just say, "Thirty minutes after the accident, the plaintiff was treated by a hospital emergency room physician." Unless the hospital is being sued or its identity is otherwise significant, naming it gets in the way of telling the story. The exact times also get in the way.

2. How to Test a Statement of the Case for Persuasiveness

While rewriting, ask yourself the following questions. They also appear on this book's website as a checklist, which you can print out.

1. Have you correctly decided which facts to include in the Statement? See the first section of this chapter.

2. Have you chosen a method of organization that tells the story persuasively? Set out the facts in a sequence that persuades and can easily be understood. Sometimes, the most effective sequence is chronological. But more often, a topical organization works better because you can use the way you organize the facts to imply the logical relationships between them. In some cases, you might try a topical organization that breaks into a chronological narrative where it's important for the reader to understand the sequence in which events happened. Use headings to break up the Statement and show how you have organized it.

3. Have you started with a punch? Begin the Statement with a short passage—one or two paragraphs—summarizing your most compelling facts and perhaps neutralizing the most unfavorable facts so that the judge understands the heart of your theory. This functions as an introduction to the story, although you don't need to call it that. For example:

> The defendant drove through a stop sign and into the plaintiff's car, putting him in the hospital for a week and disabling him from working for seven months. Every witness except the defendant testified that he entered the intersection without stopping. Although the plaintiff was driving an uninsured car with an expired registration, there was no evidence that these infractions caused the accident or contributed to the plaintiff's injuries.

Then, in the rest of the Statement, tell the story—describing in detail the facts you summarized at the beginning.

The opening passage is the most important part of the Statement. If written well, it puts the judge in a receptive frame of mind, tells the judge what facts to look for later; and creates a lasting impression. The opening passage is also one of the hardest parts of the Statement to write. But the extra time and effort are worth it. Never begin the Statement with neutral facts or unimportant facts. You can include the most unfavorable facts to neutralize them (as in the last sentence of the example above) but the introductory paragraphs are not always the best place to do this.

4. Have you reflected your theory throughout the Statement? Tightly focus the Statement on facts that advance your theory. If the Statement wanders aimlessly through the facts, the reader will not grasp your theory and may not even understand the story. Throughout the Statement, the reader should be aware of whom you represent from the way you tell the story. If the reader wonders about that, even for a paragraph or two, your Statement probably is unpersuasive. Every word should be selected to make the theory more clear. If you focus the Statement in this way, it can be surprisingly short.

5. Have you emphasized favorable facts? You can do that through organization. Readers tend to be most attentive at the beginning, least attentive in the middle, and attentive to a middling degree at the end. You can also describe the most favorable facts in detail while omitting marginal facts that would cloud the picture you want the reader to see. If a favorable fact is undisputed, you can point that out:

> Every witness, including the defendant, testified that the stop sign could easily be seen by a driver in the defendant's position (T. at 14, 35, 62, 68, 97, 132.)

You can also point to things that are missing from the record, where that helps you:

> No evidence suggested an emergency or other situation that might have justified disregarding a stop sign.

6. Have you neutralized unfavorable facts? The most effective method is to juxtapose an unfavorable fact with one or more favorable facts that show why the unfavorable fact should not hurt you. Juxtaposition is placing two things side by side. Effective juxtapositions often use "although" or "even though" contrasts. For example:

> Although the plaintiff was driving an uninsured car with an expired registration, there was no evidence that these infractions caused the accident or contributed to the plaintiff's injuries.

An unfavorable fact cannot be neutralized by tucking it away in an obscure part of the Statement. Hiding it will not make it go away.

7. Have you humanized your client? Be careful about how you refer to the parties. You could write "the plaintiff" and "the defendant" in a civil case or, in a criminal case, "the defendant" and "the State" (or "the People," "the Government," or "the Commonwealth"). More still can be conveyed by using some generic factual designation related to the issues: "the buyer" and "the seller" in a commercial dispute or "the employer" and "the employee" in a discrimination case. All those are clear enough for a reader to understand.

But how you refer to the parties can also have a persuasive effect. Many lawyers try to humanize their clients by referring to them by name while depersonalizing the opposing party ("the insurance company" or "the university"). Sometimes that works, and sometimes it doesn't. If the parties are both people, for example, it can be confusing and look unfair to call one party "Ms. Falco" and the other "the defendant."

In an appellate brief, a reader will be confused if you refer to the parties continually as "appellant" and "appellee." These designations identify only who lost in the court below. In many appellate courts, you are not allowed to use these designations inside a brief, although they appear on the cover page.[7]

Exercise I.   Storytelling

Using a case you have read in another course, develop the facts of the case into a story. Do not change or embellish the facts. Stay strictly faithful to the *substance* of what you read in the case. But develop a story that would move a listener or reader to feel or think that one party or the other should win. Use the techniques described in this chapter and in Chapter 30 [Richard K. Neumann, Jr. and Sheila Simon, Legal Writing, 2nd ed., (2011)]. Then tell the story to another student and ask that student to suggest improvements.

D.   MAKING THE FACT STATEMENT PERSUASIVE

Most courts frown on the inclusion of legal arguments in the fact statement. They frown even more on lying, even if by omission, or on stretching the truth in the way that you characterize the facts. You should include all legally

---

7. *See, e.g.,* Rule 28(d) of the Federal Rules of Appellate Procedure.

significant facts, even those that may hurt your case. Including all relevant facts is important both for "moral" reasons—your oath as an attorney requires it—and for practical reasons—your opponent will point out that you lied, and you will lose your credibility with the court.[8] Judge Morey L. Sear, of the United States District Court for the Eastern District of Louisiana, notes that "[i]f a lawyer's brief . . . fudges on the content of clear testimony, credibility is immediately destroyed. In my view, credibility is one of the most important virtues a litigator can possess."[9]

Supreme Court Justice Ruth Bader Ginsburg advises that "[a]bove all, a good brief is trustworthy. It states the facts honestly."[10] Judge Parker notes that severe distortions of the facts "will actually make me stop reading the brief and go to the district court's opinion, or even the opposing brief."[11]

Nevertheless, you can use persuasive writing techniques to tell the story from your point of view, to highlight the facts that are in your favor, and to lead the reader to draw honest and favorable conclusions about your client's case.[12]

When drafting the fact statement, remember that your reader will not be a passive recipient of information, dutifully taking in whatever you have put on the page and doing nothing more with it. Most readers—yourself included—are constantly assessing, using inductive and deductive reasoning, leaping to conclusions, and, at times, leaving the text entirely. In the argument, you will be announcing your conclusions to the reader and then, ideally, supporting them with your analysis. In the fact statement, on the other hand, you can provide information that the reader can put together to reach a conclusion. If you do it skillfully enough, the reader will have drawn a conclusion in your favor even before reaching the first page of the argument section.

For example, my father, who served in the Coast Guard in the early 1950s, tells this possibly apocryphal story about a captain and his first mate—and at least one episode of drunkenness:

> One day, when the sailors took shore leave, the first mate returned to the ship drunk. The Captain recorded this event, noting, "The first mate was drunk today" in the Captain's log. The first mate has the responsibility for keeping the log when the Captain is off duty, so he soon saw the note. He was furious; he had never been drunk before, he had been off duty when he was drunk, and he was one of a dozen drunken sailors, none of whose drunkenness was recorded in the log. He decided to retaliate. He knew he couldn't lie about the Captain, for the Captain would be seeing the log the very next day. So he wrote the simple truth: "The Captain was sober today."

If you read that log without knowing the details, you would no doubt jump to the conclusion that the Captain was *usually* drunk; thus, it was worth recording the rare occasion when he was sober. Scholars who study narrative theory note that readers who jump to conclusions probably do so due to their conscious or

---

8. *See, e.g.*, Parker, *supra* note 5, at 462.

9. Morey L. Sear, *Briefing in the United States District Court for the Eastern District of Louisiana*, 70 Tul. L. Rev. 207, 219 (1995).

10. Ruth Bader Ginsburg, *Remarks on Appellate Advocacy*, 50 S.C. L. Rev. 567, 568 (1999). *See also* Joel F. Dubina, *How to Litigate Successfully in the United States Court of Appeals for the Eleventh Circuit*, 20 Cumb. L. Rev. 1, 5 (1998/1999); Sarah B. Duncan, *Pursuing Quality: Writing a Helpful Brief*, 30 St. Mary's L.J. 1093, 1101 (1999).

11. Parker, *supra* note 5, at 462.

12. For an excellent discussion of persuasive writing techniques in fact statements, *see* Laurel Currie Oates & Anne M. Enquist, *The Legal Writing Handbook* §§17.5, 18.12 (4th ed., Aspen 2006).

unconscious awareness of "stock stories," or "schemas" that they have been accumulating all of their lives.[13] Because the state of being sober is an unremarkable fact for most people, a reader subconsciously decides that if the mate wrote "the captain was sober today," he must have done so because the captain was usually *not* sober. If we can assume that the captain was not actually a drunkard, the first mate enlisted his readers and had them tell themselves a lie on his behalf. But even though the mate told the literal truth, he is not innocent of the lie: his knowledge of human thought and behavior no doubt told him how his readers would react, and he wrote his truthful statement conscious of the untruth that would result.[14]

I am not telling you this story so that you will make your readers lie to themselves; rather, I want you to realize that whenever people read, many different thought processes come into play: they use deductive and inductive reasoning, and their own knowledge and prejudices, to fill in details and jump to conclusions. Readers jump to conclusions based not only on information that is included, but also based on information that is not included. For example, while I was in the middle of reading a novel set in and written in the nineteenth century, a new male character was described as "clean-shaven." I suddenly realized that all of the *other* male characters must have had "whiskers." I had pictured them as clean-shaven because that fit with my schema, or default image, of adult males: Presume no facial hair unless told otherwise. The author did not believe that whiskers were worth mentioning, for in her world whiskers were the default mode for adult men.

Recognize that when you are writing a statement of facts, you are telling a story. Aim to tell the story in a way that is consistent with and promotes your legal argument. As indicated above, readers sometimes jump to conclusions; those conclusions may be factual conclusions or legal ones. For example, if you are trying to persuade your reader that certain activities were or were not within an employee's "scope of employment," you might tell the story in a way that emphasizes the connection between the challenged activities and his job duties and responsibilities. To the extent that you can get your reader to conclude that the challenged activities were "just part of the job," you have gone a long way to advance your "scope of employment" argument. Storytelling can go beyond appealing just to "pathos," or a reader's emotions. When done well, it can enhance the credibility of the writer (thus appealing to "ethos") and engage the reader's logical thought processes as well ("logos").[15] Upon reading the captain and the first mate story, after all, you used logical reasoning to reach your own understanding of why the first mate wrote "the captain was sober today."

13. Linda L. Berger, *How Embedded Knowledge Structures Affect Judicial Decision Making: A Rhetorical Analysis of Metaphor, Narrative, and Imagination in Child Custody Disputes*, 18 S. Cal. Interdisc. L.J. 259, 263 (2009) ("We make sense out of new experiences by placing them into categories and cognitive frames called schema or scripts that emerge from prior experience.") (citations omitted). For further discussion of narrative theory and other persuasive writing techniques, *see* Michael R. Smith, *Advanced Legal Writing: Theories and Strategies in Persuasive Writing* (2d ed., Aspen 2008).

14. *See* Steven J. Johansen, *This Is Not the Whole Truth: The Ethics of Telling Stories to Clients*, 38 Ariz. St. L.J. 961, 992 (2006) ("left unchecked . . . [the] deception [of false stories] could be disruptive to our legal system").

15. *See* Jennifer Sheppard, *Once Upon a Time, Happily Ever After, and in a Galaxy Far, Far Away: Using Narrative to Fill the Cognitive Gap Left Behind by Overreliance on Pure Logic in Appellate Briefs and Motion Memoranda*, 46 Willamette L. Rev. 255, 256 (2009).

Legal writers can use story telling method to help their readers understand why certain parties have behaved in particular ways. Professor Ruth Anne Robbins notes that "people respond–instinctively and intuitively" to certain schemas and "character archetypes," and that lawyers should "systematically and deliberately integrate into their storytelling the larger picture of their clients' goals by subtly portraying their individual clients as heroes on a particular life path."[16] Professor Robbins advises against casting the client's opponent (or other antagonist) as a Voldemort-style villain.[17] Instead, she recommends a more benign role: the antagonist is some one who is frustrating the hero, barring him or her from achieving a goal.[18]

You may want to tell your story in terms of a quest.[19] What does your client seek? Rather than thinking in pure procedural terms–that your client wants the court to grant or deny a motion, or to affirm or reverse a decision–think in terms of your theme. In the Coors Beer case, for example, Coors wanted to give its customers truthful information about the percentage of alcohol in its beers, but it was thwarted by an outdated government regulation. The government, in contrast, sought to protect its citizens from harmful binge drinking, and it was thwarted by greedy corporations who wanted to make money by promoting excessive alcohol consumption. In *Miller v. Albright*, the petitioner could have the goal of establishing a relationship with her father, while the government seeks the right to control its borders and to determine who is eligible for automatic citizenship. A more difficult case is the case of an employee who is trying to establish individual liability of supervisors so that she can sue the person who sexually harassed her. Rather than portraying her purely as a victim,[20] the fact statement can show her as someone who wants to vindicate herself and prevent future harassment by suing her harasser directly. The defendant, in contrast, could portray himself as someone who wants to be treated as an individual and not as a corporation.

Your fact statement can identify the hero or protagonist (perhaps your client, perhaps a legislature, perhaps the constitution) and the antagonists (perhaps your opponent, or some agent of your opponent).[21] Your protagonist, though, is frustrated; its goal has been thwarted by some outside actor or problem.[22] Seen from this perspective, the antagonist can be a person, a governmental body, or an "absurd" interpretation of a statute. Your client's goal is not merely a particular court decision; rather, the goal is an experience or status *made possible* by the court's decision.

Accordingly, when you are writing your statement of the facts, review your theme and the legal conclusions you want the reader to draw, and consider how those legal conclusions relate to the facts. Recognize conclusions that you might want to lead your readers to, and conclusions you want the reader to avoid. Consider what presumptions, schemas, or "default images," could be relevant to the case generally, and to people like your client or your opponent in

---

16. Ruth Anne Robbins, *Harry Potter, Ruby Slippers and Merlin: Telling the Client's Story Using the Characters and Paradigm of the Archetypal Hero's Journey*, 29 Seattle U. L. Rev. 767, 768-69 (2006).

17. *Id.* at 788.

18. *See id.*

19. *See Id.* at 781-82.

20. *See Id.* at 779-80 (advising against portraying client as a victim).

21. Kenneth D. Chestek, *The Plot Thickens: Appellate Brief as Story*, 14 Leg. Writ. 127, 152-53 (2008) (describing strategies for choosing protagonists and antagonists).

22. Robbins, *supra n. 16*, at 778 (discussing different types of heroes, from the innocent to the warrior).

particular. For example, has your client had several drug arrests? Could your readers have certain presumptions about police officers or corporate executives that you want to reinforce or rebut? You can do this by giving details that contradict or support your readers' presumptions.

For example, if you want the court to overturn your client's criminal conviction, it might help the court to decide in your favor if it believes both that your client was treated unfairly and that your client is essentially an innocent person who was in the wrong place at the wrong time (a familiar schema). Your fact statement can include the details that will help the reader reach these conclusions independently. In *Holloway v. United States*, 526 U.S. 1 (1999), for example, counsel for Mr. Holloway had to convince the Court that it should overturn a conviction under the federal carjacking statute. The controversy centered on whether Holloway's participation in the carjacking constituted sufficient "intent to cause death or serious bodily harm." Holloway (petitioner at the Supreme Court) admittedly had been part of the carjackings, and a carjacking is a frightening crime to most people. One (student) counsel for Holloway tried to give details in the facts that would contradict the presumption that someone who would participate in a carjacking would be a violent person, and essentially tried to portray the client as an innocent who was trying to make the best of a bad situation:

Good Example

Vernon Lennon recruited Petitioner to steal cars with him. Record 156. Lennon showed Holloway the revolver that Lennon planned to carry during the commission of the robberies. Apparently, it was Holloway's job to drive the "getaway" car. Id. There is no evidence in the record that Lennon told Holloway that he planned to shoot the victims. Holloway never carried a gun during any of the robberies.
On October 14, 1994, Lennon and Holloway stole a car in Queens. Record 83-84. The car's owner sustained no injuries. The next day, the two men stole a Toyota and a Mercedes-Benz. Record 84. Holloway never even approached the driver of the Toyota; like the first driver, he escaped unharmed. Id. Lennon and Holloway both advanced toward the driver of the Mercedes-Benz, and Lennon produced his gun and threatened to shoot. Record 84. When the driver hesitated momentarily, Holloway stepped in and struck him once, before Lennon could take any action. Id. At this point, the driver surrendered his keys and fled, essentially unharmed. Id.

These details emphasize that Holloway never carried a gun and that none of the victims were shot. In the last incident, Holloway seems to become a legitimate hero; it appears that he prevented Lennon, his accomplice (or perhaps, in this telling, a bullying ringleader), from shooting one of the victims.

After you have considered your theme, the conclusions you want the reader to draw, and the schemas you might want to exploit, make a list of all of the facts that are relevant to your case. You may consult the abstract of the record, the record itself, the lower court decisions, and even the argument to come up with all of the legally (and emotionally) significant facts. (Be certain, of course, not to mischaracterize facts that were offered into evidence and rejected.) Perhaps divide your list into three parts: neutral facts, positive facts, and negative facts. As you tell your story, you can use some or all of the following persuasive techniques to highlight the positive facts and "lowlight" the negative ones.

1.   *Positions of Emphasis*

An easy and effective way to highlight information is to put it into positions of emphasis within the document. Readers subconsciously pay more attention to information that appears before or after a mental or physical break within the document. Thus, both the beginning and the ending of the fact statement are positions of emphasis, as are the beginnings and endings of any heading sections within the facts, and even the first and last sentences of paragraphs.

When writing your fact statement, strive to put your "positive facts" into positions of emphasis. You may even create positions of emphasis by inserting topical headings, by creating paragraph breaks, or by using headings to separate the introduction from the fact statement or the fact statement from the statement of the "case" (i.e., the description of the proceedings below).

2.   *Pointillism*

One way to think about the power of storytelling is to compare it to pointillism, a painting technique developed in the nineteenth century by Georges Seurat. Instead of mixing red and blue paint on his palette to make purple paint, he painted red dots next to blue dots and allowed the viewer's eye to "mix" the color. Legal writers can practice pointillism to try to control the way the reader sees information in the fact statement. If you put certain facts next to certain other facts, the reader's brain may "mix" the information to draw the conclusion that you want. When making your list of facts, try to identify facts that can be paired, either to lead the reader to draw a good conclusion or to prevent the reader from drawing a bad one. For bad facts, use the "buddy system": Make sure that every bad fact that is included in the statement is paired with a good fact that explains (or neutralizes) its presence. Certain negative facts will look better if they are juxtaposed with a good fact, or even a neutral fact that readers can use to explain to themselves why the negative fact occurred or why it is not significant. For example, in the case of *Miller v. Albright*, 523 U.S. 420 (1998), Ms. Miller, who was born in the Philippines, was trying to establish United States citizenship through her relationship with her father, a United States citizen. One reason that had been given for limiting the ability to establish citizenship in this way was the prevention of fraud. Ms. Miller's father had not been listed on her birth certificate, a "bad fact" that needed to be addressed. One writer tried to put that fact into a good context in the following way:

Good Example

Ms. Miller was born in the Philippines on June 20, 1970. App. 15. Although her birth record did not include her father's name, a voluntary paternity decree issued on July 27, 1992, by a Texas state court established Charlie R. Miller, a United States citizen, as her biological father. App. to Pet. for Writ of Cert., at 37.

Thus, the reader learns that even though the father's name was not on the birth certificate, he was willing to have paternity established by a voluntary paternity decree. This juxtaposition would encourage readers to conclude that their relationship was a legitimate one and that fraud was not an issue here.

3.   Spending the Reader's Time, Saving the Reader's Energy

To make sure that your reader remembers the positive facts in your case, make him or her spend more time and less energy on them. Use several sentences to make a point instead of crowding the information into one sentence.[23] Be as concrete as you can be when describing a positive fact so that the reader doesn't have to figure out what happened. Conversely, when you want to deemphasize a fact, don't spend much time on it, don't go into a lot of detail, and don't use concrete language. For example, in *City of Indianapolis v. Edmond*, 531 U.S. 32 (2000), a case about the constitutionality of drug interdiction roadblocks, counsel for the city of Indianapolis might describe the police procedure succinctly:

> Traffic stops consist of two simple steps: Officers verify the driver's license and registration, and then conduct a quick walk-around of the car with a narcotics-sniffing dog. Record 57a. They conduct a more thorough search *only* if the narcotics dog, plain-view, or plain-smell observation reveals a suspicion of narcotics possession, or if the driver gives explicit consent to search. Record 57a, 53a.

These two rather long sentences give a complete, but not detailed, account. The reader would have to expend energy to identify the details that this brief description implies, and more than likely would not do so. Counsel for the respondent, on the other hand, might describe the police procedure in greater detail:

> Upon entering the checkpoint, an automobile's driver and occupants are subjected to a number of examinations, which are conducted by Indianapolis police officers. Record 57a. First, the officers approach the vehicle, and the driver is asked to produce both a valid driver's license and the registration for the vehicle. Record 57a. After one officer examines and verifies this documentation, other officers scrutinize the vehicle in two ways. First, they use plain-view detection techniques, looking through the vehicle's windows. In addition, they use plain-smell methods, sniffing the air around the car as they walk around it. Both of these techniques are used to determine whether the officers can discover probable cause that would allow them to conduct a more invasive search of the automobile and its occupants.

---

23. *See also* Oates & Enquist, *supra* note 13, at 248-49 (discussing "airtime" and detail).

Record 57a. Furthermore, if the officers can persuade the driver to consent to a search, they can conduct an even more extensive search of the vehicle. Record 53a. One other method of search is used during even routine stops: A narcotics detection dog is walked around the exterior of the vehicle, in a final attempt to discover probable cause to search the vehicle for narcotics. Record 57a.

Notice how the writer has unpacked the details to state explicitly information that is implicit in the first example. In the first example, the officers "verify license and registration." These words imply request, retrieval, handing over, and inspection; the second example provides these details. The second example uses this detail to create an impression of significant intrusion on the driver and the passengers. The writer provides every detail; the reader does not have to spend any energy figuring out things on his or her own. The numerous sentences, the level of detail, and the word choice all work to create an image of a long, intrusive stop. If the reader believes in minimal police intrusion without probable cause, he or she could be halfway to a favorable conclusion merely after reading the statement of facts, for it will have created a concrete picture in the reader's mind of precisely what a "routine stop" entails.

Of course, as with any persuasive method, use good judgment. If you go overboard in either direction, you will hurt rather than help your argument.

Generally

The statement of the case in an appellate brief or a motion memorandum essentially tells the court the story of the litigation, or how the case at hand came to be before the court. While the statement of the case is similar in some ways to a statement of facts in an office memorandum, it is different in a few important aspects. First, the statement of the case includes the procedural history of the litigation as well as a statement of the facts. Second, when you include a fact in the statement of the case, you must show the reader where that information is in the record by citing to the record. Finally, and most importantly, the statement of the case is an opportunity for you to advocate for your client.

Organization

To tell the story of the litigation, the statement of the case must include a statement of facts. What facts belong in this section? You must include all facts relevant to the legal issues, whether they are favorable to your client or not. The duty of candor that lawyers owe to the court requires that you include *all* relevant facts whether they help or harm your client. Furthermore, you must include any background facts that will help the reader understand the context in which the legally relevant facts arose. Finally, the statement of the case must include any fact that you rely on in the argument section of the brief or motion memorandum.

Remember that the statement of facts should include only *facts*. It should not include any inferences that you have drawn from the facts nor should it include any legal conclusions or legal argument. While you can be persuasive in the statement of the case, and you should be, your persuasion must be subtle. If opposing counsel can take issue with the facts as you've presented them, then your bias is obvious. Thus, if opposing counsel can say that you've misrepresented a fact, then your persuasion is not subtle. So how do you subtly persuade? By crafting your facts so that they suggest the inference you want the reader to make or the legal conclusion you want the reader to reach. For instance, since you cannot ignore unfavorable facts, you must do something to minimize the harm that unfavorable fact can do your client. You can minimize the harm an unfavorable fact can do to your client by juxtaposing that unfavorable fact with a favorable fact that explains it away or lessens its impact. Thus, if your client acted in a manner that appears bad, you should couple it with a fact that shows why he or she acted in that way or with a fact that makes it seem more logical that he or she acted in that way.

For example, say you represent a client who is suing a funeral home for intentional infliction of emotional distress following an incident where employees of the funeral home dropped the casket of your client's father and disfigured his face when they flung him back into the casket. You know that the funeral home is going to argue that your client couldn't have been too distraught by what happened given that she continued on to the cemetery for the burial. The fact that your client was able to continue to the cemetery soon after the event at issue is harmful to your case. However, if you juxtapose that unfavorable fact with the fact that one of her friends who was a doctor insisted on giving her a tranquilizer before she continued on to the cemetery, you negate the harmful impact associated with the fact she was able to go to the cemetery. You suggest, without saying, that your client was able to continue on to the cemetery *only because she was sedated.*

In addition to the statement of facts, the statement of the case includes the procedural history of the case. The procedural history of the case is just that— it details the procedural steps that brought the litigation to the court. The procedural history identifies the parties to the litigation by their proper names and often describes their legal relationship to each other (e.g., lawyer-client, doctor-patient). It identifies the nature of the case or the type of action filed by the plaintiff or petitioner (e.g., a criminal case in which the defendant is charged with assault with a dangerous instrument or a civil action for employment discrimination). The procedural history also details the pertinent proceedings below (e.g., trial or a motion for summary judgment) and the disposition below (e.g., conviction of a criminal defendant, decision in favor of the plaintiff, or grant of summary judgment). If the case is before the court on appeal, the procedural history identifies the party who appealed the trial court's decision.

Where should you put the procedural history? You can either begin the statement of the case with the procedural history or you can end the section with it. Where you locate the procedural history depends on the function you want it to serve. If you begin the statement of the case with the procedural history, it will provide the reader with legal context for the facts that follow and aid the reader in making sense of the facts that you present. If you place the procedural history at the end of the section, you can use it as a transition into argument. That does not mean that you can argue in the statement of the case. It means that you may draft the procedural history in a way that allows you to articulate the basis for your client's action. For example, say you represent Lily Cromwell, an illustrator who is being sued by Major League Baseball for copyright infringement because she wrote and illustrated a graphic novel that used the image of Chief Wahoo, the mascot for the Cleveland Indians. She claims that she wrote the graphic novel to criticize Major League Baseball's use of racial stereotypes for commercial gain. The plaintiffs filed a motion for summary judgment, and you have filed a cross motion for summary judgment on behalf of Ms. Cromwell. In the motion memorandum, you plan to argue that Ms. Cromwell's graphic novel was a fair use of the image, which is an affirmative defense to a copyright infringement claim. You plan to argue that the graphic novel was a fair use of the image because it was a parody that criticized Major League Baseball's use of a racial stereotype for commercial gain. If you placed the procedural history at the end of the statement of the case, you might state it as follows:

> After becoming aware of Lily Cromwell's graphic novel, Major League Baseball and the Cleveland Indians filed suit against her for copyright infringement. Plaintiffs then filed a motion for summary judgment. Ms. Cromwell filed a cross motion for summary judgment *seeking a decision in her favor on the ground that her use of the Chief Wahoo image was for a parodic purpose and, as such, was a fair use of the image.*

Pay particular attention to the italicized language. By presenting the procedural history in this way, you are not arguing that Cromwell's use of the image was for a parodic purpose or that her use of the image was a fair use. Rather, you are stating the basis for her request for summary judgment. This distinction is important. If you simply informed the court that Cromwell's use was for a parodic purpose or was a fair use of the image, you would be making legal conclusions. You would have already decided the issues before the court. By articulating the basis for Cromwell's motion for summary judgment, on the other hand, you are simply stating facts. And facts may be included in the statement of the case.

Citing to the Record

You must cite to the record for each fact that you include in the statement of the case. In an appeal, you will cite to the record on appeal. In a trial matter, the record will consist of the pleadings, discovery, and hearing transcripts.

Though citing to the record in support of each fact included in the statement of the case seems technical, it has a persuasive impact. First, citing to the record shows the reader that the fact exists; you did not just make it up. Second, citing to the record makes the court's job easier. If you fail to cite to the record, the court will have to dig through the record to find out whether your statement is correct. This will not endear you to the court and may dampen the court's enthusiasm for ruling in favor of your client. Further, it may undermine your credibility and cause the court to view anything you say with skepticism.

The Importance of Storytelling

Why Lawyers Should Tell Stories

Rule-based reasoning is the primary form of reasoning used by lawyers. This is how we are taught to think in law school. This is what the professors mean when they say that they are teaching law students to think like lawyers. Consequently, it makes sense that rule-based reasoning, or logic, is the primary tool in a lawyer's toolbox. This means that, when drafting an appellate brief or motion memorandum, lawyers tend to focus on the legal arguments in the Argument section. They often pay little attention to the Statement of the Case.

However, cognitive research has discovered that humans comprehend concepts expressed in terms of narratives, or stories, better than those expressed as abstract principles. Practically speaking, this means that, because humans need stories to understand a series of chronological events, we tend to subconsciously arrange new experiences in story form. We do this to make sense of new experiences, to understand what happened and what will happen, and to decide what to think of what happened and will happen.

The stock story is the primary tool humans use to help them understand new experiences. Stock stories, which are also known as myths or master stories, provide ways for an entire culture to interpret certain experiences. Stock stories help us interpret and comprehend events based on the minimal facts with which we are provided because they supplement those facts with assumptions about how the world works and how the current events should play out. Thus, stock stories provide templates allowing us to predict how humans would act in a given situation, allow generalizations about the meaning of those actions, and suggest what the outcome should be in a given situation.

Stock stories can be pitfalls for the unwary lawyer. Remember that stock stories operate at a subconscious level, so we are unaware of their impact on our thinking. When presented with a new situation, we compare the facts of that situation with our collection of stock stories and select the one that most resembles the new situation. The stock story then provides meaning to the facts before us and offers an evaluation of them. However, once we have selected a stock story within which to interpret the situation, our judgments are based on the assumptions derived from the social knowledge embedded in the stock story, not from the unique facts and circumstances of the situation before us. Additionally, the outcome suggested by the stock story will seem like the only natural result of the events leading up to it. Consequently, stock stories make certain outcomes seem inevitable, guide our judgments and evaluations in new situations, and make it difficult for us to deviate from what the story has taught us about how the world operates. Consequently, this is bad news for the lawyer whose client's facts trigger a stock story that ends in a manner not favorable to the client! Therefore, a lawyer must be aware of the stock stories that may be triggered by the facts of her client's case and the potentially harmful effects that some of those stories may have on that case. Furthermore, lawyers must be able to tell an alternative story that reinforces views helpful to the client.

Given that stock stories help us make sense of new situations by telling us what to think of how and why individuals acted a certain way and how those events would and should end, they have a profound effect on the outcome of cases. Stock stories help the decision maker, whether it is a judge or jury, form his or her impression of what really happened based on the evidence presented. They affect which party's version of events the decision maker will accept; if neither party's version matches up with the selected stock story, the decision maker will either accept the version that is closest to what he or she believes happened or reject both. Further, the decision maker's understanding of what happened and why often affects which party he or she thinks should win the case and, consequently, how he or she will apply the law. It will affect how broadly or narrowly the decision maker will interpret the rules and how much he or she is willing to bend the law to the facts. As a result, the Statement of the Case is every bit as important as the Argument section, and a lawyer should spend a great deal of time crafting an effective story to supplement the more traditionally accepted rule-based reasoning employed in the Argument section. When the Statement of the Case and the Argument section work together and reinforce each other, a lawyer's advocacy will be much more sophisticated and effective. Thus, it is imperative that lawyers gain an understanding of how to craft an effective story.

Elements of a Story

Many elements help a writer tell an effective story: character, conflict, plot, point of view, setting, theme, voice, and style. Because legal writing convention requires a lawyer to use a formal style, the elements of style and voice are largely determined by legal writing conventions. Additionally, point of view (the perspective from which the story is told) is largely determined by legal writing convention. Lawyers tend to tell the story from their client's perspective. After all, it is the client's story; it only makes sense to tell it from the client's point-of-view. Finally, if a lawyer attempted to tell the story from the opposing party's point of view, it would undermine the lawyer's credibility. The lawyer is not privy to how the opposing party perceived the events that occurred, nor does the lawyer know what motivated the opposing party. While style, voice, and point of view are largely determined by legal writing convention, the remaining elements are not. Thus, this chapter will examine the elements of conflict, theme, character, setting, and plot.

Defining the Conflict

When crafting a story to explain the case, you should begin by defining the conflict. Conflict captures the reader's interest; the reader wants to understand how the conflict began and how it should be resolved. Luckily for lawyers, each lawsuit comes with a ready-made conflict. Conflict is the reason the parties are in litigation; conflict is what brought the parties before the court. But, while litigation comes with a ready-made conflict, the difficulty lies in how you *define* that conflict. Defining the conflict is essential to success because it determines whether the reader will want the conflict resolved in your client's favor.

Conflicts fall into seven categories: person versus person, person versus self, person versus society, person versus machine, person versus nature, person versus God, and person versus everyone. When deciding how to define the conflict in a legal context, you should remember that presenting the conflict as person versus person is seldom effective. This is true even with regard to causes of action that seem naturally to fall into the person versus person category, such as negligence, defamation, and breach of contract cases. Conflicts defined as person versus person are difficult to present because no person is entirely good or entirely evil. Attempts to make a client seem entirely good or the opposing party seem entirely evil will be seen as unrealistic. Presenting a party as such will harm your credibility and make everything else you say suspect. Furthermore, presenting the conflict as person versus person may cheapen the situation by making the dispute seem like nothing more than a personal dispute in which society, and the court, has no greater interest.

How should you define a conflict in a particular case? Several examples are included here. First, in criminal matters, the prosecution will define the conflict as person versus society. From the prosecutor's perspective, the defendant's criminal act did not just harm the victim; it harmed society as a whole. Defense attorneys, on the other hand, will rarely, if ever, wish to present the conflict as person versus society. Rather, defense attorneys representing clients whose behavior is induced by alcohol, drug addiction, or mental illness may find it helpful to define the conflict as person versus self. By presenting the client as struggling against addiction or mental illness, a lawyer may tap into the audience's sympathy or natural desire to provide assistance. In a criminal matter, this strategy may result in the client spending less time in prison, or receiving much needed drug rehabilitation or mental health treatment.

When dealing with an opposing party who is a powerful entity, such as the government or a large corporation, defining the conflict as person versus society or as person versus machine may be helpful. You can evoke images of a powerful entity bullying a smaller, weaker opponent (e.g., David versus Goliath). In such a situation, most readers will sympathize with and root for the underdog.

Defining the conflict as person versus society may be useful when a client is on the fringes of society or has been marginalized by society and then subjected to discriminatory laws. Any time society (through the legislature) decides that a group of persons (whether that group is defined based on a characteristic such as race, religion, gender, sexuality, etc.) has fewer rights than the majority, defining the conflict as person versus society allows you to convey the disastrous impact that the discriminatory law would have on your client's life. Thus, in civil rights or equal protection matters, where societal discrimination may be engrained in the laws, defining the conflict as person versus society allows you to focus on the devastating effects that such institutionalized discrimination will have on the lives of individuals.

On the other hand, you may wish to define the conflict as person versus machine rather than as person versus society when the opposing party is a powerful institution or leader rather than a discriminatory law. It is not difficult to envision the government, with its bureaucracy, as a cold, impassive machine that grinds along as the gears of efficiency turn. Nor is it difficult to imagine the government or a large corporation as an automaton that seeks to crush its smaller, weaker opponent under the weight of its might.

Theme

In literary writing, the theme is the main point that the story is making; it is the lesson that the author wants the reader to take away from the story. In other words, the theme is the moral of the story. In legal stories, on the other hand, the theme is your "theory of the case." It is your Argument section boiled down into a sentence or two; it is the message that you want the reader to take away from the story. In short, the theme is the reason your client should win.

A good theme makes a statement about the law, the facts, or about how the law and the facts intersect. A good theme is consistent with the facts of the case, explains away as many of the unfavorable facts as possible, has a solid basis in the law, and appeals to the reader's common sense notions of fairness. Moreover, a good theme does not ask the reader to believe that the parties or witnesses behaved in improbable ways; to do so would undermine the theme's plausibility and your credibility as an advocate. Finally, your theme should present your client in a sympathetic light.

Consequently, when you develop a theme, or theory of the case, you should consider what your client's case is *about*. Thus, theme is closely related to how the conflict is defined. When developing a theme, you should concentrate on how to finish the following statement: "My client should win because . . . ."

In seeking to finish that sentence, Professor Linda Edwards suggests that you fill in the blanks of the following statement: "This is a story about a (man) (woman) who (is) (was) . . . [describe client] . . . and who is struggling to . . . ." Once you complete the previous statements, identify a public policy that supports an outcome in your client's favor. A theme that is policy-based gives the court an additional reason to choose your interpretation of the law over opposing counsel's interpretation. Thus, when all else is equal, a good theme may help to sway the court in your client's favor.

Character Development

Character development is the most important aspect of a story. The story's conflict is relevant only to the extent it affects the characters and exposes who they really are. The way a character responds to conflict or struggles to overcome adversity reveals that character's true nature.

A variety of characters exist in any story, but the most important characters are the protagonist and the antagonist. The protagonist is the main character of the story. The protagonist is the person or institution you want the reader to empathize with and cheer on. The antagonist, on the other hand, is the person or institution against whom the protagonist struggles. The antagonist is the protagonist's adversary. Thus, when crafting a story in a legal context, your client should generally be the protagonist of the story. This is because you are trying to get the judge to rule in favor of your client, and the judge is more likely to do so if he or she empathizes with and roots for your client. If you are the prosecutor in a criminal case, you should cast the victim as the protagonist of the story.

Remember that stock stories supply a stock of characters that cast both people and things in archetypal roles. These archetypal roles include champions, companions, children, tricksters, mentors, kings, mothers, damsels in distress, and sages. Individuals as well as institutions, such as corporations, agencies, courts, legislatures, or prosecutor's offices, can fill these archetypal roles. Even an abstract concept can be a character in a legal story. The law itself, whether it is a constitutional provision, statute, regulation, policy, or legal principle from a precedent case, can be a character. Thus, you can treat a statute or legal principle as a sentient being. For example, when you have a client who is unsympathetic (say because he or she is a criminal defendant), you may make your client a proxy for a legal principle or ideal like the Fourth Amendment. In doing so, you shift the focus from the particulars of your client to the Fourth Amendment so that a ruling against your client is a ruling against the Fourth Amendment. In such a story, the Fourth Amendment, not your client, is the protagonist of the story.

Although stock stories may cast people, institutions, and ideas in archetypal roles that serve as templates for characters, you still need to develop and humanize those characters so that the reader sees them as real people with thoughts, feelings, and dreams. This is particularly important for the protagonist. If your client seems like a two-dimensional cardboard cutout, then the reader will not empathize with your client and will not wish to resolve the matter in your client's favor.

So how do you get a judge to empathize with and cheer on your client? You must humanize your client by presenting that client in a way that causes the judge to both sympathize with and like the client. To accomplish this, you have to do more than just identify the client by name and title. You have to demonstrate that the client is a valuable, productive member of society. Any number of facts can demonstrate this, including graduation from high school or college (even earning a GED), volunteer work, membership in social clubs that improve society, military service, or service to the international community (e.g., Peace Corps or the Red Cross). Employment, particularly long-term employment, can also humanize a client and make him or her seem productive, and consequently, likable. The same is true for a client who is good at his or her job (assuming that the client is not a career criminal!). Additional attributes that will make a client sympathetic and likeable include any notable achievements or awards received by the client, or if the client has overcome past adversity.

Furthermore, examining your client's goals and motivations may make him or her seem more real and more likable, but only if the reader agrees with, or at a minimum, understands those goals or motivations. Character development reveals who the parties to the litigation truly are by showing *why* they acted the way they did. If your client's goals and motivations seem sensible, then the reader will understand and possibly agree with them. Finally, presenting the client's goals and motivations may have the added benefit of appealing to the reader on an emotional level, resulting in the reader empathizing with the client.

Humanizing your client may be difficult when the client is a business or government agency. You can hardly make a client seem like a "real person" when it is not a person at all. You can overcome this problem by presenting attributes of an institutional client that make it likable and evoke empathy. For instance, if your client provides products or services that benefit society in some way, then you should make the reader aware of any such socially beneficial functions. Examples of socially beneficial products include medical equipment or pharmaceuticals. An example of a socially beneficial service is the Department of Justice's role in prosecuting crimes and civil rights violations. If an institutional client fails to provide socially beneficial goods or services, or only minimally does so, several other facts can make the client more appealing. For instance, a client that employs numerous individuals from the community or engages in philanthropy is more likable than one that does not. Additionally, as with individual clients, an institutional client that has overcome adversity to become successful or has any notable achievements will appeal to the reader. Furthermore, if the institutional client has served the country in times of need, then this will contribute to the client's likability. For example, if you represented Wal-Mart, you might let the reader know that the company shipped supplies into New Orleans following Hurricane Katrina.

When the law itself is a character in a story, you may develop its character using the same techniques used to develop the character of individuals and institutions. You can show that the law has goals and motivations, as well as notable achievements. The law can even have a flaw or suffer from some inner turmoil. Take, for example, the Fourth Amendment to the United States Constitution. The Fourth Amendment has the worthy goal of preventing the government from conducting unreasonable searches of persons and places. It seeks to protect our right to privacy, to enforce our right to be left alone. And each time the courts strike down a police practice as violative of the Fourth Amendment, that Amendment has achieved something great. And while we all know that the Fourth Amendment does not *actually* think, or want, or do anything, you can give the Amendment these qualities by presenting it as a character in a story.

Setting

The setting provides the reader with context for the story because it identifies the time and place in which the story occurs. The time when the story takes place is the historical setting for the story. The location where the story occurs is the physical setting for the story. This context helps the reader understand the events that are taking place in the story and why they are happening.

Although in literary writing the setting is limited to the historical and physical setting, in legal writing, you must also provide the factual setting for the reader. The factual setting provides the reader with facts regarding the dispute between the parties and is designed to assist the reader in understanding why and how that dispute arose. Therefore, you should include in the factual setting all "legally relevant" facts as well as any necessary or helpful background facts that the reader needs to know to make sense of the legally relevant facts. The factual setting is limited to the facts that the court may examine when making its decision. Thus, the pertinent facts will be found in the appellate record or, for motion memoranda, in transcripts of hearings, affidavits, and discovery.

Finally, just as the historical and physical settings are immutable in literary writing, the factual setting is immutable in legal writing. You cannot ignore aspects of the factual setting that may impede your arguments on behalf of the client. You cannot omit important facts or ignore unfavorable facts without sacrificing plausibility and credibility. Rather, if facts exist in the record that do not seem to "fit" with your version of events or the protagonist's character, you must find a way to explain those facts away, minimize the importance of those facts, or juxtapose those facts with other more favorable facts to lessen the harm those facts may do.

Plot

The plot is the structure of the story. The plot details not only what happened and when it happened, but it also shows cause and effect. It is important to remember, however, that the plot line is more than just a sequence of events organized to show connections between those events. The plot is the glue that holds the elements of the story together.

Naturally, all stories have a beginning, middle, and an end. The stages of plot development include an introduction, adversity, and resolution. The first stage of plot development, the introduction, provides background information about the characters, the setting, and the events. This background information provides context for the story and permits the reader to understand the story that is to come. The introduction also shows the story beginning in a state of equilibrium or tranquility. This status quo, also referred to as the "steady state," may not be perfect, but it is tolerable.

Once you have set the stage in the introduction, you are ready to introduce the adversity, or the complicating event that upsets the status quo. The adversity is the trouble that disrupts the equilibrium experienced by the protagonist in the introduction and gives birth to the conflict. This trouble may arise from one complicating event, or from a series of complicating events that build upon each other. If you represent the plaintiff or are the prosecutor in a criminal case, the adversity is caused by the defendant's actions. If you represent the defendant, the adversity is the lawsuit or prosecution, which has disrupted the defendant's equilibrium. By clearly describing the complicating events that comprise the adversity, you reveal the conflict to the reader.

The final stage in plot development is the resolution, or conclusion, of the story. In literary terms, it is referred to as the "denouement. " The resolution ensures that all the conflicts and tensions are resolved in a plausible manner. Furthermore, because readers generally like happy endings, the resolution often ushers in a return to the status quo that existed at the start of the narrative, or it may result in a new state that is tranquil and satisfying. This happy ending must be plausible and reasonable. If the resolution does not seem plausible, the reader will not be sufficiently persuaded by the story.

In the legal context, the story you tell will not have a true resolution. The resolution is what you are asking the court to do. If you represent a plaintiff, you will ask the court to restore equilibrium by awarding your client an injunction or damages. If you are the prosecutor in a criminal case, you will ask the court to restore equilibrium by convicting the defendant of the charged crime. If you represent a defendant, you will ask the court to restore equilibrium by dismissing the lawsuit or prosecution and freeing the defendant from the burden of defending against that lawsuit or prosecution and the fear of potentially losing the case.

You must draft the story so that the resolution you seek seems like the natural conclusion to the story. You should present the characters and define the conflict in such a way that the resolution you suggest seems inevitable—it is the only logical ending for the appeal or for the motion before the court. Your story should make the judge *want* to rule in favor of your client because it is the right thing to do, not just because the law demands it.

Checklist for Drafting a Statement of the Case

Generally

_____ Did you include all legally relevant facts (e.g., facts relevant to each element or factor)?
_____ Did you include all background facts necessary to understand the legally relevant facts?
_____ Did you include all unfavorable or harmful facts?
_____ Did you include all facts relied on in the Argument section?
_____ Did you include the procedural history?
_____ Did you eliminate all unnecessary facts?
_____ Did you cite to the record for each fact?
_____ Did you avoid legal analysis or legal argument?
_____ Did you avoid characterizing the facts yourself?
_____ Did you avoid drawing inferences from the facts?
_____ Did you focus on facts that advance your theory?
_____ Can the reader identify which party you represent?

Persuasion

_____ Did you emphasize favorable facts by employing the principles of primacy and latency, providing greater detail, exercising repetition, using short sentence structure, etc.?
_____ Did you deemphasize unfavorable facts by placing them in the middle of the section, a paragraph, or a sentence; providing less detail, mentioning them only once, using longer sentence structure, etc.?
_____ Did you neutralize, or explained away, unfavorable facts?

_____ Did you tell a story?

_____ Did you organize the story in a persuasive fashion (whether it is chronological, topical, or a combination of chronological and topical order)?

_____ Did you begin the story by focusing on a persuasive fact (such as the alleged wrongdoing or a character)?

_____ Is your characterization of the conflict apparent to the reader?

_____ Is the theme of your story apparent to the reader?

_____ Did you include facts that reveal the character of your client and the other parties?

_____ Did you humanize your client?

_____ Did you depersonalize the opposing party?

_____ Did you tell the story from your client's perspective (unless you had a good reason not to do so)?

Exercise.   Escape from Prison? (Developing a Theory)

Orville Bradwyn is charged with the crime of escape from prison. The state's sole witness was Benjamin Tunmeyer, a prison guard, who testified as follows.

Q: Please tell the court what you observed and did at 6:30 in the evening on the sixth of July.

A: I was checking prisoners in the dinner line. Prisoners are required to be in there at that time, and any prisoner who has not shown up for dinner is considered missing. The defendant did not appear. I then checked his cell. Some material had been put in his bed, bunched up so that it looked like somebody was asleep there. His radio had been left on. But he was gone.

Q: What did you do?

A: We searched the grounds outside the prison. We didn't find the defendant there, so we searched inside the prison—first the perimeter, and then the inside of buildings and containers where someone might hide. We finally found him in the laundry room at 7:39 P.M.

Q: What did he have with him?

A: All of his clothing.

Q: Does the prison wash the laundry of any other institution?

A: Yes, we do the laundry for the state hospital down the road. It's done in the same laundry room where we found the defendant.

Q: How is the hospital's laundry transported to and from the prison?

A: By truck. The hospital's truck brings in it in the morning and picks it up at about 8 P.M.

Q: Are prisoners permitted in the laundry room in the evening?

A: No prisoner is allowed in that room after 5 P.M. Hiding in one of the hospital's laundry bags is an obvious way to escape from the prison.

Q: What precautions are taken to prevent that?

A: At 5 P.M., a guard makes sure all prisoners assigned to work in the laundry have left, and then the door is locked. In addition, the guard opens up each laundry bag that goes to the state hospital and makes sure it has only laundry in it. Then he locks up the room and locks another door on the corridor leading to the laundry room. Nobody is inside those doors until the hospital's truck arrives about three hours later.

Q: What guard was assigned that responsibility on the night in question?

A: Me. I sent out all the prisoners and satisfactorily inspected the state hospital's bags. Then, I locked the doors and left.

Q: Was Mr. Bradwyn assigned to work in the laundry?

A: Yes. But he was not scheduled to work in the laundry room on the day in question.

Cross-examination:

Q: Are you familiar with Mr. Bradwyn's reputation among other prisoners and among corrections officers?

A: He is an exceptionally tidy person.

Q: Were there any prior occasions on which you and Mr. Bradwyn had shouting matches?

A: Yes. It's almost impossible to inspect his cell. He starts yelling the minute you touch any of his things. He says he doesn't like them moved.

Q: What was the defendant doing when you found him?

A: He was washing his clothes. No, actually, he was drying them. They were in the dryer.

Q: What items of clothing were in the dryer?

A: Both of his prison uniforms—prisoners are issued two—socks, undershirts, undershorts. They were still wet.

Q: What did you find when you searched Mr. Bradwyn's cell?

A: Letters from his family, personal photographs, letters from his lawyer, an address book.

Q: Before dinner, prisoners are free to move about outside their cells; aren't they?

A: Yes.

Q: And the same is true after dinner, isn't it?

A: Until 7:30.

After this testimony, the prosecution rested. Bradwyn moved to dismiss on the ground that the prosecution had presented insufficient evidence to convict.

Develop two theories that satisfy the criteria in Section 5.B.3. One theory should support Bradwyn and his motion. The other should support the prosecution and oppose the motion. Use the method outlined in Section 5.B.4.

The relevant statute and cases interpreting it appear below:

Criminal Code §745

If any person committed to prison shall break and escape therefrom or shall escape or leave without authority any building, camp, or any place whatsoever in which he is placed or to which he is directed to go or in which he is allowed to be, he shall be deemed guilty of an escape and shall be punished by imprisonment for a term not to exceed five years, to commence immediately upon the expiration of the term of his previous sentence.

State v. Horstman

The crime of escape is established by proof that the defendant was confined in a prison and escaped from such confinement or departed without authority from a place to which she or he was duly assigned. Unauthorized departure is the gravamen of the offense.

State v. Cahill

While incarcerated, the defendant was placed in solitary confinement for fighting with another prisoner. A guard inadvertently left the cell door unlocked. The defendant got out and was apprehended on top of the prison wall.

The defendant argues that the evidence does not prove that he committed the crime of escape because there is no evidence that he escaped from the custody of the Department of Prisons. He argues that, at most, he is guilty of the lesser crime of attempted escape.

The crime of escape was complete, however, when the defendant got out of his cell. The crime can be committed without leaving the prison as a whole. It is enough that the defendant left a place where he was confined within the prison.

State v. Liggett

The defendant was incarcerated and assigned to work in the prison shop manufacturing auto license plates. On the day in question, the defendant was reported absent from his shift in the license plate shop. After a prolonged search, he was found inside a machine in the prison cannery, using a pillow, and reading a novel.

The evidence does not prove beyond a reasonable doubt that the defendant committed the crime of escape. He failed to report for work in one part of the prison and, without authorization, spent the time in another part. That might violate prison rules and merit internal prison discipline, but it is not the crime of escape.

Exercise. Escape from Prison Exercise

Statement of the Case 1

Defendant Orville Bradwyn, a prisoner, was charged with escape from prison under Criminal Code §745, after he was discovered in an area of the prison that was off-limits to prisoners because it presented a security risk. Following evidence presented by the State at trial, defendant filed a motion to dismiss the charge for insufficient evidence to convict.

No prisoner is allowed in the prison laundry room after 5:00 p.m. because a truck arrives from the local hospital at 8:00 p.m. to pick up and drop off laundry, thus posing a security threat to the prison. Officer Benjamin Tunmeyer was the corrections officer who secured the prison laundry room on July 6, 2005. At 5:00 p.m., he inspected the laundry room, as well as the laundry bags scheduled for pickup by the local hospital, before locking down the area for the evening. Standard procedure for securing the laundry room includes making certain that all prisoners scheduled to work in the laundry that day have vacated the room and examining each bag to ensure that it does not contains stowaways, but laundry. Once the officer has determined that the laundry room is clear, the officer seals off the laundry room by locking the door to it and then locking the door leading from the corridor to the laundry room. Those doors remain locked until well after the hospital truck has departed the prison grounds.

Prisoners are allowed outside their cells from 5:00 p.m. to 6:30 p.m., when they are required to be in the dining hall. Any prisoner who fails to appear for dinner is considered missing. After dinner, prisoners are again permitted to spend time outside their cells until 7:30, when they are required to return to their cells for the evening.

The prisoner, defendant Bradwyn, was discovered missing at 6:30, when he failed to appear in the dining hall as required. Upon searching the prisoner's cell, Officer Tunmeyer discover that the prisoner's radio was on, his personal items were scattered about the cell, and material was bunched in the bed, which at first led Officer Tunmeyer to believe that someone was sleeping under the covers. After an extensive search of the prison grounds, the prisoner was later discovered at 7:39 p.m. in the locked laundry room, just 21 minutes before the scheduled arrival of the hospital truck.

Exercise.   Escape from Prison Exercise

Statement of the Case 2

Orville Bradwyn has been charged with escape from prison, stemming from an incident that occurred on July 6, 2005. Following evidence presented by the State at trial, Mr. Bradwyn filed a motion to dismiss the charge for insufficient evidence to convict.

Mr. Bradwyn is known to inmates as well as corrections officers as being a fastidious and organized person. His need for order is so great that Mr. Bradwyn becomes extremely troubled when the neatness of his cell is disturbed by others; he has often spoken to the guards and the other inmates about this. In fact, Mr. Bradwyn and Officer Benjamin Tunmeyer have engaged in shouting matches because Mr. Bradwyn does not like Tunmeyer disturbing his belongings.

Because of his proclivity to tidiness, working in the laundry room was a particularly good fit for Mr. Bradwyn. On the evening in question, instead of eating dinner at 6:30 p.m., as required by prison policy, Mr. Bradwyn was in the laundry cleaning his clothing. Intending to return to his cell, Mr. Bradwyn left the radio playing and left his other treasured belongings, including letters from his family, personal photographs, and an address book, in his cell.

On the evening in question, Tunmeyer was on duty. It was his duty to lock the two doors leading to the laundry room from the hallway and to ensure that no one was in the room prior to locking those doors. Although Tunmeyer claims that he made certain the room was clear before he locked the doors to the laundry room that evening, Mr. Bradwyn was later found in the room laundering his clothing. Additionally, despite Tunmeyer's contention that he locked the doors, there is no evidence that the locks to the laundry room doors had been tampered with.

Exercise.   *Escape from Prison Exercise Questions*

You may work alone or choose a partner or two to work with to answer the following questions.

1. Read Criminal Code §745, which carries a sentence of up to five years. What must the prosecutor prove to find Bradwyn guilty?
2. Now read the cases. Which favor the prosecutor and which favor the defendant? Why?
3. Look again at Officer Tunmeyer's testimony regarding the facts in this case. Then read the two versions of the Statement of the Case in the book and refer to them when answering the questions below.
    a. Which Statement of Case is the State's (1 or 2)?
    b. What seems to be the State's theory of the case?
    c. How did the State develop the characters of the parties and other individuals involved in this dispute?
    d. How does the State characterize the conflict?
    e. What techniques does the State use to make the outcome it is seeking seem inevitable?
    f. What other persuasive techniques did the State's attorney use?
    g. Look at Bradwyn's Statement of the Case. What seems to be Bradwyn's theory of the case?
    h. How did Bradwyn develop the character of the parties and other individuals involved in the dispute?
    i. How does Bradwyn characterize the conflict?
    j. What techniques does Bradwyn use to make the outcome he is seeking seem inevitable?
    k. What other persuasive techniques did Bradwyn's attorney use?

Exercise.   Statement of Facts

"Tell the truth, but tell it slant."

Sorting out the relevant facts:

What are the major issues in the brief?	*What facts are relevant to each of these issues?*

Deciding which facts to emphasize and which to deemphasize.
Out of the relevant facts that you indicated above:

Which facts are favorable to your client and should be emphasized (put at points of emphasis & given a lot of air time and in a lot of detail)?	Which facts are unfavorable to your client and should be deemphasized (sandwiched between positive points & summarized)?

Creating a Theme:

What facts can you use to develop and personalize your client?
How can you describe the conflict concerned in this case in a favorable manner for your client? (Remember the different types of conflicts: person v. nature, person v. person, person v. self, person v. society, person v. machine)
How can you make the resolution that you want the court to use seem just and fair?
What would be the most favorable point in time to start explaining the client's story? (At the very beginning and go through the events in chronological order? Start with recent events and then go back to the beginning and explain in chronological order? Use strictly a topical order? Explain events in chronological order under each topic?)

CHAPTER

9

Summary of the Argument

The summary of the argument follows the statement of the facts, and it signals an abrupt change. Up until this point, the writer has been describing the case, including its issues, the opinions below, and the facts. Now the writer begins to argue.

Supreme Court Rule 24.1(h) provides that the brief must include

> [a] summary of the argument, suitably paragraphed. The summary should be a clear and concise condensation of the argument made in the body of the brief; mere repetition of the headings under which the argument is arranged is not sufficient.

Only lengthy motion briefs require a summary of the argument, but they are required for almost all appellate briefs. In both motion briefs and appellate briefs, the summary of the argument can play two roles. First, the summary can serve as a roadmap to the argument as a whole. The writer should succinctly state the major arguments relied on in the brief, in the order in which they appear in the argument section. Second, the summary can be used to present a "holistic" picture of the case, focusing more on policy and equity than on black-letter law.

Judge Hamilton notes that the summary of the argument is "significant on several levels":

> First, it is the party's first opportunity to put a legal gloss on the facts. Second, it is the party's first opportunity to orient the appellate judges assigned the appeal to the theme of the party's argument. Third, and most importantly, it serves as the party's official opening statement, previewing and summarizing the key legal points the party wants to make in the argument component of the brief.[1]

A good summary should grab the reader's attention in its opening paragraph. While the statement of facts should open with a somewhat objective statement of what the case is about, the summary of the argument can be more dramatic, identifying the underlying issues that the case presents. In the case of *Rubin v. Coors Brewing Co.*, for example, counsel for the United States (Rubin) might open the summary with a declarative statement about the result being sought:

---

1. Hamilton, *supra* note 8, at 586-87.

Bad Example

Section 205(e)(2) of the Federal Alcohol Administrative Act, prohibiting alcohol content disclosure on malt beverage labels, does not violate the Free Speech Clause of the First Amendment.

While this opening is appropriately argumentative, it doesn't grab the reader's attention. To create a more dramatic opening, counsel might begin the summary by reminding the reader of the original purpose of §205(e)(2). The statute was drafted shortly after Prohibition ended; the government was seeking to prevent strength wars among brewers and to prevent beer drinkers from "forum shopping" for the most powerful beer. Counsel for the United States might bring that purpose up to date by opening the summary of the argument like this:

Good Example

Prohibition is not just a time in history that ended 60 years ago. Every day is the end of Prohibition for someone who reaches the legal drinking age.

You can be both more dramatic and more argumentative in the summary than you can in the fact statement. *Miller v. Albright* addressed the citizenship of children born outside of the United States to unmarried United States Citizens, when only one of the parents was a citizen. The issue was whether a statute could constitutionally distinguish between children of United States citizen fathers and those of United States citizen mothers. An attorney representing Ms. Miller could have opened the summary of the argument by reminding the Court of the harsh reality of the statute's distinction:

Bad Example

The issue before this Court is whether Congress may use an irrebuttable gender stereotype to impose an arbitrary time limit on the relationship between a father and his daughter.

This opening is not horrible, but it states the issue objectively when it should be arguing. Lopping off the objective opening and making a flat statement of the writer's position creates a much more effective opening sentence:

Good Example

Congress may not use an irrebuttable gender stereotype to impose an arbitrary time limit on the relationship between a father and his daughter.

Many writers clog up the summary of the argument with too much detail. This part of the document is meant to provide a *summary*. It should focus more on rules and how they apply than on detailed explanations.

In the excerpt below, from the summary of the argument in a petitioner's brief in *Minnesota v. Carter*, the author summarized a 30- page argument in two pages. The case had two main points. After introducing those points in the opening paragraph, the writer used one paragraph to lay out the first rule, then two paragraphs to apply it, followed by one paragraph on the second rule, and another paragraph to apply that rule. She ends the summary by telling the Court how she wants it to decide the case:

Good Example

Respondents did not have a reasonable expectation of privacy when they bagged cocaine in front of a partially covered window in a basement apartment. The Minnesota Supreme Court incorrectly reversed the trial court's denial of Respondents' motion to suppress. First, it erroneously ruled that Respondents had a legitimate expectation of privacy while in another's apartment for the sole purpose of illegally bagging cocaine. Second, it wrongly held that an officer conducted a search when he merely observed criminal activity in plain view from an area outside the apartment's curtilage.❶

This Court's Fourth Amendment jurisprudence demonstrates that the Minnesota Supreme Court's ruling was erroneous. In order to invoke the Fourth Amendment's protections, an individual must prove that he had a legitimate expectation of privacy. An individual possesses a legitimate expectation of privacy when he demonstrates that he has both a subjective expectation of privacy and an expectation of privacy that society is prepared to view as reasonable.❷

Respondents were sitting at an illuminated kitchen table facing a window of a ground-floor apartment and packaging cocaine. Respondents should have realized that a passerby could have looked into the apartment and noticed the illegal activity occurring within the apartment. Thus, Respondents can claim no subjective expectation of privacy.❸

Additionally, any subjective expectation of privacy Respondents possessed is not one that society is prepared to recognize as reasonable in light of longstanding social customs that serve functions recognized as valuable by society. <u>Minnesota v. Olson</u>, 495 U.S. 91, 96-97 (1990). As non-overnight guests, they lacked the connection with the premises that legitimizes an expectation of privacy. Even if shorter-term guests can claim the protection of the Fourth Amendment, only those short-term guests who are present for socially permissible and valuable reasons qualify for Fourth Amendment protection. Respondents were present only to conduct criminal business activities and therefore did not have an expectation of privacy that was reasonable in light of longstanding social customs that serve functions recognized as valuable by society.❹

Furthermore, even assuming that Respondents are entitled to invoke the Fourth Amendment's protections, no Fourth Amendment search occurred. A search occurs only when governmental agents intrude upon an area in which an individual has a reasonable expectation of privacy. A reasonable expectation of privacy is violated when an officer intrudes upon the home or its curtilage,

❶ Note how the writer lays out the two issues that the argument, and thus the summary, will address.

❷ In this paragraph, the writer lays out the basic rule that governs the first issue, identifying two sub-issues. She does not cite to authority, which is an acceptable convention in the summary of the argument.

❸ In this paragraph, the writer connects the facts to her legal conclusion that the Respondents can claim no subjective expectation of privacy.

❹ In this paragraph, the writer gives the factual details that show why society is not prepared to recognize Respondents' expectation of privacy as reasonable. These reasons reflect the organization of her argument.

❺ In this paragraph, the writer lays out in detail the rule that governs the second main issue. Again, she does not cite to authority other than the Fourth Amendment.

❻ In this paragraph, the writer applies the second rule to the facts of the case.

❼ In this paragraph, the writer sums up the two main conclusions as to the issues and connects those conclusions to her assertion that the Court should reverse the decision below.

the area immediately surrounding the home that shares the same private characteristics as the home. Conversely, there is no violation of a reasonable expectation of privacy, and therefore no *search*, when an officer merely stands outside the curtilage of a residence and observes what is in plain view.❺

In this case, the officer stood in a publicly accessible common area outside the apartment's curtilage. The officer used only his natural senses to observe what was in plain view. He conducted his observation without physical intrusion, without the use of any device, and in a manner that any member of the public could have employed. The officer's conduct violated no reasonable expectation of privacy and therefore was not a Fourth Amendment search.❻

For these reasons, this Court should hold that Respondents had no legitimate expectation of privacy in the apartment and that the observations of the officer did not constitute a search. This Court should reverse the Minnesota Supreme Court's judgment.❼

In most situations, the summary of the argument need not contain numerous citations to authority. Of course, if a case, statute, constitutional provision, or other authority is at issue, it will be mentioned; likewise, if a particular issue is largely controlled by a case or other authority, that authority may be mentioned as well. Usually, however, the focus is on legal principles rather than on the authorities that are the source of those principles.

To summarize, the summary of the argument should (1) signal the writer's theme, (2) signal the writer's major arguments and the order in which those arguments will appear, (3) focus on rules and their application rather than detailed explanations, and (4) avoid most citations to authority.

CHAPTER
10

Argument Section: CREAC Organization

A. STATE YOUR ISSUE AS A CONCLUSION

In the first "conclusion" element of the formula, the writer articulates the specific issue that is being addressed, or articulates the problem (or part or sub-part of the problem) that is being "solved" in this section of the document. The writer could articulate an issue from *Miller v. Albright*, 523 U.S. 420 (1998), by stating affirmatively what the issue is:

> Under the intermediate scrutiny test, the first issue that must be decided is whether 8 U.S.C. §1409(a) is "substantially related" to the achievement of the government's objective.

Although this method effectively tells the court the issue (and is preferable to neglecting to articulate the issue at all), it is not the best choice in a brief to a court because it is not argumentative. Generally, in persuasive writing, you should make your arguments as if they are the only reasonable resolution to the issues before the court. Therefore, it is often best to state your issues as conclusions:

> 8 U.S.C. §1409(a) is not "substantially related" to the achievement of the government's objective because it is unconstitutionally over inclusive.

If your issue is more complicated, the conclusion may be longer than just a simple sentence. You may need to provide legal or factual context to help the reader to understand how the conclusion fits into your argument. In *Minnesota v. Carter*, 525 U.S. 83 (1998), the Court was asked to determine whether an officer violated the Fourth Amendment when he observed criminal activity through the window of a basement apartment. In the example below, the writer provides factual context before using a conclusory statement to articulate the issue:

> Because Thielen was located outside the curtilage of the apartment, he was free to observe any scene in plain view. Respondents' activities within the apartment were in plain view from Thielen's lawful vantage point. Thus, Thielen's observation violated no reasonable expectation of privacy and did not constitute a Fourth Amendment search.

By stating your issue as a conclusion, you begin to focus your reader not only on the issue that you will be addressing in that section of the argument, but also on the result that your analysis of the issue will reveal.

Will My Writing Be Boring If I Use the Same Formula In Each Section?

The CREXAC formula does not provide one rubric that governs the whole argument section. CREXAC provides a rubric that can be used over and over again, any time a writer has some point to explain or prove. The argument section itself will be organized according to the unique issues and sub-issues that the case presents. CREXAC can be used, however, as a formula for your analysis of each significant issue and sub-issue within that argument. Some writers worry that their writing will be boring or overpredictable if they follow a formula like CREXAC in each section of a document. This worry is unfounded for a couple of reasons.

First, CREXAC does not tell you what to say. Instead, it recommends a particular organization for the information that readers traditionally need when analyzing legal issues. Most legal readers want to know the rule first, then understand the rule's meaning, and then see how it applies to the facts. Most judges want a simple organization; they don't want to have to struggle to find a rule that a writer "creatively" saved for the end of his or her analysis of a legal issue.

The second reason not to worry is related to the first. CREXAC is only an organizational structure. With no extra effort on your part, each section of your argument will vary from the section before according to the substance of the argument itself and the particular demands of the issue. Every issue needs a rule, but sometimes the rule is a simple quote from a statute, while at other times it is a common law rule, and at other times it is a cluster of rules that end on the particular rule that governs the narrow legal issue that is the focus of that section of the document. Similarly, the explanation of the rule and application of the rule to the facts will also vary from issue to issue.

Even if CREXAC is not the most perfect organization for the analysis of a particular legal issue or sub-issue, it will probably still be an effective organization. Thus, it is probably most practical for an attorney to assume a CREXAC organization rather than to spend precious time trying to determine what is the "best" structure for analyzing a legal issue.

Whatever organizational method you use, the elements of CREXAC provide a good checklist. In every section of the argument, the reader will always need to know the issue you're addressing, the rule that governs the issue, what the rule means, how it applies in this case, and how that application connects to your argument.

B. PROVIDE THE RULE

After you have focused the reader's attention on the issue being addressed, you should articulate the rule that governs the issue. First, let's define our terms. A rule essentially says that "if a certain condition exists, then a certain legal status results." For example:

> If you are a human being [certain condition], then you are mortal [legal status].
> If you have a duty, breach a duty, and cause compensable harm [certain condition], then you are liable in negligence [legal status].

Most rules in a brief will not be stated in "if-then" terminology. However, using the if-then structure can help you to test the rules that you include in your brief.

If your rule comes from a statute or a well-established common law test, stating the rule may be simple. Stating the rule can be more complicated, however, if there is controversy about which rule applies, or if you must use inductive reasoning to "find" your rule.

1.   Stating Established Rules

You may state the rule in a variety of ways. If the rule is derived from a statute or other enacted law, you may simply quote the pertinent language, as in this example:

> 26 U.S.C. §5861(d) provides that "[i]t shall be unlawful for any person to receive or possess a firearm which is not registered to him in the National Firearms Registration Transfer Record."

Similarly, if the rule is a well-accepted common law rule derived from a well-known authority, you may simply articulate the rule in its familiar language:

> While a person's home is, for most purposes, a place where he expects privacy, activities that are exposed "to the 'plain view' of outsiders are not protected" under the Fourth Amendment. Katz v. United States, 389 U.S. 347, 361 (1967) (Harlan, J., concurring).

If your case is more complex, stating one rule may not give the reader enough context. Some writers articulate the rule that governs a narrow situation by providing a "rule cluster" that starts with a well-accepted general rule and moves to the more narrow rule that is the focus of that section of the argument.[1] The following example is from the argument section of *Minnesota v. Carter*, a Fourth Amendment case. This section of the argument is focused on the narrow issue of whether the alleged intrusion by the government agents constituted a "search." Notice how the writer moves the reader from the general rule—the Fourth Amendment—to the narrow rule at issue, which will be the focus of this section of the argument (which, by the way, will include two subsections):

---

1. A rule cluster is appropriate when, as here, the existence and applicability of these related rules is not controversial. The discussion in Section 10.F of "Tell" issues is relevant here, because you are telling the reader what the rule is and that it is relevant in the given case. A rule cluster may also function as part of an argument's "backstory," as discussed in Chapter Ten [Mary Beth Beazley, A Practical Guide to Appellate Advocacy, 3rd ed., (2010)].

> The Fourth Amendment to the United States Constitution guarantees "[t]he right of the people to be secure in their persons, houses, papers, and effects, against unreasonable searches and seizures." U.S. Const. amend. IV. A search occurs only when governmental agents intrude upon an area in which a person has a reasonable expectation of privacy. California v. Ciraolo, 476 U.S. 207, 212 (1986). This Court will find that a Fourth Amendment search occurred only if two factors exist: (1) the location from which the observation occurred was within a complainant's zone of privacy, and (2) the government agents used extraordinary measures to accomplish the observation. See id. at 213.

Thus, although the paragraph lists three rules, the writer is focusing the reader's attention only on the last rule in the list.

2. Choosing Among Two or More Rules

Some issues are governed by well-established rules, and the court needs to decide only how, or whether, a particular rule applies to the facts of the case. Sometimes, however, a major debate between you and your opponent in the case is a debate as to which of two or more rules the court should apply to the situation. If you have to convince the court to choose the rule that you want, as opposed to the rule that your opponent wants, you must include a section in your argument devoted to proving that "your" rule is the best rule to apply. Of course, that "rule-choice" argument must be based on a rule, as well.

If a court has chosen a particular rule to apply to a situation, it has done so because it has decided that the case has certain factors or raises certain issues that the chosen rule best addresses. You might think of the basic format for a rule-choice rule as follows: "If [factors or issues] exist, then [application of designated rule] results."

Sometimes, courts state the "rule-choice rule" explicitly. For example, everyone who has taken a constitutional law course knows that when courts have to decide whether a certain governmental action is constitutional, they have at least three choices. They can apply the "strict scrutiny test" (which they apply when certain fundamental rights are implicated or the rights of a suspect class are affected); they can apply the "intermediate or heightened scrutiny test" (which they apply in a variety of situations, including situations in which laws make gender-based distinctions); or they can apply the "rational basis test" (which they apply when a law does not affect fundamental rights or make questionable distinctions). Thus, if your case is about the constitutionality of a governmental action, you and your opponent might disagree as to whether the court should apply the rational basis test or the strict scrutiny test. In that situation, your first order of business is to argue about which rule applies, using the "rule-choice rule" that governs strict scrutiny and rational basis. For example, if you believed that strict scrutiny was appropriate, that section of your argument could be based on the following "rule-choice rule":

> If a statute makes distinctions based on suspect classifications, then the strict scrutiny test applies.

Of course, even if a rule-choice rule exists, you should use a CREXAC unit of discourse to prove how it applies only if the choice of rule is in controversy. If both sides agree that the strict scrutiny test applies, for example, then the brief need not establish this fact through a CREXAC analysis. The writer can simply introduce the "strict scrutiny" section by telling the reader the rule-choice rule and stating that it results in the use of strict scrutiny before moving on to a CREXAC analysis of the strict scrutiny test itself.

Thus, if the choice of rule is not controversial, a typical argument would have one section devoted to the rule, focusing on how it should apply in the current case. If the choice of rule *is* controversial, however, the writer may need to include as many as three sections of the argument that address the rule-choice issue in some way. For example, in the first section, the writer might argue that the rule-choice rule requires that the preferred rule be applied. In the second section, the writer could argue that his or her client wins when the preferred rule is applied. In the third section, the writer could argue that his or her client wins even if the nonpreferred rule is applied. (Of course, if the result of applying the nonpreferred rule is uncontroversial, it need not be argued.)

If there are two or more competing rules and the courts have not yet labeled the "rule-choice rule," your job is to find and articulate that rule. You can "find" the rule by reasoning inductively from one or more cases in which a court has made the rule-choice decision. The section that follows explains how to use inductive reasoning to find and articulate legal rules.

3.   *Using Inductive Reasoning to Find and Articulate Legal Rules*

As many a frustrated first-year law student can attest, courts sometimes decide cases without explicitly articulating the rule that they are applying. Furthermore, sometimes the rule that they are applying can be accurately stated more narrowly or more broadly. If the cases that are analogous to your case do not contain a clear rule, or if the applicable rule as it is currently envisioned would dictate a bad result for your client, you may have to "induce" a rule. Using inductive reasoning is appropriate for finding rules of all types, not just rule-choice rules.

It is not accurate to say that you are labeling a "new" rule when you use inductive reasoning. The rule was there all along; inductive reasoning simply lets you recognize it, label it, and present it more effectively to the court.

When you use inductive reasoning to find a rule, you are trying to read between the lines of court opinions, to notice patterns that always or never predict certain results, or results that occur *only* when certain patterns are present. Authors of law review articles might observe these patterns in a vacuum, but you have a head start because you know the type of pattern you are looking for. In an advocacy document, inductive reasoning frequently begins when you distinguish your case from the cases that apparently apply.

For example, in the case *Ohio v. Robinette*, 519 U.S. 33 (1996), the issue was the constitutionality of an officer's request to conduct a drug search of a car that had been stopped for speeding. The government argued that the defendant had been free to refuse the officer's request, and so his consent was voluntary and constitutional. Many of the relevant cases addressing consent searches involved officers stopping people in airports and asking for permission to search for contraband. One student, writing a brief on behalf of Robinette, noticed a distinguishing factor between Robinette's case and the so-called air-port cases, and she used that distinction to help her to induce a more precise rule. The paragraphs below show her thinking as she moves from noticing the distinguishing factor (the way in which the police-citizen encounter began) to articulating a new rule:

> There are two types of situations in which police request consent to search—those in which the police-citizen encounter begins consensually, and those in which the police-citizen encounter begins by an assertion of legal authority. When police-citizen encounters begin consensually, courts will find the consent request valid if there was nothing in the record to suggest "that the [citizen] had any objective reason to believe that she *was not free* to end the conversation [with the officers] . . . and proceed on her way," United States v. Mendenhall, 446 U.S.544, 555 (1980) (emphasis added). On the other hand, when police request consent to search after a police-citizen encounter that began with an assertion of legal authority, the Court should use a different test, and should analyze when the defendant would have an objective reason to believe that he or she *became free* to end the conversation and proceed on his or her way. Because Newsome and Robinette's encounter began with an assertion of legal authority, and because there was no clear end to this assertion of legal authority despite Newsome's return of Robinette's license, this Court should apply the totality of the circumstances test to this case.
>
> Courts use the totality of the circumstances test to ascertain when police behavior rises to the level of a detention. See Florida v. Bostick, 501 U.S. 429, 434 (1991) ("[t]he encounter [between an officer and a citizen] will not trigger Fourth Amendment scrutiny unless it *loses its consensual nature*") (emphasis added). Courts have failed to note, however, that when a police-citizen encounter already involves legitimate force over that citizen, an inquiry as to when the encounter "rises" to the level of a detention is inapposite. . . .
>
> . . . Thus, when a police-citizen encounter begins with the police officer's assertion of legal authority over the citizen, a subsequent request to search is part of a "consensual encounter" only if the citizen has objective knowledge either (a) that the legal detention has ended, or (b) that he or she is free to refuse consent to search.

Note that this analysis is not focused on the reader; the writer is using the process of writing to figure out, or induce, the underlying legal rule. This is an example of the "cognitive" stage of legal writing. When moving from the cognitive stage to the "social perspective" stage—the stage in which you take your readers' needs into account—be sure to revise your writing with the readers' needs in mind. Regarding the example above, the writer should remember that legal readers expect to hear about the rule as soon as they learn about the legal issue. The writer discovered her rule only after reviewing several cases and considering carefully how to draw lines between those cases and her case. When presenting this argument to the reader, however, she should place the newly induced rule early in the argument:

> Because the encounter between Robinette and Officer Newsome began with an assertion of police authority—and because Robinette never knew

that the assertion of police authority had ended—cases in which this court analyzes "consensual encounters" are inapposite. When a police-citizen encounter begins with the police officer's assertion of legal authority over the citizen, a subsequent request to search is part of a "consensual encounter" only if the citizen has objective knowledge either (a) that the legal detention has ended, or (b) that he or she is free to refuse consent to search. See Florida v. Bostick, 501 U.S. 429, 434 (1991); United States v. Mendenhall, 446 U.S. 544, 555 (1980).

However you find your rule, be sure to state it explicitly early within the appropriate section of the argument. In this way, you satisfy the reader's expectations and allow him or her to understand your analysis more easily.

C.   EXPLAIN THE RULE

After you have articulated the rule, you must provide your reader with any needed explanation of the rule. Before you explain the rule, however, you must decide which part of the rule you are focusing on in the particular subsection of your argument. Usually, controversies about whether or how a rule applies will focus on certain words or phrases that are at the heart of the controversy regarding that rule. As noted in Chapter Four [Mary Beth Beazley, A Practical Guide to Appellate Advocacy, 3rd ed., (2010)], you can refer to each controversial word or phrase as a "key term" or a "phrase-that-pays." By focusing on one phrase-that-pays within each subsection of the document, you ensure that you are focusing on one issue or sub-issue at a time. Thus, after you have articulated your rule, scrutinize that rule and decide what words or phrases constitute the phrase-that-pays for that section of the document.

Identifying a phrase-that-pays for each section of your document is important because it helps you to focus your writing: Once you have identified the phrase-that-pays, you can test the analysis in each section of the formula to make sure that it relates some how to that phrase-that-pays. In the explanation section, for example, you should define the phrase that pays, explain its meaning, or show how it has been interpreted in earlier cases.

When deciding how much explanation to provide for the phrase-that pays in any particular section of your argument, consider two questions: (1) How ambiguous is the language of the phrase-that-pays? (2) How controversial is the application of the phrase-that-pays to the facts of this case? The more ambiguous and controversial the phrase-that-pays is, the more detailed your explanation should be.

Presumably, all of the issues analyzed in a brief will be controversial; if they were not controversial, they would not need to be analyzed.[2] When a phrase-that-pays is ambiguous, controversial, or both, you should "explain" its meaning, usually by illustrating how it has been applied in one or more authority cases. In the example below, the writer is arguing that an officer's behavior did

2. See discussion below and in Chapter Ten [Mary Beth Beazley, A Practical Guide to Appellate Advocacy, 3rd ed., (2010)] (regarding legal back story and roadmaps) for examples of how to deal with issues that are not controversial, but that must be included in the analysis in some way because they are necessary elements of a statute, test, or other legal rule.

not violate the Fourth Amendment because the observed activities were in plain view. The writer explains the rule by showing how the concept of "plain view"—the phrase-that-pays—has been interpreted in other cases. Notice how the writer has used the phrase-that-pays (in small capital letters in this example) in each paragraph to help the reader understand how the paragraph connects to the analysis of the legal issue:

> 2. No Fourth Amendment search occurred because the apartment interior was in PLAIN VIEW from the officer's lawful vantage point.
>
> Because Thielen was located outside the curtilage of the apartment, he was free to observe any scene in PLAIN VIEW. Respondents' activities within the apartment were in PLAIN VIEW from Thielen's lawful vantage point. Thus, Thielen's observation violated no reasonable expectation of privacy and did not constitute a Fourth Amendment search. ❶
>
> The Fourth Amendment protection of the home "has never been extended to require law enforcement officers to shield their eyes when passing by a home on public thoroughfares." California v. Ciraolo, 476 U.S. 207, 213 (1985). While a person's home is, for most purposes, a place where he expects privacy, activities "that he exposes to the 'PLAIN VIEW' of outsiders are not protected." Katz v. United States, 389 U.S. 347, 361 (1967) (Harlan, J., concurring).❷
>
> Illegal activities in PLAIN VIEW from outside the curtilage are not protected even if the police observation is specifically directed at identifying illegal activity. United States v. Dunn, 480 U.S. 294 (1987) (holding that an officer's observation into a barn was not a Fourth Amendment search, and stressing it was irrelevant that the observation was motivated by a law enforcement purpose); Ciraolo, 476 U.S. at 212, 213. In Ciraolo, the defendant was growing marijuana in a 15-by-25 foot plot in his backyard. He surrounded the yard with a 6-foot outer fence and a 10-foot inner fence. Id. at 209. Officers flew over the defendant's house in a private airplane and readily identified the illegal plants using only the naked eye. Id. The government in Ciraolo argued that the observation was analogous to looking through a knothole or an opening in a fence: "If there is an opening, the police may look." Id. at 220. This Court agreed with the government, holding that the observation was not a Fourth Amendment search. Id. The airspace was outside the curtilage of the apartment, and the Court reasoned that the scene would have been in PLAIN VIEW to any member of the public flying in the same airspace. Thus, the officers had violated no reasonable expectation of privacy. Id. at 213-14.

❶ Note statement of conclusion here.

❷ Note statement of rule here.

The length of your explanation will vary depending on how abstract and/or controversial the rule is. Probably the best way to fully illustrate the meaning of a rule is to use at least one authority that illustrates what the rule does mean in the context of acts that are similar (or nearly similar) to the facts at bar, and at least one authority that illustrates what the rule does *not* mean in the context of facts that are similar to the facts at bar.[3] In the previous example, if the writer had found a case in which the court had held that certain activities in a home

3. *See also* Laurel Currie Oates & Anne M. Enquist, *The Legal Writing Handbook* §7.9.2 (4th ed., Aspen 2006).

were *not within* plain view, the reader would have a fuller understanding of why this case must fall within the definition.

Illustrating what the phrase-that-pays means and does not mean sets the boundaries of the phrase-that-pays, and gives the application of law to facts more validity. Chapter 16 includes a discussion of how to use authority cases effectively in your explanation section.

D. APPLY THE RULE TO THE FACTS

After you have articulated the rule and explained it as needed, it's time to apply the rule to the facts (some legal writers say "applying the facts to the rule" to mean the same thing). In this step of your analysis, you are trying to show the reader how the phrase-that-pays intersects with the facts. How do the required elements or factors exist (or not exist) in your case? You should never substitute synonyms for the phrase-that-pays in any section, but particularly not in the application section.

Brief-writers often face three challenges when applying law to facts. First, some brief-writers mistakenly substitute analogies for application of law to facts. Second, for issues that are "pure" questions of law—and courts of last resort often analyze questions of law—the facts may seem to be irrelevant. Finally, when analyzing statutory interpretation issues, the writers may believe that they don't have any real "facts." This section will address each of these challenges in turn.

1. Apply Rules, Not Cases

Begin the application section of your analysis by stating affirmatively how the rule does or does not apply to the facts. Do *not* begin the application by drawing analogies; analogies may support the application of law to facts, but they do not substitute for it. Essentially, you begin your application by saying "Phrase-that-pays equals (or does not equal) our case facts." If your case is not controversial, a short passage might be enough:

> In this case, Mr. Burglar was "committing a trespass or other criminal offense" when he was bitten. Mr. Burglar was convicted of the crime of burglary in connection with the events of January 8. Burglary is considered a "criminal offense" under Ohio Revised Code §111.1111.

This writer showed the reader how the rule and its explanation intersected with the client's facts by explaining that burglary "equals" a "criminal offense" under Ohio Revised Code §111.1111.

If the issue is at all controversial, you should be sure to provide details about the record facts[4] that support your assertion about how the law applies to the

---

4. Be sure to cite to the record so that the court can verify each referenced fact. Rules about and methods for citing to the case record are discussed in Chapter 9.

facts, as in this example (the phrase-that-pays, "plain view," is in small capital letters for emphasis):

> In the case at bar, Officer Thielen merely observed a scene that was in PLAIN VIEW from his lawful vantage point. The area in which Officer Thielen stood was outside the curtilage of the apartment. While standing outside the curtilage, the officer PLAINLY VIEWED Respondents' unlawful activities. <u>See</u> Record E-2. While Officer Thielen did go to the common area outside the apartment window in response to the report from the informant, <u>see</u> Record G-11, his motivation is irrelevant. The illegal activity was in PLAIN VIEW regardless of Officer Thielen's motivation.

You may expand your application section, if needed, by drawing analogies between your client's case and the cases that you cited for authority in your explanation section:

> Like the officers in <u>Ciraolo</u>, who did not need to shield their eyes from what could be seen while traveling in public airways, Officer Thielen did not need to refrain from viewing what could be seen from the public area outside Thompson's window.

Drawing analogies or distinctions is not always necessary; sometimes the application of the rule to the facts alone will be sufficient to make your point. When appropriate, however, analogizing and distinguishing relevant authorities can help to cement the reader's understanding of how a rule operates and of how it does or does not apply to your client's case.

2.   Facts Are Relevant to Questions of Law

A legal question, or question of law, is a question about what the law should mean or how it should be interpreted. Should the law regulate all dog owners or only owners of dangerous dogs? Should the law governing "employers" include supervisors within the meaning of "employer"? Questions of fact, in contrast, ask whether the law should apply to a particular situation. Is a dog "dangerous" if it bites any person who tries to pet it? Is a person a "supervisor" if she is in charge of drawing up work schedules for all of the people in her section, but does not have the authority to hire and fire?

Even legal questions, however, are decided in a factual context. There is the hypothetical factual context of noting what will happen to certain categories of people and things if the case is decided one way or another, and there is the concrete factual context of noting what will happen to the parties in this particular case. Your application may focus on the broader legal question, but you may also want to include references to your case facts as a concrete "for instance" that shows a real-life result.

In *Miller v. Albright*, for example, a student writing for Ms. Miller argued that 8 U.S.C. §1409 used an unconstitutional overinclusive gender stereotype to deny foreign-born children of citizen fathers rights that are awarded automatically to foreign-born children of citizen mothers. In one section, the student argued that the gender-based distinction was not "substantially related" to the government's objective of conditioning citizenship on close family ties. When he applied the law to the facts, he spoke both generally about the statute and specifically about Ms. Miller and her father:

Good Example:

The gender discrimination in §1409(a) is not substantially related to the government's legitimate goal of conditioning citizenship on close family ties. Of course, §1409(a) will certainly prevent citizenship from flowing to some children who do not deserve it. The fatal flaw in §1409(a), though, is that it is over-inclusive. Section 1409(a)'s various hurdles exclude from citizenship those children—like Ms. Miller—who are deserving of citizenship under the standards of the statute due to their close family ties with their United States citizen parents.

The degree to which §1409(a) is overinclusive is a function of the degree to which the assumptions underlying §1409(a) are invalid. Thus, because the assumptions underlying §1409(a)—that paternity is hard to establish reliably and that women and men are destined to occupy different roles—are substantially incorrect, the use of these irrebuttable stereotypes is not substantially related to the government's objective.

The gender stereotypes underlying §1409(a) are the very sort of archaic generalizations that modern equal protection jurisprudence seeks to eradicate. This court has repeatedly recognized that the government "must not rely on overbroad generalizations about the different talents, capacities, or preferences of males and females." Virginia, 518 U.S. at 533 (citations omitted); see also Califano v. Goldfarb, 430 U.S. 188, 223-24 (1977). If we as a society have learned anything about gender in the twenty years since Fiallo was decided, it is that women and men may not be conclusively pigeon-holed solely on the basis of their gender.

The facts of this case support this rather obvious conclusion. Ms. Miller is twenty-seven years old. Although she is not a minor, and although she neither needs nor receives the financial support of her father, she and Mr. Miller have a close family relationship. By the terms of the stereotype underlying §1409(a), all men—including Mr. Miller—irrebuttably do not form close family relationships with their adult "illegitimate" children. To uphold the rationality of this irrebuttable stereotype is to deny the existence of Mr. Miller and those other men who, for whatever reason, form relationships with their children later in life. To uphold the validity of this irrebuttable stereotype is to deny reality. This Court should reject the validity of this irrebuttable stereotype and acknowledge that there is no substantial relationship between the use of the stereotype and the government's goal of fostering close family relationships.

Note how the writer refers to his client, Ms. Miller, in the first paragraph, and how the last paragraph uses concrete details from the case to show the court the impact its decision will have in a specific case. Not every legal issue will need such a lengthy application section or such a detailed description of the client's facts. A good writer, however, will look for opportunities to use client facts to make abstract legal principles vivid.

3. *Sometimes Statutory Language Is a Fact*

Another challenge that many student writers face when writing the application section is the problem of "no facts." If you are analyzing a statutory interpretation issue, it may seem to you that there are no facts—there is only the statute itself. Many students think of the term *facts* as referring only to tangible events, like a car accident, or a murder, or even an interrogation. For a statutory interpretation issue, however, the word *facts* refers less often to events and more often to realities like the statutory language at issue, other relevant statutory language, or the statute's legislative history. One guideline: If a rule speaks in terms of human or corporate behavior, it is likely that it applies to human or corporate events, and that's where you should look for the relevant facts. In contrast, if a rule speaks in terms of legislative behavior, it is likely that it applies to legislative events—such as the language of a statute—and that is where you should look for the relevant facts.

For example, a student writer who is arguing that Title VII's use of the word "employer" does not allow individual liability for supervisors could have several CREXAC units of discourse focused on rules of statutory interpretation. One section might be focused on the rule that words in a statute should be read consistently throughout the whole statute. She would explain that rule by showing how other relevant courts had read terms consistently in statutes. In the application section, it would be meaningless to talk about the "events" of alleged sexual harassment at the center of the lawsuit. Rather, she must focus on how the term at issue, "employer," was used in the statute as a whole, and how that use demands a particular interpretation in this case:

Good Example:

The use of the word "employer" in other sections of Title VII demonstrates that Congress did not intend that individual supervisors like Kirkby could be held liable. In §2000e-8(c), the act provides that "every employer is responsible for the execution, retention and preservation of certain employment records." Section 2000e-10 states that "every employer shall post and keep posted in conspicuous places pertinent provisions of the subchapter." Interpretation of §2000e(b) requires the court to read the word "employer" consistently throughout the act. See Holloway, 526 U.S. at 9. It is unlikely that Congress intended to impose such administrative duties on individuals in supervisory positions. It is far more reasonable to conclude that the word "employer" as used in §§2000e(b), 2000e-8(c), and 2000e-10 was intended to apply to employer-entities only.

This does not mean that event-based facts are always irrelevant to statutory interpretation questions. As they can with other legal questions, event-based facts may provide helpful illustrations of how the legal policies at issue play out in concrete situations. Writers should be aware, however, that with statutory interpretation questions, they must think about the concept of "facts" more broadly: They are applying the rule of a canon of interpretation to the fact of the existing statutory language.

E. MAKE THE CONNECTION

After you have applied the rule to the facts, you should connect the application to your argument by articulating a connection-conclusion. You may not need to begin a new paragraph if the application has been brief and the connection-conclusion is straightforward. For example,

> Therefore, because Mr. Burglar was committing a burglary when he was bitten, Mr. Angell cannot be held liable for Burglar's injuries under Ohio Revised Code §111.1111.

Stating a connection-conclusion explicitly at the end of your CREXAC analysis is an important part of the formula. Even though you stated a conclusion at the beginning of your analysis, the connection-conclusion at the end of the analysis serves a different purpose. It makes the reader aware of your conclusion, yes, but it also tells the reader that your analysis of this part of the discussion is finished and that you will soon be moving on to another point.

Furthermore, as its name implies, the connection-conclusion shows the reader how this part of the analysis fits into the argument as a whole. If a section of your argument is about a dispositive point, the connection conclusion should make the connection between that point and the ultimate result you seek. At the very least, you should connect your analysis of the phrase-that-pays (in small capital letters in the following example) to the point that was at issue in that section of the argument:

> Activities that Respondents exposed to the PLAIN VIEW of outsiders were not protected by the Fourth Amendment. Because Respondents' activities within the apartment were in PLAIN VIEW from Thielen's lawful vantage point, Thielen's observation violated no reasonable expectation of privacy.

This connection-conclusion connects the writer's point about the phrase-that-pays—"plain view"—to the point of the section, which is whether the respondents had a reasonable expectation of privacy.

F. WHEN *NOT* TO PROVIDE A CREXAC ANALYSIS

The first part of this chapter addressed how to complete a relatively thorough analysis of a legal issue. But not every issue needs a CREXAC unit of discourse. If an issue does not need the full treatment of a CREXAC, you must decide how much space, if any, to devote to the issue. As with most legal questions, an appropriate answer is "it depends." Some issues that would be controversial in one case will be obvious in another, and the depth of your analysis must change accordingly. As Figure 10.1 shows, there are four labels you can use to describe how much discussion to include for each issue or sub-issue: Ignore, Tell, Clarify (CRAC), or Prove (CREXAC):

Figure 10.1
Continuum re: how much to discuss issues that the case may present:

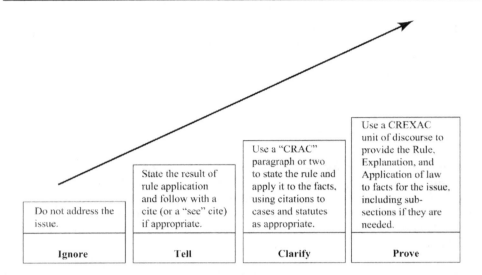

1.   Ignore Issues

Some issues are obviously *not* relevant to the analysis. Others are relevant to the analysis, but are so obviously not controversial that the writer does not need you to spend even one sentence discussing the issue. These are *Ignore issues*, that is, they are issues that you can *ignore* in your written legal analysis.

For example, suppose that the statute forbidding drunk driving in your state contains this language:

> Any person who operates any vehicle, streetcar, or trackless trolley within this state, may not, while operating the vehicle, streetcar, or trackless trolley, be under the influence of alcohol, a drug of abuse, or a combination of them, as specified in section B of this statute.

Let us presume that you work for the state prosecutor, and you have brought charges against a defendant who was arrested while sitting in the driver's seat of her car, a Chevy Impala, parked on the side of a highway. She admitted that she drank four beers earlier that evening, and sobriety tests showed an illegal level of alcohol in her blood. In order to establish that she violated the statute, you would have to prove the following elements (words signaling elements are underlined):

> Defendant is a <u>person</u> who was <u>operating</u> a <u>vehicle</u> while <u>under the influence of alcohol.</u>

In your written analysis, you would not spend any time explaining that the defendant, as a human being, is a "person" under the statute. You could ignore this issue. Likewise, in this case, you would not expend even a sentence to say "a Chevy Impala, an automobile, is a 'vehicle' under the statute." In another case, however, whether the person was operating a "vehicle" might well be at issue. In 2009, an Ohio man was arrested for operating a motorized barstool while intoxicated. In that situation, the state should not treat the "vehicle" element as an Ignore issue.

Thus, if an element is so obviously met that there could be no doubt in your reader's mind that it is satisfied in this case, you should ignore it. Do not, however, let yourself be lulled into a false belief that an issue is not controversial. For example, you might believe that "operating" a vehicle is the same as driving and presume that someone sitting in a parked car is not legally operating the car. Research, however, might well reveal that "operation" includes sitting behind the driver's seat in a car whose gearshift is in park.[5]

2. *Tell Issues*

As its name implies, a writer includes a *Tell issue* in legal analysis by *telling* the outcome of application of law to facts and then citing to authority. There are two kinds of Tell issues. The first kind is an issue that is relevant but is not controversial. The second kind of Tell issue is an issue that could have been controversial, but that has been removed from controversy by some outside means, such as a party's concession.

For example, suppose that your client, Sam Bell, is a young man who was injured while intoxicated after "hell night" activities at his fraternity. A hometown friend, Marvin Kobacker, had taken him from a supervised "drunk room" at the fraternity and later left him alone in an off-campus apartment, where he fell and injured himself. You are wondering whether Mr. Kobacker is liable to Mr. Bell.

A common law rule in your jurisdiction provides that "a person assumes a duty of care if he or she takes charge of a person who is helpless." You look at the rule and realize that two phrases-that-pay are "take charge" and "helpless." Upon doing the research, you discover that there are several factors to analyze when determining whether someone "took charge" of another person. Likewise, there are several ways to prove that a person is "helpless." At first blush, it might seem that you need to complete two separate CREXAC units of discourse. One case from the highest court in your jurisdiction, however, states unequivocally that a person who is intoxicated is "helpless" under this standard. In this situation, Mr. Bell was unequivocally intoxicated. Thus, this required element is without controversy in your case, and you can treat it as a Tell issue:

> In Vanita, a person assumes a duty of care if he or she "takes charge" of a person who is "helpless." Jenkins v. Diamond, 101 N.E.2d 104, 109 (Van. 2007). An intoxicated person is considered helpless. *Id.* at 111.

The second kind of Tell issue is one that has been removed from the controversy in some way. In a First Amendment challenge to a statute, for example, a court will use strict scrutiny to analyze a content-based restriction, while it will use a

---

5. *See, e.g., State v. Cyr*, 967 A.2d 32, 40 (Conn. 2009).

lower level of scrutiny to analyze a content-neutral restriction. If you and your opponent disagree as to whether the restriction at issue is a content-based restriction, you would probably need to use a CREXAC unit of discourse to argue that the statute does or does not impose a content-based restriction. However, if your opponent has conceded the issue—perhaps in a brief or in an oral argument to a lower court—you may treat the issue as a Tell issue, citing authority if possible:

> As the petitioner concedes, the statute at issue criminalizes speech based on its content. Pet'r Br. at 16. Accordingly, this court should apply the strict scrutiny test when analyzing its validity. <u>Cornelius v. NAACP Legal Defense & Ed. Fund, Inc.</u>, 473 U.S. 788, 800 (1985).

Tell issues can arise in different contexts, but they are most commonly found in two places in the brief: As is discussed in Chapter Ten [Mary Beth Beazley, A Practical Guide to Appellate Advocacy, 3rd ed., (2010)], they can arise in introductory material; when you are providing context for your argument as a whole, you may need to address one or more Tell issues to provide context and clear away the uncontroversial points. Second, they can arise when you are articulating the rule, either as part of a rule cluster or as an uncontroversial but significant facet of a governing rule.

3. Clarify or CRAC Issues

A *Clarify issue* is similar to a Tell issue, but it is an issue that is a shade more complex. The term *Clarify* signals that the issue needs a bit more detail in order for the reader to understand either why the issue is not controversial or why the issue is not relevant.

For example, presume that your client, Old Testament Publishers, is an employer with eight full-time employees. A plaintiff has filed a suit under both state and federal age discrimination statutes. The federal statute applies only to employers with "twenty or more employees for each working day in each of twenty or more calendar weeks in the current or preceding calendar year." In a memorandum in support of a motion to dismiss, you could conceivably treat the applicability of the federal statute as a Tell issue:

> Because Old Testament Publishers has only eight employees, the federal Age Discrimination in Employment Act does not apply. 29 U.S.C. §630(b) (defining "employer" as having "twenty or more" employees).

On the other hand, if your client were an ice cream parlor in a tourist town, its employee count might take a little more time to make clear. In that situation, the applicability of the statute would be a little more complicated, and you should treat the issue as a Clarify issue:

> Mr. Zawierucha cannot bring a cause of action under the federal Age Discrimination in Employment Act. The Act applies only to employers with "twenty or more employees for each working day in each of twenty or more calendar weeks in the current or preceding calendar year." 29 U.S.C. §630(b). Admittedly, Ice Cream Dreams sometimes employs more than twenty people. During this calendar year, it has employed twenty or more people during ten calendar weeks. For the preceding year, it employed

twenty or more people during twelve calendar weeks. Because it has never employed more than twenty employees for "twenty or more calendar weeks" in a calendar year, however, Mr. Zawierucha will be unable to bring a cause of action using this statute, and this court should accordingly dismiss Count IV of his complaint.

You might think of a Clarify issue as a CRAC issue, since it requires you to state a conclusion, state the rule, apply the rule, and provide a connection conclusion.

It is difficult to give an exact formula for distinguishing between Tell issues and Clarify issues. You may presume that "more is always better," but that is not always true. You will needlessly annoy some readers by giving a paragraph of analysis where a sentence plus citation will suffice. As you gain more experience in written legal analysis (and experience with various readers), you will develop your own sense of judgment as to the appropriate depth for your analysis. In the meantime, there are a few factors you can consider. For example, is the language in the rule abstract or highly technical? The harder the rule is to understand on its own, the more likely it is that your reader will benefit from a Clarify analysis. Is the connection between the law and the facts complex enough that you want to take the reader by the hand to make sure that the connection is evident? Are you writing about an area of law with which the court may be unfamiliar? If so, it may be worth the extra sentence or two to clarify the outcome of the issue.

4.   *Prove or CREXAC Issues*

Now we have come full circle. I use the word *Prove* to describe the kind of analysis provided in a CREXAC unity of discourse—the most in-depth type of legal analysis.[6] An issue is a *Prove* or *CREXAC issue* if (1) the issue concerns a required element of the analysis, and (2) the issue is controversial.

After you have analyzed the kinds of issues that your case presents, you should take another look at your working outline. Decide whether each issue listed is an Ignore, Tell, Clarify, or Prove issue, and mark each as appropriate. Consider whether you have omitted any issues that should be in your outline. You can leave an Ignore issue out of your outline, but you should list Tell issues, perhaps parenthetically, to make sure that you include them in your analysis.

Paradigm for an Argument

Conclusion	State the conclusion you want your reader to reach (in the heading and in the first paragraph).
Rule statement	State the applicable legal rule (in the form and structure most favorable to your client's position).
Rule explanation	Explain where the rule comes from (to satisfy your reader that the rule you've stated really is the rule).

---

6. In his text, Professor Richard Neumann uses the term "rule proof" in much the same way that this text uses the term "rule explanation." Richard K. Neumann Jr., *Legal Reasoning and Legal Writing: Structure, Strategy and Style* §10.2 (6th ed., Aspen 2009).

	Explain what the rule means (in the terms most favorable to your client's position). Rebut any counter-analysis you can weaken by a pre-emptive discussion.
Factual conclusion	State the conclusion you want your reader to reach about the facts.
Rule application	Apply the rule to your client's facts (emphasizing the favorable facts and deemphasizing the problematic facts). Rebut any counter-application you can weaken by a preemptive discussion.
Conclusion	Restate your conclusion with a one-paragraph summary of the key points supporting it.

G.   WORKING WITH THE PARADIGM

1.   *Using the Paradigm to Outline and to Begin Your First Draft*

Think of the paradigm formula for organizing proof of a conclusion of law (from Chapters 10, 11, and 12 [Richard K. Neumann, Jr., Legal Reasoning and Legal Writing: Structure, Strategy, and Style, 6th ed., (2009)]) as a tool to *help* you organize. It will also keep your material from getting out of control. Here it is again:

To prove a conclusion of law:

1. State your conclusion.
2. State the primary rule that supports the conclusion.
3. Prove and explain the rule through citation to authority, description of how the authority stands for the rule, discussion of subsidiary rules, analyses of policy, and counter-analyses. (*This is rule proof and explanation, or simply rule proof.*)
4. Apply the rule's elements to the facts with the aid of subsidiary rules, supporting authority, policy considerations, and counter-analyses. (*This is rule application.*)
5. If steps 1 through 4 are complicated, sum up by restating your conclusion.

This section describes one method of starting to work with the formula. It is only a suggestion for the first time you write. If you develop a different procedure that works better for you, use that instead.

In the method described here, you label everything so that you know where it goes and then just plug it into whatever variant of the formula best fits your situation. The first time you try this, it might seem a little awkward if you have never done anything like it before. But the second or third time, it might feel natural because it fits the way people instinctively work and because it takes less effort than other methods of organizing.

Begin by figuring out how many issues and sub-issues you have. Each one will be analyzed through a separate paradigm structure.

For each issue or sub-issue, identify the rule that is central to and governs the answer. (You might also use other rules, but for the moment focus on the rule that—more than any other—compels your answer.)

Now, inventory your raw materials. *For each issue or sub-issue,* sort everything you have into two categories: rule proof and rule application. Some methods of sorting seem to work better than others. Dividing your notes into two piles, for example, does *not* seem to work very well.

A better method is to go through your notes and write "RP" in the margin next to everything that you might use to prove that your rule really is the law and "RA" next to everything that might help the reader understand how to apply the rule. Some ideas or authorities might do both and get a notation of "RP/RA." If you have several issues or sub-issues, you can work out a method of marking them separately, such as "#3RP" for "rule proof on issue 3" or "#1RA" for "rule application on issue 1." If you have photocopied cases or printed them out, write these notations next to each part of the case that you will use. Go through your facts, too, marking the ones that are important enough to talk about during rule application. If you have been thinking about ideas that are not in your notes, write them down and note where they go.

Now, think about how all these things add up. If you have not yet drawn a conclusion, do it now. If you decided previously on a conclusion, check it against your raw materials to see whether it still seems like the best conclusion.

Ask yourself whether a reasonable argument could be made against any part of your analysis. If so, make a note of it and of where it goes. Decide whether the argument is so attractive that it would probably persuade a judge. And decide exactly *why* a judge would—or would not—be persuaded. If you decide that the argument is likely to persuade, modify your analysis accordingly. (If you cannot find any arguments at all that might work against your analysis, you may be avoiding problems that other people will later see.)

You have now completed most of the analytical process described in §6.2 [Richard K. Neumann, Jr., Legal Reasoning and Legal Writing: Structure, Strategy, and Style, 6th ed., (2009)]. And your notes are now complete enough to be organized into an outline based on some variation of the paradigm formula.

To make the fluid outline described in §6.3 [Richard K. Neumann, Jr., Legal Reasoning and Legal Writing: Structure, Strategy, and Style, 6th ed., (2009)], just assemble everything. *For each issue or sub-issue,* take a piece of paper and write four abbreviated headings on it (for example: "concl" or "sub-concl," "rule," "RP," and "RA"). (You can do this on a computer instead, if you feel more comfortable typing than writing.) Under "concl" or "sub-concl," write your conclusion or sub-conclusion for that issue in whatever shorthand will remind you later of what your thinking is (for example: "no diversity—Wharton/citizen of Maine"). Under "rule," do something similar. Under "RP," list your raw materials for rule proof. For each item listed, do not write a lot—just enough so that you can see at a glance everything you have. If you are listing something found in a case you have photocopied, a catch-phrase and a reference to a page in the case might be enough (for example: "intent to return—*Wiggins* p.352"). Under "RA," do the same for rule application. Make sure that everything you have on that issue is listed in an appropriate place on that page.

Assume that for rule proof on a certain issue you have listed six resources (cases, facts, and so on). You have not yet decided the order in which you will discuss them when you prove the rule. In most situations, the decision will be easier and more apt if you do *not* make it while outlining. The best time to decide is just before you write that issue's rule proof in your first draft. (*You do not need to know exactly where everything will go before you start the first draft.*) When you decide, just write a number next to each item ("1" next to the first one you will discuss, and so on).

When you write the first draft (§6.4 [Richard K. Neumann, Jr., Legal Reasoning and Legal Writing: Structure, Strategy, and Style, 6th ed., (2009)]), you probably will not use everything that you previously marked into one category or another. Inevitably, some material will not seem as useful while you are writing as it did when you were sorting, and you will discard it.

Keep track of what you are doing by checking off or crossing out each item in the outline as you put it into the first draft. When everything has been checked off or crossed out, you have completed the first draft of your Discussion in an office memorandum (or Argument if you are writing a motion memorandum or appellate brief).

So far, you have concentrated on making sure that all worthwhile raw materials get into your first draft. During rewriting, your focus will change. While you rewrite (§6.6 [Richard K. Neumann, Jr., Legal Reasoning and Legal Writing: Structure, Strategy, and Style, 6th ed., (2009)]), look to see where things are. If you find conclusions at the end of analysis, for example, move them to the beginning. While rewriting, ask yourself the questions in Section 10.G.2.

2.   *Rewriting: How to Test Your Writing for Effective Organization*

A well-organized presentation of analysis is immediately recognizable. Issues and sub-issues are handled separately, and each issue is clearly resolved before the next is taken up. Inside each issue and each sub-issue, the material is organized around the elements of the controlling rule or rules, and not around individual court decisions. Rule proof is always completed before rule application begins. Each issue and each sub-issue is explored through a well-chosen variation of the formula explained in this chapter. The reader is given neither too little nor too much explanation, but instead is able to read quickly and finish confident that the writer's conclusion is correct. Authority is discussed in the order of its logical importance, not necessarily in the chronological order in which it developed. Finally, the writer's organization is apparent throughout: the reader always knows where he is and how everything fits together. These things all come from sound *architecture:* from a wisely chosen building plan that the writer can explain and justify if asked to do so.

To figure out whether you have accomplished these things, ask yourself the following questions after you have written a first draft.[7]

_____
7. When marking up your work, your teacher might refer to these questions by using the number-letter codes that appear next to each question here.

i.   For each issue, have you stated your conclusion? If so, where?

State it precisely, succinctly, and in such a way that the reader knows from the very beginning what you intend to demonstrate. Some lawyers express a prediction openly ("Kolchak will not be convicted of robbery"), while others imply the prediction by stating the conclusion on which it is based ("The evidence does not establish beyond a reasonable doubt that Kolchak is guilty of robbery").

ii.   For each issue, have you stated the rule or rules on which your conclusion is based? If so, where?

If the cases on which you rely have not formulated an explicit statement of the rule, you might be tempted just to describe the cases and let the reader decide what rule they stand for. If you feel that temptation, you probably have not yet figured out yourself exactly what the rule is. And if you have not done it, the reader will not do it for you. Formulate a credible rule, and prove it by analyzing the authority at hand. (See Chapters 12, 15, and 16 [Richard K. Neumann, Jr., Legal Reasoning and Legal Writing: Structure, Strategy, and Style, 6th ed., (2009)].)

iii.   For each issue, have you proved the rule? If so, where? And do you explain the rule proof in an appropriate amount of depth?

Is your rule proof conclusory, substantiating, or comprehensive? How did you decide how much depth to use? If you were in the decision-maker's position, would you need more rule proof? Less? Is policy accounted for? (If the rule seems arbitrary, the reader will resist agreeing that it is the correct one to use. The reader will more easily agree if you at least allude to the policy behind the rule and the social benefits the rule causes.) Have you counter-analyzed attractive arguments that might challenge your choice or formulation of the rule?

iv.   For each issue, have you applied the rule to the facts? If so, where? And do you explain the rule application in an appropriate amount of depth?

Is your rule application conclusory, substantiating, or comprehensive? How did you decide how much depth to use? If you were in the decision-maker's position, would you need more rule application? Less? Is policy accounted for? Have you counter-analyzed attractive arguments that might challenge your application of the rule?

v.   Have you completed rule proof before starting rule application?

If you let the material get out of control, the result may be a little rule proof, followed by a little rule application, followed by a little more rule proof, followed by a little more rule application—and so on, back and forth and back and forth. Finish proving the rule before you start applying it. If you start to apply a rule before you have finished proving it, the reader will refuse to agree with what you are doing.

     vi.   Have you varied the sequence of the paradigm formula only where truly necessary?

If you have varied the sequence of the components of the formula, why? Was your goal more valuable than any clarity you might have sacrificed by varying the sequence? (It might have been, but your decision should be a conscious one.)

     vii.   Have you organized a multi-issue presentation so that the reader understands how everything fits together?

If you have combined separately structured explanations, did you identify separate sub-conclusions? Are the combined paradigms covered by an umbrella paradigm? Is the result crystal-clear to the reader? If not, how could it be made so? (If you are writing a persuasive motion memorandum or appellate brief, see §26.3 [Richard K. Neumann, Jr., Legal Reasoning and Legal Writing: Structure, Strategy, and Style, 6th ed., (2009)].)

     viii. Have you organized around tests and elements, rather than around cases?

Your goal is not to dump before the reader the cases you found in the library. The law is, after all, the rules themselves, and a case merely proves a rule's existence and accuracy. The cases are raw materials, and your job is not complete until you have built them into a coherent discussion organized around the applicable tests and their elements. A mere list of relevant cases, with discussion of each, is not helpful to a decision-maker, who needs to understand how the rules affect the facts. This fault is called case-by-case-itis. It is easy to spot in a student's paper: the reader sees an unconnected series of paragraphs, each of which is devoted to discussion of a single case. The impression made is sometimes called "show-and-tell" because the writer seems to be doing nothing more than holding up newly found possessions. A student not making this mistake might use five cases to analyze the first element of a test, one case—if it is dispositive—to analyze the second, three for the third, and so on, deploying cases where they will do what is needed.

     ix.   Have you avoided presenting authority in chronological order unless you have a special need to do so?

The reader wants to know what the current law is and how it governs the facts at hand. Although a little history might be useful somewhere in the discussion, you will waste the reader's time if you begin with the kind of historical background typical of a college essay. Unless there is some special need to do otherwise, present authority in the order of its logical importance, not the order in which it came to be.

x.   Have you collected closely related ideas, rather than scattering them?

If there are three reasons why the defendant will not be convicted, list them and then explain each in turn. The reader looking for the big picture cannot follow you if you introduce the first reason on page 1; mention the second for the first time on page 4; and surprise the reader with the third on page 6. If you have more than one item or idea, listing them at the beginning helps the reader keep things in perspective. It also forces you to organize and evaluate your thoughts. Sometimes, in the act of listing, you may find that there are really fewer or more reasons—or whatever else you are listing—than you had originally thought.

H.   THE PARADIGM FOR A PURE QUESTION OF LAW

Occasionally your question will be a pure question of law. You have a pure issue of law when the only issue meaningfully before the court is *what the law is*—when there is no meaningful issue before the court about how that law will *apply to the facts*.[8] You can have a pure question of law before either a trial court or an appellate court. A pure question of law arises either when procedurally the application of the law to the facts is not before the court or when the way the law would apply to the facts is uncontested.

For instance, assume that you are representing a plaintiff in a wrongful death action arising from an automobile accident in which your client's wife was killed. At the time of the accident, your client's wife was pregnant with the couple's second child, and the unborn child also died. In preparation for a jury trial, both parties prepare drafts of jury instructions which will explain the law to the jury. The parties will argue in favor of their draft instructions in a brief to the judge. In your brief, you will argue that your draft of the jury instructions accurately states the law in your jurisdiction. In such a brief, you are dealing with a pure question of law. The question of how that law will apply to the facts of your case is not yet before the court. That will be a question for the jury to decide.

This same issue also could come before the court on uncontested facts. For instance, the defendant might move for summary judgment in this same wrongful death claim, arguing that the law in your state allows recovery for the death of an unborn child only if the fetus was viable at the time of the injury. If your client's unborn child was clearly not viable at the time of the injury, your only response to the defendant's motion can be to argue that the law does (or should) allow recovery for a fetus that was not yet viable. You will be arguing a pure question of law—whether the law in your jurisdiction allows recovery for a fetus not viable at the time of the accident. The way the law will apply to your client's facts is not in dispute. The court need only decide the law.

For a pure question of law, your rule application section may be significantly shorter than the rule application section for other kinds of issues. After you

---

8. *See* pp. 293-294 [Linda H. Edwards, Legal Writing: Process, Analysis, and Organization, 5th ed., (2010)].

have fully argued your position on what the law is, explain how that law would apply to your client's case (even if this will require only a few sentences). In appropriate circumstances, you can also use the rule application section and your client's facts to demonstrate the wisdom of the policy on which you may have relied in the rule explanation section.

Sample Outline of a Paradigm for a Pure Question of Law

Rule
Rule explanation
   (full discussion; constitutes most of the section)
Rule application
   ("In this case, . . . [several sentences stating the application to your client's facts]. This result demonstrates the policy rationale underlying the rule . . . [short explanation of why the result is good.]")
   Conclusion

---

1 ISSUE - SIMPLE ANALYSIS

C   **Conclusion on the Issue**

R   **Rule**

E   **Explanation of rule**

A   **Analysis**
         Counter-Analysis

C   **Conclusion**

MULTIPLE ISSUE ANALYSIS

C   Conclusion on Umbrella Issue
           + summary of reasons = thesis paragraph

R   Umbrella Rule / Big Rule

E   Explanation of Rule

A

> ## Analysis for Umbrella Issue
>
> ### Element/Factor/Prong 1
>
> c^1 Conclusion on factor 1
>   + summary of reasons = thesis paragraph
>
> r^1 Rule for factor 1
>
> e^1 Explanation of rule
>
> a^1 Analysis for factor 1
>   • fact conclusion
>   • counteranalysis
>
> c^1 Conclusion for factor 1
>
> ### Element/Factor/Prong 2
>
> c^2 Conclusion on factor 2
>   + summary of reasons = thesis paragraph
>
> r^2 Rule for factor 2
>
> e^2 Explanation of rule
>
> a^2 Analysis for factor 2
>   • fact conclusion
>   • counteranalysis
>
> c^2 Conclusion for factor 2
>
> ### Element/Factor/Prong 3 . . .

C   Conclusion for Umbrella Issue

FACTORS ANALYSIS CREAC

C   **Conclusion** on Umbrella Issue

R   **Rule**

E   **Explanation of Rule**

General explanation of rule & factors

Factor 1–statement of factor + explanation + illustration

Factor 2–statement of factor + explanation + illustration

Factor 3–statement of factor + explanation + illustration

Statement of sub-factor 1 + explanation

Statement of sub-factor 2 + explanation

Factor 4–statement of factor + explanation + illustration

A   **Application** of Factors (all)

General application of rule (*fact conclusion*)

Factor 1–application of factor to facts

Factor 2–application of factor to facts

Factor 3–application of factor to facts

Application of sub-factor 1 to facts

Application of sub-factor 2 to facts

Factor 4-application of factor to facts

C   **Conclusion**

CHAPTER

11

Point Headings

A. FORMAT AND FUNCTION

Court rules do not give much guidance about point headings. Supreme Court Rule 24.1(h) mentions them in passing, noting that an effective summary of the argument should not merely repeat "the headings under which the argument is arranged." They are rarely mentioned at all in the limited court rules that guide motion briefs, and even then they are mentioned only in reference to related material—for example, the pleading standard that applies to a given section of the argument—and not in reference to the content of the heading itself. Nevertheless, well-drafted point headings can help both the reader and the user get the maximum benefit from the brief.

Format Requirements for Point Headings

Major contentions are labeled with roman numerals. Subpoints under roman numerals are labeled with capital letters. Subpoints under uppercase letters are labeled with Arabic numerals. Subpoints under Arabic numerals are labeled with lowercase letters. Thus:

I.
   A.
      1.
         a.
         b.
      2.
   B.
   C.

Conventional wisdom is that you should never have a "I" without a "II," an "A" without a "B," and so on. While this advice is valid (because you cannot divide something into just one section), there is an exception in written advocacy. If your argument relies on one dispositive point, that point can be labeled as a "I" even though there is no "II." (Some writers, in the alternative, simply do not label their main argument with a roman

141

numeral at all.) Note that the only exception to this point is at the roman numeral stage. You must have at least a "B" heading if you have an "A" heading, a "2" if you have a "1" heading, and so on.

Although some traditionalists may use all capital letters for the text of their roman numeral point headings and underline their capital letter point headings, these traditions no longer make sense. They come from the days before word processors; typewriters did not allow much flexibility. Unless court rules require otherwise, you should consider putting all headings (both point headings and section headings—e.g., The Summary of the Argument) in **boldfaced type** to increase their visibility and thus help the user to find particular segments of the brief.

Point headings are used as headings and subheadings within the argument section of a brief. They also appear in the table of contents; they are useful there both as a concise summary of major points for the reader and as a tool to help the user find those points. Point headings serve three functions in the body of the argument. First, they give the court easy access to the writer's basic argument. The point headings are thesis statements of the writer's argument in each section and subsection of the brief. Point headings are particularly effective as concise statements of the writer's best points because they occur in a position of emphasis within the document. Anytime the reader takes a break between one segment of a document and another (whether those segments are sentences, paragraphs, or sections) his or her attention peaks. A boldfaced heading spikes the reader's attention and makes it likely that he or she will pay attention to the information in the heading. The writer gains maximum benefit from this position of emphasis when his or her major contentions appear in the headings.

The second function of the point headings is organizational. The point headings help the reader to understand the relationships between and among the different sections of the argument, for example, that these A and B points are part of the argument related to the roman numeral II point heading, or that the writer has three main arguments as expressed in roman numerals I, II, and III. On a less substantive but equally important note, the point headings help the user to find the particular argument that he or she wants to read. Often, judges and their clerks do not read through a brief from beginning to end. Even if they do once read the brief straight through, after that initial reading they may use the brief like a reference work, and they will use the point headings to help them to find what they are looking for.

The third function of the point heading is its simplest: The point heading provides a graphic break for the reader between sections of the brief. By inserting a heading or subheading, the writer tells the reader, "You are finished with the previous point, and now you are moving on to the next point." Because reading briefs can be a daunting task, effective use of point headings can help break a long argument up into easy-to-understand (or easier-to-understand) segments. Remember that judges are more likely to be persuaded by briefs that they can easily understand. Therefore, to promote understanding, try not to have more than three or four pages without a point heading or subheading.

At this stage of the writing process, you should have already identified the main assertions you plan to make to convince the court to decide in your favor. When deciding how to arrange these assertions into headings, identify the relationships between and among those assertions. First, group the assertions that are related; second, identify the major assertions. In particular, identify the assertions that are dispositive: That is, if the court agrees with this assertion, it must decide the case in your favor.

When you first try to identify the relationships between and among your headings, your roman numeral point headings should be only dispositive assertions. This method is the most logical, and it is most likely to display an argument whose main points track the brief's questions presented. Many good attorneys do not follow this advice, however. If a case is complex, with many sub-issues related to the one dispositive assertion, the brief could end up with sub-sub-sub-subheads. In that situation, it would be preferable to eliminate the single dispositive heading and "promote" all of the other headings. Your starting point, however, should always be to identify the points that are dispositive.

B.   DRAFTING THE POINT HEADINGS

A classic point heading is a concise, persuasive statement of

1. either

   a.   a conclusion that you want the court to accept **OR**
   b.   an action that you want the court to take, **PLUS**

2. the reason that the court should take that action or agree with that assertion.

To draft your point headings, first consult your list of ultimate assertions and identify something you want the court to *do* or something the court must *conclude or agree with* to decide in your client's favor. Next, identify the reasons that support taking those actions or reaching those conclusions. If the reasons are the subparts of an argument, make each reason a separate point heading. If there are no subparts in that section of the document, "add" the reason(s) to the assertion, often with a "because."

For example, this point heading, from a respondent's brief in *Knowles v. Iowa*, 525 U.S. 113 (1998), is based on something the writer wants the court to do:

   I.   This Court should extend the search-incident-to-arrest exception to the Fourth Amendment's warrant requirement to situations in which an officer is issuing a citation in lieu of arrest.

The same point could be written in a different way, as an assertion that the writer wants the court to agree with:

   I.   The search-incident-to-arrest exception to the Fourth Amendment's warrant requirement should include situations in which an officer is issuing a citation in lieu of arrest.

The three subheadings below show the reasons that support the writer's assertion:

A.   The situation contemplated by Iowa Code §805.1(4), where an officer issues a citation in lieu of arrest, presents the same policy concerns as when an actual arrest takes place.
B.   The public interests advanced by such a search substantially outweigh the extent to which the search intrudes upon individual privacy rights.
C.   Outlawing a warrant exception for a search incident to a citation in lieu of arrest would encourage police officers to arrest more people in order to conduct searches.

Note, however, that many readers will skip point headings that are more than three lines long, or even more than two lines long. An imperfect short heading that a judge reads is better than a perfect heading that a judge skips because it is too long.

Thus, when space permits, a good point heading should (1) indicate the issue being discussed, (2) indicate your position on the issue, and (3) indicate the basic reason(s) for that position. (If needed, you can eliminate item (3) to keep the heading to a reasonable length.) Accordingly, your point headings should be full sentences, not phrases. They should be statements about how the law applies to the people or entities in your case, not abstract pronouncements about the law generally.[1] As a test, see if you could "recycle" your point heading in another brief on the same point. If so, you probably need to be more specific. In particular, you need to be more specific if your point heading could be used in your opponent's brief. For example, don't write, "The First Amendment protects freedom of speech." Instead write, "Because the First Amendment protects freedom of speech, Mr. Johnson should be allowed to distribute homemade, anonymous leaflets at a public rally."

C.   THE RELATIONSHIPS BETWEEN AND AMONG POINT HEADINGS

There can be many different types of logical relationships between and among point headings, but four are particularly common. One type of relationship exists when the main heading describes a multipart test and the subheadings discuss each of the parts in turn. For example, this set of point headings for the petitioner in *Miller v. Albright* shows how the writer believes that two parts of the intermediate scrutiny test should be applied:

I.   The use of an irrebuttable gender stereotype in 8 U.S.C. §1409(a) is not "substantially related" to the achievement of the government's

---

1. *See, e.g.,* Lynn Bahrych & Marjorie Dick Rombauer, *Legal Writing in a Nutshell* §9.5 (3d ed., West 2003).

objective, and there is no "exceedingly persuasive justification" for the stereotype's use.

    A.   8 U.S.C. §1409(a) is unconstitutionally overinclusive and, therefore, is not "substantially related" to the achievement of the government's objective.

    B.   There is no "exceedingly persuasive justification" for the use of an irrebuttable gender stereotype in 8 U.S.C. §1409(a) because less discriminatory methods would achieve the government's objective.

In the second type of relationship, the main heading makes an assertion, and the subheadings provide legal support that may or may not be formal "subparts" of the main assertion. In this excerpt from a petitioner's brief in *Minnesota v. Carter*, note how the four lettered headings make legal arguments that support heading "I." Although they are not all necessary subparts of a "reasonable expectation of privacy" argument, the reader will be more likely to agree with heading "I" if he or she agrees with the lettered subheadings:

1.   As temporary business invitees present in another's residence for the sole purpose of packaging drugs, Respondents had no legitimate expectation of privacy.

    A.   Respondents failed to meet their burden of proving that they had a legitimate expectation of privacy because they introduced absolutely no evidence regarding their status in Thompson's apartment.

    B.   Any subjective expectation Respondents might have had while temporarily in another's home for the sole purpose of conducting illegal business was not one society recognizes as reasonable.

    C.   By engaging in criminal acts in a well-lit room, directly in front of a window facing a widely used common area, Respondents exhibited no subjective expectation of privacy.

    D.   This Court should maintain its reluctance to expand the class of individuals who may claim a legitimate expectation of privacy and invoke the exclusionary rule.

In the third type of relationship, the main heading makes an assertion, and the subheadings focus on how particular facts support the main assertion:

2.   Even if the <u>Olson</u> rule extends to non-overnight guests, Respondents' expectation of privacy is unreasonable because they were present only to conduct illegal business that is not valuable to society.

    a.   Illegal drug distribution is not a longstanding social custom that serves functions recognized as valuable by society.

    b.   Respondents were present for a purely commercial purpose and were not entitled to the Fourth Amendment protection associated with the home.

The fourth common type of relationship is a relationship between "equal" headings rather than between a main assertion and its subheadings. In this relationship, the headings present alternative arguments, as in this example from a petitioner's brief in *Minnesota v. Carter*.

Good Example

1. The <u>Olson</u> rule dictates that only overnight guests have a connection to a premises that gives rise to a legitimate expectation of privacy.
2. Even if the Olson rule extends to non-overnight guests, Respondents' expectation of privacy is unreasonable because they were present only to conduct illegal business that is not valuable to society.

Using "even if" language in the second alternative point heading can help the court to understand the relationships between the headings more quickly. Despite the concerns of some students, alternative arguments are perfectly acceptable, as long as the law and the facts could reasonably support both arguments.

D.   SUMMING UP

When drafting your point headings, (1) base the headings on actions you want the court to take or assertions you want the court to accept, (2) make sure that the point headings reflect logical relationships between and among the issues in your case, and (3) make your point headings concrete assertions that incorporate the facts and law at issue in your case.

E.   DRAFTING WORKING HEADINGS

Now that you have formulated the most favorable rule you can and selected its most persuasive structure, you are ready to organize the arguments into working headings. These working headings will guide your thinking as you use the writing process to work out the best arguments. In the next stage, converting the working draft into a brief, you'll convert these working headings into the point headings and subheadings of the brief.

1.   *Organizing Arguments Under Working Point Headings*

a.   Identifying Working Point Headings

Review the rule, component by component, identifying those for which you have a reasonable argument. The next step is to identify which of these components will become point headings.

Usually, *a point heading* is the statement of your argument on a *dispositive* legal issue—that is, an independent and freestanding ground that entitles your client to the relief you seek. To tell if your argument on an element or set of elements is an independent ground for the relief you seek, ask yourself this question: If the judge agrees with me on *only* this component of the rule, is that enough to get the ruling I seek? If so, then your argument on that part of the rule will constitute a point heading.

This definition will be clearer if we look again at the burglary case. The state must prove *all* of the elements to win a burglary conviction. Thus, the defense attorney's brief need only show that any one of these elements is missing to show that the state cannot prove the burglary charge. In the defense attorney's brief, then, each challenged element will constitute an independent ground for the desired result. If the attorney challenges the state's proof on three elements ("nighttime," "intent," and "of another"), the defense attorney will have three independent, freestanding ways to win the desired ruling. The defense attorney can prevail by persuading the judge on any *one* of these elements. Therefore, the argument on each element will constitute a *point,* and the defense attorney's brief will contain three point headings.

However, the prosecution's brief in response must argue that the state can prove all of the elements of burglary. The state cannot obtain the ruling it seeks (submission of the case to the jury) simply by showing that the facts will prove any *one* element; the prosecutor's brief must show that the facts can prove *all* of the challenged elements. In the prosecutor's brief, then, each challenged element will be a subpoint. The prosecutor's brief will have only one *point* heading—a point arguing that all elements are provable. As in an office memo, having only one roman numeral is fine. Let the roman numerals identify for your reader the freestanding arguments that entitle your client to the result you seek.

So as we said, a point heading is generally a freestanding ground that will entitle your client to the relief you seek. In brief-writing, this is not a rigid rule, but rather a custom and a general principle of persuasion. In most cases, your reader will expect you to follow this method, and your case usually will be more persuasively presented if you do. Rarely will you have three free standing grounds for relief that would be more persuasively argued under a single point heading. Instead, you will want to emphasize each by giving each its own point heading. You will want the judge to know at a glance that you are correct for three independent reasons, not just one.

Occasionally, however, you may choose to treat an issue as a point heading even if it is not a freestanding ground for relief. You might want to consider this organizational variation if your case falls into one of the following categories:

- when you have a major threshold issue;
- when you are responding to a brief that has given that issue its own point heading;
- when you must win on two weighty issues that are very different from each other.

Arguing an important threshold issue. Recall that a threshold issue is one that determines the direction of the analysis from that point on.[2] For instance, the

---

2. *See* pp. 163-164 [Linda H. Edwards, Legal Writing: Process, Analysis, and Organization, 5th ed., (2010)].

question of which standard of review is appropriate would be a threshold issue. The court must decide how much deference to give to the trial court's opinion before the court can consider what decision it will make on the issues you raise.

The question of which law will govern your legal issue would be a threshold issue. Perhaps the court will have to decide whether the law of state *A* or the law of state *B* will govern the situation. Or perhaps your client's legal duty would be different depending on whether a particular statute applies to your client. For instance, under Title VII, an "employer" must not discriminate on the basis of religion.[3] The question of whether your client is an "employer" as defined by the act would constitute a threshold question.

An evidentiary or procedural issue may be a threshold issue. The court might have to decide an evidentiary or other procedural issue before it can consider your argument on the merits. The court might have to consider whether a particular document was properly admitted into evidence before considering whether the evidence was sufficient to support the trial court's opinion.

If you have a threshold issue such as one of these and if you do not have much to say about it, you can simply include it in the umbrella section of another point heading. But if you have a great deal to say about it, you might want to give it a point heading of its own.

Mirroring the organization of the opening brief. If you are filing a brief in response to another brief, you might find that the judge's understanding of your arguments will be improved if you adopt the organizational structure of the opening brief. If the judge will have read your opponent's brief, which uses three point headings, you can consider whether to respond by giving each of those three issues its own point heading in your brief as well. Be careful, though, not to concede structural decisions to your opponent too easily. Sometimes structural decisions carry important implications for persuasion.[4]

Arguing two major issues. Occasionally you will have to win on two weighty issues and the analysis of each of those weighty issues will be quite different in nature. For instance, you might have to argue that a particular statute is constitutional and also that your opponent breached its terms. While you will have to win on both of those issues, you may find that each is a very large issue, that you have a great deal to say about each, and that the nature of your argument for one is quite different from the other (constitutional principles in one case and statutory construction principles in the other). In such a case, you might want to consider giving each of those weighty issues its own point heading. However, do not rush into the decision to separate them. Often your argument on each will be strengthened by a closer association with the other, an association you can emphasize by positioning them as subpoints under a common point heading.

b. Drafting Working Point Headings

Next, draft a *working point heading* for each point. A working point heading should be a single, complete sentence that identifies and asserts the correctness of the ruling your client seeks and states how the legal rule applies to your

---

3. 42 U.S.C. § 2000e-2(b)(2000).
4. *See* pp. 262-248 for a discussion of persuasive techniques for structuring subissues.

client's facts, entitling your client to that ruling. A good way to draft working point headings is to think of the point heading in halves, using this basic formula:

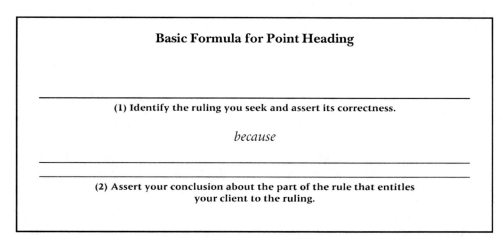

Basic Formula for Point Heading

(1) Identify the ruling you seek and assert its correctness.

because

(2) Assert your conclusion about the part of the rule that entitles your client to the ruling.

For example, assume that the defendant is challenging the state's proof on the "nighttime" element in the burglary charge. Assume further that the rule on what constitutes "nighttime" is any time between thirty minutes after sunset and thirty minutes before sunrise. The defendant's working point heading might look like this:

The burglary charge should be dismissed

[(1) Identifying the ruling you seek and asserting its correctness.]

because

the alleged breaking and entering occurred earlier than thirty minutes after sunset.

[(2) Asserting your conclusion about the part of the rule that entitles your client to the ruling.]

Don't try to identify the rule simply by a legal citation ("The motion to dismiss should be granted because the contract complies with the rule in *Smith v. Jones.*"). Articulating the key part of the rule in the working point heading will help keep your thinking focused. Also, when you later convert the working draft to a document designed for a reader, you'll need to articulate the rule. Your reader probably will not have the content of a particular statute or the holding of a particular case memorized.

2.   *Identifying and Drafting Working Subheadings*

After you have identified and drafted working point headings, turn your attention to working subheadings. The first level of subheadings should define any separate "single issues" your analysis of the point heading will cover.

a.   How to Identify a Single-Issue Discussion

Remember how to identify a "single issue." Look at your rule structure and distinguish between the parts of the rule that must be considered together and the parts that can be decided separately. The parts that can be decided separately constitute separate issues. The parts that must be considered together are all part of the same issue. Before going on, review pages 82-83 [Linda H. Edwards, Legal Writing: Process, Analysis, and Organization, 5th ed., (2010)] to be sure this concept is clear.

Use as many levels of subheadings as you need to reflect the single issues represented in the rule's structure. Even if the rule has several subparts, the facts and procedural posture of your particular assignment might place only one of those subparts at issue. If you have only one component necessary to establish the point heading, do not use a subheading. That component should be the subject of the point heading itself.

b.   Drafting Working Subheadings

The content of a working subheading can be simpler than the content of a working point heading. A subheading need not assert the entitlement to a particular ruling because the point heading already did that. The subheading can be limited to the second half of the formula for a working point heading:

> Assert your conclusion about the part of the rule that entitles your client to the ruling.

Back to the burglary example. The lack of any single element would entitle the defendant to a dismissal of the burglary charge. Therefore, every element the *defendant* challenges would constitute a point heading. If the defendant challenges the state's ability to prove three of the elements, the defendant's brief would contain three point headings, one for each disputed element.

The *prosecutor*, however, must establish all disputed elements to prevail on the motion. Therefore, the state's responsive brief (arguing that the charges should *not* be dismissed) would contain only one point heading. Because working subheadings represent each single issue necessary to establish the point heading, the state's brief would have three subheadings, one for each challenged element. The state's working point heading and subheadings would look like this.

I.   THE BURGLARY CHARGE AGAINST THE DEFENDANT SHOULD NOT BE DISMISSED BECAUSE THE EVIDENCE AT TRIAL WILL ESTABLISH ALL OF THE ELEMENTS OF BURGLARY.
A.   The evidence will show that the crime occurred in the nighttime.
B.   The evidence will show that the Defendant intended to commit a felony when he entered the house.
C.   The evidence will show that the dwelling was not the Defendant's own.

A working point heading that attempts to state the writer's position on a number of elements would be unwieldy. In such a case, the working point heading can simply make an umbrella statement covering all disputed elements, as this one does.

F.   CONVERTING WORKING HEADINGS TO THE BRIEF'S POINT HEADINGS

In the working draft, the point headings and subheadings guided you in drafting the argument. In the brief designed to persuade the judge, they will serve as a tool of persuasion. Headings can persuade because (1) they assert your position in compelling language; (2) they make visible the persuasive structure you have selected for your rule and your argument; and (3) they allow the judge to find a quick, persuasive summary of your entire argument by reading only the point headings and subheadings, either in a Table of Contents or by paging through the body of the Argument itself.

Converting your working headings to the final headings involves two steps: adding the key facts (where helpful) and editing for readability and persuasion.

1.   Adding the Key Facts

If the issue requires the application of a rule of law to your client's facts, the final version of the point headings ideally should refer to the key facts entitling your client to the desired result. For example, review the working point heading example on page 149. This working point heading simply asserts the correctness of the desired ruling and asserts your position on the part of the rule that entitles the client to the ruling. It says, "We win because the nighttime element is missing." It does not refer to the *facts* that establish that the nighttime element is missing. But to win on that issue, the defendant must apply the "nighttime" element to the facts of his case to show that the element is not met. Therefore, the final version of the "nighttime" point heading should refer to the defendant's key fact(s) on that issue.[5]

---

5. If the issue is a pure question of law, then you have no facts to add. However, the heading should still state the supporting rationale.

To convert the working headings into headings for the brief, again think of the point heading in halves, this time adding the key facts to the second half of the formula:

Final Version of Point Heading

_____

(1) Identify the ruling you seek and assert its correctness.

because

_____

_____

_____

(2) Identify the key facts **and state how they establish the correctness of the ruling.**

The second half of the point heading implicitly identifies the part of the rule that entitles your client to the result when it states how the facts establish the correctness of the ruling. Here is an example of the final version of the burglary point heading. Notice how the second half of the point heading implicitly identifies the part of the rule that determines the result.

Burglary Point Heading in the Brief

The burglary charge should be dismissed

[(1) Identifying the ruling you seek and asserting its correctness.]

because

the testimony of the bartender and other bar patrons establishes that Mr. Shaffer arrived at the house earlier than thirty minutes after sunset.

[(2) Identifying the key *facts* and stating how they establish the correctness of the ruling.]

When the point heading must cover more than one element, placing the key facts for all of those elements in one sentence along with the other required information might result in an unwieldy heading. In that situation, move the facts for each element into the subheading dealing with that element. For example, here are the prosecutor's revised headings for a brief responding to the defendant's challenge of three elements. Because the prosecutor must win on all three challenged elements to prevail, the point heading must cover all three elements with separate *sub*headings for each.[6]

I.   THE BURGLARY CHARGE AGAINST THE DEFENDANT SHOULD NOT BE DISMISSED BECAUSE THE EVIDENCE AT TRIAL WILL ESTABLISH ALL OF THE ELEMENTS OF BURGLARY.

    A.   The evidence will show that the crime occurred in the nighttime because it occurred at 6:45 P.M., more than thirty minutes after sunset.

    B.   The evidence will show that the defendant intended to commit a felony when he entered the house because he alluded to his intent to batter Mrs. Shaffer before he left the bar for her home.

    C.   The evidence will show that the dwelling was not the defendant's own because he had waived his claim to the premises and did not retain any right of access.

In summary, try to include in the final version of the point heading (or the combination of the point heading and its subheadings) the following information:

1.   the correctness of the ruling you seek,
2.   your position on the part of the rule that entitles your client to the ruling, and
3.   the key facts that establish your position on the determinative part of the rule (when helpful).

After you try to pack all of this information into one sentence, edit for readability and persuasion. The next two sections will tell you how to tame unmanageable point headings.

Exercise 1.   Evaluating the Content of Point Headings

Review the facts set out in Exercise 1, Chapter 19 [Linda H. Edwards, Legal Writing: Process, Analysis, and Organization, 5th ed., (2010)] (p. 289) and read the following versions of the "consent" point heading for Foodman's brief. Identify the point heading that contains each component for a complete point heading. For the others, identify which part is missing.

a.   Carson consented to Foodman's representation of Janoff when he did not respond to Foodman's letter.
b.   The motion to disqualify should be denied because Carson did not respond to Foodman's letter.

6. *See* pp. 150-151.

c. The motion to disqualify should be denied because Carson consented to the representation.

d. The motion to disqualify should be denied because Carson's failure to respond to Foodman's letter constituted consent to the representation of Janoff.

---

2. Editing for Persuasion

The most important quality of a persuasive point heading is readability, for the judge will not agree with a proposition she cannot understand. Editing for readability is the subject of the next section. Other strategies for persuasion impact the rhetorical structure of the point heading, and this section describes several of those rhetorical strategies.

1. Affirmative language versus negative language.   Most briefs focus on certain conduct: Is it or is it not lawful? proper? desirable? Sometimes the writer can articulate the client's position either by using affirmative language or negative language. In addition to being more readable, affirmative language generally is more forceful and appealing than negative language. Here are examples of two point headings, one using affirmative language and one using negative language.

Negative language   Carrolton's Motion for Summary Judgment should be granted because Watson is unable to show that the terms are unreasonable or that she has not breached those terms.

Affirmative language   Carrolton's Motion for Summary Judgment should be granted because the terms of the covenant-not-to-compete are reasonable and the uncontested facts establish Watson's breach.

2. Varying the structure of the point heading.   The point heading structure described in this chapter is the easiest structure for learning to draft a readable point heading. It begins with the relief you want and follows with the facts and law supporting that relief. After you have a little practice with drafting point headings, however, you can vary the formula and sometimes achieve a more persuasive version. For instance, consider these versions of the Shaffer heading. What differences in effectiveness do you notice?

Version 1

The burglary charge against Mr. Shaffer should be dismissed because the alleged breaking and entering occurred at 6:15 P.M., which was earlier than thirty minutes after sunset.

Version 2

Because the alleged breaking and entering occurred at 6:15 P.M., which was earlier than thirty minutes after sunset, the burglary charge against Mr. Shaffer should be dismissed.

Version 3

The alleged breaking and entering occurred at 6:15 P.M., which was less than thirty minutes after sunset, and therefore the burglary charge against Mr. Shaffer should be dismissed.

Tinker with the structure of the point heading until you are satisfied that it is as persuasive as it can be.

3. Phrasing alternative arguments.   When you have more than a single point heading, one or more of the headings may be an alternative argument, presented in case the judge does not agree with the first argument. The trick here is to avoid seeming to reduce the credibility of the first argument by making alternative arguments. The following example demonstrates this flaw:

I.   THE LAW OF THIS JURISDICTION DOES NOT ALLOW RECOVERY FOR THE WRONGFUL DEATH OF A FETUS, EVEN IF THE FETUS IS VIABLE AT THE TIME OF THE INJURY.

II.   THE LAW OF THIS JURISDICTION ALLOWS RECOVERY FOR THE WRONGFUL DEATH OF ONLY A *VIABLE* FETUS.

Rather than following a strong argument with a second argument that seems to undercut the first, relate alternative arguments to preceding arguments in terms that *assume the correctness* of the first argument. One way to do this is to restate the first argument expressly, like this:

I.   THE LAW OF THIS JURISDICTION DOES NOT ALLOW RECOVERY FOR THE WRONGFUL DEATH OF A FETUS, EVEN IF THE FETUS IS VIABLE AT THE TIME OF THE INJURY.

II.   EVEN IF CASE LAW COULD BE READ TO PERMIT A CLAIM FOR THE DEATH OF A FETUS, THE FETUS WOULD HAVE TO HAVE BEEN VIABLE.

Examine alternative point headings to be sure they do not undermine other arguments.

3.   *Editing for Readability*

Often the addition of the key facts to a point heading results in a long, complex, and obtuse sentence. Yet a point heading cannot persuade a judge of something the judge cannot decipher. And readability is especially important for point headings because the customary format for point headings (all capital letters) already hinders readability.

The best editing techniques for simplifying and clarifying such a point heading have already been described in sections IV through VI of Chapter 15 [Linda H. Edwards, Legal Writing: Process, Analysis, and Organization, 5th ed., (2010)]. This chapter reminds you of the techniques most important for taming point headings.

1. *Keep the subject and the verb close together.* In other words, avoid intrusive phrases and clauses.
2. *Avoid nominalizations.* Remember that nominalizations are verbs pretending to be nouns. "Investigate" is a verb, but "investigation" is a nominalization. Nominalizations require more words and make sentences harder to understand.
3. *Avoid unnecessary passive-voiced verbs.* Passive-voiced verbs make the sentence's subject something other than the actor. Passive verbs generally require more words and make sentences harder to understand.
4. *Keep the facts and reasoning at the end of the sentence.* Placing the desired result first and the facts and reasoning second generally results in a point heading that is easier to read.
5. *Avoid vague words.* Vague words cause the reader to puzzle over the writer's meaning. Purge your point headings of words like these:

this matter	with regard to
it involves	it deals with
it pertains to	it concerns

6. *Avoid negatives.* Negatives, especially multiple negatives, can make a sentence harder to understand.
7. *Use other techniques from Chapter 15 [Linda H. Edwards, Legal Writing: Process, Analysis, and Organization, 5th ed., (2010)] for reducing the number of words.*

If you have tried all of these editing techniques and still cannot produce a readable point heading, the best solution is to remove one of the items of information, generally either the key facts or the relief requested. Decide which based on persuasiveness. If the key facts are particularly persuasive, remove the relief requested; generally your reader can easily refer to the record for a reminder of the relief you request. As a last resort, remove the facts. An easily readable point heading that asserts the party's legal argument but lacks supporting facts is more persuasive than a point heading that includes the facts but can't be understood.

CHAPTER

12

Umbrella Sections[1]

For a single-issue brief where the reader needs no context, you might not need an umbrella section; but for a brief with several issues or for a single-issue brief where context would help the reader, an umbrella section can serve important functions. An umbrella section sets out the writer's organizational choices so the judge will be receptive to the writer's legal analysis.[2] In addition, by providing context, the umbrella section functions as another tool of persuasion. Ideally, a brief should *teach* the judge your argument;[3] most learners learn best when they have a context in which to place new material. An umbrella section provides the judge with the context for the heart of the argument to follow.

As you recall, an umbrella section should be concise—generally limited to one or two short paragraphs. The function of an umbrella section is to introduce the components that follow; therefore, you can use an umbrella section at the beginning of the Argument section (before the first roman numeral) to introduce the roman numeral(s), or you can use an umbrella section to introduce subparts within a roman numeral. Customary content of an umbrella section includes:

1. Summarizing the umbrella rule of law.
2. Explaining the status of any relevant elements you will *not* discuss.
3. Asserting the correctness of the ruling you seek on the elements your brief *will* discuss.
4. Identifying the relevant standard(s) of review, if any.
5. Explaining the order in which the points will be presented.

1. Summarize the rule and cite the controlling authority defining the rule. Your summary should be complete enough to give the reader a quick, clear overview of the relevant parts of the rule. Include any other principles that favorably affect the functioning of the rule, such as presumptions, burdens of proof, or policy leanings.[4]

---

1. Your teacher or law firm might ask you to use a format that includes a separate section labeled "Introduction to Argument." The content and function of this separate section are different from the content and function of the umbrella paragraphs at the beginning of the Argument section. *See* Chapter 3 for a description of the Introduction to Argument.

2. *See* Chapter 3.

3. "Teaching" the judge does not mean that the brief should employ a condescending or pedantic tone, however.

4. *See* Chapter 12 [Linda H. Edwards, Legal Writing: Process, Analysis, and Organization, 5th ed., (2010)], pp. 160-161 [Linda H. Edwards, Legal Writing: Process, Analysis, and Organization, 5th ed., (2010)].

2. Explain the status of any elements *not* discussed in the brief.   Your argument may omit some of the elements either because the element is undisputed or because it is not at issue at this stage in the litigation. If the status of these undiscussed elements might be initially unclear to your reader, identify these elements and clarify their status. If the unargued element favors your client's position and the opposing party does not contest it, say so here.

What if the element favors the opposing party, and *you* do not contest it? What if the rule contains elements on which you have no reasonable argument? Consider conceding those elements here, at the outset of the argument. Such a concession might allow you to harvest valuable credibility with your reader. A concession presents your reader with rhetorical evidence that your argument on the *contested* elements is legitimate, because you have been straightforward enough to concede the *uncontested* elements.

3. Assert the correctness of the ruling you seek on the elements your brief *will* discuss.   You can add a persuasive summary, in one or two sentences, of your argument on each element.

4. Identify the relevant standard of review.   In an appellate brief where the standard of review will not have its own labeled section, the umbrella section also may cover the standard of review. Cite to authority that supports your position on which standard applies.

If the standard will not be disputed, you can rely on minimal authority and omit lengthy explanation. If you expect the standard of review to be disputed, however, you will need to set out your authority, policy rationale, and arguments in more depth. If the discussion will be lengthy, consider making the standard of review a subheading unto itself.

As you write the argument that follows, be sure it is phrased in terms that comply with the relevant standard of review. Because the *de novo* standard does not apply any particular gloss to the question, you probably won't need to refer to it throughout the section, unless it is helpful to your argument. For the other standards of review, be sure that your argument is focused on "whether the trial court abused its discretion," or "whether the factual findings were clearly erroneous," or "whether the record contains competent evidence to support the jury's verdict."

5. Identify the elements your argument will cover and, where helpful, explain the order.   The umbrella section can summarize your argument on these elements in one or two sentences. If you anticipate that your reader will resist your chosen order, explain the choice.

Exercise 1.   Labeling the Components of the Umbrella Section

Here is an example of an umbrella section immediately before the roman numeral and an umbrella section between the roman numeral and the subsections. Identify each component of the two umbrella paragraphs.

ARGUMENT

To find the defendant guilty of burglary, the jury must find that the defendant (1) broke and (2) entered (3) the dwelling (4) of another (5) in the nighttime (6) with the intent to commit a felony therein. [citation] The defendant does not contest the sufficiency of the evidence to establish the first four of these elements. The defendant challenges only whether the breaking and entering occurred in the nighttime and whether the defendant had formed the requisite intent when he entered the dwelling. This brief will show that the evidence establishes these final two elements as well.

I. THE BURGLARY INDICTMENT AGAINST THE DEFENDANT SHOULD NOT BE QUASHED BECAUSE THE EVIDENCE WILL ESTABLISH BOTH CHALLENGED ELEMENTS OF BURGLARY.

To defeat a motion to quash the indictment, the state need only show that a reasonable jury *could* consider the expected trial evidence and find each challenged element present. [citation] The state's expected trial evidence more than meets this standard.

A. The Evidence Will Show That the Crime Occurred in the Nighttime.
    [one discussion organized according to the paradigm]
B. The Evidence Will Show That the Defendant Intended to Commit a Felony When He Entered the House.
    [one discussion organized according to the paradigm]

A. PROVIDING CONTEXT WITH LEGAL BACKSTORY AND A ROADMAP

When one of my daughters was in the fourth grade, she wrote a paper on the Ottawa people. Her teacher told her she had to begin with an introduction, so she wrote, "Hello, here is my paper on the Ottawa people." The introductory material that you provide in a brief to a court is not as simple, but it should be almost as direct.

Professor Linda Edwards has used the term "umbrella paragraphs" to describe the combination of introductory material and roadmap paragraphs that appear—or should appear—at the beginning of most arguments.[5] In introductory material, the writer generally includes any information that is needed to provide context, that is common to all of the subpoints, or that will connect the subpoints to the writer's thesis. Figure 12.1 shows where the umbrella paragraphs should appear. Generally, any time you break a section

---

5. Linda Holdeman Edwards, *Legal Writing: Process, Analysis, and Organization* 69-74, 133-37, 160-61 (5th ed., Aspen 2010).

Figure 12.1

I.   **First Major Point**

[legal backstory relevant to A, B, & C and roadmap foreshadowing A, B, & C]

A.

B.

[legal backstory relevant to 1 & 2 and mini-roadmap foreshadowing 1 & 2]

     1.

     2.

C.

II. **Second Major Point**

[legal backstory relevant to A & B and roadmap foreshadowing A & B]

A.

B.

III. **Third Major Point**

---

down into further subsections, you should provide some sort of introduction and roadmap. Sometimes these items can be combined in one paragraph, while at other times you may need two or three paragraphs. Note that it would be extremely unusual to need more than a page for your umbrella.

Many brief writers mistakenly believe—consciously or subconsciously—that they do not need to provide the court with an introduction within the argument. The court knows the law, they believe, and it can read the facts and then figure out how this case fits in the scheme of things. And on one level they are right; the court could figure it out, with enough time. But good legal writing doesn't make readers figure things out: it provides them with the information they need when they need it. And at the beginning of the argument, legal readers need two things: They need to know what's already happened, and they need to know what's coming. You must write the legal backstory to tell them what has already happened, and a roadmap to tell them what's coming.

1.   *What's Already Happened: The Legal Backstory*

"What's already happened" is not just the facts and the procedure in the case (although certainly, readers do need this information, which you have no doubt supplied in the Fact Statement). I'm talking about what has already happened "in the law." Where did this issue come from? How has it been spending its time? If the law is a seamless web, what part of the web are we looking at right now? Perhaps, rather than thinking of the law as a seamless web, you should think of it as a complicated movie. Thus, the beginning of any argument can be thought of as the middle of the movie. And the court just came in late, sat down next to you, and whispered, "What's happened so far?"

To explain what has happened "so far," you need to provide the legal backstory, as succinctly as possible and with citations as appropriate. By doing so, you provide the reader with vital context for the rest of the argument. If you are saying that the defendant did not have a reasonable expectation of privacy, don't dive into the reasonable expectation of privacy analysis, presuming that the reader knows how it is relevant to the plaintiff's rights. Instead, set the argument in the context of the Fourth Amendment. Likewise, if you are arguing that the public policy exception to the employment-at-will doctrine does not apply, make sure that you tell the reader what the employment-at-will doctrine is. Further, if there is a split in the circuits, don't make the court figure that out five pages later; tell that important detail right away.

Broadly stated, the reader should be able to glean four elements from the legal backstory:

1. **The question that this part of the document is answering.** If you are writing the backstory for the whole argument, you should address the question that the whole document is answering. If you are providing backstory for just one part of the argument, focus on that part alone. In almost every situation, you should state this question as an argumentative declaration, as in, "The plaintiff's complaint should be dismissed because supervisors cannot be held individually liable under Title VII."

2. **The legal rule or standard that is at the root of the issue being addressed in that part of the document.** Many legal arguments are about the meaning of a particular word or phrase within a constitutional provision, statute, or legal rule. Even when there is a thick layer of judicial gloss on the original rule—as there is, for example, on the First Amendment—you should still note (or quote) the pertinent part of the First Amendment before moving to the concept of, for example, the existence of a chilling effect in a particular case.

3. **How the legal issue in this case (or section of the argument) relates to the rule.** After stating the rule that is at the root of your controversy, move from that rule to the rule or sub-rule currently at issue. The concept of the "rule cluster," which was discussed in Chapter 10, may be appropriate here, as there may be a direct progression from one rule to the next. In contrast, the legal issue in your case may be a sub-part of the main rule.

4. **The current status of that issue in the relevant jurisdiction, if needed.** Although this piece of the umbrella is not always needed, for some cases its inclusion is crucial. Most umbrellas will make evident how the rule operates in general. Include more details about the rule's status if there are any controversies about this rule that are relevant to your argument. For example, perhaps you are arguing that the court should allow an exception to a particular rule when circumstance C exists. To identify the current status of the rule, you might point out that the court has previously created exceptions for circumstance A and circumstance B. In addition or in the alternative, there might be a split in the circuits as to the issue. If you are writing to a court other than the United States Supreme Court, it might be appropriate to point out that sister states or sister circuits have adopted a particular rule but that your particular jurisdiction has not yet done so.

Be honest in the legal backstory. For example, if there is a split in the circuits, it might be tempting to point out only that certain other courts have decided the case the same way you want the court to decide this one. Your credibility would suffer, however, when the court reads your opponent's brief and discovers the truth. In contrast, if you begin by laying out the complete backstory, you will do much to help the court and to burnish your own image as an honest dealer.

Note how this writer accurately identifies contrasting authorities in this legal backstory:

Good Example

❶ This sentence tells the court the question that the document will ultimately answer.

❷ Here is the legal rule at the root of the issue.

❸ This sentence tells how the legal issue in the case relates to the legal rule: the issue is about the meaning of the word "employer" as it relates to supervisors. The sentence also begins to tell the reader the current status of the issue in the relevant jurisdiction: the court has not decided it yet.

❹ Here, the writer provides more information about the current status of the legal issue, noting that there is a split in the circuits.

❺ Note that, although the writer honestly portrays the split in the circuits, she is appropriately argumentative, ending the

Gary Kirkby cannot be found individually liable as an employer under Title VII.**❶** Title VII defines an employer as "a person engaged in an industry affecting commerce who has fifteen or more employees . . . and any agent of such a person." 42 U.S.C. §2000e(b) (2001).**❷** Neither the Supreme Court nor the First Circuit has addressed the specific question of whether a supervisor is an "employer" for purposes of individual liability under Title VII.**❸** Morrison v. Carleton Woolen Mills, Inc., 108 F.3d 429, 444 (1st Cir. 1997) (declining to consider whether Title VII provides for individual liability); Scarfo v. Cabletron Sys. Inc., 54 F.3d 931, 951-52 (1st Cir. 1995) (because the law on the point of individual liability has not been decided in the First Circuit, the district court did not commit plain error when it held that a supervisor could be liable).

Differing interpretations of the phrase "and any agent" in the definition of employer have engendered a split in the federal circuits regarding whether Title VII provides for individual liability. E.g., Tomka v. Seiler Corp., 66 F.3d 1295, 1313 (2d Cir. 1995) (concluding Title VII does not provide for individual liability); Wyss v. General Dynamics Corp., 24 F. Supp. 2d, 202, 206 (D.R.I. 1998) (finding that individual liability is appropriate under Title VII).**❹** The vast majority of circuits deciding this issue have determined that Title VII was intended only to impose vicarious liability on employers. E.g., Tomka, 66 F.3d at 1313.**❺**

The backstory for subsections within the argument may be much shorter. Sometimes, the backstory may require nothing more than a sentence. You may need slightly more detail if, for example, you are analyzing a part of a rule that itself has multiple parts. The following example of legal backstory comes from a motion to dismiss a negligence cause of action. In the main backstory, the writer had laid out the four-part test for negligence in the relevant jurisdiction (duty, breach, causation, damages) and then noted that there were two grounds for dismissal: First, the defendant in the case owed no duty to the plaintiff under the circumstances. Second, even if the defendant did owe a duty, the complaint did not plead sufficient facts as to the causation issue. The excerpt below provides the backstory for the causation issue. Because the writer has stated earlier the rule at the root of the case, the backstory here need only refer to it:

> Even if this court finds that plaintiff will be able to establish a legal duty, it should dismiss the complaint because the plaintiff will not be able to establish causation.**❶** To survive a motion to dismiss as to causation, a complaint must plead sufficient facts for both causation in fact and legal cause.

<u>McGuffin v. Blanchard</u>, 426 S.E.2d 802, 804 (Vanita 1993).❷ This complaint has not done so. First. . . . ❸

By referring specifically to the causation element (and the legal duty element), the writer has ensured that the reader will be able to understand what rule is at the root of the controversy for this part of the argument. The status of the rule is not controversial, and so the writer merely relates the two parts of her analysis to the causation rule.

Whether your legal backstory is simple or complex, providing it will go a long way toward helping the reader to understand the rest of the argument.

2.   *What's Coming Next: The Roadmap*

Roadmap paragraphs follow the legal backstory. And roadmaps are the opposite of what you whisper to some one who wants to know what's going on in a movie because a good road map will be full of spoilers; it will tell the reader exactly what's going to happen in the argument. For purposes of narrative reasoning, roadmaps are important because the backstory has set up a problem: the roadmap literally shows the court how it can solve the problem.[6]

Roadmap paragraphs are important in the template because they help confirm, and sometimes establish, the reader's expectations for the document. A good roadmap will also reveal the writer's position on the points to be addressed in the relevant sections or subsections. By writing an effective roadmap, the writer tells the reader how "far" this part of the document extends— how many points does the writer talk about before stopping? In addition, an effective roadmap lays out the document's large-scale organization by telling the reader the order in which the writer will address the main points. Even a poorly-organized document will be easier to understand if the writer has provided a good roadmap.

It is tempting to skip this step, but providing this material makes your brief more effective by reducing the reader's suspense. If the reader sees a "I" heading, followed immediately by an "A" heading, for example, he or she does not know how many subheadings will follow or how the subheadings connect to the writer's main point. By writing a backstory and a roadmap, the writer provides "Bacon links" for the reader so that the connections are obvious.

Although many writers are familiar with the law review style of roadmap paragraphs (e.g., "this article will address three issues"), roadmaps in court documents can and should be more sophisticated. A simple technique is to provide the legal backstory and then use the decision maker's needs as the focus of the roadmap,[7] as in the following example based on *Miller v. Albright,* 523 U.S. 420 (1998):

> I. Section 1409(a) Is an Unconstitutional Denial of Equal Protection as Guaranteed by the Fifth Amendment's Due Process Clause.

paragraph by noting that more of the circuits are on her side. This case is set in the District of Rhode Island; if she were on the other side of the case, she might note that although there is a split in the circuits, courts within the District of Rhode Island are on her side.

❶ This sentence tells the reader the question that this part of the document answers. Note how it also shows how this issue connects to the previous issue: these are alternative grounds on which the court can grant the motion.

❷ This sentence tells the reader how the issues under discussion (causation in fact and legal cause) relate to the general rule regarding causation, and how they operate in this context in a motion to dismiss.

❸ At this point, the writer is shifting from backstory to roadmap.

---

6. *See* Kenneth D. Chestek, *The Plot Thickens: Appellate Brief as Story,* 14 Leg. Writ. 127, 155-56 (2008) ("The 'road map' paragraphs . . . describe where the legal issues will be encountered in the remainder of the brief. They serve both as 'foreshadowing' of the conflict to raise in the coming pages and as a neat transition to the 'rising action' portion of the plot.").

7. *See* Laurel Currie Oates & Anne M. Enquist, *The Legal Writing Handbook* §21.2.1 (4th ed., Aspen 2006).

❶ Here is the
rule–a statute–
that is the root of
the controversy.

❷ Here is
information
about the
current status of
the legal rule, i.e.,
how it is
currently being
interpreted by
the Court.
❸ Here is
more
information
about the status
of the legal rule.

❹ In this
paragraph, the
writer is
identifying a
second rule that
is at the root of
the controversy:
the rule about
how to interpret
statutes that
discriminate on
the basis of
gender.
❺ Part one of
the roadmap.
❻ Part two of
the roadmap.

The statute at issue in this case, 8 U.S.C. §1409(a), classifies foreign-born children of a United States citizen and a noncitizen into three groups: (a) those whose parents are married, (b) those whose parents are unmarried and who have a United States citizen for a mother, and (c) those whose parents are unmarried and who have a United States citizen for a father.❶ Children in the first two groups—those whose parents are married and those with a United States citizen mother—are United States citizens by birthright. See 8 U.S.C. §1401(g). Children in the last group—those whose parents are unmarried and who have United States citizen fathers—may receive their fathers' citizenship only after clearing several statutory hurdles.❷

Even when paternity has been established by "clear and convincing evidence," and even assuming that the father was a United States citizen at the time of the child's birth, a child in this third group will still be denied citizenship unless (a) the father agrees in writing to support that child until age 18, *and* (b) the child is "legitimated" before he or she reaches the age of 18, *or* the father acknowledges paternity before the child reaches the age of 18, *or* the father's paternity is established by adjudication before the child reaches the age of 18.❸

Section 1409(a) illegally discriminates against children of United States citizens based on the marital status of their parents and on the sex of their citizen parent. For more than 25 years, this Court has consistently applied a heightened scrutiny to state statutes or state constitutional provisions which have classified persons based on gender. See, e.g., J.E.B. v. Alabama, 511 U.S. 127, 140 (1994) (citing cases). Similarly, for almost 20 years, this Court has applied a heightened scrutiny to those state statutes which have classified persons based on their "legitimacy." See, e.g., Pickett v. Brown, 426 U.S. 1, 6-9 (1983) (citing cases). In reviewing federal legislation, this Court has also demanded that Congress satisfy a higher standard than the traditionally deferential one for classifications based on either legitimacy, see id. at 8 (quoting Trimble v. Gordon, 430 U.S. 762, 767 (1977)), or based on gender. See, e.g., Rostker v. Goldberg, 453 U.S. 57, 66-70 (1981).❹

Because of its questionable classifications, §1409(a) should be subjected to a heightened scrutiny despite the great deference normally due congressional authority to enact immigration legislation.❺ Section 1409(a) cannot survive this level of scrutiny because neither its gender-based classifications❻ nor its legitimacy classifications are supported by "exceedingly persuasive" justifications, nor does either classification substantially further an important governmental interest.

This roadmap paragraph does not include enumeration but indicates that the writer will first address which test applies and then address the argument that neither classification within the statute—the classification based on gender nor the classification based on legitimacy—can survive the test. Notice how the roadmap foreshadows the points made under the three subheadings within that section of the document:

A. This Court should apply a heightened scrutiny to §1409(a) consistent with the Fifth Amendment's equal protection guarantee.

B. Section 1409(a) does not survive the heightened scrutiny that this Court has applied to gender-based classifications.

C. Section 1409(a) does not survive the heightened scrutiny that this Court has applied to legitimacy-based classifications.

Some writers provide a roadmap to the entire argument within the summary of the argument. They then provide mini-roadmaps—as the writer in the previous example has done—to each complex section of the document (i.e., each section of the document that has further subparts). The structure of the headings will dictate the structure of the roadmap paragraphs. If there are two main headings, there should be two points in the overall roadmap. If a main heading section contains three subsections with subheadings, then the mini-roadmap that introduces that section should have three points. Do not provide too much detail in a roadmap. For example, if your main roadmap lays out the elements of duty and causation, do not include sub-parts of the causation issue in the main roadmap; they are properly included in the roadmap to the causation section.

Although the writer in the example above chose not to use enumeration (perhaps because there had been several other sentences with enumeration in the backstory), enumeration almost always makes roadmap paragraphs more effective. The user's eye is drawn to numbers on a page, and it is easy for the reader to see how the points relate to each other. The previous roadmap paragraph could be enumerated with a few simple changes:

> This Court should reverse the decision below for three reasons: (1) because of its questionable classifications, §1409(a) should be subjected to a heightened scrutiny despite the great deference normally due congressional authority to enact immigration legislation; (2) the gender based classifications in §1409(a) cannot survive heightened scrutiny; and (3) the legitimacy-based classifications in §1409(a) cannot survive heightened scrutiny.

Whether you use enumeration or not, your roadmap should be argumentative. An ineffective roadmap will say, in essence, "this court must decide three issues: (1) whether to rule for or against my client as to issue one . . . " Because you know how you think the court should come out, make that hoped-for result the premise of your roadmap, as in the previous examples, saying in essence: "This Court should rule in favor of my client for three reasons." You should also review your headings and roadmaps to make sure that the roadmaps predict exactly the points you will address and that they echo language that you will use when you address each point. You should not copy and paste your exact headings into the roadmap, but the roadmap should certainly include words and phrases—particularly phrases-that-pay—that appear in the headings. The roadmap will create expectations in the reader; by using similar language in the roadmap and the headings, you can reassure the reader that you are fulfilling those expectations and make it easier for the user to find needed information.

CHAPTER

13

Articulating Persuasive Rules & Rule Explanations

A.   IDENTIFYING VALID AUTHORITY

When you are writing a brief to a court, you are trying to convince it to do something. On a basic level, your argument consists of assertions that will convince the court to decide in your favor—if it agrees with those assertions. The court will be much more likely to agree with your assertions if it believes in the validity of the authorities you cite as support for your assertions.

The "validity" of each authority depends on several factors. When you are deciding what authorities to cite, realize that most judges are not interested in breaking new ground or making new law: They are interested in not getting reversed. Thus, part of your job is to reassure them that the result you seek is consistent with the mandatory authorities that govern their jurisdiction. Every time you cite to an authority that is not mandatory, the judge may be thinking, "Why do I care about this?" If you are writing to a court of last resort, like the United States Supreme Court, realize that—even though that court has the power to make new law—its first instinct is to look to its own decisions for authority rather than to lower court authorities. If you are writing to a trial court or to an intermediate court of appeals, its first instinct is to look to decisions of the court or courts that have the authority to reverse its decisions.

This principle does not mean that you should ignore nonmandatory authorities; rather, it indicates that you should *first* identify any mandatory authorities because they will have more validity than nonmandatory authorities. The more valid the authorities you cite, the more weight the authority will have with the court. Nonmandatory authorities can persuade, but because they have less weight, you should be sure that your reader knows why he or she should care about the authority. For example, you may be able to use nonmandatory authorities to show how various courts have applied a particular rule from the mandatory authority, particularly if the lower court decisions are more on point than the decisions of the mandatory authority.

Because each case is decided based on the facts and issues unique to it, the validity of an authority can vary depending on both the court you are arguing to and the facts of the case before the court. Therefore, when assessing the validity of authorities during your research, consider the relevance of the facts, the legal issues, and the source of the authority.

1. *Relevant Facts*

First, consider what types of facts might be relevant, and look for authorities that relate to those types of facts. Remember that research is recursive; you may not know what facts are legally significant until after you have completed some of your research. Keep an open mind, and revisit your facts frequently (e.g., by reviewing your abstract of the record). Some cases with similar facts will be easy to recognize, but be sure to consider the different levels of similarity. This is where the lessons of the abstraction ladder become important: Thinking about your facts at various levels of abstraction can help you to recognize facts from other cases whose relevance is not apparent. If your client is seeking to ban smoking in the workplace, for example, you should not limit your research to cases in which plaintiffs tried to ban smoking in the workplace. You might look for cases dealing with other types of toxic fumes in the workplace, other types of dangers in the workplace, or other situations in which an employee tried to enforce public health laws (or other laws) in the workplace.

As noted above, you may have to broaden your concept of what a "fact" is. Many law students think of facts as events that involve human beings—the details of a contract negotiation, a car accident, or a termination of employment. In a statutory construction case, however, the language of a statute can be a "fact" that is significant to your argument. Likewise, the way that particular language within a statute operates can also be a "fact"—or a category of facts—that you need to be aware of so that you can look for similar categories of facts when you conduct your research. For example, if you are arguing that the word "employer" in the Family and Medical Leave Act includes "supervisors" as well as the entity-employer, it may be a legally significant fact that Congress used the terms "employer," "person," and other words in particular ways within certain provisions of the Act. A relevant category of facts in this case could be the way that the legislature used words in the statute. Accordingly, you might find relevant cases that discussed how Congress used a variety of words in a variety of contexts. You may miss the significance of these facts if you limit the concept of "facts" to your client's behavior in the workplace and the conversations the supervisor had with your client before the termination.

2. *Relevant Legal Issues*

Second, consider what types of legal issues might be relevant. Obviously, when choosing authority cases, the more on-point the issue, the better. If your issue involves the meaning of a federal statute, for example, cases interpreting the statute would certainly be relevant. But you might also consider looking for cases that have interpreted other statutes that either use similar (or identical) language or govern similar legal problems. If your client has sued under the Americans with Disabilities Act, for example, you might search for cases interpreting similar aspects of Title VII. Likewise, if your client is being accused of wrongfully discharging an employee in violation of a contract, other categories of wrongful discharge cases can be helpful as well. Further, if your case has several possible sub-issues, authorities that address a sub-issue might be highly relevant for that sub-issue even though they might not be relevant to every issue in your case. For example, if you are analyzing a torts issue, a case addressing foreseeability might be relevant to your case even if the particular tort at issue in that case is irrelevant.

B.   COMPARING THE PRECEDENTIAL VALUE OF EACH AUTHORITY

Cases serve as precedent for the legal rules they articulate. This status as precedent underlies the claim that the case is an authority binding on a future court. However, not all cases carry the same degree of precedential value. The degree of deference a court will give to any particular case will depend on a number of factors.

Because your task is to predict what a court will do, you must always be sensitive to the relative precedential values of the authorities you find. However, when you find seemingly inconsistent authorities, the relative precedential weight of each becomes particularly significant. To measure the relative precedential values of the authorities you are working with, ask the following questions for each authority:

1.   Primary Authority: Is This Authority Really "Law"?

Some authorities are "law," and some are simply commentary on the law or suggestions about what the law ought to be. Authorities that actually are law are called "primary authorities." Authorities that are explanation or commentary on primary authorities are called "secondary authorities."

Primary authority is created by an entity that has the legal power to create law, and it is in one of the forms used to create law. In addition to federal and state constitutions, three basic kinds of law exist: (1) case law created by courts, (2) statutory law created by legislatures, and (3) administrative law created by governmental agencies. All three of these kinds of authorities are "law." Situations governed by Michigan law are governed by the Michigan Constitution and by the statutes the Michigan legislature creates. They are governed by the case law the Michigan courts create. They are governed by the administrative law the Michigan state agencies create. They are also governed by applicable federal case law, statutes, and administrative law. All of these sources are primary authority.

Secondary authority comes in many forms. You may already be familiar with some secondary sources such as treatises or hornbooks on particular subject areas, legal encyclopedias, or law review articles. These sources are created by private individuals, organizations, or businesses. They may help you locate primary law or understand it better once you have found it. For some, respect for the author or for the drafting process will cause judges to pay deference to the source's content, but those private individuals, organizations, or businesses do not have the authority to create law. So, generally, when a secondary source conflicts with a primary source from that jurisdiction, the primary source controls.

2. *Mandatory Authority: Is This Authority Binding?*

Not all primary authorities will bind the Georgia court that will ultimately decide Watson's question. For instance, an Iowa statute or case opinion would not bind the Georgia court. The Georgia court may find the Iowa opinion persuasive, perhaps because of the strength of its reasoning or because it represents the rule in a majority of jurisdictions or because the judge who wrote the opinion is particularly well respected; but the Georgia court would not be *required* to follow it. The Iowa court will be explaining Iowa law, and Georgia is not bound to follow Iowa law. Thus the Iowa opinion would be *persuasive* authority, not *mandatory* authority.

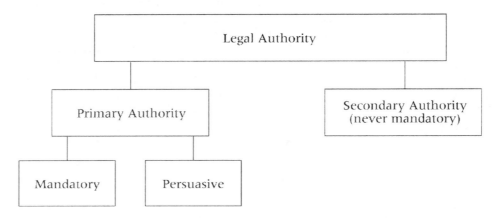

Probably you have already learned about the structure of court systems from your legal research text. Here is a summary of the way this structure affects the determination of whether a primary authority is mandatory or persuasive.

Each state has two court systems—a state system and a federal system. Each of those systems has a trial-level court and at least one appellate-level court. The federal court system is the same for each state. It is structured like this:

Highest appellate court	United States Supreme Court
Intermediate appellate court	United States Court of Appeals (for that circuit)
Trial-level court	United States District Court (for that district)

A case is filed in the trial court, here the District Court. Subsequently, it may be appealed to the intermediate appellate court, the Court of Appeals for that circuit. Finally, under certain circumstances it may be appealed to the Supreme Court, the highest appellate court in the federal system.

State court systems follow a similar pattern, though the courts may have different names. Cases are filed first in the trial court and then may be appealed to an intermediate appellate court (if one exists) and ultimately to that state's highest appellate court.

On issues of state law, the decisions of a state's highest court are mandatory authority for all other courts of that state, as well as for all federal courts applying that state's law. The state's highest court is not bound by its own decisions.

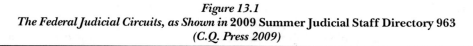

Figure 13.1
The Federal Judicial Circuits, as Shown in **2009 Summer Judicial Staff Directory 963**
(C.Q. Press 2009)

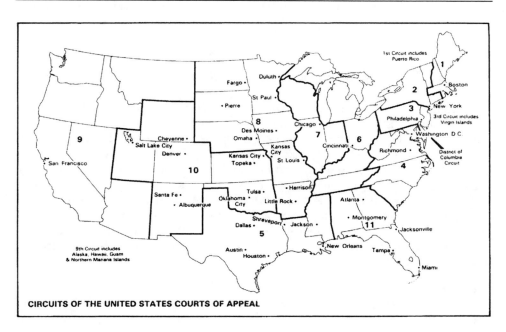

Its role as a developer of the law requires it to be free to overrule itself. However, reluctance to change the law without compelling reason causes even the highest court to pay great deference to its own prior holdings.

Decisions of intermediate appellate courts are binding on trial courts within the geographic boundaries of the intermediate appellate court's jurisdiction. Decisions of courts from other states or of federal courts, including the United States Supreme Court, are persuasive but not mandatory.

On issues of federal law, decisions of the United States Supreme Court are binding on all federal and state courts in the country. Decisions of the intermediate-level federal appellate court (the United States Court of Appeals for that particular circuit) are binding on all federal district courts in that circuit. Figure 13.1 shows the geographic jurisdictions of the federal circuit courts of appeal.

Decisions of federal intermediate appellate courts and federal trial courts on issues of federal law are not mandatory authority for state courts. However, as a practical matter, state courts generally give the opinions of those courts significant weight. This is particularly true of state courts within the geographical boundaries of the particular federal court.

3.   Subsequent Treatment: Is This Authority Still "Good Law"?

Before relying on any authority, you must update it to find out whether it is still valid authority, still "good law." A case opinion can be reversed by a higher court or overruled (expressly or implicitly) by a later opinion in a different case.[1] A statute can be repealed or amended by a later statute. The effect of a statute may be limited or even expanded by a later court ruling interpreting the statute. A court may have nullified the statute on constitutional grounds. Your research text will explain how to update your sources. Never rely on any authority you have not updated.

4. What Other Characteristics May Affect the Persuasive Value?

Mandatory authority is, of course, binding. However, occasionally you may find two conflicting sources of mandatory authority. For instance, you may find a statute and a conflicting case opinion from the jurisdiction's highest court. If the legislature has enacted a statute governing a particular issue, a court is bound by it. A court can declare a statute invalid if the statute suffers from some constitutional infirmity; but if the statute is valid, it controls. However, courts often interpret statutes—they tell us what the statute means. If the subsequent opinion interpreted the statute in a particular way, the opinion's interpretation of the statute takes precedence.[2] In that sense, the opinion controls the statute.

For nonbinding case law, precedential value can be affected by a number of other factors, including the following:

1. The relative level of the issuing court.   The more prestigious the court, the more persuasive its opinions. For instance, a decision of the United States Supreme Court is powerful persuasive authority, even when it is not mandatory.

2. The date of the opinion.   All other things being equal, more recent opinions carry more persuasive value.

3. The strength of the opinion's reasoning.   A well-reasoned opinion is more persuasive than a poorly reasoned opinion. An opinion that includes a thorough discussion of policy is more persuasive than an opinion that simply applies existing legal authorities without exploration of the policy rational for the rule.

4. The subsequent treatment of the opinion by other authorities.   Later authorities, both primary and secondary, may comment on your authority. For instance, later case opinions may discuss and rely on the case you are evaluating. Conversely, a later opinion may question or reject the reasoning of the earlier case. Legal writers may comment on the case in treatises or law review articles. An opinion that has received favorable notice usually will carry greater persuasive weight than an opinion that has received no notice or critical notice.

5. Whether the court's statements about your issue are part of the holding or dictum.   Statements that are dicta are not as persuasive as statements that are part of the holding.[3]

---

1. An opinion is reversed when that *same* case is appealed to a higher court and that court reverses the opinion of the court below. Once a case has completed the litigation process and is closed, it cannot be reversed except by reopening proceedings in that same case. However, the opinion in that case can be overruled. An opinion is overruled if, in a later opinion in a *different* case, the issuing court or a higher court recants the law set out in the earlier opinion.

2. If the legislature disagrees with the court's interpretation, the legislature can amend the statute to correct the court's interpretation.

3. *See* Chapter 4, section V [Linda H. Edwards, Legal Writing: Process, Analysis, and Organization, 5th ed., (2010)].

6. How factually similar the opinion is to the facts of the present situation.
The more similar the facts of the two situations, the more sure the judge can be
that the authority was meant to apply to situations like the present one.

7. The number of subscribing judges.   Most federal intermediate-level
appellate cases are decided by a panel of the court, usually three judges. Far less
frequently a case will be decided by all judges of that court (the court sitting en
banc). En banc opinions are binding on future panels of the same court. They
are generally more persuasive to other courts than are panel decisions. Unani-
mous opinions are more persuasive than split decisions. A majority opinion
generally is more persuasive than a concurring opinion, which is in turn more
persuasive than a dissenting opinion.

Be careful with concurring or dissenting opinions. Look to see if the statement of law you are interested in is part of the disagreement between the concurring or dissenting opinion and the majority opinion. If so, the statement in
the concurring or dissenting opinion may actually establish that what it says is
not the law, since the opinion is disagreeing with the majority opinion on that
point and it is the majority opinion that controls.

En banc opinion	An opinion issued in a case heard by all of the judges of that particular court.
Majority opinion	An opinion subscribed to by a majority of the judges who heard the case.
Concurring opinion	An opinion that agrees with the result reached by the majority opinion but for reasons differ-ent from those of the majority opinion.
Dissenting opinion	An opinion that disagrees with the result reached by the majority opinion.

8. Whether the opinion is published.   If the opinion does not appear in an
official collection of published opinions (an official case reporter), it is not
"published." In many jurisdictions, an unpublished opinion has no precedential value, and some courts have local rules that prohibit citing or relying on an
unpublished opinion. However, other courts will give some credence to an
unpublished opinion on the theory that stare decisis should still operate, even
with regard to unpublished opinions. Even if the court declines to give the
unpublished opinion any precedential weight, an unpublished opinion may
still help you predict how that same court would approach a similar situation.

9. The reputation of the particular judge writing the case opinion.   Some
judges have earned particular respect separate from the position they hold.
The opinions of those judges may have added persuasive value.

10. Trends in the law.   If you can discern a trend among other courts in the
nation or in your state, opinions consistent with that trend may have greater
precedential value than inconsistent opinions. For instance, if, over the past several years your state's highest court has been extending the liability of

manufacturers in various situations, a case opinion consistent with that trend may have more precedential weight than an opinion that questions that trend.

C.   RECONCILING THE AUTHORITIES

Your second method for dealing with inconsistent cases is to reconcile the cases. You may be able to combine the language in the cases into one rule of law. This process is called "synthesizing" or "harmonizing" opinions. Often you will discover that a more careful reading of the court's language can resolve the apparent conflict. Perhaps you initially misread one opinion. Perhaps one opinion uses careless language. If so, the way the court *applied* the rule it articulated may help you see what the court really meant. Or the rule in one case may actually be a more complete explanation of one of the elements of the rule from the other case.

If you conclude that the language from the opinions really does set out different rules, ask yourself whether these seemingly inconsistent legal rules are meant to apply to different situations. Analysis that leads to a conclusion that the rules in two opinions apply to different situations often is called "distinguishing" cases. As you reexamine the cases, you may find factual or procedural differences that lead you to realize that the rules articulated in the cases are meant to apply to different kinds of situations. For example, one rule may apply when a business is a "lending institution" and the other rule may apply to other kinds of businesses. Perhaps one rule is meant to be an exception to the other. If the rules are meant to apply to different situations, then the rule in one of the cases will apply to your client's case while the other will not.

In attempting to reconcile cases, you will be looking for clues to tell you whether one of these resolutions is possible. You must reread carefully all of the language in the seemingly conflicting opinions. You must look for later cases that may resolve the seeming inconsistency. Even if the later cases do not mention the inconsistency, these later cases will probably articulate and apply a rule. As you study the way these later cases articulate and apply the law, you may find clues about whether one of these reconciliations is possible.

Finally, you may find that both rules are potentially applicable to your client's situation and that they are not reconcilable. As you have already learned, lawmakers seldom *mean* to maintain two inconsistent rules in a single jurisdiction. Yet, such a situation is possible. Two courts of equal rank may adopt differing rules until a higher court resolves the difference of opinion. Or perhaps in an area of constitutional analysis, the Supreme Court may apply different tests, particularly while the members of the Court are trying to reach consensus on the issue. If the clues you have found lead you to believe that both rules cover your issue, your task is to predict which rule the judge is more likely to apply. You may consider such factors as the direction in which the court seems to be moving, which rule is better reasoned, and which rule produces a more reasonable result under the facts of your case.

No matter which resolution you reach, remember that if you are struggling with the large-scale organization of your first draft, you are struggling with formulating the rule. If you are struggling with formulating the rule, you have not yet mastered the authorities. When you are sitting in front of the computer keyboard, you will be on your own. No teacher will be there to offer advice about how to get past a thinking or writing roadblock. Your first draft structure can offer important counsel. Don't forget to listen to it.

D.   FORMULATING AND STRUCTURING A FAVORABLE RULE

Creating the working draft of a brief is much like creating the working draft of an office memo. At each stage of the process of writing your brief, you should review the appropriate chapters in Part I of this book.[4] But a brief also must persuade. It must meet its reader—the judge—wherever she is and move her to the spot where the client needs her to be. In addition to presenting an honest, accurate, and clear legal discussion, the brief-writer also must (1) formulate the most favorable rule possible, a rule that will present the client's story most compellingly; (2) order the points and subpoints to maximize persuasive impact and write out compelling arguments under each section; and (3) use the facts to tell a compelling story.

These tasks are among the most challenging and interesting parts of a lawyer's job, but they do complicate the writing process. The rule you first formulate may be well reasoned and faithful to the sources, but might not be particularly favorable. You want the rule to give maximum legal significance to your client's strongest facts and to limit the legal significance of your client's weakest facts. How well does your rule measure up? Will your formulation of the rule help or hurt your client?

If you are troubled by the prognosis for your client under your first rule formulation, you'll need to think again about the rule. You might be able to formulate a better one.

1.   Formulating a Favorable Rule

You have two primary methods for dealing with a case seeming to set out a troublesome rule: (1) You can try to discount the troublesome case, or (2) you can try to reconcile its language with your client's position. An advocate can use a number of ways to discount or reconcile a case. Here, roughly in the order of their force, is a list of some of the primary ways:

1. Appeal to stronger authority.   You might be able to discount the opinion by trumping it with stronger authority. For instance, remember that mandatory authority controls over persuasive authority.[5] The opinion of a higher court

---

4. Chapters 2 through 6 [Linda H. Edwards, Legal Writing: Process, Analysis, and Organization, 5th ed., (2010)] have described analyzing the sources of law on your client's legal issue, formulating a rule from those sources, and outlining the rule that will organize a working draft. Chapters 7 through 10 [Linda H. Edwards, Legal Writing: Process, Analysis, and Organization, 5th ed., (2010)] have described writing a draft, explaining the law from the sources you found, and applying that law to the facts of your client's case.

5. *See* Chapter 5 [Linda H. Edwards, Legal Writing: Process, Analysis, and Organization, 5th ed., (2010)].

overrides the opinion of a lower court of the same jurisdiction. The opinion of the highest state court overrides the opinion of a federal court applying state law. A more recent opinion usually carries more weight than an older opinion.[6]

Sometimes you will find no mandatory authority, but only persuasive authority from other jurisdictions. Authorities from other jurisdictions are likely to disagree. While legal analysis is never a matter of mere "nose counting," it helps your case if you can claim majority support for your proposed rule, especially if the majority is substantial. Then you can appeal to "the great weight of authority."

One of the rules you find articulated by the persuasive authority might have been the settled law on this issue for many years. The antiquity of such a well-settled rule might give it greater persuasive authority than a more recent holding, particularly if that more recent holding is not carefully reasoned and thoroughly discussed in the opinion. On the other hand, several recent holdings could constitute a "modern trend" in the law, and thus might have greater persuasive authority than an older rule. When persuasive authorities are in conflict, there is no rigid formula for deciding which rule is more persuasive. You are free to argue for the greater merit of the rule you prefer.

2. Distinguish the facts.   You can sometimes argue that the law articulated by the troublesome case does not apply to your client's situation. You do this by showing that your client's facts are different from the facts of the troublesome case, *and* by showing that the differences are legally significant. It is best to show that your factual distinctions are significant in light of the express reasoning of the precedential case. You will be looking for language that either states or implies that the law in that opinion was meant to apply to a factual situation different from your client's situation. But if you cannot find express support for this argument in the opinion, appeals to reason, common sense, and justice can also support a claim that a factual distinction is material.

3. Distinguish the policy.   Your case might be factually different from both the favorable and unfavorable precedents. Your task then is to show that the policy considerations of the favorable authorities—and not those of the unfavorable authorities—apply to your client's case. The policies behind a rule are the goals to be served or the problems to be avoided by that rule. For instance, the policies behind a rule imposing liability on a homeowner for maintaining an attractive nuisance would include the goal of protecting children from dangers they are not yet old enough to realize.

4. Reinterpret the opinion.   Carefully reread the opinion and all other authority from the jurisdiction asking yourself whether you have misread the opinion's troublesome language. Look particularly at the terms the opinion uses to be sure that your initial understanding of their meaning is the meaning the court intended. Ask yourself whether the court has simply used language carelessly. Did the court really mean to be saying something different from the law articulated by the other cases? Read any cases the court said it was following.

One of the best ways to check the court's articulation of the law is to measure what the court *said* against what the court *did*. The court might have articulated

---

6. Always check to be sure that the opinion has not been reversed or overruled, either expressly or by implication.

a statement of law carelessly or unclearly, but rendered a result consistent with your client's needs. The court's discussion of the application of that law to the facts of the case before the court might yield good clues about what the court really meant. You may be able to formulate the rule of the case more favorably than you initially thought.

5. Attack the bad authority; defend the good.   You can sometimes demonstrate that the law articulated in the troublesome opinion is not well reasoned, that it does not lead to a just result, or that it is not in keeping with current developments of the law. You probably won't persuade a lower court to reject the controlling decision of a higher court expressly, though this occasionally happens. A court may, however, reject persuasive authority. Even where you are attacking controlling authority, you might be laying the groundwork for an appeal in which you will ask the higher court to reverse existing law.

Let's look at an example of how some of these strategies might work. We'll use a variation of the Watson covenant-not-to-compete example. You recall that Sharon Watson was a sales employee of Carrolton Company. She was interested in leaving Carrolton to form her own company that would compete with Carrolton. Thus, she needed to know the likelihood that Carrolton could enforce the covenant.

Now, suppose that Watson decided to leave Carrolton and begin her own competing business. The history of her decision goes like this: Originally Carrolton had been owned by Watson. Since its founding it has been the only retailer of in-home health care equipment in the area. Consequently, it does a large volume of business each year and is profitable.

One year ago Watson sold Carrolton to its present owners. She stayed on, accepting employment in a sales position for the company. She agreed to the covenant-not-to-compete as one of the terms of the sale. The covenant applies only to making sales contacts, not to any other aspect of the business. The covenant restricts her only in the three counties closest to the company headquarters. The covenant restricts her for three years after leaving Carrolton's employ.

When Watson owned Carrolton, she used a reasonable markup so that customers paid fair prices. She tried to be responsive to customer needs in other ways as well. She viewed the business as a responsible commercial citizen of the community. However, the new owners of Carrolton have taken a different approach to the business. They are aware of the lack of competition in the area, and therefore have substantially raised prices. They are not concerned about customer requests and complaints, knowing that customers have nowhere else to go for the health care equipment they need. Watson became increasingly frustrated as she watched the slow destruction of the business reputation she had built over many years. She also saw in this situation an entrepreneurial opportunity.

For these reasons, Watson has left Carrolton and formed Acme. Acme has begun to compete with Carrolton, and Watson has begun to make sales contacts for Acme. Start-up costs for a health care equipment retailer are high. Ms. Watson is dealing with those costs in two ways: She has incurred substantial personal debt to pay some of the costs, and she has postponed some of the costs by planning to start small, selling equipment in only several of the categories of products currently sold by Carrolton. In the first two years of business, Acme will do well to break even. It cannot expect to garner more than 20 percent of Carrolton's business in the particular products it will sell and none of Carrolton's business in the other categories. The loss of that much business would still leave Carrolton with healthy profits.

Carrolton has filed suit against Watson, seeking to enforce the covenant-not-to-compete. You represent Watson. You must write a brief setting out the law the court should apply in deciding whether to enforce the covenant. As Watson's lawyer, you want to prevent Carrolton from enforcing the covenant. Therefore, you'd like to set out a rule of law that Carrolton would find harder to meet.

Recall that your research had led you to *Coffee System of Atlanta v. Fox* and *Clein v. Kapiloff*.[7] Reread these two cases, which can be found in Appendix A.

In Chapter 4 [Linda H. Edwards, Legal Writing: Process, Analysis, and Organization, 5th ed., (2010)] we first formulated this rule from *Fox*:

A covenant is enforceable if all of the following elements are reasonable:

1.   the kind of activity that is restrained;
2.   the geographic area where it is restrained; and
3.   the time period of the restraint.

Then in Chapter 5 [Linda H. Edwards, Legal Writing: Process, Analysis, and Organization, 5th ed., (2010)] we formulated this rule from *Clein*:

To be enforceable, a covenant-not-to-compete:

1.   must be supported by sufficient consideration, and
2.   must be reasonable. The test for determining reasonableness is:
   a.   whether the covenant is reasonably necessary to protect the interests of the party who benefits by it;
   b.   whether it unduly prejudices the interests of the public; and
   c.   whether it imposes greater restrictions than are necessary.

We worked with synthesizing these two cases, and finally formulated the following rule:

I.   IS   THE   WATSON   COVENANT-NOT-TO-COMPETE ENFORCEABLE?
   The covenant is enforceable if the contract is valid in all other essentials and if the activity restrained, the geographic area of the restraint, and the time period of the restraint are all reasonable.
   A.   Is the contract valid in all other essentials, including sufficiency of consideration?

---

7. *See* Appendix G [Linda H. Edwards, Legal Writing: Process, Analysis, and Organization, 5th ed., (2010)].

> [Discuss any relevant cases pertaining to contract essentials including *Fox* and *Clein*.]
>
> B.   Is the kind of activity restrained reasonable?
>   [Discuss any relevant cases pertaining to the nature of the restrained activity, including *Fox* and *Clein*.]
>
> C.   Is the geographic scope reasonable?
>   [Discuss any relevant cases pertaining to the geographical limits of a restrained activity, including *Fox* and *Clein*.]
>
> D.   Is the duration of the restraint reasonable?
>   [Discuss any relevant cases pertaining to the duration of a restraint, including *Fox* and *Clein*.]

Having formulated this rule, you begin your analysis. You do not need to worry about the other contract essentials because they are not at issue in Watson's case, so you set about to find all of the Georgia cases that give clues about the relevant prongs of the *Fox/Clein* test: the reasonableness of what is restricted, where it is restricted, and how long it is restricted.

As you begin organizing and writing your working draft, you notice that Watson's case is not looking good. You have found many Georgia cases upholding restrictions of the same kind, geographic scope, and duration as the Watson-Carrolton covenant. Should you simply advise your client to give up, close down her new business, and go job hunting so that she can try to repay the debts she incurred for startup expenses?

Watson's case might look much different, though, under some of the language from the rule you originally formulated from *Clein*. If the judge could assess Carrolton's need for the covenant, the judge might find that Watson's competition during the period of the restraint would do little harm to Carrolton. If the judge could consider the interests of the public, the judge would probably conclude that the public has a significant interest in the benefits that would result from competition with Carrolton. If the judge could consider whether the restrictions are larger than necessary to protect Carrolton, the judge might be more willing to refuse enforcement of the covenant.

Moreover, as an advocate, you know that it is important to present the judge with a sympathetic and compelling personal story, a set of *facts* that will make the judge want to agree with your client's argument on the *law*.[8] Generally, though, you may present to the judge only the facts that have *legal* significance—that is, only the facts the judge needs to know to apply the relevant rule of law. If the Georgia rule only compares the terms of the Watson-Carrolton restraint to the terms of restraints enforced by past Georgia cases, without regard to the needs of the public and the parties, then your ability to tell the judge Watson's full story is impaired. You cannot present her compelling personal goals and the strong public policy that represent the heart of Watson's position.

So, you need to find a way to articulate the Georgia rule in a form that includes the *Clein* considerations for the needs of the public and of both

---

8. *See* Chapter 22 [Linda H. Edwards, Legal Writing: Process, Analysis, and Organization, 5th ed., (2010)].

parties. Yet you cannot ignore the way the *Fox* opinion seemed to set out the Georgia test. *Fox* is mandatory authority, it is a more recent opinion than *Clein*, and its holding has not been overturned. What can you do?

Recall from Chapter 5 [Linda H. Edwards, Legal Writing: Process, Analysis, and Organization, 5th ed., (2010)] that you have already searched for a way to argue that the *Fox* rule does not apply to your client's factual situation. The only possible distinction you noticed was the distinction that the *Fox* covenant was part of an employment contract, whereas the *Clein* covenant, like the Watson covenant, was part of the sale of a business. However, you found that the test for determining enforceability would be the same. Further, you found that covenants made as part of the sale of a business are *more* easily enforced than those made as a part of an employment contract. Because this is not the result you want, you do not pursue this distinction.

Your next option is to ask yourself what the court must have meant by the troublesome language, that is, the language seeming to restrict the test to the elements of the covenant. Does the language of the *Fox* opinion really exclude the parts of *Clein* you want to use? In other words, did the court in *Fox* really *mean* to be saying that a judge is not supposed to consider the interests of the public or the situation of the parties when deciding whether to enforce a covenant? You also look for clues beyond the seemingly conflicting language. Has a later opinion already discussed and explained the seeming inconsistency?

Fox does not discuss the particular interests of the restrained party. The opinion does not reject that consideration expressly, but neither does it seem to consider those interests in deciding the case before it. By quoting from an earlier case, however, *Fox* does describe the *public's* interests as part of judging reasonableness.

This is your clue. Perhaps what seemed to be a *complete* statement of a test for deciding the enforceability of a covenant was really just a part of the test. Perhaps it was merely the identification of the aspects of the restraint that the court should examine. You read the *Fox* language again and this time you notice that the opinion introduces the list as "elements" the court has considered in determining whether a covenant is "reasonable."

Now you're onto something. If the *Fox* opinion's list of three only identifies the *elements* (the terms) of the covenant that the court should examine, and if the *standard* that each aspect must meet is reasonableness, then perhaps the *Fox* opinion does not mean to be setting out the complete, exclusive statement of how to decide enforceability of a covenant. After all, we would still need to know *how* a court is to judge whether the elements of the covenant (what, where, and how long) are reasonable. *Fox* itself implicitly supports this understanding: After *Fox* sets out the list of three elements, the opinion goes on to consider each element of the covenant before it. In the process of examining the reasonableness of the nature, scope, and duration of the restraint, *Fox* seems to discuss "reasonableness" in part by reference to the interests of the public and the needs of the restraining party.

In other words, perhaps in *Fox* the Georgia Supreme Court intended to list the *terms* of the covenant a court should test for reasonableness, but not *what factors* to use to judge the reasonableness of those terms. If so, then the *Fox* opinion did not purport to list the factors for judging reasonableness. It merely gave us some good clues by letting us "listen in on" the factors it chose to use in deciding the case before it.

More fortunate yet, two of the three factors you want to salvage from *Clein* (the interest of the public and the needs of the restraining party) were mentioned in the *Fox* opinion. And because *Fox* does not announce that its "reasonableness" analysis of the *Fox* covenant is exclusive, you can argue that a judge can consider the remaining factor you'd like to include, the needs of the restrained party. You even notice some language from another portion of *Clein* that supports consideration of the needs of the restrained party: "The agreement must be considered with reference to the situation, business and objects of the parties in light of all of the surrounding circumstances." As a matter of fact, this language seems to give you a chance to identify other relevant and helpful factors as well.

So, it looks as if you can formulate a rule that harmonizes the *Fox* and *Clein* opinions more favorably for Watson's case. First, try to state your rule using *simple* sentences. When you have several items, include "and" or "or" to indicate whether all must be considered. After each part of your statement of the rule, indicate the source of that part of the rule. You might come up with something like this:

A covenant-not-to-compete is enforceable only if it is reasonable. [*Fox* and *Clein*]

The terms of the covenant that must be reasonable are (1) the kind of activity restrained, (2) the geographic scope of the restraint, and (3) the duration of the restraint. [*Fox*]

The way a court judges "reasonableness" is by considering (1) the needs of the restraining party [*Fox* and *Clein*], (2) interests of the public [*Fox* and *Clein*], (3) the needs of the restrained party [*Clein*], and (4) all other circumstances [*Clein*].

Notice how much stronger Watson's legal arguments are because she can argue that the covenant is unreasonable in *her* case (based on the needs of the parties and interests of the public) rather than simply by comparing the terms of her covenant with the terms of the covenants enforced in other cases. Because you looked for the ambiguities in the language of the controlling opinions, you have been able to formulate a rule more favorable than the one you initially thought *Fox* and *Clein* set out.

Notice also how this formulation of the rule allows you to put Watson's whole story before the judge. Because you were paying attention to your client's story, you formulated a rule that gives legal significance to Watson's best facts. The combination of narrative and rule-based reasoning has made this result possible.

Finally, notice how the struggle to find a way to articulate a more favorable rule has actually led you to a more complete and more accurate understanding of the law.

One word of caution: *Credibility is essential to advocacy*. The more a judge feels pushed by an argument and the closer to the limits of credibility the lawyer's formulation of a rule comes, the more a judge will resist the brief-writer's purpose. Even more important, once a brief-writer's formulation of a rule has

crossed the credibility line, once the judge believes that the brief-writer is proposing a rule that the sources can't reasonably be said to support, the judge will
tend to reject everything else the lawyer offers. Thus, a brief-writer is better off
proposing a slightly less favorable rule than running the risk that the judge will
decide that the writer's proposed rule is outside the bounds of any reasonable
construction of the statutes and case law.

2. *Structuring a Favorable Rule*

a. Subparts

After you have *formulated* a favorable rule, your work with the rule still might
not be done. You must take your statement of the rule and *structure* it in the way
most helpful to your client. By "structuring the rule," we mean organizing the
rule into a structure (an outline format) like those described in Chapter 2
[Linda H. Edwards, Legal Writing: Process, Analysis, and Organization, 5th ed.,
(2010)]. The primary task of rule-structuring is identifying the rule's subparts
and their relation to each other. Often the rule's structure will be inherent in
the way the authorities state the rule, and you will not have choices to make.
The burglary rule is an example of such a rule.

But sometimes the authorities will leave you more latitude in identifying the
rule's subparts, and you can exercise that latitude to your client's advantage.
Keep in mind that the subparts you identify will probably become the organizational groupings for your discussion, either formally, as subheadings, or informally, as the organizational scheme within rule explanation and rule
application. So you want to look for subparts that (1) emphasize and deemphasize the material in a helpful way, and (2) appeal to the reader's interest and
thus claim more of the reader's attention.

The parts of the rule that become subheadings in the final draft are especially
important. Recall two major characteristics of how subheadings function: (1)
Subheadings emphasize their own content and obscure other content, and (2)
subheadings often serve as the reader's mechanism for keeping score.

i. *Choosing Subheadings for Emphasis*

Subheadings emphasize their own content and deemphasize other content.
Therefore, issues that are favorable to the writer ideally should be stressed in
the subheadings, while less favorable issues are addressed less conspicuously in
the body of the brief. Using a subheading ensures emphasis of that part of the
analysis by providing visibility, repetition, and substantive focus. Further,
emphasizing a particular part of the rule necessarily draws attention *from,* and
therefore deemphasizes, parts not used as subheadings.

As long as the subheadings fairly and completely cover the rule, a reader will
seldom ponder what the writer's other choices for subheadings might have
been—that is, why some elements were broken out separately and others
lumped together; why some exceptions were given subheadings and others
mentioned in sections on the basic rule. Even if other choices for subheadings
occur to a reader, the reader will not mentally reorganize the argument according to that other possible set of subheadings. So, the selection of subheadings is

another decision the advocate must make, another choice invisible to the reader but effective upon the reader nonetheless.

Strategic selection of subheadings, then, requires the writer to identify the facts and law the writer wishes to emphasize and deemphasize, the facts and law that help most and that hurt most. Much of this process of identifying strong and weak facts and law will be unique to each client's case and to each legal issue. However, some general principles apply. Recall the characteristics of judges as readers. Remember, for instance, the power of the equities and of social policy. Remember the natural attraction of readers to facts. Remember that judges care about how today's ruling could limit or enhance their ability to "do justice" in tomorrow's case. Such characteristics of judges apply to each case and give you some good standards for evaluating choices of subheadings, no matter what the characteristics of the particular facts and law.

ii. Subheadings as a Tallying Mechanism

Subheadings are the reader's tallying mechanism. Recall that readers, whether they realize it or not, keep score. This process is particularly true when the reader encounters separately identified categories—that is, subheadings. A reader tends to stop at the end of the discussion of a subheading and do a little preliminary evaluation of the strength of that subheading. The reader will mentally label each subheading as either "weak" or "strong."

To make this tallying mechanism work to your advantage, try to maximize the *number* of strong subsections and minimize the *number* of weak subsections. Look for ways to break the stronger part of your case into several strong arguments with separate subheadings. Look for ways to lump the weaker parts of your case into as few subheadings as possible. Not only does this minimize the number of weaker points, but sometimes several weaker points, combined, can become one stronger point. A reader will be far more convinced by one strong argument than by a series of weak ones.

b. Example: Structuring a Favorable Rule from *Fox* and *Clein*

Fox and *Clein* cases appear in Appendix A of this book.

Once again, let's consider an example to see how this process works. We'll use the rule we most recently formulated from *Fox* and *Clein*.

A covenant-not-to-compete is enforceable only if it is reasonable. [*Fox* and *Clein*]

The terms of the covenant that must be reasonable are (1) the kind of activity restrained, (2) the geographic scope of the restraint, and (3) the duration of the restraint. [*Fox*]

The way a court judges "reasonableness" is by considering (1) the needs of the restraining party [*Fox* and *Clein*], (2) interests of the public [*Fox* and *Clein*], (3) the needs of the restrained party [*Clein*], and (4) all other circumstances [*Clein*].

Notice that this formulation of the rule gives you two options for structuring the rule: You can organize the rule by the terms of the covenant to be judged or by the interests used to judge them.

Terms of Covenant	*Interests*
I. REASONABLENESS OF COVENANT	I. REASONABLENESS OF COVENANT
A. Activity restrained [Discuss interests of parties and public.]	A. Needs of restraining party [Discuss activity, territory, and time.]
B. Territory restrained [Discuss interests of parties and public.]	B. Needs of public [Discuss activity, territory, and time.]
C. Time restrained [Discuss interests of parties and public.]	C. Needs of restrained party [Discuss activity, territory, and time.]
	D. Any other circumstances [Discuss activity, territory, and time.]

Both structures are accurate representations of the rule. But notice the difference in emphasis. How well does each set of subheadings accomplish your goal of emphasizing and deemphasizing in a strategically helpful way? Ask yourself which structure will focus more attention on the arguments most helpful to Watson. The structure on the left, organized by the *terms* of the covenant, will focus the judge's attention on what is restrained, where it is restrained, and how long it is restrained. Watson's facts on those comparisons are not compelling. Her covenant restrains only limited activities in a limited geographical area for a limited time.

The structure on the right, organized by the *standards* for judging reasonableness, will focus the judge's attention on how little Carrolton needs the restraint, on how the public's interests are hurt by it, and on how much Watson would be hurt by it. Watson's facts on these standards are stronger.

How well does each set of subheadings accomplish your goal of appealing to your reader's interest and therefore keeping the reader's attention? Notice that the set on the left emphasizes uninteresting facts (categories of jobs and numbers of counties and years) whereas the set on the right emphasizes compelling facts about people. Notice that the set on the right emphasizes equities and social policy—topics of interest to many judges. Notice, too that the set on the right emphasizes the breadth of factors the judge may consider in deciding this case, thus appealing to the judge's concern about the effect of this ruling on deciding future cases.

Your decision here is easy; the rule structure on the right is the better choice. This rule structure will form the structure of your legal discussion.

In Chapter 4 [Linda H. Edwards, Legal Writing: Process, Analysis, and Organization, 5th ed., (2010)] we formulated a rule directly from *Fox*. In Chapter 5 [Linda H. Edwards, Legal Writing: Process, Analysis, and Organization, 5th ed., (2010)] we formulated a somewhat different rule from *Fox* by harmonizing it with *Clein*. Now we have formulated a third rule from *Fox* and *Clein*. Further, we have structured this third rule in two ways, ways so different that they seem like two distinct rules rather than merely two ways of structuring the same rule. Each of these rule statements and structures is supportable from the two cases we have worked with. Let this example of the diversity of rule formulations be another reminder of the pliability of many rules of law.

3. Rule Formulation and Structuring in a Responsive or Reply Brief

Usually the party seeking relief files an opening brief; then the opposing party files a responsive brief. Generally the party who filed the opening brief then can file a reply brief. Rule formulation and structuring require some additional decisions when you are writing a responsive or reply brief.

a. Responsive Brief

Every litigator has this common experience: You are sitting at your desk working on the matters of the day. The mail arrives, and you open an envelope from a law firm representing an opposing party. There you find a motion asking for some ruling—a ruling either harmful or downright fatal to your client's position. Your anxiety level starts to rise. A brief accompanies the motion, and you quickly read it. "Uh oh. We may be in trouble!" you think. "Does the law really say that? Do the facts really establish that? Oh no! Am I going to lose this case? How will I explain this to my client?"

The first thing you do is find the cases cited in the opening brief and start to read them. "Oh good," you think. "This might not be quite as bad as I thought. I can argue that this case doesn't apply because . . . and this statute doesn't apply because. . . . " You switch on your computer, put your opponent's brief on top of all those case reporters stacked, open, on your desk, and start to tackle your opponent's brief, point by point and case by case. Your anxiety level starts to decrease as you take apart your opponent's arguments. Before long you've got a draft. You read it over, do some editing, feel much better, and file it.

This common scenario might make the lawyer feel better, but unfortunately it seldom results in a strong responsive brief. The scenario leads the lawyer into three traps: (1) being unable to see other, more favorable rule formulations or structures, (2) allowing the opponent's argument to remain the center of the judge's attention, and (3) conceding that the opponent's brief should be the one the judge uses as the overall exposition of the law governing the issues.

First, when the lawyer organizes the responsive brief by responding to the opponent's points, the lawyer has accepted the opponent's rule structure. This mistake can be particularly serious because the party who controls the structure of the argument stands a much better chance of controlling the outcome. The Watson-Carrolton example above demonstrates this basic principle of advocacy.

This is not to say that the responding attorney should always formulate or structure the rule differently from the opening brief. The rule structure from the opponent's brief might be the only available option, it might be as favorable as the other options, or it might even be the best structure for the responding lawyer's arguments. In such cases, use the same structure because your brief won't have to ask the judge reading the briefs to shift from one structure to another. The important principle here is to remember to *ask* whether the opponent's rule formulation and structure constitute the most favorable options. If so, use them, but make the decision consciously, after considering the options, rather than unconsciously by assuming the opponent's structure.

Second, even if the authorities will not support any other, more favorable rule formulation or structure, a responsive brief written like the one in our scenario never has a chance to present its own message in a coherent and powerful way. It spends its pages trying to poke holes in the opponent's arguments rather than affirmatively establishing the strength of its own arguments. Thus the judge's attention remains centered on the opponent's arguments.

Finally, if the content of the responsive brief primarily refers back to the arguments set out in the opening brief, the judge cannot use the responding attorney's brief as the primary exposition of the law, but rather must use the opening brief as the basic point of reference for the legal analysis. The responding attorney would be in a far better position if the judge at least had the option to choose the responsive brief as the starting point for deciding what the law is. And if the responsive brief is better written and researched, the judge will probably do just that.

So what would be a better scenario than the one described above? Try this instead: Your day is interrupted by the arrival of a brief accompanying the motion from an opposing party. You panic. This time, however, instead of frantically trying to respond to the brief, you take a deep breath and put the opening brief aside for a few days. You work on other matters, using your focus on them to distance yourself from the arguments you read in the opening brief. Then you return to the task of responding to the brief, beginning by researching the issue as if you were going to file an opening brief seeking the opposite ruling— as if the opposing brief had not been filed. You use your standard methods for finding authority. Some of the authorities you find will have appeared in the opening brief, but probably some will be new. When you have found the relevant authority, you formulate and structure the most favorable rule you can.

At this point, you check to be sure that you have read all the cases your opponent has cited, updated them, and read the main authorities on which those cases relied. You can now use your critical reasoning to devise ways to minimize the damage those cases can do to your position.

Next, you write a draft of an argument *as if you were writing an opening brief seeking the ruling you want.* When you have your own analysis written out, you convert that draft of an argument to the argument section of a responsive brief. Now you insert your specific responses to the opponent's points into *your affirmative argument.* Place these responses after your own affirmative arguments in the draft rather than ahead of them. With a little editing here and there, you'll have a stronger responsive brief than did the first lawyer described above.

b.   Reply Brief

A reply brief allows the writer of the opening brief to accomplish three important but potentially inconsistent goals: (1) to counter the arguments made in the opponent's responsive brief, (2) to return the judge's attention to the writer's own arguments, and (3) to avoid irritating the judge by *unduly* rehashing material from the opening brief. (A little repetition is necessary so the important arguments, obscured by pages devoted to less important points, will not fade from memory.) The particular challenge of the reply brief is to accomplish these three goals in the same document.

Use the structure from your opening brief, and write a summary of the heart of *your* argument. Then, just as described above for a responsive brief, insert your responses to the opponent's points into the summary of your affirmative argument. Generally, these responses should go after your own arguments in the draft rather than ahead of them. If you do need to intersperse your responses within your own points, be sure that the emphasis remains on your points.

Reasserting your own structure is particularly important if the responsive brief has used a different (presumably less favorable) structure. If the reply brief can pull the argument back to your large-scale structure, incorporating the opponent's points into that structure and rebutting them there, it stands a far better chance of retaining control of the argument.

If the judge reads the briefs in the order of filing, the reply brief-writer controls the material the judge reads last and therefore material the judge might remember longest. The chance to control the "last word" is a powerful strategic opportunity. Draft a compelling summary of your main points, getting right down to the nub of the matter and showing why your position is the best resolution of the issue. Try to keep your summary short so you won't lose the judge's attention and so the rhetorical impact of your summary won't be diffused over too many pages.

E.   ILLUSTRATIVE NARRATIVES IN RULE-BASED ANALYSIS

Without the concrete instances the general proposition is baggage, impedimenta, stuff about the feet.

—Karl Llewellyn, *Bramble Bush*

In Chapter 2 [Michael R. Smith, Advanced Legal Writing: Theories and Strategies in Persuasive Writing, 2nd ed., (2008)], we saw that the concept of logos in the context of persuasive legal writing refers to efforts to persuade through legal reasoning based on established legal authorities. We also saw that most of the skills you learned in your introductory persuasive writing course—the skills of effectively communicating legal analysis—can technically be classified as logos skills (even though it is unlikely they were labeled as such). Because you already have substantial training in logos skills, this text's treatment of the logos process will be limited to some advanced aspects.

This chapter explores the cognitive dimensions of a writing technique employed by many legal writers when communicating rule-based analysis: setting out not only the relevant rule, but also an illustration of how the rule was applied in a precedent case, prior to applying the rule to the facts of the present matter. Consider the following examples of this technique, set out in the context of excerpts from two hypothetical appellate briefs:

EXAMPLE 13-1

Under California law of statutory construction, "[w]here a statute referring to one subject contains a critical word or phrase, omission of that word or phrase from a similar statute on the same subject generally shows a different legislative intent." Craven v. Crout, 163 Cal. App. 3d 779, 783, 209 Cal. Rptr. 649, 652 (1985); *accord e.g. Hennigan v. United Pac. Ins. Co.*, 53 Cal. App. 3d 1, 8, 125 Cal. Rptr. 408, 412 (1975). *In* Craven, *for example, the plaintiff in a medical malpractice suit was awarded a lump-sum judgment of more than one million dollars by the superior court. 163 Cal. App. 3d at 781, 209 Cal Rptr. at 650. Two months after the judgment was entered, the defendants filed a request with the superior court to have the damages paid by periodic payments pursuant to California Civil Procedure Code section 667.7 (West 1985), which allows a trial court to order periodic payments of awards issued in medical malpractice actions.* Craven, *163 Cal. App. 3d at 781, 209 Cal Rptr. at 650-51. The trial court granted the defendants' request, and the plaintiff appealed claiming that the superior court lacked the power to modify the original judgment of a lump-sum payment after it was entered.* Id. *at 781-82, 209 Cal Rptr. at 650-51.*

In resolving this issue, the court noted that while section 667.7 was silent on the issue of whether a superior court has the authority under that section to amend an award after final judgment has been entered, a separate provision, California Civil Procedure Code section 85 (West 1985), expressly authorizes "municipal courts" to amend their money judgments at any time, even after final judgment. Craven, *163 Cal. App. 3d at 783, 209 Cal Rptr. at 652. Applying the rule of statutory construction quoted above, the court concluded that the fact that section 85 expressly allows for the modification of a money award by a municipal court after final judgment and "section 667.7 contains no similar language is an unmistakable indication that the Legislature did not intend that section to authorize modification of an entered judgment."* Id. *at 783-84, 209 Cal Rptr. at 652. Thus, the court reversed the order of the superior court that provided for periodic payments by the defendants.* Id. *at 785, 209 Cal Rptr. at 653.*

The issue in the present case is whether California's criminal statute on vandalism requires the state to prove "lack of permission" as an element of the offense. The vandalism statute, California Penal Code section 594 (West 1999), does not expressly state that "lack of permission" is an element of the offense. However, the defendant in this case argues that this element should be read into the statute and that because the prosecution did not prove this element at trial, his conviction should be reversed.

A review of California's Penal Code reveals that "lack of permission" has expressly been made an element of other crimes. Robbery, for example, is defined as "the felonious taking of personal property in the possession of another, from his person or immediate presence, and *against his will*, accomplished by means of force or fear." Cal. Penal Code sec. 211 (West 1999) (emphasis added). Similarly, rape is defined as "an act of sexual intercourse accomplished with a person not the spouse of the perpetrator . . . [w]here it is accomplished *against a person's will* by means of force, violence, duress, menace, or fear." Cal. Penal Code sec. 261 (a) (2) (West 1999) (emphasis added). And, regarding the poisoning of animals, California Penal Code sec. 596 (West 1999) (emphasis added) provides, "Every person who, *without the consent of the owner*, willfully administers poison to any animal . . . is guilty of a misdemeanor." The omission of language in section 594 making lack of permission an element of vandalism, when such language has been inserted in other criminal statutes to make lack of permission or consent an element of the offenses, is indicative of a legislative intent not to make lack of permission an element of vandalism.[9]

EXAMPLE 13-2

Another factor this Court considers in determining whether the prolonged pretrial detention of a criminal defendant violates his due process rights is the complexity of the case. **This Court has held that if the delay in bringing a defendant to trial is attributable to the complexity of the case, as opposed to the misconduct or inaction of the prosecution, this factor will support a finding that the extended pretrial detention of the defendant is not a violation of due process.** *See e.g. United States v. Gonzales Claudio,* 806 F.2d 334, 341 (2d Cir. 1986) *(finding that because of the complex nature of the case, which involved 20 defendants, events that occurred in numerous locations, and hundreds of audio cassettes, video cassettes, and documents that had to be translated from Spanish to English, this factor supported a finding that the prolonged pretrial detention of the defendant did not violate his due process rights); United States v. El-Hage,* 213 F.3d 74, 80 (2d Cir. 2000).

In the present case, much of the delay in bringing this case to trial is attributable to its inherent complexity. The defendant is charged along with seven codefendants with numerous counts of embezzlement and transporting stolen vehicles across state lines. Coordinating the proceedings on this many charges with this many defendants has been a laborious process. Moreover, witnesses and evidence relevant to the case are scattered over four states. Finally, as to the embezzlement charges, the process of reviewing the volumes of financial documents relevant to these charges has been unavoidably time consuming. Thus, much of the delay in this case is attributable, not to misconduct on the part of the prosecution, but to the complex nature of the case itself, and these facts support a finding that the defendant's due process rights will not be violated by his continued pretrial detention.

These two excerpts illustrate the writing technique of supplementing a legal rule with an illustrative narrative from a precedent case. In each of these excerpts, the rule is indicated in **bold** type and the illustration in *italics*. In Example 13-1, the rule involves a canon of statutory construction. An illustration of the rule is set out in the text of the discussion before the rule is applied to the facts of the present case. In Example 13-2, the rule involves one factor of a weighing test that federal courts consider in determining whether pretrial detention violates a defendant's due process rights. An illustration of the rule is

---

9. This illustration was developed from *In re Rudy L.,* 29 Cal. App. 4th 1007, 34 Cal. Rptr. 864 (1994). Some language from *Rudy* has been quoted without indication.

set out as a parenthetical in the citation of an applicable case before the rule is applied to the facts of the case before the court.

This technique of providing a narrative illustration of a rule before applying the rule is fairly common in persuasive legal writing. Despite its popularity, however, it has not been analyzed in much depth. In this chapter, then, we will analyze in detail the communicative and persuasive functions of illustrative narratives in rule-based analysis. To this end, we will turn to the field of cognitive psychology. We will see that cognitive psychology theory indicates that the human brain processes stories and narratives more effectively than abstract propositions and rules. We will also see that this discovery by cognitive psychologists has great significance to us as legal writers, for illustrative narratives are not merely stylistic devices; they are important communicative devices that facilitate a reader's understanding of abstract rules. Thus, we will see that communicating rule-based analysis using narrative illustrations is effective (if not essential) because it allows us to tap into the fundamental way that the human brain processes information. In the end, with a fuller appreciation of the cognitive dimensions of illustrative narratives, we will discuss how we as legal writers can use this technique even more effectively to communicate the analysis in our persuasive documents.

1. *Communicating Rule-Based Analysis in Legal Writing: The Problem, The Answer, and the Impact*

a. **The Problem: The Paradox of Rule-Based Analysis**

As a "country of laws, not men," our system for resolving legal disputes is based primarily on rule-based analysis: the process of applying established legal rules to the facts of a specific dispute.[10] Despite its preeminence in legal reasoning, however, rule-based analysis suffers from a major shortcoming: It is inconsistent with the fundamental way the human brain processes information.

From a cognitive standpoint, rule-based analysis involves the mental process of applying a legal principle, stated in the form of an abstract rule, to the facts of a specific case. Recent developments in cognitive psychology suggest, however, that humans do not think effectively in terms of abstract general propositions.[11] This realization presents quite a paradox for legal writers. On the one hand, our system for resolving legal disputes relies heavily on the application of general rules to the facts of a specific case (that is, rule-based analysis). On the other hand, our brains (in particular, the brains of our readers) do not easily understand and process ideas expressed in the form of general propositions. Thus, legal advocates constantly face a dilemma inherent in the system. We are forced to reason based on general rules, yet rules as concepts are cognitively flawed.

10. *E.g.* Linda H. Edwards, *The Convergence of Analogical and Dialectic Imaginations in Legal Discourse*, 20 Leg. Stud. Forum 7, 10 (1996). The rules employed in rule-based analysis can come from a variety of sources, such as statutes, administrative rules and regulations, and case law.

11. *See generally* Steven L. Winter, *The Cognitive Dimension of the Agon Between Legal Power and Narrative Meaning*, 87 Mich. L. Rev. 2225 (1989) [hereinafter Winter, *The Cognitive Dimension*]; Steven L. Winter, *Transcendental Nonsense, Metaphoric Reasoning, and the Cognitive Stakes for Law*, 137 U. Pa. L. Rev. 1105 (1989).

b.   The Answer: The Cognitive Dimensions of Illustrative Narratives

As we just discussed, cognitive theory indicates that the human brain does not effectively process abstract rules. According to cognitive psychologists, humans understand concepts expressed in the form of stories or narratives better than they understand concepts explained as abstract principles. That is, narrative as a mode of communication is more effective than general propositions. As Steven L. Winter has stated, "[N]arrative . . . corresponds more closely to the manner in which the human mind makes sense of experience than does the conventional, abstracted rhetoric of the law."[12]

A short answer to the question of why narrative has such communicative power is that a person learns through story in the same way that he or she learns through experience. Starting at infancy, human beings learn by interacting with and experiencing the world around them. And because life is continual and occurs over the passage of time, much of learning by experience happens as events, ideas, and concepts build on each other. A person is basically the protagonist in the story that is his or her own life. And much of what we learn is learned by chronologically experiencing related events that build on each other.

Story as a mode of communication functions in the same way. Just as life involves experiencing the chronological passing of related events, stories too, by definition, involve a chronological telling of related events. When we hear a story, we place ourselves in the role of the protagonist. "We imagine ourselves as the protagonist and picture ourselves in the protagonist's shoes as we proceed from introduction to conclusion."[13] And we learn from this experience in the same way we learn from our participation in our own lives. As Winter states,

> [narrative] engage[s] the audience in the cognitive process by which it regularly makes meaning in its day-to-day world. . . . [T]he process of making sense of the projected experience of the story [is] mimetic of the process by which humans always make meaning. The audience "lives" the story-experience, and is brought personally to engage in the process of constructing meaning out of another's experience.[14]

Thus, "narrative's communicative capacity is rooted in the way that the mind interprets, processes, and understands information."[15] The most fundamental way that we learn and process information is through living the experience. Stories communicate in the same way and thus take advantage of the most fundamental way in which humans process and understand information. For this reason, narrative has a communicative advantage over general propositions. As Winter puts it,

> The grounding of all human cognition in experience means that there is a greater cognitive "clout" to images from lived experience as compared to propositional formulations that attempt to "literalize" their meaning. The dramatic image of

---

12. Winter, *The Cognitive Dimension, supra* n. 3, at 2228. It is beyond the scope of this chapter to delve in-depth into how cognitive theory explains the effectiveness of narrative as a mode of communication. If you are interested in these cognitive principles, read Winter's fascinating works and the numerous sources referenced therein.

13. *Id.* at 2272.

14. *Id.* at 2277.

15. *Id.* at 2271.

[narrative] has a communicative power that is unmatched by the "equivalent" propositional statement.[16]

What does all of this mean for the legal writer who must communicate rule-based reasoning? As we have seen, rule-based reasoning is indispensable to legal discourse. Yet, as we have also seen, the human mind does not effectively process general principles. Consequently, legal writers should heed this information from cognitive theory and combine illustrative narratives with rules when communicating rule-based analysis. When a legal writer must communicate rule-based analysis, the writer, knowing the cognitive limitations of the human mind, should consider supplementing a statement of the general rule with a narrative that illustrates how the rule operated in a precedent case.

We see this strategy of combining a general proposition with an illustrative narrative in everyday conversations. Frequently, a person trying to explain a point will supplement an abstract statement with an illustration or example. Similarly, "how to" books on all subjects (including this one) frequently supplement their abstract descriptions with illustrations. This general tendency to supplement propositions with illustrations is a manifestation of an innate sense held by all humans that general propositions alone lack communicative force and precision.

It is not surprising then that, as we saw in the beginning of this chapter, some legal writers already employ the strategy of combining rules with illustrative narratives when communicating rule-based analysis. Again, the existence of this writing strategy is a manifestation of an instinctive sense on the part of some legal writers that many concepts cannot be adequately explained by a rule alone. Thanks to cognitive theory, however, we now know why this is true. Consequently, with this knowledge from cognitive psychology, we as legal writers can now approach the communication of rule-based analysis more consciously and strategically. The use of illustrative narratives should no longer be a result of accident or intuition; the use of illustrative narratives should be the result of conscious choice in view of our knowledge of the cognitive limitations of rules and the cognitive benefits of narrative.

c.   The Impact: In-Text and Parenthetical Illustrations

The answer to the inherent communicative problems with rules is to supplement them with illustrative narratives. Traditionally in legal writing this has been accomplished by incorporating illustrative narratives with rules in one of two ways: (1) through in-text-illustrations, or (2) through parenthetical illustrations.

Consider the following two examples of legal discussions analyzing the same substantive point using rule-based analysis. In Example 13-3, narrative illustrations of the applicable rule appear in the *text* of the discussion, immediately following the statement of the rule. In Example 13-4, the illustrations of the rule appear as *parentheticals* within the citations of the applicable cases. (In both examples, the rule is set out in **bold** type and the illustrations are set out in *italic* type.)

---

16. *Id.* at 2276-77.

EXAMPLE 13-3

The first factor Georgia courts consider in deciding whether to bar a tort suit between married parties is whether allowing the suit will foster marital disharmony and disunity between the parties. The Georgia Supreme Court has recognized that, "[a] truly adversary tort lawsuit between husband and wife, by its very nature, would have an upsetting and embittering effect upon domestic tranquility." *Robeson v. International Indemnity Co.*, 282 S.E.2d 896, 898 (Ga. 1981). Consequently, most tort suits between spouses will be barred for this reason. *See id.* **However, the Georgia Supreme Court has also held that if the facts of the case indicate that marital harmony will not be disrupted by an interspousal suit, this consideration will not require that the suit be barred.** *See Harris v. Harris*, 313 S.E.2d 88, 90 (Ga. 1984); *Jones v. Jones*, 376 S.E.2d 674, 675 (Ga. 1989).

In Harris, *for example, the case involved a personal injury suit between parties who were legally married, but who had been living in a state of separation for ten years. 313 S.E.2d at 89-90. The Supreme Court held that the "marital disharmony" factor did not require that the suit be barred because "there was, realistically speaking, no 'marital harmony' to be protected by application of the interspousal immunity rule."* Id. *at 90. Similarly, in* Jones, *the Georgia Supreme Court held that a tort suit between the estate of a deceased spouse and a surviving spouse was not barred under the doctrine of interspousal immunity. 376 S.E.2d at 676. In analyzing the "marital disharmony" factor, the court stated, "First, and most obviously, there can be no marital harmony to foster when one spouse has died."* Id. at 675.

EXAMPLE 13-4

The first factor Georgia courts consider in deciding whether to bar a tort suit between married parties is whether allowing the suit will foster marital disharmony and disunity between the parties. The Georgia Supreme Court has recognized that, "[a] truly adversary tort law suit between husband and wife, by its very nature, would have an upsetting and embittering effect upon domestic tranquility." *Robeson v. International Indemnity Co.*, 282 S.E.2d 896, 898 (Ga. 1981). Consequently, most tort suits between spouses will be barred for this reason. *See id.* **However, the Georgia Supreme Court has also held that if the facts of the case indicate that marital harmony will not be disrupted by an interspousal suit, this consideration will not require that the suit be barred.** *See Harris v. Harris*, 313 S.E.2d 88, 90 (Ga. 1984) (*holding that a suit between spouses who had been separated for ten years was not barred under the "marital disharmony" factor because there was no marital harmony to be protected*); *Jones v. Jones*, 376 S.E.2d 674, 675 (Ga. 1989) (*holding that a suit between the estate of a deceased spouse and a surviving spouse was not barred under the "marital disharmony" factor because "there can be no marital harmony to foster when one spouse has died"*).

As the above examples illustrate, narrative illustrations of rules can be inserted into the text of a discussion or into citation parentheticals. Later in this chapter we will discuss some guidelines for writers to consider when deciding between these two approaches.

2. The Communicative Functions of Illustrative Narratives

In the preceding discussion, we saw that illustrative narratives facilitate the communication of abstract rules because they are more consistent with the way the human brain processes information. A closer look at illustrative narratives, however, indicates that they can actually serve several specific communicative functions.

a. Illustration for Elucidation

The most important function that can be served by illustrative narratives is explaining the substance of a rule. As we previously discussed, many legal concepts are too nebulous or complex to be fully understood in the form of an abstract rule. Thus, one possible function of an illustrative narrative is to elucidate the meaning of a rule by providing an example of how the rule operated in a precedent case. The narrative puts the rule in concrete terms and thereby makes it more understandable. Consider the following example:

EXAMPLE 13-5

Another factor federal courts consider in determining whether the unauthorized use of copyrighted material is permissible under the "fair use" doctrine is whether the alleged infringer's use of the copyrighted material is "transformative." If the use is transformative, this will support a finding that the use is fair. To constitute a "transformative use" the alleged infringer's use must add something new to the original material and thereby alter its purpose, meaning, or character. *See e.g. Campbell v. Acuff-Rose Music, Inc.*, 510 U.S. 569, 579 (1994); *Religious Tech. Ctr. v. Netcom On-Line Communication Servs., Inc.*, 923 F. Supp. 1231, 1243 (N.D. Cal. 1995); *Belmore v. City Pages, Inc.*, 880 F. Supp. 673, 677-78 (D. Minn. 1995).

The *Belmore* case provides a good illustration of what is meant by "transformativeness." In that case, the plaintiff, a policeman, wrote an article entitled "Tale of Two Islands" and published it in the local police federation newspaper. *Belmore*, 880 F. Supp. at 675. The article was written in the form of a fable and portrayed a dispute between the inhabitants of two fictitious neighboring islands—one populated by clean, considerate, industrious people and the other populated by lazy, dirty, dishonest people. *Id.* at 675, 681 app. Subsequently, the local Minneapolis newspaper, City Pages, without the permission of the plaintiff, reprinted the entire fable in an article criticizing it as evidence of racism in the local police department. *Id.* at 675. The author of the fable then sued City Pages for copyright infringement. *Id.* In analyzing whether City Pages' verbatim copying of the plaintiff's fable was fair use, the court considered, among other things, whether the defendant's use was transformative. *Id.* at 677-78. The court noted that City Pages added new expression to the fable by incorporating the fable into a longer article that criticized it and the local police department. *Id.* at 675, 678. The court also noted that City Pages altered the character and purpose of the fable. City Pages' purpose in using the fable was to set it out for criticism and to offer it as evidence of racism in the police department, a purpose quite different than that of the original author. *Id.* at 678. Thus, the court found that the use was transformative and that this factor supported a finding that the copying by City Pages was fair use. *Id.*

The above example involves the "fair use" defense to copyright infringement. As the example indicates, one factor federal courts consider in determining fair use is whether the use of the copyrighted material by the alleged infringer was "transformative." The example begins by setting out the definition of "transformativeness" as a general proposition. This general definition, however, is vague and ambiguous. The concept of "transformativeness" is difficult to understand as an abstract rule. Consequently, the example supplements the rule with an illustration from the *Belmore* case. It is only through this illustration that one gains an appreciation of what is meant by a "transformative use of copyrighted material."

Such is often the case with abstract rules. They are frequently incapable of clearly and accurately conveying complicated legal concepts. Thus, the first and primary function of illustrative narratives is to help communicate the substance of abstract rules.

b. Illustration for Elimination

Illustrative narratives can also serve to eliminate possible misinterpretations of general rules. Because general rules are limited in their capacity to communicate precisely, they can sometimes be susceptible to multiple interpretations. A writer can eliminate interpretations other than the one he or she intends by supplementing the rule with an illustration. Consider this example:

EXAMPLE 13-6

In order for a criminal victim to recover restitution under Florida Statutes section 775.089(1)(a), the victim must show that the expenses in question are sufficiently connected to the crimes of which the defendant was convicted. *See e.g. State v. Williams*, 520 So. 2d 276, 277-78 (Fla. 1988); *Faulkner v. State*, 582 So. 2d 783, 784 (Fla. 5th Dist. Ct. App. 1991); *Jones v. State*, 480 So. 2d 163, 164 (Fla. 1st Dist. Ct. App. 1985). In *Faulkner*, the court reversed a restitution order that required the defendant to reimburse two burglary victims for items taken during a burglary of their home and not recovered. 582 So. 2d at 784. Although there was evidence in the record that the defendant was involved in the burglary, he was not convicted of that crime. The defendant was convicted only of dealing in stolen property. The court concluded that the missing items were related to the burglary itself, not the offense of which the defendant was actually convicted—dealing in stolen property. Thus, restitution was inappropriate. *Id.*; *see also Jones*, 480 So. 2d at 164 (finding that a defendant could not be held responsible for the cost of repairing a window broken during a burglary committed by the defendant when the defendant was convicted only of dealing in stolen property and not the burglary itself).

In the foregoing example, the general rule states that restitution under the relevant statute is appropriate only where the expenses in question are connected to the crimes of which the defendant was "convicted." Without the illustrations from the *Faulkner* case and the *Jones* case, a reader may not appreciate the significance of the word "convicted" in this rule. A reader might interpret this rule as merely requiring that the expenses be related to the crimes the defendant *committed* or the crimes with which the defendant was *charged*. Only by the inclusion of the illustrations does the reader appreciate the significance and importance of the word "convicted." To a less-than-careful reader, the general rule is susceptible to multiple interpretations. Thus, the illustrations serve to eliminate the inaccurate interpretations of the general rule.[17]

The function of *eliminating* erroneous alternative interpretations of a rule is slightly different from the first function of *elucidating* a vague rule. The elucidation function applies when a rule is too complex or vague to conjure up *any* clear meaning in readers' minds. The rule is understandable in general only through a narrative illustration. The elimination function, on the other hand, applies when the rule appears to make sense on its face, but is actually susceptible to erroneous interpretations. In such cases, the illustrations eliminate the possible erroneous interpretations and highlight the correct one. Consider the following additional example of illustration for elimination:

EXAMPLE 13-7

Another factor federal courts consider in determining whether the unauthorized use of copyrighted material is permissible under the "fair use" doctrine is whether the alleged infringer's use of the copyrighted material had a negative impact on the potential market of the original work. Federal courts generally hold that if the copying of copyrighted work by an alleged infringer has an adverse impact on the commercial market for the original work, this factor will strongly support a finding that the alleged infringer's use of the material is not fair use. *See e.g. Campbell v. Acuff-Rose Music, Inc.*, 510 U.S. 569, 590 (1994); *Consumer Union of United States, Inc. v. General Signal Corp.*, 724 F.2d 1044, 1050-51 (2d Cir. 1983); *Religious Tech. Ctr. v. Netcom On-Line Communication Servs., Inc.*, 923 F. Supp. 1231, 1248 (N.D. Cal. 1995).

In *Religious Tech. Ctr.*, the defendant copied and posted on the Internet a number of copyrighted works owned by the Church of Scientology for the purpose of criticizing the works and the Church in general. 923 F. Supp. at 1238-39. The

---

17. I have created hypothetical problems using this rule in a number of my introductory legal writing classes. I have found that many, many students do not at first appreciate the significance of the word "convicted" in the rule. It is only by reading a number of cases in which the result turned on this word that the students come to appreciate its significance. This anecdotal evidence supports the idea that some general rules are susceptible to misinterpretation and that this misinterpretation can be eliminated upon seeing how the rule works in actual cases.

Church then sued the defendant for copyright infringement. *Id.* at 1239. In analyzing whether the defendant's copying of the Church's works was permissible under the fair use doctrine, the court considered, among other things, whether the copying by the defendant had a negative effect on the marketability of the original works. *Id.* at 1248-49. The court noted that the only relevant inquiry under this factor was whether the posting of the works on the internet usurped the demand for the original works—that is, whether the posting diminished the public's need to purchase these works from the Church. *Id.* at 1248. The court specifically held that if the defendant's criticism of the materials and the Church caused a reduction in the sale of the works, this was beyond the focus of this factor. The court stressed that this factor is only concerned with whether the *copying* affected the market, not whether the defendant's criticism affected the market. *Id.* at 1248 n. 19.

In the above example, the general rule is as follows: If the copying of copyrighted work by an alleged infringer has an adverse impact of the commercial market for the original work, this factor will strongly support a finding that the alleged infringer's use of the material is not fair use. This rule is relatively straightforward and appears to make sense on its face. However, based on a simple reading of the rule, a reader may not appreciate that it is not enough that the market of the original work was negatively affected by the infringer's use; it must also be shown that the negative impact was caused by the *copying.* A quick reading of the rule may suggest that any negative impact on the market of the original work is sufficient under this factor. It is only by reading the illustration from the *Religious Tech. Ctr.* case that the reader can appreciate the significance of the wording "If the *copying* . . . has an adverse impact . . . " Again, the illustration has the function of eliminating an erroneous interpretation of the general rule.

c.   Illustration for Affiliation

The third function that narrative illustrations can serve in rule-based analysis is to make a rule more meaningful to a reader by explaining it in familiar terms. Rules are often sterile abstractions of general legal concepts, personally meaningless to a reader. Because of the abstract nature of rules, a reader can often feel removed and detached from a rule. Illustrative narratives can help a reader to appreciate a rule more fully by putting the rule in a familiar context, thereby creating a closer connection between the reader and the general rule. Consider this example:

EXAMPLE 13-8

Another factor federal courts consider in determining whether the unauthorized use of copyrighted material is permissible under the "fair use" doctrine is whether the copyrighted work is primarily informational or creative. The courts generally "broaden the protection of those works that are creative, fictional, or highly original and lessen the protection for those works that are factual, informational, or functional." *Religious Tech. Ctr. v. Netcom On-Line Communication*

Servs., Inc., 923 F. Supp. 1231, 1246 (N.D. Cal. 1995); *accord e.g. Campbell v. Acuff-Rose Music, Inc.*, 510 U.S. 569, 586 (1994); *Harper & Row, Publishers, Inc. v. Nation Enters.*, 471 U.S. 539, 563 (1985). From a policy standpoint, federal courts have reasoned that there is less of a need to disseminate works of fiction than factual works. Consequently, less copying will be allowed for fictional works than for factual works. *See e.g. Harper & Row*, 471 U.S. at 563. In terms of this factor then, if the work copied by an alleged infringer is a creative, highly original work, this consideration will weigh against a finding of fair use. Conversely, if the original work is primarily informational, this factor will weigh in favor of fair use. *See e.g. id.*; *Campbell*, 510 U.S. at 586; *Consumers Union of United States, Inc. v, General Signal Corp.*, 724 F.2d 1044, 1049-50 (2d Cir. 1983) (finding that because the material in the magazine *Consumer Reports* is primarily informational rather than creative, this consideration supported a finding of fair use by an alleged infringer).

In the above example, the general rules by themselves are probably understandable to a reader. Thus, an illustration is not required to communicate the substance of the rules. However, the illustration regarding *Consumer Reports*, a magazine with which many people are familiar, puts the rule in a familiar context. Consequently the rule seems less abstract and gains personal significance for the reader. Consider these additional examples of illustration for affiliation:

EXAMPLE 13-9

To establish duress as a defense to a contract under Florida law, the party alleging duress must show that he or she acted "involuntarily" in entering into the contract. *See e.g. McLaughlin v. State Dep't of Natural Resources*, 526 So. 2d 934, 936 (Fla. 1st Dist. Ct. App. 1988); *City of Miami v. Kory*, 394 So. 2d 494, 497 (Fla. 3d Dist. Ct. App. 1981). One factor Florida courts consider in determining whether a person involuntarily entered into a contract is the fairness of the contract itself. If the resulting contract is grossly unfair to the person claiming duress, this will support a finding that the person acted involuntarily in signing the contract. *See Berger v. Berger*, 466 So. 2d 1149, 1151 (Fla. 4th Dist. Ct. App. 1985) (finding that because a property settlement agreement between divorcing spouses gave the wife nothing, this factor supported a finding that the wife signed the agreement involuntarily).

EXAMPLE 13-10

From *Johnson v. Automotive Ventures, Inc.*, 890 F. Supp. 507, 511 (W.D. Va. 1995) (some citations omitted):

In the spirit of protecting expression without stifling ideas, courts have refused to extend [copyright] protection to short phrases. *See Takeall*, 1993 WL 509876, at 509878 (holding that the slogan "You've got the right one, uh-huh" "fails to evince the requisite degree of originality to entitle it to copyright protection and is a short expression of the sort that courts have uniformly held uncopyrightable").

In the above examples, illustrative narratives are not essential to understand the general propositions. Yet the illustrations are helpful to readers because they put the rules into a familiar context. In Example 13-9, the general rule regarding the fairness of a contract allegedly made under duress is made more meaningful to a reader by the inclusion of the illustration from the *Berger* case. The fact scenario of the *Berger* case—a husband pressuring his wife to sign an unfair separation agreement—is more vivid and real for the reader than is the abstract, impersonal rule. Similarly, the reference to Diet Pepsi's famous slogan "You've got the right one, uh-huh" in Example 13-10 provides the reader with a concrete illustration of the types of short phrases deemed unworthy of copyright protection. These examples demonstrate how illustrative narratives can serve an affiliation function by which they make general rules more vivid and meaningful to a reader.

d.   Illustration for Accentuation

Illustrative narratives can also serve to emphasize the operative effect of a general rule. Consider the following examples:

EXAMPLE 13-11

Under Rule 9(B) of the Local Rules of Appellate Procedure, an appellant's brief may not exceed 30 pages. *See* Loc. R. 9(B); *see also State v. Untied,* No. 00-CA-32, 2001 WL 698024, at *8 (Ohio Ct. App. June 5, 2001) (refusing to address "appellant's Ninth, Tenth, Eleventh or Twelfth Assignments of Error as these assignments of error are contained in the portion of appellant's brief that exceeds the page limit under Loc.R. 9(B)").

EXAMPLE 13-12

The statute of limitations of 28 U.S.C. 2401(b) relevant to tort actions filed against the United States is strictly enforced. *See e.g. McDuffee v. United States,* 769 F.2d 492, 493-94 (8th Cir. 1985) (dismissing under 28 U.S.C. 2401(b) a complaint that was filed one day late and reversing the holding by the lower court that barring the suit offended "notions of fair play").

In Example 13-11, the general rule regarding the limit on the length of appellate briefs is emphasized with a dramatic illustration from the *Untied* case.

The court in that case completely disregarded the portions of the appellant's brief that exceeded the 30-page limit. Similarly, the illustration from the *McDuffee* case in Example 13-12 highlights in dramatic fashion the rigidity of the statute of limitations under 28 U.S.C. 2401(b). These examples demonstrate how narrative illustrations of general rules can serve to accentuate and emphasize the operative effect of a rule.

As we discussed previously, narratives communicate effectively because readers of narratives tend to project themselves into the stories as protagonists. As the reader learns of the circumstances that befall the person in the narrative, the reader empathizes with the person and imaginatively experiences the circumstances himself or herself. Thus, as we can see from reading Example 13-11 and Example 13-12, narratives can provide unparalleled emphasis. Imaginatively experiencing a dramatic or startling event indicative of the operation of a legal rule can indelibly imprint that legal concept in the mind of a reader.

Exercise 13-1   Understanding the Functions of Illustrative Narratives

- Illustration for Elucidation
- Illustration for Elimination
- Illustration for Affiliation
- Illustration for Accentuation

1. Above is a summary of the functions illustrative narratives can serve in rule-based analysis. Find an example of each type in a judicial opinion. Because a single illustrative narrative can serve more than one function simultaneously, your choice for each type should have that specific function as its *dominant function*. The examples you choose can be either in-text illustrations or parenthetical illustrations.
2. Write an essay analyzing your examples. For each example, your essay should (a) explain why the relevant discussion in the judicial opinion involves rule-based analysis; (b) explain why the example is an illustration of the category you believe it represents; and (c) to the extent that the example serves more than one function, explain its other functions. Attach copies of the relevant judicial opinions to your essay.

---

3.   How a Parenthetical Functions as a Narrative

While it is clear how an in-text explanation of a precedent case functions as a illustrative narrative, it is less clear how a one-sentence parenthetical qualifies as a "narrative." A narrative, after all, is a story; and one may wonder how one sentence can possibly constitute a story. The answer lies in the fact that while a parenthetical is only one sentence, it has the ability to conjure up a complete narrative by tapping into and building on stock stories already in the reader's mind.

According to cognitive psychologists, all people have mental storehouses of *stock structures* (also called *idealized cognitive models*) that help them make sense of and respond to the world in an efficient manner. Stock structures are generic, idealized models that are formed in the mind and that represent common social situations, social phenomena, people, places, and objects. Conjuring up and relying on these idealized mental structures allows us to encounter common social situations without having to reevaluate them from scratch. Professor Steven Winter offers this example of a stock structure:

> Suppose, for example, we enter a restaurant, seat ourselves, and are then confronted by a human with pad and pencil. Does this stranger want to hear our life stories? Challenge our right to enter the premises? Take our bet on the afternoon race? Any of these are possible and, on particular occasions, may in fact be the case. Yet, we "know" automatically that the person is asking for our order because we have unreflexively assumed a "restaurant scenario" which organizes our understanding of the events around us.[18]

Professor Gerald Lopez explains the role of stock structures in everyday meaning-making:[19]

> To understand . . . the world, [humans] depend heavily on "stock stories," "stock characters" and "stock theories"—knowledge of events, people, objects, and their characteristic relationships organized and represented by a variety of "stock structures." Some stock structures result from direct personal experiences; others are entirely vicarious. . . . Together these stock structures form an interpretive network: What goes on in [a given situation] is never approached sui generis, but rather is seen through these stock structures. Once the principal features of a given phenomenon suggest a particular stock structure, that structure shapes our expectations and responses. This use of stock structures resolves ambiguity and complements "given" information with much "assumed" information. [These stock structures] "help us carry out the routine activities of life without constantly having to analyze or question what we are doing."[20]

When a legal writer includes a parenthetical illustration of a rule, the writer activates several stock structures in the reader's mind. The reader reflexively uses these stock structures to make sense of the parenthetical and, in turn, to make sense of the rule that is being illustrated. Consider the following example of a discussion that employs parenthetical illustrations:

EXAMPLE 13-13

The third element under Colorado's burglary statute requires that the place entered by the defendant be a "dwelling." §18-4-502. A "dwelling" is defined under Colorado's penal code as "a building which is used . . . by a person for habitation." Colo. Rev. Stat. §18-1-901(3)(g) (Lexis 2006). **Colorado courts have held that places of temporary habitation qualify as "dwellings" for the purposes of the burglary statute.** *See e.g. People v. Germany*, 41 Colo. App. 304, 308,

---

18. Winter, *The Cognitive Dimension, supra* n. 3, at 2233.
19. Gerald P. Lopez, *Lay Lawyering*, 32 UCLA L. Rev. 1, 5-6 (1984).
20. *Id.* at 3.

586 P.2d 1006, 1009 (1978) (holding that a patient's hospital room was a dwelling under Colorado's burglary statute); *People v. Nichols*, 920 P.2d 901, 902 (Colo. App. 1996) (holding that a county prisoner's jail cell qualified as a dwelling under Colorado's burglary statute).

The rule set out in **bold** type in this example is potentially a bit vague to a reader because the reader may have difficulty understanding what is meant by the phrase "temporary habitation." Recognizing the ambiguity of the rule and in anticipation of the potential confusion it may cause, the writer has included two parenthetical examples of "temporary habitation," one referring to a case involving the burglary of a hospital room and one referring to a case involving the burglary of a jail cell.

Principles of cognitive psychology reveal how these parentheticals help a reader to understand the rule by conjuring up relevant illustrative narratives in the reader's mind. The first parenthetical, for example, activates several stock structures in the reader's mind that, when put together, create an illustrative narrative that explicates the rule:

1. *The stock structure for "patient's hospital room."* The reference to "patient's hospital room" in the first parenthetical activates in the reader's mind the stock structure for hospital room. The reader reflexively pictures the characteristics of a generic hospital room: its appearance, its furnishings, its atmosphere, its smell, etc. Moreover, the reference to "patient" forces the reader to picture the room as being occupied by some generic person who is receiving medical treatment of some sort. Most important, the reader also pictures the prototypical function of a hospital room—its use for temporary habitation by a patient (usually for just a few days) while he or she receives medical treatment. Indeed, with regard to the rule under discussion, this "temporary habitation" idea is the key stock feature of a hospital room that the reference is designed to conjure up in the reader's mind. Thus, whether these stock structures are based on the reader's personal experience or on vicarious information (such as by watching television shows or movies), the reference to "patient's hospital room" in this parenthetical evokes in the reader's mind the generic scene of a hospital room that is temporarily occupied by a patient.

2. *The stock structure for "burglary."* Similarly, the reference to "burglary" in the parenthetical conjures up in the reader's mind the prototypical concept of someone sneaking into another person's geographical area and stealing something or committing some other crime in that area. Unless the reader has been a victim of burglary him- or herself, this stock structure likely comes from a variety of vicarious sources, such as from reading or viewing crime novels, movies, and television shows; from seeing news accounts; from the discussion of burglary in this document leading up to this point; or from reading other burglary cases (the intended reader is a lawyer, after all). Combining these first two stock structures, the reader pictures in his or her mind a general, "idealized" story of some person burglarizing some patient's temporary hospital room.

3. *The stock structure for an appellate case.* As mentioned earlier, the target audience of the above example of legal writing is the law-trained reader. Lawyers, by their training and practice, have certain stock structures in their minds that are unique to (or at least prevalent among) members of that group. One such stock structure is that for an appellate case. In the above example, the hospital room

parenthetical is incorporated into a citation to a judicial case, namely the *Germany* case decided by the Colorado Court of Appeals. Through this reference, the law-trained reader knows that the parenthetical is a summary of the appellate court's holding in a specific case. The reference also activates in the reader's mind the stock story of how a case reaches an appellate court and leads to a decision by that court. Working off of the other stock structures, the reader pictures a person burglarizing the hospital room of a temporary patient and subsequently being arrested for burglary. The reader also pictures the defendant being convicted of burglary in a trial court. Next, the reader pictures the defendant appealing the conviction to an appellate court and raising the issue, perhaps among others, of whether the temporarily occupied hospital room qualifies as a "dwelling" of the victimized patient. This issue addressed on appeal by the *Germany* court becomes clear to the reader as the stock structure of a temporarily occupied hospital room is juxtaposed against the word "habitation" in the definition of dwelling. Because the word habitation itself evokes the stock structure of a permanent home or residence, and because this stock structure conflicts with the stock structure of a hospital room, the reader immediately appreciates the issue addressed on appeal: whether the temporary use of a hospital room is habitation.

4. *The stock structure for parentheticals in legal writing.* The final stock structure activated in this example is the stock structure for the functions of parentheticals in legal writing. As a person who is trained in legal reading and legal writing, the reader of the passage has in his or her mind a stock structure for the concept of a parenthetical itself. The law-trained reader knows what parentheticals in case citations are and the relationship between the parenthetical and rest of the discussion. Specifically, the reader knows, based on traditional legal writing form, that the parenthetical is designed to supplement the stated rule and to serve as an illustration of how the cited case applied the rule to the facts of a specific case.

Thus, with a short parenthetical and by tapping into preexisting stock structures, the writer conjures up in the reader's mind an elaborate narrative of an intruder burglarizing a patient's hospital room, being prosecuted for and convicted of burglary, and finally appealing the issue of whether a hospital room qualifies as a dwelling for the purposes of Colorado's burglary statute. To this activated "stock" information, the writer adds the "new information" that the court in this case did in fact hold that the hospital room qualifies as a dwelling under the burglary statute (despite its nature as a place where one resides only temporarily). Thus, the court's holding is explained quickly and efficiently by tapping into stock information and combining it with essential new information. With just a single sentence, the writer has communicated to the reader the whole story represented by the cited case. The reader also knows based on the stock function of parentheticals in legal writing that the activated narrative is an illustration of the rule stated immediately prior to the case citation. Consequently, the story helps the reader understand the general rule expressed by the writer—that Colorado courts have held that places of temporary habitation qualify as "dwellings" for the purposes of the burglary statute. The same cognitive process is activated with the second parenthetical regarding the burglary of a jail cell.

This is the essence of a parenthetical illustration. It conjures up a complete story in the reader's mind by activating relevant stock structures and combining that information with new information about the court's holding within that fact scenario. This story is then available to the reader as an illustration of the abstract rule to help the reader understand the rule.

4.   *Choosing Between In-Text Illustrations and Parenthetical Illustrations*

As we saw above in Section I.C., illustrative narratives can be placed either in the text of a discussion or in a parenthetical within the cites to relevant authority. How as a legal writer do you decide where to put your narrative illustrations? Answering this question involves several considerations.

First, as a threshold question, the writer must ask himself or herself whether an illustration of the relevant rule should be included at all. Sometimes a rule is so vague as a general proposition that it cannot be understood by the reader without an illustration. In these situations, an illustrative narrative of the rule is imperative. However, even where the rule is understandable by itself, without an illustration, the writer should consider whether an illustration would nevertheless benefit the reader in any of the ways discussed in Section 13.E.2 above. Some rules are plain and simple enough not to require an illustration. However, considering the cognitive problems with rules and the cognitive advantages of narrative illustrations, a writer would be better off in most cases erring on the side that affords better communication: the inclusion of an illustration of the rule.

The second consideration is the importance of the rule to the issue under discussion. If the rule is dispositive of or otherwise plays a major role in resolving the entire issue being addressed, then the writer should most definitely include an illustration of the rule from a precedent case and should place that illustration in the text of the discussion. If a single rule from a precedent case answers the entire issue, the reader generally expects (and is entitled to) a full explanation of that rule, and this includes a textual explanation of how the rule was applied in a precedent case.

If a writer has decided to include an illustration of a rule and the rule is not dispositive of the whole issue (but merely relevant to one aspect of the issue, like a single element or factor), the writer must next consider whether the illustration can be explained effectively in a single sentence. If so, the writer can include the illustration as a parenthetical. If not, the illustration should be placed in the text of the discussion. As we have seen in the earlier examples, and as we will see more specifically below in connection with the discussion of guidelines in drafting parenthetical illustrations, parentheticals are limited to one sentence. Thus, if an illustration cannot be explained in a single, relatively short and understandable sentence, then it must be explained in the text.

Finally, a writer must consider the overall length of the document. All courts have rules limiting the page length of submitted briefs. Furthermore, the prevailing standard for modern legal writing requires that writers be concise and to the point. Lengthy illustrative narratives can be inconsistent with both of these requirements. Consequently, a brief writer often faces a dilemma. On the one hand, a premium is placed on brevity; on the other, communication principles derived from cognitive psychology suggest that merely stating rules may not be enough. A legal writer must balance these competing considerations when drafting a brief. In many cases, the compromise will be to use parenthetical illustrations, which can provide the reader with an illustrative narrative without adding significant length.

The following exercises—Exercise 13-1, Exercise 13-2, and Exercise 13-3—are designed to give you practice in evaluating whether an illustrative narrative should be included in the discussion of a point governed by a rule in a case and, if so, whether the illustration should be explained in the text or in a parenthetical. These exercises are designed to be completed together. The full effect of the assignment is only achieved by completing (a), (b), and (c).

Exercise 13-1   Choosing Among Rule-Based Analysis Techniques

Write a short essay analyzing which of the following versions of this point is most effective in terms of the concepts discussed in Section 13.E.4 of this chapter.

Version 1: Rule Only

Another factor Florida courts consider in determining whether a worker is an "employee" or an "independent contractor" is who supplies the worker's tools. If the worker supplies his or her own tools, this factor will support a finding that the worker is an independent contractor, as opposed to an employee. *See e.g. Kane Furniture Corp. v. Miranda*, 506 So. 2d 1061, 1065 (Fla. 2d Dist. Ct. App. 1987); *T & T Communications, Inc. v. Department of Labor and Employment Sec.*, 460 So. 2d 996, 998 (Fla. 2d Dist. Ct. App. 1984). In the instant case, Ms. Green provided her own musical instrument when playing with the Miami Symphony Orchestra. This fact supports a finding that Ms. Green is an independent contractor, rather than an employee, of the orchestra.

Version 2: Rule with Parenthetical Illustration

Another factor Florida courts consider in determining whether a worker is an "employee" or an "independent contractor" is who supplies the worker's tools. If the worker supplies his or her own tools, this factor will support a finding that the worker is an independent contractor, as opposed to an employee. *See e.g. Kane Furniture Corp. v. Miranda*, 506 So. 2d 1061, 1065 (Fla. 2d Dist. Ct. App. 1987) (finding that because a carpet installer supplied his own installation equipment in performing his work, this factor supported a finding that he was an independent contractor); *T & T Communications, Inc. v. Department of Labor and Employment Sec.*, 460 So. 2d 996, 998 (Fla. 2d Dist. Ct. App. 1984). In the instant case, Ms. Green provided her own musical instrument when playing with the Miami Symphony Orchestra. This fact supports a finding that Ms. Green is an independent contractor, rather than an employee, of the orchestra.

Version 3: Rule with In-Text Illustration

Another factor Florida courts consider in determining whether a worker is an "employee" or an "independent contractor" is who supplies the worker's tools. If the worker supplies his or her own tools, this factor will support a finding that the worker is an independent contractor, as opposed to an employee. *See e.g. Kane Furniture Corp. v. Miranda*, 506 So. 2d 1061, 1065 (Fla. 2d Dist. Ct. App. 1987); *T & T Communications, Inc. v. Department of Labor and Employment Sec.*, 460 So. 2d 996, 998 (Fla. 2d Dist. Ct. App. 1984).

In *Kane*, the plaintiff brought a wrongful death action against Kane Furniture Corporation after the plaintiff's wife was killed in a collision with a vehicle owned and operated by a carpet installer that worked for Kane Furniture. 506 So. 2d at 1063. Because an employer can be held responsible only for the torts of an employee, and not for the torts of an independent contractor, the court had to determine whether the installer was an employee of Kane or an independent contractor. *Id.* at 1063-67. In analyzing this issue, the court considered, among other factors, whether the employer or the worker supplied the worker's tools. *Id.* at 1065. The court reasoned that because the worker supplied his own installation equipment, this factor supported a finding that the worker was an independent contractor. *Id.*

In the instant case, Ms. Green provided her own musical instrument when playing with the Miami Symphony Orchestra. This fact supports a finding that Ms. Green is an independent contractor, rather than an employee, of the orchestra.

Exercise 13-2   Choosing Among Rule-Based Analysis Techniques

Write a short essay analyzing which of the following versions of this point is most effective in terms of the concepts discussed in Section 13.E.4 of this chapter.

Version 1: Rule Only

Estoppel will not be applied against a state agency for misrepresentations of "law," as opposed to misrepresentations of "fact." *See e.g. Dolphin Outdoor Advertising v. Department of Transp.*, 582 So. 2d 709, 710 (Fla. 1st Dist. Ct. App. 1991); *Austin v. Austin*, 350 So. 2d 102, 105 (Fla. 1st Dist. Ct. App. 1977); *Brown v. Richardson*, 395 F. Supp. 185, 190 (W.D. Pa. 1975).

In the instant case, a representative of the Florida Department of General Services addressed a group of applicants for certification as state contractors and misrepresented the statutory requirements for certification. Because this misrepresentation was a misrepresentation of law, as opposed to a misrepresentation of fact, the Department of General Services cannot be bound by estoppel to these erroneous statements.

Version 2: Rule with Parenthetical Illustration

Estoppel will not be applied against a state agency for misrepresentations of "law," as opposed to misrepresentations of "fact." *See e.g. Dolphin Outdoor Advertising v. Department of Transp.*, 582 So. 2d 709, 710 (Fla. 1st Dist. Ct. App. 1991); *Austin v. Austin*, 350 So. 2d 102, 105 (Fla. 1st Dist. Ct. App. 1977) (holding that the Florida Division of Retirement was not bound by estoppel to an erroneous statement of law made in a pamphlet distributed by the Division that explained the features of the new Florida retirement statute); *Brown v. Richardson*, 395 F. Supp. 185, 190 (W.D. Pa. 1975).

In the instant case, a representative of the Florida Department of General Services addressed a group of applicants for certification as state contractors and misrepresented the statutory requirements for certification. Because this misrepresentation was a misrepresentation of law, as opposed to a misrepresentation of fact, the Department of General Services cannot be bound by estoppel to these erroneous statements.

Version 3: Rule with In-Text Illustration

Estoppel will not be applied against a state agency for misrepresentations of "law," as opposed to misrepresentations of "fact." *See e.g. Dolphin Outdoor Advertising v. Department of Transp.*, 582 So. 2d 709, 710 (Fla. 1st Dist. Ct. App. 1991); *Austin v. Austin*, 350 So. 2d 102, 105 (Fla. 1st Dist. Ct. App. 1977); *Brown v. Richardson*, 395 F. Supp. 185, 190 (W.D. Pa. 1975). In *Austin*, for example, the wife of a deceased state employee challenged the distribution of the decedent's retirement benefits by the Florida Department of Administration. 350 So. 2d at 103-04. The department decided that the benefits should be distributed to the beneficiaries designated by the decedent before his death. *Id.* In support of her claim of entitlement to the benefits, the plaintiff pointed out that a pamphlet published by the Department of Administration explaining the features of the new Florida retirement statute specifically stated that a surviving spouse would receive benefits even if the surviving spouse was not a designated beneficiary. *Id.* at 105. Although this statement in the pamphlet was erroneous, the plaintiff claimed that the Department was bound by the statement and was estopped from denying her benefits. *Id.*

In analyzing this claim, the court held that the statement in the pamphlet was not a misrepresentation of "fact" as required for estoppel; it was a misstatement of the law. *Id.* The court further held that the state cannot be estopped through mistaken statements of "law" as opposed to misstatements of "fact." *Id.* Thus, the court concluded that the plaintiff's estoppel claim was invalid. *Id.*

In the instant case, a representative of the Florida Department of General Services addressed a group of applicants for certification as state contractors and misrepresented the statutory requirements for certification. Because this misrepresentation was a misrepresentation of law, as opposed to a misrepresentation of fact, the Department of General Services cannot be bound by estoppel to these erroneous statements.

Exercise 13-3   Choosing Among Rule-Based Analysis Techniques

Write a short essay analyzing which of the following versions of this point is most effective in terms of the concepts discussed in Section 13.E.4 of this chapter.

Version 1: Rule Only

The second element of the absolute immunity afforded to defamatory statements made during the course of a judicial proceeding requires that the statements have some relevance to the proceeding. *See e.g. Wright v. Yurko*, 446 So. 2d 1162, 1164 (Fla. 5th Dist. Ct. App. 1984); *Sussman v. Damian*, 355 So. 2d 809, 811 (Fla. 3d Dist. Ct. App. 1977).

In the instant case, Mr. Black's defamation suit stems from statements made by Mr. Carreson during a settlement conference regarding Mr. Carreson's negligence suit against Mr. Black. Mr. Carreson's suit alleges that Mr. Black negligently caused an automobile accident between the parties. At the settlement conference between the parties and their respective attorneys, Mr. Carreson accused Mr. Black of being intoxicated at the time of the accident. As this statement is related to the negligence suit, the second element of the absolute immunity is established.

Version 2: Rule with Parenthetical Illustration

The second element of the absolute immunity afforded to defamatory statements made during the course of a judicial proceeding requires that the statements have some relevance to the proceeding. *See e.g. Wright v. Yurko*, 446 So. 2d 1162, 1164 (Fla. 5th Dist. Ct. App. 1984); *Sussman v. Damian*, 355 So. 2d 809, 811-12 (Fla. 3d Dist. Ct. App. 1977) (finding that a statement by an attorney (Sussman) to another attorney (Damian) during a deposition that Damian was a "damned liar" was relevant to a legal proceeding as required for immunity because the statement was made during the deposition and concerned whether Damian's client had produced documents subject to discovery in the case, whereas, Damian's statements to Sussman after the deposition accusing Sussman of mishandling client funds were not privileged because they were in no way relevant to the pending lawsuit).

In the instant case, Mr. Black's defamation suit stems from statements made by Mr. Carreson during a settlement conference regarding Mr. Carreson's negligence suit against Mr. Black. Mr. Carreson's suit alleges that Mr. Black negligently caused an automobile accident between the parties. At the settlement conference between the parties and their respective attorneys, Mr. Carreson accused Mr. Black of being intoxicated at the time of the accident. As this statement is related to the negligence suit, the second element of the absolute immunity is established.

Version 3: Rule with In-Text Illustration

The second element of the absolute immunity afforded to defamatory statements made during the course of a judicial proceeding requires that the statements have some relevance to the proceeding. *See e.g. Wright v. Yurko*, 446 So. 2d 1162, 1164 (Fla. 5th Dist. Ct. App. 1984); *Sussman v. Damian*, 355 So. 2d 809, 811 (Fla. 3d Dist. Ct. App. 1977). In *Sussman*, two attorneys, Robert Sussman and Vincent Damian, sued each other for defamation for statements made by the attorneys while representing adverse parties in a civil suit. In a deposition on the civil suit, the attorneys began to argue over whether Mr. Sussman's client had produced certain relevant documents. After Mr. Damian insisted that the documents had not been produced, Mr. Sussman called Mr. Damian a "damned liar." The deposition then terminated. *Sussman*, 355 So. 2d at 810.

Sometime later, after attending a hearing related to the suit, the attorneys got into another argument in the hallway and elevator of the courthouse. At that point, Mr. Damian attacked Mr. Sussman's professional integrity and accused him of improperly handling client monies and trust funds in matters unrelated to the pending lawsuit. Subsequent to this, Mr. Sussman filed his defamation action against Mr. Damian. Mr. Damian then filed a counterclaim for defamation based on the statement made at the deposition. *Id.* at 810-11.

In analyzing the respective defamation claims by the attorneys and whether the statements were protected by the absolute immunity for statements made during a judicial proceeding, the appellate court addressed whether the statements were "relevant to the judicial proceeding" as required by the immunity doctrine. *Id.* at 811-12.

Regarding Mr. Sussman's statement made during the deposition, the court concluded that it was relevant to the lawsuit because it concerned whether Mr. Sussman's client had produced documents subject to discovery in the case. *Id.* at 811. The court concluded that although Mr. Sussman's statement was "intemperate and unprofessional," it was nevertheless absolutely privileged in a defamation action. *Id.* Regarding Mr. Damian's statements made in the hallway and elevator of the courthouse, the court reasoned that the statement was in no way relevant to the pending lawsuit. Accordingly, it was not absolutely privileged. *Id.* at 812.

In the instant case, Mr. Black's defamation suit stems from statements made by Mr. Carreson during a settlement conference regarding Mr. Carreson's negligence suit against Mr. Black. Mr. Carreson's suit alleges that Mr. Black negligently caused an automobile accident between the parties. At the settlement conference between the parties and their respective attorneys, Mr. Carreson accused Mr. Black of being intoxicated at the time of the accident. As this statement is related to the negligence suit, the second element of the absolute immunity is established.

---

5.   Guidelines for Drafting Parenthetical Illustrative Narratives

Drafting an in-text illustration is relatively straightforward, but drafting an effective parenthetical illustration involves meeting a number of technical requirements. In this section, we will review guidelines for drafting effective parenthetical illustrations of legal rules.

a.   Specific Guidelines for Drafting Parenthetical Illustrations

i.   *The Location of Parenthetical Illustrations*

A parenthetical illustration should be inserted into the citation of the case to which it applies. In the citation, the parenthetical statement should follow the parenthetical that contains the date of the opinion (with a space but no punctuation between the parentheticals).[21] In a basic case citation, for example, the parenthetical statement should be located as follows:

Case Name, Vol. Rptr. Page (Ct. Date) (Parenthetical Illustration).

If the case citation includes subsequent history, the parenthetical statement should precede the reference to the subsequent history.[22]

Case Name, Vol. Rptr. Page (Ct. Date) (Parenthetical Illustration), Subsequent History.

---

21. *See* The Bluebook: *A Uniform System of Citation* Rule 1.5 (18th ed. 2006); *see also* Darby Dickerson, Association of Legal Writing Directors, *ALWD Citation Manual: A Professional System of Citation* Rule 46.2 (3d ed. 2006) [hereinafter "*ALWD*"].

22. *See The Bluebook, supra* n. 13, at Rule 10.6 & 10.7; *ALWD, supra* n. 13, at Rule 46.2.

In short citation form, the parenthetical comes at the end of the cite.

> *Short Case Name*, Vol. Rptr. at Page (Parenthetical Illustration).

> *Id.* at Page (Parenthetical Illustration).

In a citation sentence that includes more than one case, the parenthetical should be included in the citation of the case to which it applies. Thus:

> *Case #1 Name*, Vol. Rptr. Page (Ct. Date) (Parenthetical Illustration for Case #1); *Case #2 Name*, Vol. Rptr. Page (Ct. Date).

ii.   *Start with a Present Participle*

A parenthetical illustration ordinarily begins with a *present participle*—a verb ending in "ing"—that modifies the cited case by explaining some action by the court in the case.[23] Common present participles used to begin parenthetical illustrations are *finding, holding, reasoning, ruling, stating, concluding*, and the like.

Two exceptions exist to this rule. First, parenthetical illustrations need not begin with present participles when they enumerate a series of related illustrations set up by the text sentence. The *Bluebook* offers this example.

EXAMPLE 13-14

Such standards have been adopted to address a variety of environmental problems. *See, e.g.*, H.B. Jacobini, *The New International Sanitary Regulations*, 46 Am. J. Int'l L. 727, 727-28 (1952) (health-related water quality); Robert L. Meyer, *Travaux Preparatoires for the Unesco World Heritage Convention*, 2 Earth L.J. 45, 45-81 (1976) (conservation of protected areas).[24]

In this example, a text sentence sets up the list of illustrations that are included in parentheticals with the cites. When listing a series of illustrations like this, writers need not begin each parenthetical illustration with a present participle.

The second exception occurs when the parenthetical illustration consists of a full-sentence quote from the applicable case.[25] Consider the following example:

EXAMPLE 13-15

Another factor federal courts consider in deciding whether to grant a motion for change of venue is the convenience of the alternative forums to the parties. Federal courts have held, however, that this factor supports rejecting the motion for transfer if the effect of the transfer is simply to shift the

---

23. *See The Bluebook, supra* n. 13, at Rule 1.5; *ALWD, supra* n. 13, at Rule 46.3.
24. *See The Bluebook, supra* n. 13, at Rule 1.5.
25. *See id.* at Rule 1.5; *see also ALWD, supra* n. 13, at Rule 46.3.

inconvenience from the defendant to the plaintiff. *See e.g. Graff v. Qwest Communications Corp.*, 33 F. Supp. 2d 1117, 1121 (D. Minn. 1999); *K-TEL Int'l, Inc. v. Tristar Products, Inc.*, No. CIV 00-902, 2001 WL 392405, at *8 (D. Minn. March 28, 2001) ("Based on the fact that a transfer to New Jersey would only serve to shift the inconvenience between the parties, this court concludes that this factor weighs in favor of maintaining this action in Minnesota.").

In this example, the parenthetical illustration was generated from a quote from the case itself. In such instances, it is not necessary to begin the illustration with a present participle. Be forewarned, however; only rarely is a court so kind as to provide a ready-made sentence that can be used as a parenthetical illustration. In the large majority of cases, writers must construct the illustration themselves. It follows then that in the large majority of the cases writers must begin any parenthetical illustration with a present participle.

iii.   *Provide a Factually Specific Illustration*

Because the parenthetical should provide the reader with a narrative illustration of how the stated rule was applied in a specific factual context, it should refer to specific facts of the cited case. However, because the reader will not necessarily have read the cited case, factual references should be stated in somewhat general terms. This means, for example, using indefinite articles "a" and "an" instead of the definite article "the" when referring initially to specific facts of the cited case, referring to the parties of the case by descriptive titles rather than by proper names, and so on. These two considerations appear to be contradictory: be specific, but be general at the same time. With practice, however, it will make more sense. The parenthetical illustration should be specific enough to evoke relevant stock structures in the reader's mind as discussed in Section 13.E.3 of this chapter. It should not be so general that it merely restates the general rule. By the same token, however, the illustration should not include references to facts that require reading the case to be understood. The examples in this chapter will help you develop a feel for how parenthetical illustrations can be drafted to satisfy these two considerations.

iv.   *Explain the Illustration in the Context of the Rule Being Discussed*

The substance of the parenthetical illustration should be given a specific context. That is, the illustration should explain what the court decided in the *context* of the general legal proposition being discussed. The example below under "Common Mistakes" will help to clarify this point.

v.   *Begin the Parenthetical Statement with a Lowercase Letter*

Because the parenthetical statement is part of the overall citation sentence, it should begin with a lowercase letter, not a capital letter.[26] An exception to this

---

26. *See The Bluebook, supra* n. 13, at Rule 1.5; *see also ALWD, supra* n. 13, at Rule 46.3.4

rule occurs when the parenthetical illustration consists of a full-sentence quote from the applicable case.[27] Look again at Example 13-15 above, in which the quotation in the parenthetical illustration begins with a capital letter.

vi.   *Limit the Parenthetical Illustration to One Sentence*

A parenthetical illustration should not include more than one sentence. (In fact, because it begins with a present participle, the parenthetical illustration is actually a sentence fragment.) If it is not possible to effectively explain an illustration using a single understandable sentence, the illustration should be placed in the text of the discussion rather than in a parenthetical.

vii.   *Do Not Include Ending Punctuation*

The parenthetical statement should not end with any punctuation mark inside the closing parenthesis.[28] Again, parenthetical illustrations consisting of full-sentence quotations are an exception to this rule. Example 13-15 demonstrates the use of ending punctuation in a parenthetical quotation.

viii.   *The Number of Illustrations*

It is not necessary to give parenthetical statements for each case cited for the general proposition. If you feel that the reader would benefit from more than one illustration, however, it is permissible to include parentheticals for more than one of the cited cases.

b.   **Common Mistakes in Drafting Parenthetical Illustrations**

i.   *Common Mistake #1: Putting the Rule in a Parenthetical*

One common mistake made by legal writers in using parenthetical illustrations is putting the statement of the applicable rule in the parenthetical rather than in the text of the discussion. This happens most frequently when the writer provides a transition to the point, but fails to state the actual rule in the text. Let's look at a revised version of Example 13-2 as an illustration:

Not Effective: Another factor this Court considers in determining whether the prolonged pretrial detention of a criminal defendant violates his due process rights is the complexity of the case. *See e.g. United States v. Gonzales Claudio*, 806 F.2d 334, 341 (2d Cir. 1986) (holding that if the delay in bringing a defendant to trial is attributable to the complexity of the case, as opposed to the misconduct or inaction of the prosecution, this factor will support a finding that the extended pretrial detention of the defendant is not a

27. *See The Bluebook, supra* n. 13, at Rule 1.5; *see also ALWD, supra* n. 13, at Rule 46.3.4
28. *See The Bluebook, supra* n. 13, at Rule 1.5; *ALWD, supra* n. 13, at Rule 46.3.

> violation of due process); *United States v. El-Hage*, 213 F.3d
> 74, 80 (2d Cir. 2000).

Because the first sentence merely serves as a transition, this discussion is not effective. The actual rule is never stated in the text of the discussion; it has been relegated to a parenthetical. As discussed previously, the rule should be stated in the text; the parenthetical should supplement the rule by illustrating how the rule was applied in a specific factual context. Compare the foregoing example to Example 13-2.

ii.   Common Mistake #2: Restating the Rule in a Parenthetical

Another common mistake is merely restating the general rule in the parenthetical. Consider the following example:

Not Effective: Another factor this Court considers in determining whether the prolonged pretrial detention of a criminal defendant violates his due process rights is the complexity of the case. This Court has held that if the delay in bringing a defendant to trial is attributable to the complexity of the case, as opposed to the misconduct or inaction of the prosecution, this factor will support a finding that the extended pretrial detention of the defendant is not a violation of due process. *See e.g. United States v. Gonzales Claudio*, 806 F.2d 334, 341 (2d Cir. 1986) (holding that if the delay in bringing a defendant to trial is attributable to the complexity of the case, this factor will support a finding that the extended pretrial detention of the defendant is not a violation of due process,); *United States v. El-Hage*, 213 F.3d 74, 80 (2d Cir. 2000).

This example is not effective because the parenthetical merely restates the rule already stated in the text; it adds nothing new. This parenthetical comment should be either deleted or redrafted to supplement the rule by illustrating how it was applied to the facts of the cited case. Again, compare this to Example 13-2.

iii.   Common Mistake #3: Stating the Parenthetical Illustration in Overly Broad Terms

The third common mistake is stating the parenthetical in terms so general that it constitutes merely a restatement of the general rule already stated in the text. Consider this example:

Not Effective: Another factor this Court considers in determining whether the prolonged pretrial detention of a criminal defendant violates his due process rights is the complexity of the case. This Court has held that if the delay in bringing a defendant to trial is attributable to the complexity of the case, as opposed to the misconduct or inaction of the prosecution, this factor will support a finding that the extended pretrial detention of the defendant is not a violation of due process. *See e.g. United States v. Gonzales Claudio,* 806 F.2d 334, 341 (2d Cir. 1986) (finding that because the case was of a complex nature, this factor supported a finding that the prolonged pretrial detention of the defendant did not violate his due process rights); *United States v. El-Hage,* 213 F.3d 74, 80 (2d Cir. 2000).

This example is ineffective because the parenthetical is so general that it adds little to the rule itself. Such broad statements do not constitute narrative illustrations and serve little function.

iv.   *Common Mistake #4: Stating the Parenthetical Illustration in Overly Specific Terms*

A fourth common mistake is stating the parenthetical in terms so factually specific that it is difficult to understand without reading the referenced case. Most often this mistake involves a writer referring to the parties of the precedent case by their proper names rather than using descriptive titles. When writing a parenthetical, keep in mind that it must make sense to someone who has not read the referenced case.

v.   *Common Mistake #5: Failing to Place the Parenthetical Illustration in Context*

The fifth common mistake writers make when composing parenthetical illustrations is to fail to indicate the relevant context in the parenthetical. This occurs when a writer summarizes what the court decided too narrowly, without making it clear how this finding fit into the court's analysis of the general rule being discussed. Consider the following example:

Not Effective: Another factor this Court considers in determining whether the prolonged pretrial detention of a criminal defendant violates his due process rights is the complexity of the case. This Court has held that if the delay in bringing a defendant to trial is attributable to the complexity of the case, as opposed to the misconduct or inaction of the prosecution, this factor will support a finding that the extended pretrial detention of the defendant is not a violation of due process. *See e.g. United States v. Gonzales Claudio,* 806 F.2d 334, 341 (2d Cir. 1986) (finding that the case was of a complex nature because it involved 20 defendants, events that occurred in numerous locations, and hundreds of audio cassettes, video cassettes, and documents that had to be translated from Spanish to English); *United States v. ElHage,* 213 F.3d 74, 80 (2d Cir. 2000).

This parenthetical regarding the *Gonzales Claudio* case is ineffective because, while it tells the reader that the court found the case to be of a complex nature, it does not explain how this finding affected the court's decision on the due process issue. This finding of the court has not been put into the context of the general legal proposition being discussed. The reader has no idea whether the *Gonzales Claudio* case is even a "due process" case, or whether it has been taken completely out of context. The parenthetical illustration should not only tell the reader that the court found the case to be complex; it should also explain that this fact weighed in favor of a finding that the defendant's due process rights had not been violated. Compare the above example to Example 13-2.

F.   USING QUOTATIONS EFFECTIVELY IN CASE DESCRIPTIONS

Quotations can be used very effectively to provide proof and support for the brief-writer's assertions. When using quotations from cases, however, it's good to keep a couple of points in mind. First of all, you should usually paraphrase rather than quote language from cases. Quotation marks draw the reader's attention, and you want to save that special attention for important statements. Generally, use direct quotations only when you are stating rules or other language at issue, or when you are justifying a conclusion you have drawn about the meaning of an authority. Of course, whether you are quoting or paraphrasing, be sure to provide appropriate citations.[29]

Writers' problems with quotations from cases tend to fall into the two categories of "not enough" and "too much." Some writers drop quotations into their arguments without giving the reader enough information about the case. Without sufficient context, the quotation is meaningless. Other writers give the reader too much quoted language, leaving the reader to complete the writer's job of sifting through the language and sorting out its meaning. Police your writing to avoid these problems.

1.   *Not Enough Context*

Legend has it that Marie Antoinette once said, "Let them eat cake!" If you don't know the context of that remark, she sounds like a pretty nice person. She sounds a lot less friendly, however, once you learn that she supposedly said it while looking down at the peasants in the street who were crying for bread.

Keep Marie in mind when you are tempted to drop a pithy quote from an obscure case into the middle of your rule explanation section. If the judge doesn't know what that court was looking at—i.e., the issue, the rule, and the facts—when it made that statement, he or she can't begin to understand the significance of the quote without looking the case up. And since most judges don't have time to read the cases cited in the briefs, the quote may have a

29. See Section 6.5.1 [Mary Beth Beazley, A Practical Guide to Appellate Advocacy, 3rd ed., (2010)] for information on when to provide citations.

negative impact: The judge will be annoyed at being given insufficient or misleading information.

Thus, when using a quotation from a case, be sure you have provided the reader with the type of context mentioned in Section 6.1 [Mary Beth Beazley, A Practical Guide to Appellate Advocacy, 3rd ed., (2010)]. Do not drop a quotation into your argument like a chocolate chip into batter:

Bad Example

This Court has noted that generalizations "concerning parent-child relations . . . become less acceptable as the age of the child increase[s]." <u>Caban v. Mohammed</u>, 441 U.S. 380, 382 (1979). Thus, the gender-based generalizations in this case are invalid.

An altered quotation with an unaccompanied citation does not fill the court with confidence about the validity of your argument. Instead, include the details that will give context for the quotation:

Good Example

As far back as 1979, this Court struck down a statute that characterized parent-child relationships between unwed fathers and their children differently from those of unwed mothers. <u>Caban v. Mohammed</u>, 441 U.S. 380, 382 (1979). While conceding that unwed mothers might be closer to their children at birth, the Court stated that the generalization would become "less acceptable as a basis for legislative distinctions" as the age of the child increased. <u>Id</u>.

Quotations can also be used effectively in a parenthetical:

> As far back as 1979, this Court struck down a statute that characterized parent-child relationships between unwed fathers and their children differently from those of unwed mothers. <u>Caban v. Mohammed</u>, 441 U.S. 380, 382 (1979) (noting that any generalizations would become "less acceptable as a basis for legislative distinctions" as the child grew older).

By making a quotation part of a coherent case description, you make it more likely that the quotation will do the job of convincing the court that the case stands for the proposition you say it does.

2. *Too Much Quoted Language*

Some writers are so enamored with the court's language that they are loathe to paraphrase. Instead, they simply provide page after page of excerpted quotes and let the reader determine the significance of the quoted language.

"Overquoting" creates two problems. First, the writer is not doing his or her job. The writer is not supposed to provide the raw material to the readers and let them sort out what it all means. The writer's job is to research the law, synthesize the available information, and write up the analysis in a way that allows the reader to understand the situation with a minimum of effort.

The second problem is related to the first. A reader—a judge in this context—who is constantly asked to consume and digest lengthy quotations may lose the thread of the argument. As a practical matter, many readers (including some of the people reading this book) skip long quotations. Judges who are reading briefs may do so because they know that the quotation says nothing about the case currently before the court; instead, it talks about another case, which must some how be connected to the current case. Writers who overuse long quotes frequently do so because they have not figured out that connection and thus cannot make the connection within the argument. They compensate by giving the reader background reading that may, with luck and some work, allow the reader to reach the conclusion that the writer espouses. Since the writer, rather than the reader, is supposed to do the work, it is usually ineffective to use lengthy quotations.

The following example is from a student-written brief written in the case of *Chicago v. Morales*, 527 U.S. 41 (1999). In that case, the city of Chicago argued in favor of the constitutionality of a statute that allowed the arrest of people who "loitered" with gang members and who refused to disperse on police order. The writer of the following example apparently wanted the reader to use the quoted language to draw the conclusion that laws that promote "peace and quiet" are constitutional:

Bad Example

This Court has provided almost absolute protection to speech of a political nature. In 1969, the Court found the arrest of demonstrators for disorderly conduct to be unconstitutional under the First Amendment. Gregory v. Chicago, 394 U.S. 111, 116 (1969). The Court made this finding in favor of political speech even though the picketers' actions led to a disruption of the peace and quiet of a neighborhood by picketing in front of the mayor's home.Id. at 111. A concurring opinion stressed the lawfulness and peacefulness of the demonstration as well as the petitioners' First Amendment right to engage in that activity.Id. at 121 (Black, J., concurring). However, Justice Black also declared:

> Plainly, however, no mandate in our Constitution leaves States and governmental units powerless to pass laws to protect the public from the kind of boisterous and threatening conduct that disturbs the tranquility of spots selected by the people either for homes, wherein they can escape the hurly-burly of the outside business and political world, or for public and other buildings that require peace and quiet to carry out their functions, such as courts, libraries, schools, and hospitals.

Id. at 118 (Black, J., concurring). Therefore, even if loitering were treated as a fundamental right, Petitioner possesses a significant, legitimate interest in limiting criminal street gang members' right to loiter for no purpose.

Readers who skipped the quote would have no way of knowing where the writer's "therefore" came from. Even readers who read the quote would have to figure out for themselves the significance of the quoted language. If you are tempted to use a lengthy quotation, try one of two tactics to help ensure that your readers will understand your message.

The first and perhaps most obvious solution is to try to shorten the quote. Start by underlining the language that is most significant to your argument:

> Plainly, however, <u>no mandate in our Constitution</u> leaves States and governmental units powerless to pass laws to protect the public from the kind of boisterous and <u>threatening conduct</u> that <u>disturbs the tranquility</u> of spots selected by the people either for homes, where in they can escape the hurly-burly of the outside business and political world, or for public and other buildings that require peace and quiet to carry out their functions, such as courts, libraries, schools, and hospitals.

Then, quote only the underlined material (after removing the underlining), and incorporate a paraphrase of the rest of the quotation into your argument:

Good Example

This Court has provided almost absolute protection to speech of a political nature. <u>Gregory v. Chicago</u>, 394 U.S. 111, 116 (1969). In <u>Gregory</u>, the Court found the arrest of demonstrators for disorderly conduct to be unconstitutional under the First Amendment.<u>Id</u>. The Court made this finding in favor of political speech even though the picketers' actions led to a disruption of the peace and quiet of a neighborhood by picketing in front of the mayor's home.<u>Id</u>. at 111. A concurring opinion stressed the lawfulness and peacefulness of the demonstration as well as the petitioners' First Amendment right to engage in that activity.<u>Id</u>. at 121 (Black, J., concurring). However, Justice Black also declared that "no mandate in our Constitution" prevents states from passing laws that protect the public from "threatening conduct" that "disturbs the tranquility" of homes or certain public buildings.<u>Id</u>. at 118 (Black, J., concurring). Therefore, even if loitering were treated as a fundamental right, Petitioner possesses a significant, legitimate interest in limiting criminal street gang members' right to loiter for no purpose.

In the alternative, you may determine that the lengthy quote is absolutely necessary for your argument. If this is the case, promote the effectiveness of the quotation by articulating the conclusions you want the reader to draw from it and putting those conclusions into the body of your argument. I recommend using what I refer to as a *Katie Couric Introduction*[30] before the quotation.

---

30. Previous editions of this text have referred to a "Tom Brokaw Introduction," but since Mr. Brokaw has now retired from full-time newscasting, I have changed this label accordingly.

A Katie Couric Introduction is an introduction that focuses the reader's attention on the point the writer is using the quotation to prove or establish. I call it that because Katie Couric and other newscasters constantly introduce little snippets of interviews or public events. In much the same way, a long quote is a little snippet of an opinion or other legal document. Legal writers, unfortunately, often give readers unfocused introductions like, "The Court noted," or, as in the previous illustration, "Justice Black also declared." In contrast, newscasters almost never give introductions like, "The President said," or "The Senator noted." Instead, they give the audience some context and essentially tell them what to listen for when they hear the quoted language.

The illustration below is from a broadcast in which Katie Couric excerpted pieces of interviews with Captain Chesley Sullenberger and other crew members of U.S. Airways flight 1584. Captain Sullenberger and the crew achieved fame in 2009, when they safely landed a disabled jet on the Hudson River and safely evacuated all of the passengers. The excerpt below is from the beginning of the story, and it focuses on Captain Sullenberger's feelings when he realized the danger of the situation. Notice how the (italicized) language leading up to the quotation gives the audience context and prepares it for what is to come:

Good Example

KATIE COURIC: When U.S. Airways flight 1549 landed in New York's Hudson River on January 15th, what seemed destined to be a tragedy became an extraordinary tale of success and survival. By the time all 155 people were pulled from the icy waters by a flotilla of rescue boats, a story began to emerge of a highly trained pro with a cool demeanor who had deftly guided his doomed aircraft to safety. In an instant, Captain Chesley "Sully" Sullenberger found himself at the heart of an uplifting news story people all over the world wanted to celebrate. In February, *just two weeks later, Captain Sullenberger gave his first account of the harrowing five minutes in the sky over New York City:*

CAPTAIN CHESLEY SULLENBERGER: It was the worst, sickening, pit-of-your-stomach, falling-through-the-floor feeling I've ever felt in my life. I knew immediately it was very bad.[31]

In the same way, you should prepare your audience for a long quotation by stating the conclusion you want the reader to draw from it:

Good Example

However, Justice Black also pointed out that governments can prohibit certain behaviors in public places to protect the public:

---

31. Video available at http://www.cbsnews.com/video/watch/?id=4784012n&tag=mncol;lst;1 (last accessed May 5, 2010).

Plainly, however, no mandate in our Constitution leaves States and governmental units powerless to pass laws to protect the public from the kind of boisterous and threatening conduct that disturbs the tranquility of spots selected by the people either for homes, wherein they can escape the hurly-burly of the outside business and political world, or for public and other buildings that require peace and quiet to carry out their functions, such as courts, libraries, schools, and hospitals.

<u>Id</u>. at 118 (Black, J., concurring). Therefore, it is possible for municipalities to protect both the Constitution and the peace and quiet of their communities with appropriate legislation.

Use a Katie Couric Introduction to help the reader to get the most out of lengthy quotations. The focused introduction will encourage the reader to read the quote by directing his or her attention and making it easier to understand the point of the quotation. Even if the reader does skip the quote, the writer has still articulated the point of the quotation in a place that the reader will see it and in a way that the reader can understand.

CHAPTER

14

Developing Arguments Generally

A. DEVELOPING PERSUASIVE ARGUMENTS

1. *What Is an Argument?*

Arguments are the primary tool lawyers use to persuade people to do things. *An argument is a group of ideas arranged logically to convince a reader or listener to do a particular thing or to adopt a particular belief.*

That would *not* include excited utterances from drivers after a fender-bender in a parking lot. The drivers might sound argumentative, but they are really ventilating anger, neither of them having any hope of persuading the other. Nor does it include the pushy expression of one's view on news, fashion, sports, or gossip. In daily life, many people are eager to state their opinions. But they seem to do it just so that you know what they think—and not with the intent of changing your mind.

Uncapitalized, "argument" means a contention designed to persuade. Capitalized, it means the largest portion of a motion memorandum or appellate brief. There might be many arguments in an Argument.

In designing an argument, your initial question should be "What will make the reader or listener want to agree with me?" A good argument will *affect* the audience. It leads readers or listeners through reasoning so convincingly that, at the end, they are pleased to be persuaded.

Arguments can be expressed ("the defendant committed negligence by running a red light and hitting my client's car") or implied, usually by reciting the facts in a way that suggests the argument ("my client entered the intersection with a green light and was hit sideways by the defendant, whose light was red"). This chapter explains how to make expressed arguments in the Argument portion of a motion memorandum or a brief. Chapters 29 and 30 [Richard K. Neumann, Jr., Legal Reasoning and Legal Writing: Structure, Strategy, and Style, 6th ed., (2009)] explain how to make implied arguments in a Statement of the Case and in a Question Presented.

Most disputes are two-sided in the sense that each side can make credible arguments, and it takes real work for the judge or jury to choose between them. Here is an example from a nonlitigation setting: hypothetical testimony before a Congressional committee on whether to impose a tariff on shoelaces:[1]

A new and stiff tariff should be imposed on imported shoelaces. We do not ask for a ban on the import of foreign shoelaces. All we ask for is a chance to compete fairly. Foreign shoelace manufacturers pay their workers only a small fraction of what workers in our shoelace factories are paid, and that is why their shoelaces are so much cheaper than ours. Unless imported shoelaces are taxed on the boat or at the border, they will become so cheap that our own domestic shoelace manufacturers will be driven into bankruptcy. Our own hard-working employees will lose their jobs, leaving their families destitute and adding to the unemployment problem. And if our own domestic shoelace manufacturing industry disappears, our country will become completely dependent on imported shoelaces. If imported shoelaces were cut off in war or other national emergency, we would have no source of new shoelaces, which means that eventually most shoes would become unwearable. Every soldier has to lace up boots to go into combat. Most of the office and factory workers have to tie shoelaces to get to work in the morning. Without shoelaces every domestic industry would eventually come to a halt. Please do not let our domestic shoelace industry become extinct.

Imported shoelaces should not be subject to a tariff. The American consumer already pays too much for shoelaces. If they are so essential that everyone needs them, they should cost less. We cannot artificially protect every domestic industry that faces hard foreign competition. If we tried, the cost of living to the American consumer would go up because it is impossible for people to live without buying imported goods. A tariff might save some American jobs, but it would destroy others because some people make their living importing shoelaces. If the American shoelace manufacturers cannot compete without the help of a tariff, their industry should become extinct and its people and capital directed toward some business that Americans really can do better or cheaper than foreign producers. And the country is not going to be brought to its knees because it doesn't have shoelaces. It is extremely difficult to imagine any national emergency that could cut off a supply of imported shoelaces. And if a national emergency ever did that, it would also cut off the supply of so many other imports that shoelaces would be the least of our worries.

If a controversy is *evenly* two-sided, the person who must choose the winner—usually a court, but here a legislature—will have a hard time deciding because the arguments on each side are attractive. Your job is to make your arguments

1. A tariff is a tax on imported products. It makes the import more expensive when sold to the consumer. Arguments like these have been made whenever Congress has considered tariff and trade bills. (The examples here were vaguely inspired by testimony regarding the 1962 Trade Expansion Act but not about shoelaces.) This is a hypothetical. Please do not assume that imported shoelaces are now specially taxed, or that the domestic shoelace industry has any trouble competing with imports, or that a domestic shoelace industry even exists. The parallel block quotes are just examples of how arguments work against each other.

better than the adversary's, or to make the adversary's arguments worse by find-ing their weak points, or—preferably—to do both of these things. This chapter explains how.

2. What Judges Expect from Written Argumentation

You already know some things about how judges think: in our system of litiga-tion the lawyers (and not the judge) frame the issues, develop the theories and arguments, and adduce the evidence. Judges are busy people who view any assertion skeptically and who must make many decisions in short periods of time. Thus, they need complete but concise arguments that can be quickly understood.

In addition, there is so much litigation now that courts are increasingly dependent on written arguments submitted by attorneys. Many—perhaps most—appeals today are decided without oral argument and without any other personal contact between attorneys and judges. On appeal, the written brief bears the primary burden of persuading the court. A similar evolution is occur-ring in trial courts. It is not unusual today for a judge to complete a case without a trial, without a hearing, without an oral argument, without a conference in chambers, and solely on the basis of the attorneys' written submissions in con-nection with a motion to dismiss or a motion for summary judgment.

Judges are evaluated on their skill at the *art* of judging—not on whether they know all the law. Although judges know a great deal about rules of procedure (which they use constantly), they usually know much less about individual rules of substantive law (which come up less often). And in most courts judges cannot specialize in particular areas of substantive law: they must decide any case you bring before them. Unless a case turns on parts of the law about which a judge has thought deeply lately, the judge depends on the attorneys to explain what the law is and how it governs the case. And a judge knows nothing at all about the facts of a case except for what can be learned through the attorneys and their evidence.

Judges will want you to *teach* them your case. Think of a motion memoran-dum or appellate brief as a *manual on how to make a particular decision* (and—by implication—on how to write the opinion that justifies that decision). A lawyer who can show the court how the decision should be made, laying out all the steps of logic, stands a much better chance of winning.

If done in a respectful tone, this is not as presumptuous as you might think. If you have prepared properly, you will know much more about the decision than the judge will. But teach the court without insulting its intelligence, and do so in the clearest and most concise manner possible. Judges find it hard to rule in your favor if you are condescending or waste their time.

3. Argumentation Techniques

> *A carefully prepared, carefully stated, lawyer-like written argument is a work of art and a joy forever.*
>
> —*E. Barrett Prettyman*

A convincing argument is not just a random collection of stray comments that sound good for the client. Those kinds of comments might be useful raw materials, but they become an argument only when they coalesce into a coherent presentation that influences the audience. Here is how to do it:

1. Design a compelling theory and back it up with compelling arguments.
2. Include both motivating arguments and justifying arguments.
3. Limit your contentions to those that have a reasonable chance of persuading the court.
4. Organize to emphasize the ideas that are most likely to persuade.
5. Make your organization obvious.
6. Give the court a clear statement of the rule or rules on which the case turns.
7. Rely on an appropriate amount of authority with appropriate amounts of explanation.
8. Explain exactly and in detail how the law governs the facts.
9. To the extent they advance the theory, make the facts and people involved come alive on the written page.
10. "Tell the judge exactly what will happen in the real world if he decides for you or for your opponent."[2]
11. Reinforce the theory with carefully chosen wording.
12. Confront openly your weaknesses and your opponent's strengths.
13. Enhance your credibility through careful editing and through the appearance of the memorandum or brief.
14. Make it easy for the judge to rule in your favor.

Each of these techniques requires strategic decisions on your part. If you think these decisions through carefully, you should be able to explain your work by answering the litany of strategy questions in §24.2.

You will find the following material easier to understand if you read the motion memorandum in Appendix F [Richard K. Neumann, Jr., Legal Reasoning and Legal Writing: Structure, Strategy, and Style, 6th ed., (2009)] before continuing here.

1. Design a compelling theory and back it up with compelling arguments.   Until you provide proof, a judge will not believe anything you say. In litigation writing, proof is a well-argued theory that compels a decision favorable to your client. You can develop a theory through the process described in Sections 5.B.4-5.B.5. And the quality of your theory can be measured by the criteria set out in Section 5.B.3. But even a good theory does not sell unless it is argued.

A persuasive argument is neither extravagant nor belligerent. To a judge, extreme statements sound unreliable. Because judges are experienced, professional skeptics, they are rarely fooled by inaccurate or farfetched statements, and when they find such a statement in an argument, in their view a dust of untrustworthiness settles over the theory and the lawyer involved. Judges usually have what Hemingway, in another context, called "a built-in, shock-proof, shit detector."[3] Because you cannot afford to be seen as unreliable, you need to be

---

2. Hollis T. Hurd, *Writing for Lawyers* 61 (Journal Broad. & Commun. 1982).
3. *Writers At Work: The Paris Review Interviews, Second Series* 239 (George Plimpton ed., Penguin 1965).

similarly equipped so that you can examine—with a judge's skepticism—each statement you contemplate making. In addition to the skills explained here, it helps to have a mature and thorough understanding of human nature (some of which can be acquired in law school, even if it is not listed in the catalog).

A good theory and good arguments are reasonable and accurate, appear reliable, and make your client's victory appear *inevitable*—either because the higher courts will reverse any other result, or because it is the only right thing to do, or both. The feeling of inevitability is a judge's selling point. It is reached by laying out for the judge every step of logic so that the advocate's conclusion becomes more and more irresistible as the argument proceeds. A judge knows when the selling point approaches, because the job of deciding seems to grow easier.

2. Include both motivating arguments and justifying arguments.   Both are needed to persuade.

A motivating argument is one that causes a judge to *want* to decide a case in a particular way. It causes the judge to feel that any other decision would be unjust. Motivating arguments tend to be centered on facts or a combination of facts and policy. Greatly oversimplified, the following are the primary motivating arguments in the sample motion memorandum and appellate briefs in the appendices:

Appendix F [Richard K. Neumann, Jr., Legal Reasoning and Legal Writing: Structure, Strategy, and Style, 6th ed., (2009)]:	The defendant created a risk of irreversible harm to the health of 130 children by mishandling a toxic substance which he could have handled safely using well accepted techniques.
Appendix G [Richard K. Neumann, Jr., Legal Reasoning and Legal Writing: Structure, Strategy, and Style, 6th ed., (2009)]:	The defendant was only following her doctors' treatment plan for a recognized illness, and the law should leave her alone.
Appendix H [Richard K. Neumann, Jr., Legal Reasoning and Legal Writing: Structure, Strategy, and Style, 6th ed., (2009)]:	The defendant and his friends had misrepresented their true identities, and a crime-ridden society is threatened when people do that.

(In all three appendices, notes in the margins show you where motivating arguments are being made.)

A justifying argument is one that shows that the law either requires or permits the result urged by the arguer. Justifying arguments are centered on legal rules or on a combination of rules and policy. Again oversimplified, the following are the main justifying arguments in the sample motion memo and briefs in the appendices:

Appendix F [Richard K. Neumann, Jr., Legal Reasoning and Legal Writing: Structure, Strategy, and Style, 6th ed., (2009)]:	The evidence satisfies the test for summary judgment in a negligence case.
Appendix G [Richard K. Neumann, Jr., Legal Reasoning and Legal	The defendant was not disguised within the meaning of the statute.

Writing: Structure, Strategy, and Style, 6th ed., (2009)]:
Appendix H [Richard K. Neumann, Jr., Legal Reasoning and Legal Writing: Structure, Strategy, and Style, 6th ed., (2009)]:

And if she was, the statute would violate the constitutional right to privacy. The defendant was disguised within the meaning of the statute. And the statute does not violate the constitutional right to privacy.

The first year of law school is designed, among other things, to teach you how to make justifying arguments. (You probably understood something of motivating arguments even before you came to law school, although you will learn more about making them.)

In judicial opinions, justifying arguments are usually developed in much detail while motivating arguments are only hinted at. The hints are found most often in the court's recitations of the facts. Have you had the feeling, while reading the first few paragraphs of an opinion, that you knew how the case would be decided before the court had told you—and even before the court had begun to discuss the law? If so, it was probably because you noticed in the fact recitation clues about which facts had motivated the court.

Why do you need both motivating arguments and justifying arguments? A motivating argument alone is not enough because even a motivated judge is not supposed to act without a solid legal justification. Judges understandably want to feel that they are doing a professional job of judging, and they can be reversed on appeal if they fail to justify their actions within the law.

And a justifying argument alone is not enough because, in a large number of cases, a justifying argument, without more, will not persuade. The law can usually be interpreted in more than one reasonable way. When a judge is given a choice between two conflicting justifying arguments, each of which is reasonable, the judge will take the one she or he is motivated to take. (Judges are, after all, human.) Remember what Karl Llewellyn wrote: "rules *guide*, but they do not *control* decision. There is no precedent the judge may not at his need either file down to razor thinness or expand into a bludgeon."[4] (See §15.6 [Richard K. Neumann, Jr., Legal Reasoning and Legal Writing: Structure, Strategy, and Style, 6th ed., (2009)].)

Many beginners have more difficulty developing motivating arguments than they do with justifying arguments. Before starting law school most of us have already had a fair amount of experience justifying our own beliefs. But that is not the same as getting inside another person's thinking and *causing* her or him to *want* to do something. To motivate, we need to learn not only a new argument style, but also a new *process* of creating arguments. That is because the process of creating justifying arguments is different from the process of creating motivating arguments.

[In a college course, Kathleen wrote a paper on the] question "Is American Sign language (ASL) a 'foreign language' for purposes of meeting the university's foreign language requirement?" Kathleen had taken two years of ASL at a community college. When she transferred to a four-year college, the chair of the foreign languages department at her new college would not allow her ASL proficiency to count for the foreign language requirement. ASL isn't a "language," the chair said summarily. "It's not equivalent to learning French, German, or Japanese."

4. K. N. Llewellyn, *The Bramble Bush* 180 (Oceana 1930).

Kathleen disagreed, so [in a different course she decided to write a paper on this issue]. While doing research, she focused almost entirely on subject matter, searching for what linguists, brain neurologists, cognitive psychologists, and sociologists had said about the language of deaf people. Immersed in her subject matter, she was [not very] concerned with her audience, whom she thought of primarily as her classmates and the professor [who taught the class in which she was writing the paper. They] were friendly to her views and interested in her experiences with the deaf community. She wrote a well-documented paper, citing several scholarly articles, that made a good case to her classmates (and the professor) that ASL was indeed a distinct language.

Proud of the big red A the professor had placed on her paper, Kathleen returned to the chair of the foreign language department with a new request to count ASL for her language requirement. The chair read her paper, congratulated her on her good writing, but said her argument was not persuasive. He disagreed with several of the linguists she cited and with the general definition of "language" that her paper assumed. He then gave her some additional (and to her fuzzy) reasons that the college would not accept ASL as a foreign language.[5]

This is a common experience when justifying insights are used in an attempt—often unsuccessful—to influence real-world decision-making. The ideas that made sense in the library and sounded wonderful to colleagues are ignored by the person who makes a decision, whether that person is an administrator (as here) or a judge.

It would be easy for Kathleen to dismiss the chair of the foreign language department as a nincompoop, but for two reasons she cannot and should not do that. First, she cannot get around the fact that he has the power of decision. The only way she can get her ASL work to count for the foreign language requirement is *to change his mind*. For this issue, he is the judge.

Second, he might have sincere concerns that deserve to be addressed. Does Kathleen know what they might be? At this point, she does not. Her paper focused on the issue itself, and the only audience she imagined was a friendly one. She avoided thinking about the unfriendly audience, even though the skeptical audience—the department chair—is the only one that can make the decision. We would like to forget about the skeptical audience, but if we want action, we have to *concentrate* on that audience.

How can Kathleen find out what the department chair's concerns might be? How can she address them?

Spurred by what she considered the chair's too-easy dismissal of her argument, Kathleen decided . . . to write a second paper on ASL—but this time aiming it directly at the chair of foreign languages. Now her writing task falls closer to the persuasive end of our continuum. Kathleen once again immersed herself in research, but this time it focused not on subject matter (whether ASL is a distinct language) but on audience. She researched the history of the foreign language requirement at her college and discovered some of the politics behind it (an old foreign language requirement had been dropped in the 1970's and reinstituted in the 1990's, partly—a math professor told her—to boost enrollments in foreign language courses). She also interviewed foreign language teachers to find out what they knew and didn't know about ASL. She discovered that many teachers [inaccurately] thought ASL was "easy to learn," so that accepting ASL would allow

5. John D. Ramage & John C. Bean, *Writing Arguments: A Rhetoric with Readings* 10-11 (4th ed., Allyn & Bacon 1998).

students a Mickey Mouse way to avoid the rigors of a real foreign language class. Additionally, she learned that foreign language teachers valued immersing students in a foreign culture; in fact, the foreign language requirement was part of her college's effort to create a multicultural curriculum.

This new understanding of her target audience helped Kathleen totally reconceptualize her argument. She condensed and abridged her original paper. . . . She added sections showing the difficulty of learning ASL (to counter her audience's belief that learning ASL was easy), and literature (to show how ASL met the goals of multiculturalism), and showing that the number of transfer students with ASL credits would be negligibly small (to allay fears that accepting ASL would threaten enrollments in language classes). She ended her argument with an appeal to her college's public emphasis (declared boldly in its mission statement) on eradicating social injustice and reaching out to the oppressed. She described the isolation of deaf people in a world where almost no hearing people learn ASL and argued that the deaf community on her campus could be integrated more fully into campus life if more students could "talk" with them [in their own language]. Thus, the ideas included in her new argument, the reasons selected, the evidence used, the arrangement and tone all were determined by her primary focus on persuasion.[6]

Kathleen's first paper was limited to justifying arguments because it did no more than provide a logical rationale that could support a decision in her favor—if the department chair were inclined to rule as she wanted. It lacked motivating arguments because it did not address the concerns of the department chair.

The second paper included both kinds of arguments and thus was good lawyering. She got inside the decision-maker's thinking and showed him that his own values and needs would benefit from doing what she wanted. Purely justifying arguments remained—because they are needed to justify a decision in her favor—but they receded in importance and were joined by policy arguments with which the department chair could sympathize as well as arguments that addressed genuine practical problems that had made him skeptical.

3. Limit your contentions to those that have a reasonable chance of persuading the court.
You might be tempted to throw in every good thing you can think of about your theory and every bad thing about your adversary's theory, assuming that all this cannot hurt and might help. That is "shotgun" writing, and it hurts more than it helps. Instead, focus sharply on the strong contentions. Develop them fully, and leave out the weak ones. As Holmes put it: "strike for the jugular and let the rest go."[7] That creates a document that is more compact but explores more deeply the ideas on which the decision will be based.

A good argument begins by subduing the judge's skepticism into a general feeling of *confidence* that the theory can be relied on, and then, on that foundation of confidence, it builds a feeling that your client is the *inevitable* winner. Weak contentions interfere with this. They excite skepticism, rather than quieting it. If a judge believes that you have indiscriminately mixed unreliable contentions with seemingly attractive ones, the judge's natural temptation is to dismiss the whole lot as not worthy of confidence, for the same reason that a person considering the purchase of a house justifiably suspects the integrity of the entire structure after cracked beams are found in the attic. Just as it is the

6. *Id.* at 11.
7. Oliver Wendell Holmes, *Speeches* 77 (Little, Brown & Co. 1934).

builder's job to select only sturdy materials, so it is the lawyer's job—and not the judge's—to separate out the weak ideas before the memorandum or brief is submitted. A judge has neither the time nor the inclination to delete all the suspect material and then reassemble the remainder into something sturdier.

When you determine whether a contention has a reasonable chance to persuade, you are, of course, making a predictive judgment. A "reasonable chance" does not mean certainty and, in a case where you have nothing better, might not even mean probability. To be worth making, however, a contention should have the capacity to seem tempting and attractive to a judge.

4. Organize to emphasize the ideas that are most likely to persuade.   Remember that you will make both motivating arguments and justifying arguments. Justifying arguments can be organized through the paradigm formula you have already learned because they are proofs of a conclusion of law. Motivating arguments, on the other hand, are more often appeals to a human sense of justice or pragmatic policy needs. When you add motivating arguments, you may vary the paradigm formula in radical ways (many of which would not work in predictive writing). In part, that is because motivating arguments should be introduced very early in a presentation, preferably in the first paragraph.

To merge motivating and justifying arguments, do this: First, write a justifying argument structured in the paradigm format you have already learned (Chapters 10-13 [Richard K. Neumann, Jr., Legal Reasoning and Legal Writing: Structure, Strategy, and Style, 6th ed., (2009)]). Then start adding motivating arguments wherever they seem relevant to what you have already written. Finally, write an opening paragraph that sums up your motivating arguments. (This is illustrated in the memorandum in Appendix F [Richard K. Neumann, Jr., Legal Reasoning and Legal Writing: Structure, Strategy, and Style, 6th ed., (2009)] and in the appellate briefs in Appendices G and H. See the notes in the appendix margins.) With more experience, you will be able to write motivating and justifying arguments at the same time, or even to write the motivating argument before you write the justifying argument.

The opening paragraph that introduces the motivating argument should precede all statements of rules, proof of those rules, and rule application. Word for word, the opening paragraph is the most powerful argumentative passage you can write. It is worth rewriting and rewriting again many times until it introduces your motivating arguments in the most persuasive way.

Why is it so important to introduce the motivating arguments first? There are several reasons. Most importantly, it tracks the way many judges think. They act on what motivates them (unless it cannot be justified). Motivation is established first, the need to justify afterward. Moreover, early impressions tend to color how later material is read, and, like most people, a judge reads most carefully at the beginning. In addition, because judges are so busy, they expect the strongest material first. If they find themselves reading weak material early, they assume that nothing better follows and stop reading altogether.

(You probably read a newspaper in the same way: you expect the most important or most entertaining material near the beginning of a story, and when you have had enough, you stop reading and go on to something else. Newspaper editors know that, and newspaper stories are written with the least valuable material at the end, so that readers can decide how much of a story to read. Just as your method of reading a newspaper would be thrown off if the most valuable material were strewn randomly throughout the story, so a judge's method of reading a memorandum or a brief would become muddled if the strongest arguments might appear anywhere.)

Thus, judges will expect you to get immediately to the point. A judge quickly becomes impatient with long prefatory passages of historical background because that kind of material usually does not help in making a decision. (Even in a constitutional case where the issue is the drafters' intent one or two centuries ago, the historical material is part of the argument, not a preface to it.) An argument—and even a predictive memorandum—written in the style of a law review article is considered especially offensive because law review writing aims to be densely encyclopedic and is not focused to assist decision-making.

Michael Fontham has said that the "best strategy is to strike quickly, establish momentum, and maintain the advantage through a forceful presentation of contentions selected for their persuasive effect."[8] Focus the reader's thoughts on the ideas that can cause you to win.

In general, the most persuasive sequence is to present first the issues on which you are most likely to win; within issues, to make your strongest arguments first; and, within arguments, to make your strongest contentions and use your best authority first.

For example, if your adversary must prove that a five-element test has been satisfied, and if you think that your adversary's proof is weakest on element number three, do not argue the elements in the order in which they are listed in the controlling statute. Argue number three first because as far as you are concerned, it is the controlling element. (Your adversary, however, might do either of two things. She might argue them in exactly the order listed in the statute, to build a feeling of cumulating persuasion. Or if some elements are extremely easy to prove, she might get them out of the way first and then concentrate on the ones where the battle is concentrated.)

Sometimes, however, the logic of the dispute requires that the strongest material be delayed to avoid confusing the court. Some arguments are simply hard to understand unless preceded by less punchy material. In these situations, you must weigh your need for clarity against your need to show merit from the start.

5. Make your organization obvious.   You cannot afford to let the judge grope for clues about how your contentions are related to each other. Instead, use the techniques of forceful writing[9] to help the judge see your focus. Very soon after you begin to discuss each issue, tell the judge exactly what your theory is. Use a thesis sentence to state each contention before you begin to prove it. And use transitional words and phrases to show how your contentions are cumulative:

> There are three reasons why . . . First, . . . Second, . . . And finally, . . .

> Not only has the defendant violated . . . , but she has also . . .

6. Give the court a clear statement of the rule or rules on which the case turns.   That rule might not be exactly as stated in the cases to which you cite. In fact, the

8. Michael R. Fontham, *Written and Oral Advocacy* 108 (Wiley 1985).
9. See §19.3 [Richard K. Neumann, Jr., Legal Reasoning and Legal Writing: Structure, Strategy, and Style, 6th ed., (2009)].

cases might enforce the rule without stating it at all, and you might have to figure out what the rule is from the court's reasoning, particularly the way it treats the facts. (See §3.2 [Richard K. Neumann, Jr., Legal Reasoning and Legal Writing: Structure, Strategy, and Style, 6th ed., (2009)].)

The judge who reads your Argument needs what Karl Llewellyn called the advocate's "own clean phrasing of the rule," together with "a passage which so clearly and rightly states and crystallizes the background and the result that it is *recognized* on sight as doing the needed work and as practically demanding to be lifted into the opinion."[10] Particularly in appellate courts, judges know that they will have to write an opinion justifying their decision, and that the opinion should be as convincing as possible to the parties, to the bar, to the public, and to any still higher court to which the decision could be appealed. That is a hard task where a gap in the law must be filled. The judge who asks in oral argument in a gap-filling case, "Counselor, what rule would you have us enforce?" really wants to know how—if the lawyer prevails—the court should word the second component of the paradigm formula when it writes the opinion.

As you already know, for any given rule, the authority can usually be interpreted to support several different formulations from broad to narrow. In choosing one formulation over another, balance two separate factors. First, out of any given set of authority, some rule formulations are more likely than others to be accepted by a court. And second, some formulations more logically support the client's position. The trick is to find a formulation that does both.

7. Rely on an appropriate amount of authority with appropriate amounts of explanation. To rule in your favor, a court would need to believe that you have provided sufficient authority, although the typical judge is unwilling to tolerate an exhaustive explanation of every case you cite. How do you steer a middle course between underciting and overciting and between underexplaining and overexplaining?

Begin by predicting the amount of citation and explanation a skeptical but busy judge would need. Then carefully study the available authorities. Place in a "major authority" category those that are likely to *influence* the court and in a "peripheral" category those that are merely somewhat related to the issue. Think in terms of cause and effect: if you had to make the judge's decision, which authorities would be most likely to have an effect on you, *even an effect adverse to your client's position?* Those are the authorities you must discuss, and many of them are best discussed in detail. Peripheral authorities should eventually be discarded unless they are needed to fill holes in your argument not settled by the major authorities.

The quantity of authority and the volume of explanation will depend on how much is needed to clarify the issue involved, how disputed that issue is, and how important it is to your theory. At one extreme, an idea may be so complex, so disputed, and so critical that it must be supported by a comprehensive explanation, filling many pages, of major authorities. At the other extreme, if the court is apt to be satisfied with a mere conclusory explanation, you should limit citation to one or, at the very most, two cases. If an idea is undisputed and routine, such as an uncontested procedural test, it should be enough to cite, with little or no explanation, the most recent decision from the highest court in the

---

10. Karl N. Llewellyn, *The Common Law Tradition: Deciding Appeals* 241 (Little, Brown & Co. 1960) (emphasis in original).

jurisdiction that has invoked the test. (For example, notice how the test for summary judgment is proved in the memorandum in Appendix F [Richard K. Neumann, Jr., Legal Reasoning and Legal Writing: Structure, Strategy, and Style,
6th ed., (2009)].)

The point is to give the court confidence that you are right without tiring its
patience.

8. Explain exactly and in detail how the law governs the facts.   A court rules for
one party over another not merely because the law is abstractly favorable, but,
more importantly, because the law and facts *combine* favorably. The judge often
reaches the selling point only where the law and facts are finally combined—
woven together—to show that what the writer wants is inevitable. Beginners
sometimes devote so much attention to the law that they overlook the final step
of arguing the facts—weaving the law into the facts to show the court precisely
how the decision should be made. After all the work of explaining the law, a
beginner might assume that the application to the facts is obvious, but it hardly
ever is. Do not assume that merely mentioning the facts is enough: *show* the
court exactly how the determinative facts require the decision you seek.

***9. To the extent they advance the theory, make the facts and people involved come
alive on the written page.***   As the judge looks at the facts of your case, you want
her or him to see more than a chronological recitation of events. Instead, you
want the judge to see something that reveals character and causation. An illustration of the difference between those two things is from E. M. Forster's classic
lectures on fiction.[11] When we read "The king died, and then the queen died,"
we might see in the mind's eye either no image or at best an image of stick-like
figures without personality. But when we read "The king died, and then the
queen died of grief," we see instead an image of at least one real human being:
she may be wearing fairytale-like clothing, but she is genuinely suffering as real
people do.

When a judge, reading an argument, visualizes stick figures or no image at
all, the case seems boring and unimportant, and the judge is not motivated to
rule in your favor. But the judge begins to take sides if she or he can visualize
real people doing real things to each other.

Before you begin to write, make a list on scratch paper of the determinative
facts. You will have to discuss those facts to make your argument, and that is
where your opportunities occur. For each fact, ask yourself what the fact illustrates about the *people* involved: does it show who is an innocent victim, who is
predatory, who is inexcusably foolish, and so forth. For each fact, ask yourself
further what the fact illustrates about *what happened*: does it show the events to
have been accidental, caused by one person's carelessness, the result of another's greed and cunning, and so on. Only by knowing what each fact reveals can
you tell the client's story in a compelling way.

When you describe these facts in your writing, do not characterize them with
emotion-laden words. Although a fact is determinative because the law coldly
makes it so, a judge can form a human reaction to it, simply because judges prefer to make decisions that are fundamentally fair. On the other hand, a judge's
professional self-image is naturally offended by an argument that reads like
political oratory or a story in a tabloid newspaper. *Vividness* is not the same as

11. E. M. Forster, *Aspects of the Novel* 86 (Harcourt Brace 1927).

luridness, which demeans an argument and the judge who reads it. If a fact will seem compelling to a court, that fact will speak for itself. All you will need is a calm description of the fact, in simple words and with enough detail to make the picture vivid. When reading the Argument in the memorandum in Appendix F [Richard K. Neumann, Jr., Legal Reasoning and Legal Writing: Structure, Strategy, and Style, 6th ed., (2009)], you may have thought that the painter was irresponsible—but the writer never called him that. Instead, the writer simply described what happened so that *you* formed that opinion. (Forster did not say that the queen loved the king. He only told you why she died.)

10. *"Tell the judge exactly what will happen in the real world if he decides for you or for your opponent."* [12] In a trial court, that usually means showing the judge how the parties have been affected by the dispute, how they would be affected by the relief you seek, or how in some other way what you seek is fundamentally fair.

In an appellate court, where precedent makes law, it also means showing the court how you should prevail from a policy standpoint. Not only must you show the court that your client deserves individually to win, but you also must demonstrate that what you want makes sense in other cases as well because the decision will become precedent. If a court must choose between competing rules, for example, you should spend more than a little effort showing that the rule you urge is better than others. Even where the law is settled and the question is how to apply it, a court is still less likely to rule in your favor if the court lacks confidence that what you want is, in a very general sense, a good idea.

Prove policy with authority. Some policy is openly announced in decisions and statutes, but more often it is implied. For example, courts everywhere like solutions that are easily enforceable, promote clarity in the law, are not needlessly complex, and do not allow true wrongdoers to profit from illegal acts. Other policy considerations may differ from state to state. In Arizona, for example, public policy disfavors solutions that interfere with development of land for homes and industry, while in Vermont policy prefers conservation, the environment, and preservation of agriculture. Some states favor providing tort remedies even at some risk to judicial efficiency, although in others the reverse is true. Still other policy considerations differ from era to era. Some activities once greatly favored in the law—such as the building and operation of railroads in the nineteenth century—now enjoy no special treatment, while other things—such as a woman's reproductive control over her own body—are now protected in a way they once were not.

Lawyers tend to introduce policy-based arguments with phrasings like the following:

> This court should reject the rule urged by the defendant because it would cause . . .

> Automobile rental companies [or some other category of litigants] should bear the risk of loss because . . .

> Not only is the order requested by the plaintiff not sanctioned by this state's case law, but such an order would violate public policy because . . .

---

12. Hollis T. Hurd, *Writing for Lawyers* 61 (Journal Broad. & Commun. 1982).

Remember, however, that policy arguments are used to reinforce argument from authority. Only where authority is unusually sparse should policy arguments play the predominant role in a theory.

11. Reinforce the theory with carefully chosen wording.   Choose words in part for the effect they should have on the reader. Simple, concrete words can paint the pictures on which your theory is based. In the memorandum in Appendix E [Richard K. Neumann, Jr., Legal Reasoning and Legal Writing: Structure, Strategy, and Style, 6th ed., (2009)], notice how facts are described almost entirely in short, everyday words with very specific meanings. And notice how the word *toxic* is used to remind the reader that although lead paint seems innocuous, it is not.

Readers see scenes where writers have given concrete descriptions to build on. The knack is, first, to isolate the very few facts that are essential to the scene because they will motivate the reader or are determinative under the law, and then to describe those facts in words that are simple and concrete enough for the desired image to come quickly into the reader's mind. This is not simple and concrete:

> Where contamination has occurred, lead dust can be ingested by young children through frequent and unpredictable hand-mouth contact during play.

This is:

> If the floor inside a building or the soil outside is contaminated with lead dust, young children can literally eat lead because they frequently and unexpectedly put their hands and other things in their mouths while playing.

Did you see a more vivid image when you read the second example?

You can do harm with words that claim too much. The first example below is actually less persuasive than the second:

> It is obvious, therefore, that the defendant clearly understood the consequences of his acts.

> Therefore, the defendant understood the consequences of his acts.

In the first example, "It is obvious" and "clearly" supply no extra meaning. Instead, they divert the reader's attention from the message of the sentence. Judges assume that expressions like these are used to cover up a lack of logical proof.

Your references to the parties should be clear to the reader, but the way you refer to the parties can also advance your theory. For example, suppose Eli Goslin, the client in the office memo in Appendix C [Richard K. Neumann, Jr., Legal Reasoning and Legal Writing: Structure, Strategy, and Style, 6th ed., (2009)], were to sue Herbert Skeffington. (The office memo explains why.) In a later motion memorandum or appellate brief, the plaintiffs lawyer would refer to his client with dignity as "Mr. Goslin." Even if his neighbors might know him to treat people and pets vilely and to have vicious opinions that offend all decent-minded folk, he is a sympathetic figure in litigation as long as the court knows him to be "Mr. Goslin," the elderly widower who only wants to live out his last days in his own home. And Goslin's lawyer might frequently refer to Herbert Skeffington as "the nephew" or "the defendant," with no dignity other than his role as nephew and with no personality other than what he reveals about himself through the way he treats his uncle. While he is the shadowy "nephew," it is easier to think him capable of deceit, greed, and cold-bloodedness. But if the judge were to think of him as Mr. Skeffington—and to think of the other interlopers as Mr. Skeffington's wife Amelia and their children Wendy and Tom, aged respectively eight and four—it is a little harder to think ill of them.

It can work the opposite way, too. In the motion memo in Appendix F [Richard K. Neumann, Jr., Legal Reasoning and Legal Writing: Structure, Strategy, and Style, 6th ed., (2009)], the plaintiff's lawyer always refers to the defendant with dignity as "Mr. Raucher." The defendant's conduct is criticized, but he is never demeaned personally. And this refusal to demean can make his conduct look more starkly unacceptable because the issue is cleanly what he did and not him. That is not so in Goslin's situation: the issue there really is the nephew and his character.

But your first obligation when referring to parties is to do so in a way the court will understand. In general, you have three ways: by name ("Trans-Continental Airlines"), generically by the party's out-of-court role ("the airline"), or by the party's in-court role ("the defendant").

Once the reader knows who has sued whom, the clearest references are by name. (Most modern courts write their own opinions that way.) If you represent a person in conflict with a large organization, it might help humanize your client to use the client's name while referring to the opponent generically ("Ms. DiMateo asked the airline for an earlier flight"), but only after introducing the organization by name and telling the reader that you will be using a generic designation: "Ms. DiMateo sued Trans-Continental Airlines ('the airline') afterf. . . . " But if Trans-Continental has a terrible reputation for service, its name might do more than a generic reference to create sympathy for your client.

In trial courts, the parties' in-court roles ("plaintiff," "defendant") are usually clear to the reader but lifeless. Appellate courts, on the other hand, will become confused if you refer to the parties as "the appellant" or "the appellee," and many prohibit it, preferring instead references to the parties' roles in the trial court ("plaintiff," "defendant") or their out-of-court roles ("the taxpayer," "the employee").[13]

12. Confront openly your weaknesses and your adversary's strengths.   Hiding from problems will not make them go away in the night. You have to confront and defeat them. "Be truthful in exposing . . . the difficulties in your case," an appellate judge has written. "Tell us what they are and how you expect to deal with them."[14] If you do not do that, the court will assume that you have no arguments worth making on the subject.

---

13. *See, e.g.,* Rule 28(d) of the Federal Rules of Appellate Procedure.
14. Roger J. Miner, *Twenty-five "Dos" for Appellate Brief Writers,* 3 Scribes J. Leg. Writing 19, 24 (1992).

Ask yourself four questions. First, which cases and statutes favor your adversary? Second, which facts work to your adversary's advantage? Third, what are your adversary's strongest arguments? (Your adversary *does* have strong arguments; otherwise, the case would not be worth litigating.) And fourth, what will your adversary say to fight against your arguments? The answers to these questions identify your adversary's strengths. After you know what those strengths are, read §25.5 to find out what to do about them.

13. Enhance your credibility through careful editing and through the appearance of the memorandum or brief. Help the judge to trust you. Understandably, judges do not trust easily. Their decisions are important ones, and you will always face at least one opposing attorney with another theory to sell. A judge will more readily trust you if you appear to be careful, thorough, and professional. For that reason, a document is more persuasive if its appearance is flawless.

A well-written memo or brief can earn warm gratitude and respect from a judge.[15] Where one side in a case has produced fine writing and the other has done the opposite, a court can draw invidious comparisons and be influenced accordingly:

> If counsel for Phipps had asked us to direct dismissal of the complaint, we might well have done so, as we could do even [now] in the absence of such a request. [Citations omitted.] However, in light of counsel's inadequate and intemperate brief, . . . we shall not do so. In contrast, we compliment counsel for Mrs. Lopez on her excellent and helpful brief. . . .[16]

Beginners in law often underestimate how much bad writing upsets judges. To give you a flavor of how strongly judges feel about this, read the explanatory parentheticals in the footnote attached to this sentence.[17]

---

15. "We express our appreciation to Ellen M. Burgraff, Esq., . . . for her excellent brief and argument in this case." *Swanger v. Zimmerman*, 750 F.2d 291, 294 n. 3 (3d Cir. 1984). "As Mr. Nevin [appellant's lawyer] says in his excellent brief . . . " *United States v. Moore*, 109 F.3d 1456, 1465 (9th Cir. 1997). "The court expresses its appreciation to appellant's counsel for submitting excellent briefs on this appeal." *Johnson v. Stark*, 717 F.2d 1550, 1551 n. 2 (8th Cir. 1983). "We commend assigned counsel for his excellent briefs and argument." *United States v. 4492 South Livonia Rd.*, 889 F.2d 1258, 1271 (2d Cir. 1989).

16. *Lopez v. Henry Phipps Plaza South, Inc.*, 498 F.2d 937, 946 n. 8 (2d Cir. 1974).

17. The following are only a few of the many cases in which judges have embarrassed or punished lawyers for poor writing or violating court rules on briefs or memoranda: *Kano v. National Consumer Coop. Bank*, 22 F.3d 899, 899 (9th Cir. 1994) (ordering a lawyer to pay sanctions of $1,500 for violating page limit, double-spacing, and typeface rules); *DCD Programs, Ltd. v. Leighton*, 846 F.2d 526, 528 (9th Cir. 1988) (suspending a lawyer for misrepresenting the record below); *Jorgenson v. Volusia County*, 846 F.2d 1350, 1351 (11th Cir. 1988) (affirming the district court's punishing lawyer "for failing to cite adverse, controlling precedent"); *Gardner v. Investors Diversified Capital, Inc.*, 805 F. Supp. 874, 875 (D. Colo. 1992) ("The amended complaint . . . is replete with misspellings, grammatical aberrations, non sequiturs. . . . "); *P. M. F. Services, Inc. v. Grady*, 681 F. Supp. 549, 550-51 n. 1 (N.D. Ill. 1988) ("With callous disregard for the reader, plaintiff's counsel" refers to the parties in confusing ways and "uses possessives without apostrophes, leaving the reader to guess whether he intends a singular or plural possessive, etc. Such sloppy pleading and briefing are inexcusable"); *Green v. Green*, 261 Cal. Rptr. 294, 302 n. 11 (Cal. App. 1st Dist. 1989) (ordering appellant to pay appellee's attorney's fees in part because of "the slap-dash quality of [his] briefs"); *In re Hawkins*, 502 N.W.2d 770, 770-72 (Minn. 1993) (publicly reprimanding lawyer and ordering him to attend remedial instruction because of, among other things, "his repeated filing of documents rendered unintelligible by numerous spelling, grammatical, and typographical errors"); *Slater v. Gallman*, 339 N.E.2d 863, 865 (N.Y. 1975) (imposing costs on appellant because of a verbose and unfocused brief); *Frazier v. Columbus Bd. of Educ.*, 638 N.E.2d 581, 582 (Ohio 1994) (dismissing appeal because appellant's jurisdictional memo exceeded page limit).

Edit out every form of intellectual sloppiness: inaccuracies; imprecision; incorrectly used terms of art; errors with citations and other matters of format and layout; mistakes with the English language, its spelling and punctuation; typographical errors; and empty remarks that do not advance the argument (such as rhetorical questions and irrelevant histories of the law). Any of those would suggest a lawyer who cannot be relied on—and judges will be quick to draw that inference.

14. Make it easy for the judge to rule in your favor. "The first rule of advocacy is to make your argument understandable."[18] Judges are overburdened with so many cases that you must assume a certain amount of fatigue. If a memorandum or brief is frustrating, it will be ignored. Instead, submit a document that is easy to read and use. Think about the problems a judge would have with the document, and solve them before submission. Not only should the writing be clear, concise, and focused sharply on the issue at hand, but the type should be easy to read; margins should be large enough that each page does not look oppressively dense; and headings should look like headings (and not like part of the text). A visually inviting document is more likely to be read with care.

4. Argumentation Ethics

The rules of professional ethics place limits on what you are permitted to do in argument.

First and most basically, a lawyer is forbidden to "[k]nowingly make a false statement of law or fact" to a court.[19] The whole system of adjudication would break down if lawyers did not speak honestly to courts.

Second, a lawyer is required to inform a court of "legal authority *in the controlling jurisdiction* known to the lawyer to be *directly adverse* to the position of the [lawyer's] client and not disclosed by opposing counsel."[20] The system of adjudication would suffer immeasurably if courts could not depend on lawyers to give a full account of controlling law. (Section 25.5 explores ways to comply with this requirement while least damaging your case.)

Third, a lawyer is not permitted to advance a theory or argument that is "frivolous" except that a lawyer may make a "good faith argument for an extension, modification or reversal of existing law."[21] In a legal system like ours, where "the law is not always clear and never is static," the rules of ethics permit a lawyer to advance theories and arguments that take advantage "of the law's ambiguities and potential for change."[22] But a frivolous theory or argument—one that stands little chance of being adopted by a court—is unfair to courts and to opposing parties because it wastes their time, effort, and resources.

Separate court rules—procedural, rather than ethical in nature—also punish lawyers who make frivolous arguments. In federal trial courts, for example, every "written motion, or other paper" must be signed by an attorney, whose signature certifies "that to the best of the [signer's] knowledge, information,

18. *American Iron & Steel Institute v. Environmental Protection Agency,* 115 F.3d 990 (D.C. Cir. 1997).
19. Rule 3.3(a)(1) of the Model Rules of Professional Conduct.
20. Rule 3.3(a)(2) of the Model Rules of Professional Conduct.
21. Rule 3.1 of the Model Rules of Professional Conduct.
22. Comment to Rule 3.1 of the Model Rules of Professional Conduct.

and belief, formed after inquiry reasonable under the circumstances . . . the claims, defenses, and other legal contentions therein are warranted by existing law or by a nonfrivolous argument for the extension, modification, or reversal of existing law or the establishment of new law."[23] Where that standard is violated, the court has the power to impose monetary fines on the offending lawyer.[24] Similar rules govern in appellate courts.[25]

B.   HARVESTING ARGUMENTS FROM NONMANDATORY AUTHORITIES

If you are writing to a trial court, you need to know first whether a mandatory authority governs the issue directly. If you are writing to a court of last resort, or if there are no mandatory authorities that are directly on point, you may need to look beyond mandatory authorities. First, if you are in a state court or in a federal court other than the Supreme Court, you should determine whether your jurisdiction is within the mainstream. If your jurisdiction is the first to tackle a new interpretation of the law, or a new cause of action entirely, one side or the other may be able to argue that it is now time to return to the old way of doing things. Conversely, if all or most of your sister jurisdictions have made a jurisprudential change, one side can argue that it is time for this jurisdiction to make the change as well.

Whether you are arguing to a trial court, an intermediate court of appeals, or a court of last resort, you need to decide whether to cite nonmandatory, or even nonjursidictional, authorities. If your jurisdiction is within the mainstream and if authorities within your jurisdiction are sufficiently on point to answer your legal question, there may be no need to cite authorities outside of that jurisdiction. If your jurisdiction is out of the mainstream or if there are no authorities that are directly on point, you may want to consult nonmandatory or nonjurisdictional authorities as well.

If you have not already done so, now is a good time to identify "foundational search terms": These are unique statute numbers or legal phrases that always pull up on-point authorities. They may pull up other authorities as well; I call them *foundational* search terms because they include the fundamental, or foundational, legal terms that are relevant to a particular legal issue. Often, you will discover foundational search terms as part of your research, so don't be surprised if you can't identify them until well into your research. For example, if you were arguing that an employer should ban smoking in the workplace, you would discover the term *safe workplace* in a relevant statute. Both the statute number and the term *safe workplace* could be good *foundational search terms*. A Boolean search that looked for the statute number *or* the term *safe workplace* would be a broad search, but if you limit it to the mandatory authority database,[26] you would be sure to find every case in which the court of last resort in your jurisdiction addressed the issue of safe workplaces.

23. Fed. R. Civ. P. 11.
24. *Id.*
25. For example: "If a court of appeals determines that an appeal is frivolous, it may . . . award just damages and single or double costs to the appellee." Fed. R. App. P. 38.
26. For example, Lexis and Westlaw have search techniques that would allow you to limit your search to just the highest court in the particular jurisdiction.

Search the foundational search terms in your mandatory database to make sure you have the last word on how the court of last resort has interpreted the crucial word, phrase, or statute at issue. You should review each case from within the last few years to make sure that you are up to date on the mandatory authority. In addition, you should find the most recent cases in your jurisdiction to have addressed the issue in any way, even if they were not decided by the court of last resort. If your search pulls up too many hits, try using the *when* clause from your research question to help you to identify fact-based search terms to add to your search, which will help you discover the authorities that are most on point. In the smoke-in-the-workplace case, for example, you could add "cigarette or tobacco or smoking or smoke or fumes" to narrow your search.

If there are relevant authorities in your jurisdiction but no authorities that are sufficiently on point, plug your fact-based foundational search into databases outside your jurisdiction. In this way you may be able to discover any cases that are on-point as to issues and facts and that can therefore serve as persuasive authority. Although these cases would be a *source* of an argument rather than an authority for it,[27] courts often find on-point authorities to be helpful guideposts, even when they are not mandatory.

Further, you may be able to "harvest" effective arguments from nonmandatory authorities both within and outside your jurisdiction. When I refer to *harvesting* an argument, I am suggesting that you use the raw materials from an argument or an analysis and then figure out how to *make* that same argument to your court. Harvesting an argument from a nonmandatory or nonjurisdictional authority is a very different thing than *citing* an argument from such an authority. When you harvest an argument, you let nonmandatory or nonjurisdictional sources help to direct your research.

Suppose, for example, that you are arguing that the Americans with Disabilities Act (ADA) forbids your client's employer from requiring her to submit to medical testing. You are arguing the case in a motion brief in a circuit that has no mandatory authority governing the issue. The statutory section at issue, 42 U.S.C. §12112(d)(4)(A), provides:

> Prohibited examinations and inquiries
> A covered entity shall not require a medical examination and shall not make inquiries of an employee as to whether such employee is an individual with a disability or as to the nature or severity of the disability, unless such examination or inquiry is shown to be job-related and consistent with business necessity.

You are arguing that the term *employee* in this section means "any employee," while your opponent is arguing that the term means only "qualified individuals with disabilities." In your research, you discover a case from a nonmandatory authority that looks at the ways that the terms *employee* and *qualified individual with a disability* are used throughout the statute. That court alludes to statutory and regulatory language that supports your conclusion:

> A plaintiff need not prove that he or she has a disability unknown to his or her employer in order to challenge a medical inquiry or examination under 42 U.S.C. §12112(d)(4)(A). In contrast to other parts of the ADA, the statutory language

---

27. Chapter 16 explains the difference between "sources" and "authorities."

does not refer to qualified individuals with disabilities, but instead merely to "employees." 42 U.S.C. §12112(d)(4)(A).

McGuffin v. Bernard, 444 F. Supp. 2d 455, 472 (S.D. Ohio 2009).[28]

A writer who merely *cited* that nonjurisdictional case as authority would not use it effectively:

Bad Example

The United States District Court for the Southern District of Ohio has observed that the term "employee" in 42 U.S.C. §12122(d)(4)(A) must refer to all employees and not just to those employees who are qualified individuals with disabilities. McGuffin v. Bernard, 444 F. Supp. 2d 455, 472 (S.D. Ohio 2009). It noted that Congress had used the phrase "qualified individual with disabilities" in other sections of the ADA and could have done so in §12122(d)(4)(A) if it so desired. Id. Therefore, when the ADA forbids medical inquiries directed to "an employee," the term must mean. . . .

To harvest the argument effectively, the writer should let the nonmandatory source direct further research. The writer should observe that the court based its analysis—at least implicitly—on a governing rule that says that when Congress uses the same term in more than one section of a statute, the term should be interpreted consistently, and when Congress chooses a different term, it must have intended the term to mean something different. This observation should lead the writer to conduct research to find an appropriate rule in the mandatory jurisdiction. But that is not enough. It would be ineffective to merely cite the mandatory rule and state the same conclusory analysis. Instead, the writer should also research the language of the statute and figure out how best to apply the rule regarding consistent interpretation of terms to the "fact" of the statutory language:[29]

Good Example

When Congress uses one term in one part of a statute and a different term in another, this court should assume that different meanings were intended. Cucilich Industries v. Perek, 599 F.3d 947, 955 (18th Cir. 2009). In Cucilich Industries, the Eighteenth Circuit analyzed the Carriage of Goods by Rail Act and noted that "Congress chose to use different terms in [the Act] when referring to the 'shipper' in conjunction with other parties, on the one hand, and the 'shipper' alone, on the other." Id. at 956. Accordingly, the court refused to interpret the term "shipper" in one clause in the same way that it interpreted the phrase "shipper, receiver, or holder of bill of lading." Id. at 958.

---

28. The language from this fictional case is adapted from *Lee v. City of Columbus*, 644 F. Supp. 2d 1000, 1011 (S.D. Ohio 2009).

29. The example mentions fictional case law that is adapted from *Sosa v. Alvarez-Machain*, 542 U.S. 692, 712 (2004) and *APL Co. Pte v. UK Aerosols Ltd.*, 582 F.3d 947, 952 (9th Cir. 2009).

When Congress chose to use the term "employee" in 42 U.S.C. §12112(d)(4)(A) of the ADA, it did so in order to refer to all "employees" of the employing entity, and the term should not be interpreted to mean "qualified individual with a disability." The terms "employee" and "qualified individual" are defined separately in the Act, at §§12111(4) and 12111(8), respectively. Section 12114(c) specifies limits that can be imposed on "employees," while other sections speak specifically to qualified individuals with a disability. Section 12122(b)(5)(A), for example, notes that discrimination against a "qualified individual on the basis of disability" includes not making reasonable accommodations for "an otherwise qualified individual with a disability." Similarly, §12112(b)(5)(B) forbids denying employment in certain circumstances to "an otherwise qualified individual with a disability." Accordingly. . . .

Thus, one way to "harvest" an argument is to unpack a relevant legal conclusion from a nonmandatory source. Do some research to find a mandatory rule that would lead to that conclusion, and articulate it and explain it appropriately. Then, apply that rule completely and effectively to the appropriate facts in your client's case.[30]

If you believe that the court you are writing to would find the nonmandatory source to be meaningful, you could include a "see also" citation[31] to that authority, but you should not presume that one is appropriate. In the alternative, if the area of law were novel or the facts or legal issues in the nonmandatory cases were particularly relevant, the writer might follow the citations to the mandatory authorities with a discussion of the nonmandatory authority, perhaps beginning the discussion by noting, "This is just the approach taken by the Fifteenth Circuit in a very similar case. . . . "

To sum up, when designing and executing your research plan, think ahead, but be ready to explore new leads as you learn more about your case and its issues.

C.   CHOOSING ISSUES RESPONSIBLY

One of the first ways that advocates establish their credibility is by arguing only those issues—and cases—that are worthy of argument. Most law students cannot choose which issues to argue, but they can choose how many arguments to make. Soon, they will be choosing the issues, as well as deciding whether a case or a motion is worth filing or whether an appeal is worth pursuing. You should appeal any case and make any argument that has a credible chance of a positive result, but use good judgment when making those decisions, and

---

30. Of course, it is vitally important to note that plagiarism rules vary greatly in academic settings and in litigation settings in practice. In an academic setting, if you "harvest" an argument from an authority, you should always note the source of the argument. When writing litigation materials in an academic setting, the best course might be to drop a footnote and indicate the nonmandatory source of the argument. Some teachers might give you permission to remove the citation, but presume that you should include the citation unless instructed otherwise.

31. The Sample Motion Brief in Appendix C [Mary Beth Beazley, A Practical Guide to Appellate Advocacy, 3rd ed., (2010)] uses this technique.

remember the busy courts to whom you are arguing. A marginal argument weakens the advocate's present and future credibility; a brief that addresses fewer issues argued well is better than a brief with many issues argued poorly.

Judge Patricia Wald, of the United States Court of Appeals for the District of Columbia Circuit, notes: "Confident counsel should almost always go for broke and rely on their one or two best arguments, abandoning the other 9-10 wish-list entries. . . . The fewer arguments you make the more attention they will get from us in preparing and disposing of your case."[32] Judge Pierce notes that trial judges make "relatively few mistakes" and that a brief that asserts a half-dozen or more key points of error may "needlessly divert" the judge's attention from the more compelling grounds, with the result that the court's ability to recognize the validity of any one of the grounds "decreases significantly."[33] Similarly, former Chief Justice Burger has noted that "a brief that raises every colorable issue runs the risk of burying good arguments."[34] Judge Wiener advises that counsel should "[d]ecide which legal arguments are key to resolving the issues of the case in your client's favor," and should "[f]orce" themselves to "omit fringe issues and far-out theories; they will only dull the thrust of your appeal and obscure the potentially winning points."[35] Finally, Judge Parker notes that you do a disservice to your client when you raise too many issues on appeal, noting that if you raise 20 issues and give them all "equal [time]—and therefore, short-shrift," you may fail to convince the court that the district court "committed just one error which justifies some relief for your client."[36]

Thus, when choosing issues and arguments, restrict your brief to those that are best supported by both the law and the facts. Not every error is worthy of appeal, or even of argument. Before arguing about an error in the trial court, identify a causal link between the error and the court's judgment against your client; without that link, the error is irrelevant. Before filing a motion, identify a valid purpose for that motion. While some motions may be filed as a method of narrowing issues rather than in a bona fide attempt to dispose of the whole case, be sure that you are not wasting the court's time. Further, remember that the validity of each individual argument has an impact on the whole brief. Every specious argument chips away at your overall credibility. When all the arguments are legitimate, on the other hand, the stock of the whole brief and of counsel rises.

32. Patricia M. Wald, 19 *Tips from 19 Years on the Appellate Bench*, 1 J. App. Prac. & Process 7, 11 (1999).

33. Lawrence W. Pierce, *Appellate Advocacy: Some Reflections from the Bench*, 61 Fordham L. Rev. 829, 835-36 (1993).

34. *Jones v. Barnes*, 463 U.S. 745, 751-52 (1983).

35. Jacques L. Wiener, Jr., *Ruminations from the Bench: Brief Writing and Oral Argument in the Fifth Circuit*, 70 Tul. L. Rev. 187, 194 (1995).

36. Parker, *supra* note 2, at 460.

CHAPTER

15

Organization

A. CHOOSING AN ORDER FOR THE ARGUMENTS

1. *Ordering Point Headings*

Your draft already has working point headings, but you have not yet decided the *order* in which they should appear. While no one right order exists, the most common choices for ordering point headings are (1) ordering by strength on the law, (2) ordering by strength on the equities, (3) ordering by the reader's priorities, and (4) ordering by familiarity.

a. Order by Strength on the Law

If one or two points are significantly stronger on the law than the others, you will nearly always want to order them by strength, placing the strongest point first. You already have a good idea of the virtues of this order. A reader's attention to the argument is greatest at the beginning and drops off rapidly after the first few pages. Judges are busy and want to see the strongest arguments first. As a matter of fact, some busy judges might read carefully only the first fifteen pages or so. Because the first fifteen pages include the Introduction and Statement of Facts, such a judge is reading carefully only the first eight to ten pages of the Argument. Judges usually presume that the strongest argument is first, and thus prejudge the subsequent arguments as even weaker.

b. Order by Strength on the Equities

Some arguments rely primarily on rules of *law* and some rely primarily on the equities, that is, on *facts* that speak to the judge's sense of justice. If your points are of relatively equal legal strength, you may choose to order them according to their equitable (factual) strength. You will be able to identify which is which

243

by asking yourself, "Which of these points really sounds like an appeal to justice? Which convinces me that one or more of these parties *should* win, as opposed to which party is *supposed* to win?"

If you have a point that relies heavily on the equities, you should capitalize on those favorable equities up front. A reader whose sense of justice is already convinced will be much more willing to accept your legal analysis. Such a reader will *want* you to be right on the law. You can capitalize on the equities in two ways: by placing the point strongest on the equities first or by placing it last. If your points are relatively equal in legal strength, you might decide to order your points by their equitable strength, placing the strongest first.

However, strange as this might sound, sometimes you can capitalize more effectively on a point with favorable equities by placing it last. This makes more sense when you remember that your reader will read the brief's Fact Statement before reading the Argument section. In Chapter 22 [Linda H. Edwards, Legal Writing: Process, Analysis, and Organization, 5th ed., (2010)] we will see that a brief-writer can make an argument implicitly (especially an equitable one) by doing a careful job on the brief's Statement of Facts. The Statement of Facts precedes the Argument section. It tells the story of the events that led to the pending issues. It should make no express reference to the law, and yet it might well be the section of the brief with the most potential for persuasion. Of course your argument section must still make the argument expressly, but a well-drafted Fact Statement could allow you to present the reader with the equities even earlier than the first legal argument.

In such a case, placing the point with favorable equities last has additional advantages. First, it lets the favorable facts convince your reader without any express argument from you. This can work well because the Fact Statement does not seem like the argument of a litigant and thus the reader's level of skepticism is not as high as when reading an express legal argument.

Second, leaving space between the presentation of the facts and the argument you will make about them allows the reader to reach the desired conclusion before you articulate it. Thus, she might think of the conclusion as primarily her own. As you recall from Chapter 3, a reader clings more tenaciously to a position she thinks she reached herself than to a conclusion first argued by another. Then, when the reader encounters the argument articulated by the writer at the end of the Argument section, the writer's argument will seem to confirm the reader's own well-grounded conclusions.

c. Order by Your Reader's Priorities

Occasionally your brief will have a point heading with priority in the mind of your reader, the judge. This priority will stem from the judge's preference for basing a judicial opinion on some kinds of legal rulings rather than on others. For instance, courts normally decide issues on jurisdictional grounds first, on procedural grounds second, and on substantive grounds last. Judges often prefer to decide issues on narrow grounds rather than on broad grounds. When both a constitutional ground and a nonconstitutional ground are dispositive, constitutional jurisprudence requires courts to decide as many of the issues as possible on the nonconstitutional ground.

Because your reader will have these preferences, you must take them seriously when choosing an order for your point headings. If the issues with priority for the judge also happen to be your strongest arguments, your decision is easy—order the points according to the judge's priorities. However, if your client's position on the judge's priority argument is weak, you must decide whether you can afford to place it first. Usually your best choice will be to place your strongest points first, but to use an umbrella section to assure the judge that your argument will address the other point as well.[1] Of course, you will not want to announce that you have placed that point last because your client's position on it is weak, but rather that your client's argument on the first point is so dispositive that consideration of the remaining point may be unnecessary.

d.   Order by Familiarity

Recall from Chapter 11 [Linda H. Edwards, Legal Writing: Process, Analysis, and Organization, 5th ed., (2010)] that the order of the elements of some legal rules has become familiar to law-trained readers. Judges, however, seldom expect to see a preordained order in a brief because they are used to seeing points ordered by strength. For brief-writing, ordering by familiarity is useful if your points are of relatively equal legal and equitable strength and if your reader has no particular priorities for considering the issues.

2.   *Ordering Subheadings*

Subheadings have three primary functions in a brief. First, they provide your reader with an easily identifiable road map of your argument. Second, they allow your reader to pause for a moment, and thus invite increased attention levels at the beginning and end of each subsection.[2] Third, they make visible the persuasive rule structure you formulated.

The working draft has already identified the primary subheadings.[3] Now, as you convert the working draft to the Argument section, order subheadings of equal rank according to the organizational principles described above for point headings.

Usually, further subdivisions are not necessary and can even be confusing. Occasionally, however, when the discussion under a subheading is long or complex, further divisions within the discussion can help the reader follow the argument. If you need additional demarcation to help your reader follow the argument, you can subdivide by any logical categories. The first level of subheadings, however, should match the issues addressed by the brief and should reflect rather than obscure the rule's structure.

---

1. *See* pp. 301-159 [Linda H. Edwards, Legal Writing: Process, Analysis, and Organization, 5th ed., (2010)].

2. *See* Chapter 11 [Linda H. Edwards, Legal Writing: Process, Analysis, and Organization, 5th ed., (2010)], pp. 150-151 [Linda H. Edwards, Legal Writing: Process, Analysis, and Organization, 5th ed., (2010)].

3. *See* Chapter 19 [Linda H. Edwards, Legal Writing: Process, Analysis, and Organization, 5th ed., (2010)], pp. 150-151.

B.   HANDLING CONCESSIONS AND REBUTTALS

Many legal arguments entail two potential troublespots: concessions and rebuttals of the opponent's argument. While both enable the court to fully understand the case, they also distract from the affirmative argument you want to make on the client's behalf. Hence, both should be handled with care.

1.   *Concessions*

The need to present a concession arises when the two sides concur on a point and that point favors your client's opponent. Concessions may be handled several ways. The first two are true concessions, while the third is a limited-purpose concession.

First, you may by omission implicitly concede the point, neither stating the point nor presenting an argument to the contrary. For example, you could note that the issue concerns a statute and begin your argument with a discussion of the exceptions, implicitly conceding that your client's case falls within the scope and general rule of the statute.

Other techniques for handling concessions involve explicit statements of the conceded point. In the technique known as "confession and avoidance," you state the conceded point but move on to an argument that nullifies the harmful impact of the concession. For example, you could state that the client's conduct falls within a statutory definition, yet argue that the client's conduct is permitted by a statutory exception.

In a third technique known as "assuming arguendo," you state the conceded point for purposes of the present argument only, and you emphasize that the point is not conceded beyond the present argument. For example, you would argue first that your client is outside the scope of the statute, then assume arguendo that the client falls within the statute's scope to show how its conduct is governed by a statutory exception.

Whenever you are stating a concession, you would use the methods described in this chapter to deflect the reader's attention from the concession. For example, you could allocate little space to the concession, place it in a dependent clause, or state it in passive voice or nominalization. Indeed, if you deem the concession unnecessary to the logical flow of your argument, you could place it in a footnote. Meanwhile, you would allocate more space to your argument responding to the concession, place that argument in the main clause, or use active voice to express it.

In the sample briefs in the HomeElderCare case, several concessions appear. HomeElderCare implicitly conceded that its social workers are not licensed as lawyers; its argument proceeds directly from a quotation of the unauthorized practice statute to the prohibition against giving legal advice (at page 385). Figure 15.5 presents two explicit concessions; note how affirmative arguments tightly frame both concessions.

C. RULE APPLICATION FOR RULES WITH FACTORS OR GUIDELINES: ADVANCED TECHNIQUES

The organizational pattern usually best for the rule *explanation* of a rule with permissive subparts (factors or guidelines) is organizing according to the factors.[4] However, a writer can organize the rule *application* section of the paradigm in several different ways. These organizational decisions can significantly affect the persuasiveness of a brief.

1. First Organizational Option: By Factor

Because rule application generally mirrors rule explanation, the factor-by-factor pattern often organizes rule *application* as well. The working draft using this pattern would explain the factors, one by one, and then apply them one by one:

I. A LAWYER MUST EXERCISE THE SAME STANDARD OF CARE THAT WOULD BE EXERCISED BY A REASONABLE AND PRUDENT LAWYER PRACTICING IN THAT JURISDICTION.

   Paradigm

Rule explanation:

- first factor
- second factor
- third factor
- etc.

   Rule application:

- first factor
- second factor
- third factor
- etc.

Conclusion

Consider, for example, this statute governing a judge's decision on child custody in a divorce:

As between the parents, custody is to be decided according to the best interests of the child. The court may consider the following factors in deciding the best interests of the child:

4. *See* Chapter 9 [Linda H. Edwards, Legal Writing: Process, Analysis, and Organization, 5th ed., (2010)].

Figure 15.5
Concessions and Rebuttals

Confession and Avoidance (in Mr. Nelson's brief)

The *Gardner* rule must be applied in "a common sense way which will protect the public and not hamper or burden that public interest with impractical and technical restrictions which have no reasonable justification." [citation omitted] The restriction on social workers preparing living wills may burden the social worker who wishes to practice law. [confession] But the restriction is not impractical or merely technical; it is more than reasonably justified when viewed from the proper perspective—the client's. [avoidance]
(Sentences developing the client's perspective follow.)

Assuming arguendo (in the HomeElderCare brief)

To avoid the rendering of legal advice, HomeElderCare policy calls for the social worker to suggest that the client consult an attorney if the client wishes to deviate from the form or has legal questions. Thus, the social worker did not provide legal advice. [affirmative argument]
However, even if the social worker touched on legal matters, [concession for purposes of proceeding], the service would not constitute the unauthorized practice of law under Minnesota case law. [next affirmative argument]

Rebuttal (in a footnote in the HomeElderCare brief)

As it does for all its services, HomcElderCare charged a fee for its living will services. [factual introduction] The charging of a fee should not render this service the practice of law [Mr. Nelson's argument], any more than the charging of a fee for home maintenance services would render that service the practice of law. *Cf. Cardinal v. Merrill Lynch Realty/Burnet, Inc.* . . . . [rebuttal]

---

1. the fitness of each parent
2. the appropriateness for parenting of the lifestyle of each parent
3. the relationship of the child to each parent
4. the placement of other children
5. the child's living accommodations
6. the district lines of the child's school
7. the proximity of extended family and friends
8. religious issues
9. any other factors relevant to the child's best interests

In rule application, the writer *could* simply apply each factor, one by one, just as the rule explanation explained each factor.
    To evaluate this choice, look first at the effect of organizing rule application according to the statute's list of factors. Recall that readers keep score. Recall that keeping score, factor by factor, implicitly tends to equalize the importance of the factors; yet few readers will compensate consciously for the effect of this phenomenon. Thus, organizing according to the statute's list of factors tends to equalize the emphasis on favorable and unfavorable factors.

Second, organizing according to the list will expose any weaknesses of the client's facts on any particular factor. Such an organization limits flexibility. The writer cannot combine weaker factors with stronger factors that may offset the particular weakness. Nor can the writer identify a strategic theme (sometimes called a "theory of the case") and use the organization of the legal argument as one way of explaining this theme to the judge.

The *theory of the case* is your version of what really happened or what the case is really about. It usually has a theme that incorporates and makes sense of the facts proven at trial. For instance, in the child custody case, one theory of the case might be that the father is an unfit parent. A different theory of the case would be that the father is a fit parent, but that the mother would be a better custodial parent for this particular child at this particular time. These theories would use the same facts to tell different stories about the case. These different theories would require significantly different strategies, both in writing and in many other aspects of handling the case.

If you suspect that organizing rule application by the list of factors might not be your best choice, ask yourself (1) if the statute and its context offer any other possibilities for categories and (2) what categories you would like to use if the statute hadn't created any. For our custody example, both inquiries will give you other possibilities.

2. *Second Organizational Option: By Party*

The procedural context of this statute offers at least one other organizational choice because the statute operates when the judge is deciding which parent will be awarded custody. Thus, one option is to organize the rule application by party. Such a discussion, written on behalf of the mother, might look like this:

I. BEST INTERESTS OF THE CHILD

As between the parents, custody is to be decided according to the best interests of the child. The court may consider the following factors in deciding the best interests of the child: [list]

Rule explanation [explaining the factors one by one]
Rule application:

- Interests served by awarding custody to mother:

  [Discuss, in the best light possible, the statute's identified factors that favor the mother. Since the statute allows consideration of other factors, discuss also any unidentified factors that favor the mother.]

- Interests served by awarding custody to father:

  [Discuss, in a less favorable light, the factors that favor the father. Compare these to the interests served by awarding custody to mother, showing that the latter outweighs the former.]

We cannot fully evaluate an organizational plan without reference to the facts and legal authorities controlling the particular case. Yet we can observe at least four advantages of this organization, even without reference to facts and authorities. First, this organization would be flexible; it would allow the writer to combine factors, to emphasize and deemphasize, and to advance a theme within each subsection. The writer could communicate a primary theme about the advantages of placement with the mother and could communicate a different primary theme about the disadvantages of placement with the father. Second, this organization has the appearance of objectivity. It is the classic "on the one hand this; on the other hand that" structure. Because its *structure* appears neutral, it might reduce the reader's skepticism.

Third, it immediately equalizes the score being kept by a reader. If the majority of the statute's identified factors would favor the opposing party, using this "balancing" format invites the reader to keep score using a much more favorable method. Finally, this organization might be the one most like the judge's natural thought process on this issue. Thus, if the brief-writer has used this organization and has already laid out the analysis in this format, the judge could choose to use that writer's analysis (rather than the opposing writer's analysis) as the starting point for the judge's own reasoning about the issues.

This organizational plan looks like an interesting option—one the brief-writer will want to consider. First, though, the writer must finish identifying other possible plans.

3. *Third Organizational Option: By Theme*

Recall that the second question on page 249 invited you to be more creative. It asked you to imagine that the statute did not identify a set of categories and to decide what categories you would prefer.

Here is the brief-writer's best chance to think about themes. In the final analysis, why should this child be placed with the mother? Why not the father? If the lawyer steps back even further from the categories of the statute, the real heart of the client's position is likely to appear. For instance, perhaps the court-appointed social worker has identified this child's two greatest present needs as stability and a sense of control over his own fate in the midst of this frightening process of divorcing parents. You can see how the statute's identified factors and probably a number of other, unidentified factors would fit under these two categories. You could organize the statute's factors (and any others you want to add) beneath categories defined by these two identified needs. The application section might look like this:

I. BEST INTERESTS OF THE CHILD

As between the parents, custody is to be decided according to the best interests of the child. The court may consider the following factors in deciding the best interests of the child: [list]

Rule explanation [explaining the factors one by one]
Rule application:

Child's need for stability [Discuss each factor that impacts stability:]

- Personal fitness of each parent to provide stability [Argue that placement with the mother would provide more stability because she has a more stable personality, keeps daily activities on a predictable schedule, etc.]
- Personal lifestyle of each parent as it affects stability [Argue that the father travels sometimes and would need either to take the child with him or leave him in the care of a baby-sitter, who would be a new person in the child's life.]
- Relationship of the child to each parent as it affects stability [Argue that, while the child cares deeply for each parent, the child has spent more time with his mother than with his father.]
- Living accommodations as they affect stability [Argue that, while the father's new home is nicer, the mother will be living in the former family home and the child would not have to move.]
- District lines of the child's school as they affect stability [Argue that, while the father's new house is closer to the child's school, stability counsels for having the child continue to ride the same school bus with the same group of children.]
- Any other factors relevant to stability

Child's need for sense of control over his own fate

- Personal fitness of each parent as it affects the child's sense of control [Argue that, while both are fit parents, the mother is more likely than the father to allow the child to make decisions in appropriate areas of the child's life.]
- Other factors affecting the child's sense of control [Argue that the child has decided that he wants to operate a paper route and placement with the father would interfere with his ability to carry out that decision, etc.]
- Any other factors relevant to sense of control.

Such a fact discussion organizes by *theme* or theory of the case rather than by factors. This organization is the most flexible of the three. First, it allows the most room for combining the discussions of some factors, so that they strengthen each other, while isolating other factors, to expose the weakness of the other party's position.

Second, and even more important, this organization allows the writer to mold the statute to suit the client's goals in the particular case. The writer can identify, apart from the statute, this particular child's greatest needs. After these particular needs are identified (and who could argue that the child does *not* need stability and some sense of control?), the fact discussion reorganizes the statute's identified factors, and any others as well, around these strategically identified needs.

Third, this organization allows the writer to emphasize larger and more compelling categories than the factors listed in the statute. Thus, the writer can pit these larger needs of the child against the individual factors that favor the other party. For instance, assume that the father has moved close to the child's grandparents, and placement with the father would have the advantage of proximity to the grandparents. Under this organization, the writer could weigh the child's need for stability against the advantage of proximity to the grandparents rather than weighing the child's need to avoid changing schools against the advantage of proximity to the grandparents. The judge is more likely to agree that, although proximity to grandparents is nice, the need for stability in a child's life is a vital.

Using themes or facts to organize the rule application part of a legal discussion is an advanced writing technique. Although it will sometimes be the most effective choice, take care not to use it unless you are sure that you understand the rule itself and that the rule's meaning will remain identifiable in your organization.

CHAPTER

16

Analogies and Distinctions

A. USING LANGUAGE PRECISELY WHEN ANALOGIZING AND DISTINGUISHING CASES

Analogizing and distinguishing relevant authority cases can be a vital part of the application sections of your argument. By showing the reader how a case is like or unlike a relevant case, a writer can convince the reader to apply the rule in a way that will achieve the desired result. Note that your application section should not *begin* with the analogy or distinction. Instead, begin with an explicit assertion about how the law applies to the facts (generally, "phrase-that-pays equals or does not equal case facts"). Use the relevant cases to support that assertion. Do not begin your application this way:

Bad Example

This case is like <u>McGuffin</u>.

Instead, begin by telling the reader how the law applies to the facts:

Good Example

Mr. Pillion had a reasonable expectation of privacy. Like the defendant in <u>McGuffin</u>, . . .

Your case analogies and distinctions will be most effective if they are *precise*. Do not analogize a specific fact to a whole case:

Bad Example

Like <u>Robinson</u>, the Defendant here had committed an arrestable offense.

This comparison is inapt because one defendant, by definition, cannot be "like" a whole case. Make your analogy or distinction specific. Compare defendants to defendants, and other actors and things to their specific counterparts in the authority case. These illustrations make the comparisons explicit:

Good Examples

In the present case, Respondents, like the defendants in <u>Lewis</u> and <u>Hicks</u>, were present on property for the sole purpose of conducting criminal business.

Like the officer in <u>Lewis</u>, Officer Thielen observed only activities that were a necessary part of Respondents' illegal business. During the entire time Officer Thielen watched the apartment occupants, the occupants did nothing but divide and package cocaine. <u>See</u> Record at E-2, G-14.

Unlike the car at issue in <u>Rakas</u>, an apartment is a private dwelling not normally open to the public view.

These examples also provide details from the client's case that make the analogies vivid. The writer must do more than make the bare statement that "this case is like (or unlike) *McGuffin*" if the reader is to see the connection or the disconnection between the two cases. In the next example, the writer takes care to provide the details that will clarify the distinctions between the two cases:

Good Example

Unlike the defendant in <u>Katz</u>, who argued that he sought privacy by closing the door to his phone booth, Respondents introduced no evidence of conduct that demonstrated an intent to keep their activities private. Though the blinds were drawn, there is no indication that Respondents drew them. <u>See</u> Record at E-2, E-10. On the night in question, Respondents were present in a first-floor apartment that had several windows <u>at</u> ground level. Record G-26. The windows faced a public area that apartment residents and nonresidents frequented. Record G-69, G-70. As darkness fell in early evening, Respondents sat illuminated under a chandelier light at a table directly in front of one of these windows. Record G-13. Only a pane of glass and a set of blinds that featured a series of laths, Record G-50, separated Respondents from the adjacent common area. On the night in question, the blinds, though drawn, had a gap in them; the gap was large enough for a citizen who passed by and an officer who stood a foot or more from the window to view easily the entire illuminated interior scene. Record G-13.

Individuals in Respondents' position would have known and expected that a passerby could look through the gaps in the blinds and see into the illuminated kitchen. Thus, Respondents could not have actually expected that their illegal activities would go unnoticed.

This application is somewhat long, but the details are necessary for the reader to understand how the law applies to the facts. Although analogies and distinctions are not always needed, make sure that when you do include them, you focus them on the specific people or things that you want to compare. Second, make sure that you provide the details that allow the reader to understand both the comparison and the application of law to facts.

CHAPTER

17

Policy Arguments

A. MAKING POLICY ARGUMENTS

1. Why Policy Is Especially Important in an Appeal

Policy matters in an appellate court for two reasons. First, when a court enforces a rule of law, it tries to do so in a way that accomplishes the policy behind the rule. In any court—trial or appellate—your odds of winning increase if you can show that the decision you want would achieve important public goals.

Second, a substantial part of an appellate court's work is clarifying ambiguous law and making new law. The higher up you go in the appellate system, the more that is true. Clarifying the law and making new law are virtually the only things the U.S. Supreme Court does. When a court makes law in this way, it tries to do so consistently with policies that are already accepted in the law (or should be).

When you appear before a court in a law-making case, judges will naturally ask questions like this: What rule of law would a decision in your favor stand for (remembering that it would become binding precedent)? In what words would that rule be most accurately expressed? If the court does as you request, how would the law in the future treat facts that are similar to—but not exactly the same as—yours? What would be the practical effects in the courts, in the economy, and in society as a whole? Why is the rule you advocate better than the one your adversary urges?

In your brief, make policy arguments that would answer these questions persuasively.

2. Types of Policy Arguments

The following article will help you choose public policies and argue them.

TEACHING STUDENTS TO MAKE EFFECTIVE POLICY ARGUMENTS IN APPELLATE BRIEFS

Ellie Margolis
9 Perspectives 73 (2001)

. . . While there are several different types of policy arguments, all policy arguments share the common attribute of advocating that a proposed legal rule [or a proposed interpretation of a statute or constitutional provision] will benefit society, or advance a particular social goal (or conversely, that the proposed rule [or interpretation] will cause harm and should not be adopted). . . . Thus, all policy arguments involve an assessment of how a proposed rule will function in the real world. . . .

A.   JUDICIAL ADMINISTRATION ARGUMENTS

. . . These are arguments about the practical administration of the rule by the courts. The goal at the heart of these arguments is a fair and efficient judicial system. . . .

The dual goals of fairness and efficiency are sometimes at odds, however. This tension gives rise to the first type of judicial administration argument, the "firm vs. flexible rule" argument. The argument for a firm rule is that a clear, specific standard will be easy for the court to administer, and therefore promote efficiency. A firm rule also promotes fairness by leaving little room for judicial discretion and leading to more consistent application, which makes it easier for [the public] to understand the rule and act accordingly [because of the] adoption of a clear, precise rule. The "flexible rule" argument, on the other hand, focuses more heavily on fairness. The argument for a flexible rule is that flexibility will allow the court to . . . take into account the individual circumstances of each case[, which would be] more responsive and fair. . . .

There are three other judicial administration arguments that focus primarily on efficiency. These can be made individually or combined with the firm/flexible rule arguments. The first is the "floodgates of litigation" argument.[*] This argument asserts that a proposed rule, if adopted, will inundate the court with lawsuits. . . .

The second of these arguments is the "slippery slope" argument [which] asserts that if the proposed rule is adopted, the court will not be able to prevent its application to a broader and broader set of cases. First it will be applied to one new circumstance, then another, leading the court to hear a whole range of cases it had never intended to entertain [—and may additionally] lead to a large number of frivolous claims. . . .

The final judicial administration argument asserts that a proposed rule, even if firm, is so complex that it will be impossible to administer efficiently[,] . . . making it difficult [for the public] to understand and comply with the law [and] undermin[ing] judicial efficiency by requiring a large number of judicial resources in order to resolve claims under the rule.

---

*This argument is much overused and used inappropriately. Over the years, I have seen many student briefs making "floodgate" arguments because the students knew they should make some kind of policy argument and this was the only one they could think of. While this argument still has value it should be used selectively, and only where truly appropriate.

B.   Normative Arguments

. . . Although there is a significant overlap between different types of normative arguments, they can be broken down into roughly three categories: moral arguments, social utility arguments, and corrective justice arguments. Normative arguments tend to appear more "political" in nature because, in today's complex society, there is rarely widespread social consensus on issues of morality or other social good. As a result, the goal of a normative policy is not always as obvious or easy to establish as the goal in a judicial administration argument.

Moral arguments generally take the form of asserting that a particular rule should be adopted because it is consistent with generally accepted standards of society. . . .

. . . Under [a social utility] argument, the advocate asserts that a proposed rule will serve a social good and benefit society, or conversely, that it will undermine a social value and harm society [—because it] either deters or encourages conduct that affects . . . public health, public safety, economic health, [or] national security. Social utility arguments are particularly useful in tort law cases. . . .

[A] corrective justice argument . . . centers on the goal of fairness and asserts that as between two innocents, the one that caused the damage should be responsible. . . . In common law cases of first impression, [when] the court is being asked to establish a new cause of action, [especially in torts,] corrective justice arguments could be very useful.

C.   Institutional Competence Arguments

. . . These are arguments about which branch of government (generally the judiciary or the legislature) should address a particular issue. . . .

[Although a legislature is the primary creator of new law, u]nder the common law method, judges have the power to fill in gaps in the law and formulate new rules . . . creating the potential for arguments over whether an issue is better suited to the courts or the legislature.

An argument that an issue is better suited for the courts focuses on the nature of courts as institutions set up for resolving individual disputes. . . . The argument would emphasize the court's ability to [act on the facts before it when the legislature has not acted and to learn facts from] witnesses and make objective determinations of credibility. . . .

The argument that the legislature is better suited . . . asserts that the courts are not competent to resolve the issue because . . . the legislature [is better able] to reflect changes in public opinion, and to hold hearings and gather complex and varied facts that may not be relevant in the [narrow] context of litigation. . . .

D.   Economic Arguments

. . . One form of economic argument focuses on the efficient allocation of resources. . . . For example, a rule might be desirable because it spreads loss over a large segment of the population. On the other hand, a defendant trying to avoid liability in a products liability suit might argue that the cost of such liability will be passed on to the public, ultimately punishing those the rule was designed to benefit.

Another form of economic argument asserts that a cost-benefit analysis dictates that a rule should be adopted. Under this analysis, the arguer must show that the economic benefits of a rule outweigh the costs of implementing it. . . . The key to a cost-benefits analysis is the determination of the factors going into the cost. In addition to obvious costs, such as the monetary costs of fixing a defective part, costs such emotional damage can be factored in. . . .

A third type of economic policy argument is that the proposed rule will have a positive or negative effect on economic efficiency and affect the operation of the free-market economy[, asserting, for example,] that a proposed rule would either promote or inhibit competition. . . .

3. How to Make a Policy Argument

The preceding section of this chapter describes the most frequently used policies. Look at the cases and statutes you have found in your research. What policies do they enunciate? When you write the brief, make policy arguments in three steps:

Step 1: Identify one or more public policies that a decision in your favor would further. Tell the court exactly which policy or policies you want the court to be guided by.

Step 2: Persuade the court that the policy or policies you have identified are valuable. Your adversary will urge competing policies. Show that yours are more important. It's not enough just to say yours are worth more. Prove it with argument.

Step 3: Show exactly how a decision in your favor will further the policy or policies you have identified. Don't assume that the court will understand how. Explain it *specifically.*

Policy arguments are much stronger if supported by authority. If the policy you urge has already been recognized by the courts in other cases, cite and explain those cases. If the legislature has adopted the policy in enacting statutes that are not directly related to your case, cite those statutes and explain how they reflect the policy you are urging. If you have only a few cases or statutes, try to find secondary authority, such as treatises and law review articles, that explain policies that should govern your case. You might also cite and explain nonlegal sources that show a genuine public need. For example, if you argue that the courts should adopt strict tort rules assigning liability for contamination with industrial chemicals, you can cite scientific studies showing the presence of PCB's and other toxic chemicals in the food supply.

When a court is being asked to clarify the interpretation of a statute, the court is not free to attach to the statute any policy the court likes. Instead, the court must use the policy the legislature adopted when it enacted the statute. Sometimes that policy is expressed in the statute or the legislative history. If not, the court (with your assistance) must figure out what policy the legislature probably adopted.

When making a policy argument, use the terminology you find in the cases and statutes in preference to the terminology used in this chapter. You will be able to recognize a normative policy when you see one in a case or statute. But when you argue that policy to a court, refer to it in the way the cases or the statutes do. Or simply say in plain language what you mean: "This rule would be consistent with standards of behavior generally accepted throughout society. Specifically, . . . " The terms "normative argument," "social utility argument," and "corrective justice argument" rarely occur in the case law, although many statutes and thousands of cases have adopted policies that can be categorized as normative, social utility, or corrective justice. Courts and law school teachers sometimes use different words to refer to the same policies. When writing for a court, use the wording that judges use.

You might also avoid telling a court that it is a less competent institution than a legislature. It would be more diplomatic to say that the legislature is "in a better position" to decide whether to adopt the rule of law urged by your adversary, or that the decision is a type that "should be reserved to" the legislature. (Then show why.)

B.   PERSUADING USING POLICY-BASED REASONING

Section II [Linda H. Edwards, Legal Writing: Process, Analysis, and Organization, 5th ed., (2010)] reminded you to identify the relevant policy rationales, especially those favorable to your client, and to explain why they support your client's desired result. Courts are virtually always willing to consider important policy rationales. Policy-based reasoning is especially important when you are asking the court to adopt a new rule or to change an existing rule.

Of course, the best sources for identifying relevant policies are the authorities themselves. However, you might also be able to identify some relevant policies simply by using your own common sense. Once you have had a little practice in using policy-based reasoning, you will find it an extraordinarily effective tool of advocacy. To help you get started, here is a list of some common policy rationales:

1. As between two parties, the law should place the risk of liability on the party most able to prevent a loss.
2. As between two parties, the law should place the risk of liability on the party most able to insure against it.
3. As between two parties, the law should place the risk on the party who already bears similar risks and therefore whose legal and practical situation will be least affected by the risk.
4. Where the bargaining positions of certain kinds of parties are grossly disparate, the governing rule should protect the weaker party.
5. The law should not impose a liability that might limit the ability of people to engage in a particular business in the future, especially if the business provides a socially desirable service.
6. The rule should place the burden of proof on the party with the easiest access to the evidence.

7. The governing rule should be workable in light of the practical realities of day-to-day life. It should incorporate a realistic view of human psychology and business custom.

8. The governing rule should not create a legal standard that is easily subverted by knowledgeable and crafty individuals and businesses.

9. Stability in the law is desirable. The law should not change unless the need for the change is clear.

10. The realities of modern life have changed significantly (explain how). The law must be willing and able to change and adapt to changing circumstances.

11. A governing rule should encourage moral behavior in society, such as honesty, fair dealing, and altruism. It should discourage morally questionable behavior, such as greed, scheming, and taking advantage of others who are particularly vulnerable.

12. The law should resist the temptation to rush to the rescue when a refusal to intervene will encourage people to be diligent and responsible in handling their economic and legal affairs.

13. A rule should not create additional costs for a person or an industry unless the harm to be prevented justifies the imposition of those costs.

14. A governing rule should not add impediments to the free transfer of assets and the ease of doing business.

15. A governing rule should maximize individual freedom.

16. A governing rule should be concrete enough to allow people to predict whether the conduct they contemplate will be considered lawful and, therefore, to conform their conduct to the law.

17. A governing rule should be flexible enough to allow future courts enough flexibility to achieve a fair result in individual future circumstances.

18. A governing rule should be concrete enough to insure that future adjudications will be based on objective criteria rather than on prejudices of the decision-maker.

19. It is appropriate for the law to require a higher standard of conduct from a commercial party than from an individual not engaged in a particular business.

20. The governing rule should defer to the expertise of decision-makers most able to decide wisely.

21. A court should adopt a rule that is as consistent with established custom as possible since customs become established because, over time, people have discovered that they work well.

Naturally, you will want to focus on policy rationales that support your client's desired result. In the rule explanation section of your argument, explain these rationales and show why they are desirable. Then in the rule application section, you'll apply to your client's situation not only the relevant legal authorities but also the relevant policy rationales. Explain why your client's desired result would best serve the relevant policy rationales and would not unduly impinge on competing policy concerns.

C.   EVOKING FAVORABLE EMOTIONS AND VALUES

Persuading people requires an understanding of how they respond to emotional as well as logical arguments.[1]
         —John C. Shepherd and Jordan B. Cherrick

In Chapter 2 [Michael R. Smith, Advanced Legal Writing: Theories and Strategies in Persuasive Writing, 2nd ed., (2008)], we saw that under the principles of classical rhetoric the concept of pathos refers to efforts to persuade by appealing to an audience's emotions. We also saw that pathos actually encompasses two separate processes: *emotional substance* (persuading by evoking emotions regarding the substance of the matter under discussion) and *medium mood control* (persuading by evoking a favorable mood through the way an argument is presented). In Chapter 2 [Michael R. Smith, Advanced Legal Writing: Theories and Strategies in Persuasive Writing, 2nd ed., (2008)], we explored in some detail the role of the medium mood control aspect of pathos in persuasive legal writing. This chapter begins our exploration of emotional substance.

1.   The Relationship Between Emotions and Values

Although classical rhetoricians defined pathos as persuading by appealing to an audience's emotions, contemporary psychologists and morality theorists would likely define pathos—if they were asked—as persuading by appealing to an audience's *values*. Recent literature on the nature of human emotions indicates that emotions are essentially byproducts of values. A *value* is defined as "an enduring belief that a specific mode of conduct or end-state of existence is ... preferable to an opposite or converse mode of conduct or end-state of existence."[2] An *emotion*, on the other hand, is primarily an outward or physiological manifestation of a commitment to a value.[3] Thus, when an advocate appeals to an audience's emotions, the advocate is actually appealing to the values that underlie and generate those emotions.

Consider, for example, a situation in which an advocate attempts to evoke in an audience anger toward an opposing party's cruelty to an animal. What the advocate is really attempting to do in this situation is to tap into the audience's value supporting the well-being of animals and its aversion to animal cruelty. If the advocate is successful at evoking anger in this situation, the success will have been achieved because (1) the targeted audience appreciated the described value, and (2) the advocate's strategy for activating the value and generating a corresponding emotion was effective.[4]

---

1. John C. Shepherd & Jordan B. Cherrick, *Advocacy and Emotion*, 138 F.R.D. 619, 619 (1991) (reprinted in 3 J. ALWD 154, 154 (2006)).
2. Milton Rokeach, *The Nature of Human Values* 5 (The Free Press 1973).
3. *See generally, e.g.*, Martha C. Nussbaum, *Emotions as Judgments of Value*, in *Upheavals of Thought: The Intelligence of Emotions* 19 (Cambridge U. Press 2003).
4. Even the medium mood control component of pathos (evoking favorable emotions through the style with which an argument is presented) is actually connected to values. The reason an effective writing style evokes favorable emotions in a reader is because most readers *value* such a style.

In view of the intrinsic link between emotions and values, our discussion of pathos in the context of contemporary legal persuasion will depart slightly from the terminology used by classical rhetoricians. Rather than speaking primarily in terms of emotions, this discussion will focus on the roles of both emotions and values in the persuasive process.

2. Two Types of Substantive Pathos Strategies: Fact-Based Persuasion and Policy-Based Persuasion

a. Fact-Based Persuasion

The process of persuading through emotions and values takes two forms in legal advocacy. The first form is *fact-based persuasion*. Under fact-based persuasion, a legal advocate attempts to persuade his or her audience by strategically explaining and emphasizing particular facts in the matter at hand that are designed to evoke favorable emotions in the audience. Telling the facts of a matter in such a way as to evoke sympathy for one's client or, alternatively, telling facts designed to evoke anger toward an opposing party's behavior are common examples of this strategy. Fact-based persuasion is designed to implicate values and evoke emotions that will motivate the audience/decision-maker to decide in the advocate's client's favor.

Consider the example of fact-based persuasion by Judge Solomon Liss of the Maryland Court of Special Appeals, who wrote the opinion in the case of *Springham v. Kordek*.[5] In *Springham*, the adult surviving children of an abandoned mother sued their estranged father after he attempted, following his wife's death, to sell the family home and retain all of the proceeds. The facts of the case showed that the father had abandoned his wife and four minor children years earlier and that the children, upon reaching adulthood, helped their mother make the mortgage payments on her home. The mortgage on the home was in the names of both the mother and the father; thus, the children's efforts to avoid foreclosure benefitted both their mother and their absentee father. After the mother died, the father reentered the scene to claim the property and to sell it. The children then filed suit to enjoin the father's sale of the property and to impose a lien on the property as subrogees for the mortgage payments they had made.

The trial court ruled in favor of the father, and the children appealed. The main issue on appeal was whether the children had gained rights as subrogees or whether they had acted as mere "volunteers" or "intermeddlers," who were not entitled to rights of subrogation. The appellate court reversed the trial court and held that the children did acquire lien rights under Maryland's law of subrogation.

Although Judge Liss, in writing the judicial opinion, justifies the court's decision with extensive legal analysis based on established legal authorities (logos), he also persuades the audiences of this opinion that the court decided correctly by evoking the emotions of anger and astonishment toward the father's behavior of abandonment and ingratitude. Judge Liss begins his opinion with a

5. 462 A.2d 567 (Md. Spec. App. 1983).

literary allusion[6] and a compelling statement of the facts that are specifically designed to evoke these negative emotions toward the father:

> Shakespeare, in his tragedy "King Lear," portrayed the bitterness of a parent plagued by ungrateful children. In Act I, IV 283, Lear laments,
>
>> Ingratitude, thou marble hearted fiend,
>>> More hideous, when thou shows't thee in a child,
>> Than the sea monster.
>
>
> And again, in Act I, IV 312, Lear cries out,
>
>> How sharper than a serpent's tooth it is
>> To have a thankless child.

> This case illustrates that ingratitude is not the sole prerogative of ungrateful children.
>
> Stephen C. Kordek, the appellee herein, and Edith Kordek were married in Maryland on March 31, 1940. Four children were born as a result of the marriage. The parties remained together until March 25, 1971, when Stephen left his wife and minor children. So far as the record discloses, the appellee made no payment for maintenance or support of his wife and/or children after he left the marital home in 1971. Edith continued to live in the family home at 980 Dalton Avenue, Baltimore County, Maryland, from the date her husband left the premises. In 1978, Edith found herself unable to continue to make the mortgage payments and pay the expenses on the property. The mother thereupon requested the children to make the monthly mortgage payments in the amount of $120.24 per month and to preserve, maintain and repair the property owned by Edith and Stephen as tenants by the entireties. Stephen was not advised of the request and did not make any request of the children. Edith died on April 18, 1981, and Stephen, as the surviving tenant by the entirety, became the sole owner of the property. The appellee, promptly after the wife's death, entered into a contract for the sale of the property in the amount of $33,000.
>
> On August 3, 1981, the children of the appellee, who are the appellants herein, . . . filed a bill of complaint in the Circuit Court for Baltimore County in which they sought to enjoin the sale of the property and to impress it with a lien for the monies expended by them at the request of Edith.[7]

A number of times in the opinion Judge Liss refers to the appellee's deceased wife as the "abandoned" mother. Moreover, later in the opinion, Judge Liss again expressly evokes anger toward the father's ingratitude. In responding to the father's argument that the children had acted as intermeddlers who "'interfered' with his liability for the debt," Judge Liss states,

> The appellee perhaps gives his children less credit than they deserve. It is obvious that they knew that by making the mortgage payments they protected not only their mother but their father as well. To suggest that the father has shown less than the minimum of gratitude which might be expected is to state the obvious.[8]

---

6. Judge Liss's reference to *King Lear* is actually a "thematic" literary reference. We will explore the persuasive power of thematic literary references in Chapter 13.

7. *Id.* at 568.

8. *Id.* at 570 & n. 3.

The *Springham* opinion is a clear example of a judge (as a legal writer) engaging in fact-based persuasion. The fact that the father was ungrateful for the children's efforts to save his property was not legally relevant to the issue of subrogation raised by the case. Yet, Judge Liss endeavored to convince readers of the opinion that the court had acted correctly by evoking negative emotions toward the father for this behavior. Most people value gratitude and disapprove of ingratitude. Thus, by emphasizing the father's ungrateful behavior, Judge Liss was able to tap into this value and to generate the attendant emotions in his audience. These emotions cause readers to "root" against the father as they read. In the end, readers of this opinion are not surprised (and may even feel relieved) when they learn that the court ruled against the father.

While the *Springham* case is an example of a judicial opinion writer engaging in fact-based persuasion, legal practitioners, such as brief writers, engage in this strategy, as well. In the context of writing briefs, fact-based persuasion can be express or implied. Express fact-based persuasion would involve a discussion in the Argument section of a brief that expressly tells the reader why certain emotional facts, and the values they implicate, support a result in the case. While such express emotional arguments are sometimes used, many attorneys only imply emotional persuasion in their legal writing. The most common example of implied emotional persuasion occurs in the Statement of Facts section of a trial or appellate brief. As you undoubtedly learned in your introductory legal writing courses, the Statement of Facts section of a trial or appellate brief is the section where the legal writer sets out the facts of the matter under consideration. As a general rule, a legal writer is not allowed to argue in the Statement of Facts section. Nevertheless, the Statement of Facts provides a legal writer with the opportunity to make an implied emotional argument through the strategic inclusion, organization, and phrasing of certain facts. An effective Statement of Facts contains implied fact-based persuasion by including with the legally relevant facts helpful emotional and background facts and by organizing and phrasing the facts in a way that evokes the desired emotion in the reader. Later in this chapter we will explore specific strategies for maximizing the effects of fact-based persuasion.

Exercise 17-1   *Understanding Fact-Based Persuasion*

Find an example of fact-based persuasion in a judicial opinion. Write an essay explaining how the writer of the opinion engages in fact-based persuasion. Use the discussion of the *Springham* opinion above as a guide for your essay. Attach a copy of the judicial opinion to your essay.

---

b.   Policy-Based Persuasion

The second form of legal persuasion based on an appeal to values is *policy-based persuasion*. Policy-based persuasion involves a legal advocate explaining how a particular decision or outcome in the matter at hand would harm or benefit the public good.[9] It is readily acknowledged that a decision by a court not

---

9. *E.g.* Linda H. Edwards, *The Convergence of Analogical and Dialectic Imaginations in Legal Discourse*, 20 Leg. Stud. Forum 7, 10 (1996).

only affects the parties to that particular case but also affects other people by serving as precedent on the issue raised in the matter. Case precedent is law, and when a case precedent is established, people in general conform their behavior to that precedent, just as they conform their behavior to other laws. Policy arguments take advantage of this precedential quality of judicial decisions by focusing on the effect the court's decision in the present matter will have on future behavior and situations.

Consider this simple example of policy-based persuasion: Assume that a particular jurisdiction recognizes the doctrine of interspousal immunity, which generally bars tort suits between spouses. Assume further that a court in this jurisdiction is presented for the first time with the issue of whether interspousal immunity bars a suit between parties who were married at the time of the tort but who were divorced at the time the tort suit was filed. The advocate for the plaintiff would likely argue that the immunity does not bar the suit because the parties are no longer married. The advocate for the defendant, however, could counter with a policy argument.

Defense counsel could argue that if the suit were allowed, the court's decision would set a precedent that a victim of an interspousal tort can get around interspousal immunity and sue if he or she divorces before filing suit. Such a precedent would cause future victims of interspousal torts to view divorce as a means of getting around interspousal immunity and may even encourage divorce. If a victim of an interspousal tort is forced to decide between staying married and being barred from recovery, on the one hand, and divorcing and being allowed to recover damages, on the other hand, it is safe to assume that some spouses would choose the latter option. This is particularly true for couples who may have been experiencing marital difficulty before the tort occurred. Rather than trying to resolve the difficulties and save the marriage, the plaintiff spouse may view the ability to sue for the interspousal tort as the determining factor in a decision to divorce. Thus, a decision for the plaintiff in the present case would actually create an incentive to divorce on a societal scale. To avoid setting such a precedent, the policy argument concludes, the court should rule in favor of the defendant and bar the suit under interspousal immunity. This is the essence of policy-based persuasion.

As this illustration demonstrates, legal advocates use policy arguments as persuasive strategies by raising policy implications that motivate the decision-maker to decide in the advocate's favor. Indeed, policy arguments can be presented in the negative or the positive. A *positive policy argument* entails an advocate explaining to a court how a decision in his or her favor would have a positive impact on society (or some segment thereof). A *negative policy argument*, on the other hand, is more of a rebuttal argument and entails an advocate explaining how the opposing party's position would harm the public good. The interspousal immunity illustration above is an example of a negative policy argument. Both negative and positive policy arguments serve to motivate the decision-maker to favor the advocate's position.

Policy arguments are classified as "pathos" arguments because they persuade by tapping into an audience's values. Positive policy arguments, for example, persuade by motivating the decision-maker to decide in a way that would further or promote valued consequences. Similarly, negative policy arguments persuade by motivating the decision-maker to avoid consequences that are contrary to one's values. In the interspousal immunity example, for instance, the argument that a decision for the plaintiff would create an incentive to divorce is designed to tap into the decision-maker's value regarding the virtuousness of marriage and the corresponding aversion to divorce. Because a decision for the plaintiff may have the effect of encouraging divorce, this argument motivates the decision-maker to render a decision that would avoid that negative consequence.

While both fact-based persuasion and policy-based persuasion involve appeals to an audience's values, they function quite differently. As we saw in the previous section, fact-based persuasion endeavors to evoke favorable values (and their attendant emotions) by focusing on the facts surrounding the specific matter at hand. Policy-based persuasion, by contrast, endeavors to evoke favorable values by looking beyond the parties and facts of the matter at hand and focusing on the potential precedential impact of the present decision.

A more formal illustration of policy-based persuasion will better demonstrate how it works in legal advocacy and how it differs from fact-based persuasion. In the case of *Murken v. Solv-Ex Corporation*,[10] the plaintiffs filed a class action securities fraud suit in New Mexico against Solv-Ex Corporation and others alleging that the defendants had perpetrated a fraud involving the sale of Solv-Ex stock. One of the defendants, the investment firm DMG, agreed to a settlement with the plaintiffs and entered into a settlement agreement. After the plaintiffs and DMG had reached a settlement but before the trial court could formally approve it, other parties filed a motion to intervene in the class action. The trial court denied the motion to intervene, and the interveners appealed. While the appeal on the denial of the motion to intervene was pending, and over the objections of the interveners, the trial court issued its final approval of the settlement agreement between the original plaintiffs and DMG. From this decision, the interveners appealed, arguing that the trial court lacked jurisdiction to approve the settlement while their appeal on the denial of the motion to intervene was pending.

The primary issue presented to the New Mexico Court of Appeals by the *Murken* case was whether the trial court lost jurisdiction to approve a settlement agreement in the class action suit while potential interveners in the suit were appealing the trial court's denial of their motion to intervene. This issue was one of first impression in New Mexico. In arguing that the trial court had jurisdiction, the parties to the settlement agreement (the original plaintiffs and defendant DMG) argued numerous legal theories based on established civil procedure law and class action law (i.e., logos arguments). The plaintiffs and DMG also made a policy argument. They argued that if the appeals court were to hold that a trial court in a class action suit loses jurisdiction during the pendency of an appeal on motion to intervene, such a holding could lead to delay and gamesmanship in future class action suits. More specifically, these parties argued that such a precedent would give parties claiming to be interveners the power to delay a class action suit indefinitely by filing a motion to intervene, no matter how frivolous, and then appealing the denial of the motion.

Ultimately, the Court of Appeals ruled against the interveners and held that the trial court did have jurisdiction to approve the settlement agreement. In reaching this conclusion, the Court of Appeals found the plaintiffs and DMG's policy argument to be persuasive:

We have also considered the policy arguments raised by Plaintiffs and Defendant DMG. They point out that if we were to rule in Appellants' [interveners'] favor on this question, we would be creating the possibility that an appeal of any

10. 136 P.3d 1035 (N.M. App. 2006).

intervention motion, no matter how frivolous, could be used to delay proceedings in the district court indefinitely. We agree that this possibility further counsels against a holding that the district court lacked jurisdiction in this case.[11]

The *Murken* example illustrates clearly the difference between policy-based persuasion and fact-based persuasion. The plaintiff and DMG did not attempt to persuade by presenting a compelling version of the facts of the matter that would evoke favorable emotions in the appellate judges. Rather, they looked past the facts and outcome in this case and focused on the potential precedential impact of the court's decision. What's more, the policy argument in *Murken* is an example of a negative policy argument. The plaintiffs and DMG did not argue that a decision in their favor would set a precedent that would lead to good consequences. Rather, they argued that a decision in the opposing parties' favor would set a precedent that would lead to negative consequences: namely delay and gamesmanship in class action suits. This argument was designed to implicate the decision-makers' values regarding judicial efficiency and fair play as well as their corresponding aversion to judicial delay and the strategic abuse of procedural rules. The activation of these values, in turn, was designed to motivate the decision-makers to decide in a way that would further these values and avoid the undesirable alternative. And we know by the court's express statement that the argument had this exact effect.

3.   Distinguishing Between Logos and Pathos

a.   The Clear Division in Law Between Logos and Pathos

Understanding the concept of pathos in the context of contemporary legal writing is actually easier than understanding the concept of pathos in the context of classical rhetoric theory. This ease in understanding stems from the fact that the distinction between pathos and logos is much clearer in law than it is in the context of classical rhetoric.

In Chapter 2 [Michael R. Smith, Advanced Legal Writing: Theories and Strategies in Persuasive Writing, 2nd ed., (2008)], we saw that classical rhetoric principles were first developed for Greco-Roman citizens some 2500 years ago to help them argue and persuade more effectively in social, political, and economic debates in various societal institutions such as the forum, the church, and the marketplace. Even today, most classical rhetoricians focus on persuasion in the contexts of various political and social situations rather than in the context of legal practice. As we also saw in Chapter 2 [Michael R. Smith, Advanced Legal Writing: Theories and Strategies in Persuasive Writing, 2nd ed., (2008)], classical rhetoricians define *logos* as the process of persuading based on logic and define *pathos* as the process of persuading based on emotion. In the context of political or social debates, however, the line between an argument based on logic (logos) and an argument designed to evoke emotion (pathos) can be blurry. Consider, for example, a debate over whether one's country should go to war with another country. In the context of this debate, assume that one debater argues that war should be waged because the security of the nation depends on it. When one looks at this argument under classical

11. *Id.* at 1039-40.

rhetoric principles, it is difficult to classify it as a logos argument or a pathos argument because it is unclear whether it is designed to persuade based on logic (the need for national security), emotion (such as patriotism or fear for one's safety), or both.

The blurry distinction between logos and pathos also appears in the persuasive efforts of television commercials, which were also explored in some detail in Chapter 2 [Michael R. Smith, Advanced Legal Writing: Theories and Strategies in Persuasive Writing, 2nd ed., (2008)]. Consider, for example, a commercial that attempts to persuade consumers to purchase a product based on the argument that it will keep the consumer's family safe. Is this a logical argument (logos) or is this an emotional argument (pathos)? Really, it could be viewed as either.

By contrast, the division between logos and pathos is quite clear in the context of the law and legal writing.[12] In Chapter 2 [Michael R. Smith, Advanced Legal Writing: Theories and Strategies in Persuasive Writing, 2nd ed., (2008)], we defined logos in the context of legal writing as the process of persuading through legal reasoning based on established legal authorities. Thus, logos in law does not refer to any argument based on logic. Rather, it refers more limitedly to efforts to persuade a legal audience based on the application of established legal authorities (such as statutes and cases) to the issue at hand. On the other hand, pathos in the context of legal writing refers to efforts to persuade based on arguments that go beyond the relevant legal authorities, such as arguments based on the emotional facts of a legal matter (i.e., fact-based persuasion) and arguments based on the public policy implications of a particular course of action (i.e., policy-based persuasion). In simple terms, a pathos argument in law is one in which an advocate says, either expressly or impliedly, "Beyond what the law requires, a decision in my client's favor is compelled by the values implicated by the matter."

b. Distinguishing Between Pathos Policy Arguments, Logos Policy Arguments, and Quasi-Logos Policy Arguments

Because we have defined logos in the context of legal persuasion as arguments based on established legal authorities, it is necessary to differentiate between policy arguments based on legal authority and those based purely on an appeal to values. Most of the literature on the role of policy in legal persuasion suggests that all policy arguments persuade in basically the same way: by pointing out how a decision in the present case will benefit or harm the public good. In terms of classical rhetoric theory, however, there are two distinct types of policy arguments—pathos policy arguments and logos policy arguments—and these two types of policy arguments persuade in very different ways.

Pathos policy arguments are like those that we have discussed so far in this chapter. They go beyond the relevant legal authority on an issue and focus on the precedential impact of the matter at hand and the values implicated by those potential consequences. These types of policy arguments are pathos arguments

---

12. In fact, under classical rhetoric theory, persuasion in the context of law is treated completely separately from persuasion in the context of social or political debates. *See e.g.* Edward P. J. Corbett & Robert J. Connors, *Classical Rhetoric for the Modern Student* 17-18 (4th ed., Oxford U. Press 1999).

because they are not based on legal authorities; they are based on an appeal to the decision-maker's foresight and values.

Logos policy arguments, by contrast, involve policy arguments based on preexisting statements of policy in the law relevant to the issue at hand. Many statutes include express statements about the public policy goals of the statutes. Likewise, many legal rules announced by courts include express statements by the courts about the policies the rules are designed to promote. Legal advocates often make policy arguments based on these express statements of policy underlying the rules at issue. Such policy arguments, however, are not the type of policy arguments we have been discussing in this chapter because they are based, not on original, previously unforeseen policy implications, but on preexisting statements of policy. As such, they are logos arguments.

Logos policy arguments do not persuade by evoking values implicated by the precedential impact of the case. Logos policy arguments persuade primarily by pointing out how the advocated outcome is consistent with a preexisting express statement of policy. Thus, as a general matter, logos policy arguments persuade the same way all logos arguments persuade: through formal logic based on established law. Unlike with pathos policy arguments, a decision-maker presented with a logos policy argument often will not ask himself or herself in any meaningful way whether he or she agrees with the policy underlying the rule at issue or whether that policy is consistent with his or her values. The decision-maker often will simply accept the policy as a given, mandated by the applicable law, and focus instead on the more formal mental inquiry of how the stated policy relates to and affects the issue at hand.

To say that logos policy persuasion is always a matter of dispassionate logic would be an overstatement, however. A judge often has some discretion in determining whether the law on an issue is unclear enough to even warrant the consideration of the underlying policy. Likewise, even when the policy underlying a legal rule is implicated, judges often have discretion in determining the specific relevance and application of that express policy to the issue at hand. In situations such as these, in which a judge views the application of a rule's underlying policy as a judgment call rather than a mandate, the values implicated by the express policy statement become more important in the persuasive process. In these situations, the judge will not simply apply the policy statement to the issue. Instead, the decisions on whether to refer to the underlying policy and how that policy applies to the issue at hand will be significantly influenced by how strongly the judge agrees or disagrees with the values implicated by the policy. Thus, in situations where a judge views the application of a rule's express policy as a discretionary judgment, the persuasive process is a complex combination of pathos (values) and logos (logic).

That being said, however, policy persuasion based on an express statement of policy is more often than not a matter of formal rather than value-based reasoning. When a rule of law includes an express statement of the policy the rule is designed to promote, judges generally try to interpret the rule in away that effectuates its policy. Thus, unlike with pathos policy arguments, an advocate employing a logos policy argument generally does not have to worry about whether the judge will agree that the values implicated by the issue are important. An authoritative source—either a legislature or court—has already determined and announced through the express policy statement that those values are important. The judge will often accept that determination and will focus more on how best to promote those values (i.e., policy) in the matter at hand.

All of the examples of policy arguments presented so far in this chapter are examples of pathos policy arguments. For the purpose of comparison, consider this example of a logos policy argument: In the case of *In the Matter of J.S.*,[13] the Pennsylvania Department of Public Welfare filed a petition under Pennsylvania's Mental Health Procedures Act (MHPA)[14] to declare an individual, J.S., to be "severely mentally disabled" and to recommit him to involuntary inpatient treatment in the Philadelphia State Hospital. The MHPA defines the term "severely mentally disabled" to mean that "as a result of mental illness, [a person] poses a clear and present danger of harm to others or to himself."[15] The MHPA also creates the position of "mental health review officer" and provides that petitions for involuntary commitment can be heard by a judge of the Court of Common Pleas or by a mental health review officer. The Department's petition for the recommitment of J.S. was heard by a mental health review officer, who denied the petition. The Department then filed with the Court of Common Pleas a petition for review of the mental health review officer's action.

Counsel for J.S. challenged the Department's petition for review, arguing that the Department lacked standing to bring it. The MHPA provides that when a petition for involuntary commitment is heard by a mental health review officer, "*the person made subject to treatment* shall have the right to petition the court of common pleas for review of the [officer's action]."[16] The Act is otherwise silent on the right to petition for the review of a mental health review officer's action. Counsel for J.S. argued that the quoted provision allows only "the person made subject to treatment" (i.e., the patient) to seek review of a mental health review officer's action and that the Department therefore lacked standing to bring its petition for review. The Court of Common Pleas agreed and refused to entertain the Department's petition for review. The Department appealed this decision of the Court of Common Pleas to the Commonwealth Court of Pennsylvania.

On appeal, the Department made several arguments based on the language of the MHPA that it had standing to seek a review of the mental health review officer's action in the Court of Common Pleas. The Department also made a policy argument based on the express policy underlying the MHPA. Section 7102 of the MHPA, entitled "Statement of Policy," provides as follows:

> It is the policy of the Commonwealth of Pennsylvania to seek to assure the availability of adequate treatment to persons who are mentally ill, and it is the purpose of this act to establish procedures whereby this policy can be effected. The provisions of this act shall be interpreted in conformity with the principles of due process to make voluntary and involuntary treatment available where the need is great and its absence could result in serious harm to the mentally ill person or to others.[17]

The Department argued that this express policy underlying the MHPA supported a finding that the Department had standing to seek review of the mental health review officer's action. The Commonwealth Court agreed, and on this specific point stated the following in its opinion:

13. 597 A.2d 750 (Pa. Cmmw. 1991).
14. *Id.* at 750 (citing the MHPA as 50 P.S. §§7101-7503).
15. *Id.* at 751 (discussing 50 P.S. §7301 (a)).
16. *Id.* at 752 (quoting 50 P.S. §7109) (emphasis added).
17. 50 Pa. Consol. Stat. Ann. §71-2 (West 2007).

Further, the express policy of the MHPA supports a conclusion that petitioners such as [the Department] may seek review by the court. Section [7102] of the MHPA . . . provides in part:

> The provisions of this act shall be interpreted in conformity with the principles of due process to make voluntary and involuntary treatment available where the need is great and its absence could result in serious harm to the mentally ill person or to others.

> . . . The purpose of the MHPA to provide treatment where the need is great could be thwarted if the act were interpreted to prevent a petitioner such as [the Department] from seeking review by the court to point out possible errors by the mental health review officer.[18]

Ultimately, the Commonwealth Court decided for the Department and reversed the Court of Common Pleas' decision that the Department lacked standing to seek review of the mental health review officer's action.

This discussion in *In the Matter of J.S.* is an example of a logos policy argument. The Department could have focused on the potential precedential impact of the court's decision and argued that upholding the Court of Common Pleas' narrow interpretation of the MHPA would lead to missed determinations of mental disability and, consequently, to harm to mentally ill persons or members of the public. Such an argument would have been a pathos policy argument. Instead, however, the Department made a similar but more compelling logos policy argument by framing its argument in terms of the express statement of the policy underlying the MHPA.

Although logos policy arguments and pathos policy arguments differ from each other, there is a third type of policy argument that contains characteristics of both. For lack of a better term, we will call these policy arguments quasi-logos policy arguments. *Quasi-logos policy arguments* involve a legal advocate taking an express statement of policy from one area of the law and arguing for its relevance and application to another area of the law. Consider as an example the policy discussion in the case of *Commonwealth v. Fenstermaker.*[19] In this case, the Pennsylvania Supreme Court was faced with the issue of whether a newspaper had a common law right of access to affidavits of probable cause executed in support of an arrest warrant. In analyzing this issue, the court looked to the policies underlying a comparable area of law: public access to criminal trials. Specifically, the *Fenstermaker* court referred to its own decision in the prior case of *Commonwealth v. Contakos,*[20] in which the court specifically set out the policies behind the rule for public trials as follows:

> The historical basis for public trials . . . can be briefly summarized as follows: generally, to assure the public that justice is done even-handedly and fairly; to discourage perjury and the misconduct of participants; to prevent decisions based on secret bias or partiality; to prevent individuals from feeling that the law should be taken into the hands of private citizens; to satisfy the natural desire to see justice done; to provide for community catharsis; to promote public confidence in government and assurance that the system of judicial remedy does in fact work; to promote the stability of government by allowing access to its workings, thus

18. *In the Matter of J.S.*, 597 A.2d at 753.
19. 530 A.2d 414 (Pa. 1987).
20. 453 A.2d 578 (Pa. 1982).

assuring citizens that government and the courts are worthy of their continued loyalty and support; to promote an understanding of our system of government and courts.[21]

The *Fenstermaker* court then applied these policies to the issue before it:

Although the instant case does not involve the issue presented in *Contakos*, to wit, the propriety of limitations upon public access to the courtroom itself, . . . many of the same considerations command recognition of a common law right of access to the affidavits sought by [the newspaper in this case]. Specifically, from a policy standpoint, public inspection of arrest warrant affidavits would serve to discourage perjury in such affidavits, would enhance the performance of police and prosecutors by encouraging them to establish sufficient cause before an affidavit is filed, would act as a public check on discretion of issuing authorities thus discouraging erroneous decisions and decisions based on partiality, and would promote a public perception of fairness in the arrest warrant process.[22]

In the end, and largely because of these policy considerations, the *Fenstermaker* court held that a newspaper in Pennsylvania does have a common law right of access to arrest warrant affidavits.

This use of policy in *Fenstermaker* is not an example of a pathos policy argument because the policy considerations discussed by the court were not raised originally in connection with the issue of that case. Likewise, the use of policy in *Fenstermaker* is not an example of a logos policy argument because the express statements of policy relied on by the *Fenstermaker* court were not announced previously in connection with the law on public access to arrest affidavits. The policies relied on by the *Fenstermaker* court were previously announced in connection with the different but analogous area of law of public access to criminal trials. Thus, this is an example of a quasi-logos policy argument: The court looked to express statements of policy from one area of the law and applied them to a new area of law.[23]

Legal advocates regularly employ quasi-logos policy arguments. Legal advocates often find policy statements announced for one issue or area of the law and argue for their relevance and application to another issue or area of the law. In fact, legal advocates often develop quasi-logos policy arguments through reverse engineering. Often an advocate will first develop a pure pathos policy argument by recognizing potential policy consequences implicated by his or her issue. The advocate will then look for an authoritative statement (either a judicial statement or a legislative statement), unconnected to the governing rule, that expressly acknowledges the importance of the policies and values implicated by the issue. If the advocate finds such an authoritative statement, the advocate can then cite that authority in connection with his or her policy argument, making it a quasi-logos policy argument. Although the policy statement cited by the advocate may have been expressed in a completely different context, it nevertheless strengthens the advocate's argument because it serves as authoritative recognition of the importance of the policy as a general matter.

---

21. *Fenstermaker*, 530 A.2d at 417 (quoting *Contakos*, 453 A.2d at 579-80).
22. *Id.* at 417-18.
23. The policy discussion in *Fenstermaker* is also an example of a *positive* policy argument. The court's argument points out how allowing public access to arrest warrant affidavits will lead to positive consequences for the general public.

From a persuasion standpoint, quasi-logos policy arguments fall somewhere between pathos policy arguments and logos policy arguments. A quasi-logos policy argument tends to be more compelling than a pure pathos policy argument because an authoritative source—either a legislature or a court—has already acknowledged the importance of the stated policy. Thus, the advocate has authoritative support, and not just his or her lone opinion, that the policy and values implicated by the matter are in fact important. On the other hand, a quasi-logos policy argument is generally not as compelling as a pure logos policy argument because the policy statement was not made specifically as a guide for interpreting the legal rule under discussion. Thus, the decision-maker may feel less compelled to effectuate that policy than he or she would in the context of a pure logos policy argument.

Exercise 17-2   Understanding Different Types of Policy Arguments

1. For each of the three types of policy arguments discussed in the previous section—pathos policy arguments, logos policy arguments, and quasi-logos policy arguments—find one example in a judicial opinion. Hint: One way to locate cases that contain policy discussions is to conduct a computer search in a case law database using the words "policy" or "public policy" as your search terms.
2. Write an essay analyzing the three examples of policy arguments you found. In particular, for each example, explain why it fits into the category you assigned it and explain the persuasive functions it serves in the opinion in which it was found. Use the discussions of the examples of policy arguments in this chapter as guides for your essay. Attach copies of the three judicial opinions to your essay.

---

4.   How Pathos Supplements Logos

As is evident from the previous discussion, the pathos process of persuasion is different from the logos process of persuasion. Nonetheless, the two processes can and should work together. Logos strategies (i.e., arguments based on legal authorities) explain why a decision in an advocate's favor is compelled by the law. Because legal decision-makers (such as judges) are required to render decisions consistent with established law, logos arguments serve to justify a particular decision in terms of the law. Pathos strategies, by contrast, persuade by evoking favorable emotions and values. These emotions and values serve to motivate the decision-maker to decide the matter in a way consistent with those emotions and values.

Richard K. Neumann, Jr., explains more fully how, in the development of advocacy strategies, pathos strategies (which he calls "motivating arguments") can be (and should be) used to support and supplement logos arguments (which he calls "justifying arguments"):

> *Include both motivating arguments and justifying arguments.* Both are needed to persuade.
>
> A motivating argument is one that causes a judge to *want* to decide a case in a particular way. It causes the judge to feel that any other decision would be unjust.

Motivating arguments tend to be centered on facts or a combination of facts and policy. . . .

A justifying argument is one that shows that the law either requires or permits the result urged by the arguer. Justifying arguments are centered on legal rules or on a combination of rules and policy. . . .

Why do you need both motivating arguments and justifying arguments? A motivating argument alone is not enough because even a motivated judge is not supposed to act without solid legal justification. Judges understandably want to feel that they are doing a professional job of judging, and they can be reversed on appeal if they fail to justify their actions within the law.

And a justifying argument alone is not enough because, in a large number of cases, a justifying argument, without more, will not persuade. The law can usually be interpreted in more than one way. When a judge is given a choice between two conflicting justifying arguments, each of which is reasonable, the judge will take the one she or he is motivated to take. (Judges are, after all, human.)[24]

5.   The Inverse Relationship Between Logos and Pathos

Even though, as we just saw, pathos strategies often supplement logos strategies, the two processes actually have an inverse relationship. From an advocate's perspective, this relationship perhaps is best expressed through the following maxims:

The stronger one's logos, the less important one's pathos.

The weaker one's logos, the more important one's pathos.

If a legal advocate has very strong arguments based on binding legal authorities, it is less important that the advocate have compelling emotional facts and/or strong policy arguments. If, on the other hand, an advocate merely has persuasive, non-binding legal arguments, the pathos process of persuasion and the values implicated by the matter will be extremely important to the advocate. In the former situation, the advocate doesn't really need to motivate the decision-maker to view the matter as the advocate sees it, because the applicable legal authorities alone compel a result in the advocate's favor. In the latter situation, however, the law does not compel one clear answer, and thus, the advocate must motivate the decision-maker to agree with the advocate's position.

Not surprisingly, this inverse relationship between logos and pathos applies to the decision-maker, as well. If the law on a legal issue and its application to the matter at hand are clear, the emotional facts and values implicated by the matter will be less significant in the decision-making process. Judges will rarely ignore clear and compelling arguments based on binding authority (logos), even in the face of contrary compelling emotional facts or policy (pathos). If, on the other hand, the law on a legal issue or its application to the matter at hand is unclear, then pathos will play a significant role in the decision-making process. If the law on an issue is unclear, the decision-maker is forced to render a decision based on what he or she believes is "right." In the absence of clear, binding law, a decision is "right" if it comports with one's values. Thus, when

24. Richard K. Neumann, Jr., *Legal Reasoning and Legal Writing: Structure, Strategy, and Style* 319-21 (5th ed., Aspen Pub. 2005).

the law on an issue is unclear, a judge is more open and receptive to arguments that explain how a particular decision in the matter will reward or promote favorable values or punish or discourage undesirable behavior: to wit, pathos.[25]

Because of this inverse relationship between logos and pathos, pathos strategies—fact-based persuasion and policy-based persuasion—tend to play a more significant role in following types of issues:

- Questions of first impression (issues for which there is no existing binding rule in the jurisdiction in question).
- Issues governed by a rule that is binding but which is vague or unclear.
- Issues governed by a rule that is clear but whose application to the facts of the present matter is unclear.
- Issues governed by a clear rule announced previously by the same court but which may be ripe for overruling.

In all of these scenarios, the issues cannot be resolved through logos reasoning alone. Granted, the advocates in these situations would likely offer some nonbinding logos arguments, such as arguments based on analogy, arguments based on authority from nonbinding jurisdictions, or arguments based on canons of statutory construction. But, the logos process of persuasion alone does not compel or require a specific result. Thus, with these types of issues, pathos plays a very significant role in the decision-making process.

6.   *Guidelines for Employing Pathos Strategies*

The following discussion sets out guidelines that will help legal advocates employ pathos more effectively.

a.   **Employing Both Fact-Based Persuasion and Policy-Based Persuasion in a Single Document**

Because fact-based persuasion and policy-based persuasion operate differently, it is possible for a legal advocate to employ both in a single document. An advocate should not view these two forms of pathos as an either/or choice. Legal matters often involve facts that lend themselves to fact-based persuasion as well as policy implications that lend themselves to policy-based persuasion. Thus, legal advocates should watch for opportunities to employ both processes in their persuasive documents. A document that contains the effective use of both processes is more persuasive than a document that contains only one.

b.   **Policy-Based Persuasion Is Often More Compelling Than Fact-Based Persuasion**

While both forms of pathos can be effective, policy-based persuasion tends to have a greater impact on judges than fact-based persuasion. The reasons for this

---

25. A similar inverse relationship exists between logos and ethos: The murkier the law is, the more reliance the decision-maker will put on the advocates' credibility. *See* Chapter 7 [Michael R. Smith, Advanced Legal Writing: Theories and Strategies in Persuasive Writing, 2nd ed., (2008)], Section I.A [Michael R. Smith, Advanced Legal Writing: Theories and Strategies in Persuasive Writing, 2nd ed., (2008)].

preference for policy are based in the ideals of the American legal system. Our legal system prides itself on being a "system of laws, not men." One aspect of this ideal is the notion that legal matters will be decided by impartial, dispassionate decision-makers. The America legal system disfavors ad hoc decision-making by judges based on the emotional components of a particular case. The judge's role is to render judgments based on the established law. And when a judge is faced with a gap in the law, the judge's duty is to fill that gap in a way that serves the greatest public good.

Rendering a decision based on the emotional facts of a particular matter, or even being influenced by such facts, is inconsistent with the ideals underlying our legal system. Truth be told, fact-based persuasion is an argument for ad hoc decision-making: decide this case based, not on broad principles, but on the particular emotional facts presented. It is not surprising then that judges often view emotional factual arguments as inappropriate. Policy-based persuasion, on the other hand, is more consistent with the ideals of the adversary system because policy considerations, by definition, look beyond the facts and parties of the present matter and focus on the general public good. Thus, policy arguments often have greater persuasive impact than fact-based persuasion.

This discussion, however, is not intended to suggest that fact-based persuasion is irrelevant to legal persuasion. (Otherwise, it would not be covered in this chapter.) Despite the ideals underlying the legal system, judges are human, and humans can be and often are influenced by emotion. As we have seen earlier, when the law on an issue is unclear, the judge will take the position that he or she is most motivated to take. While policy arguments can serve as effective motivators, the emotional facts of the case can as well. A judge is this situation may not even realize why he or she is more motivated in one direction than the other. Likely, it is a complex combination of the values implicated by the facts of the case and the values implicated by the policy consequences of the case. Thus, despite the ideals underlying the legal system, the emotional facts of a case can and do play a role in the decision-making process.

c. Strategies for Maximizing Fact-Based Persuasion

The following is a brief discussion of specific strategies for maximizing the effects of fact-based persuasion.

i. Imply Your Emotional Arguments

As we saw above, judges may view overt emotional arguments as inconsistent with their role in the legal system and, thus, as inappropriate. Even worse, as Kathryn M. Stanchi has pointed out, judges may even be insulted by such arguments, because they may "imply that judges are susceptible to rash, irrational judgments as opposed to considered, reasoned ones."[26] And it is never a good idea for legal advocates to insult the very person they are trying to persuade. Thus, legal advocates should be subtle in their efforts at fact-based persuasion. Generally, this means that advocates should avoid overt emotional arguments in the Argument section of their briefs. Instead, as was discussed previously in

---

26. Kathryn M. Stanchi, *Feminist Legal Writing*, 39 S.D. L. Rev. 387, 397 (2002).

Section II.A, advocates are generally better off implying their emotional arguments through well-crafted Statements of Facts.

ii.   Tell a Compelling Story

Undoubtedly, the most effective way for an advocate to evoke emotions based on the facts of a matter is to present the facts in the context of a compelling story. Much has been written in recent years about the compelling nature of an effective narrative and how the skills of effective storytelling can enhance a lawyer's efforts at fact-based persuasion. An in-depth discussion of the techniques for crafting an effective narrative is beyond the scope of this text. Thus, I encourage you to read two ground-breaking works in this area. The first is Brian J. Foley and Ruth Anne Robbins's article, *Fiction 101: A Primer for Lawyers on How to Use Fiction Writing Techniques to Write Persuasive Facts Sections.*[27] This article explores the elements of an effective story—character, conflict, resolution, organization, and point of view—and the application of these elements to the Facts Sections of court briefs. The second work is Ruth Anne Robbins's article, *Harry Potter, Ruby Slippers and Merlin: Telling the Client's Story Using the Characters and Paradigm of the Archetypal Hero's Journey.*[28] This article explores the "hero's journey" archetype, which is ubiquitous in literature, and explains its relevance to persuasive legal writing. More specifically, this article explains how an advocate can portray a client's story as a hero's journey and, by doing so, tap into and make use of universal themes and expectations in the audience's mind. These two works explore the power of narrative and specific techniques legal advocates can use to harness this power in their own writing.

iii.   Expressly Identify the Value or Values Implicated by the Story

A third technique for maximizing the effects of fact-based persuasion is to expressly state the value or values implicated by the client's story. Many legal advocates tell their clients' stories with the goal of highlighting certain emotional facts, yet never actually label the conduct or values they seek to highlight. As a consequence, many Facts Statements leave the reader with only a general impression of the conduct the writer intended to highlight. A more effective technique is for legal advocates to actually label the conduct they seek to emphasize. If an advocate wants to portray his or her client as being brave or loyal or trustworthy or whatever, the advocate should not only set out the facts that reflect that characteristic (although the advocate should do that as well). The advocate should also specifically label the conduct as brave, loyal, trustworthy, and so on. Likewise, if an advocate wants to portray the opposing party as being disrespectful and greedy, the advocate should expressly use those labels as he or she tells the facts that reflect those characteristics. Expressly labeling conduct in this way provides the reader with a context for the highlighted facts and helps the reader process the facts in the way the writer intended. Without such labels, the reader may be left with only an amorphous, undefined feeling about the described conduct.

27. 32 Rutgers L. J. 459 (2001).
28. 29 Seattle U. L. Rev. 767 (2006).

Consider, for example, the facts statement by Judge Liss in the *Springham* case, which was discussed in Section II.A above. Judge Liss told the story of a father who abandoned his family and who, upon return, was ungrateful for his children's efforts in saving the family home. Rather than simply telling the facts that demonstrated abandonment and ingratitude, Judge Liss actually labeled the father's conduct with those express terms. By using these labels, Judge Liss was assured that his readers would consciously connect the father's conduct with the values implicated by that conduct.

d.   Strategies for Maximizing Policy-Based Persuasion

The following is a brief discussion of specific strategies for maximizing the effects of policy-based persuasion.

i.   *Opt for Logos Policy Arguments*

Section III.B of this chapter introduced three basic types of policy arguments:

- *Logos policy arguments*: Policy arguments based on express statements of policy for the rule that governs the issue at hand;
- *Quasi-logos policy arguments*: Policy arguments based on express statements of policy that are unconnected to the rule governing the issue at hand; and
- *Pathos policy arguments*: Policy arguments unsupported by legal authority and based only on the potential precedential impact of the matter at hand.

As we saw in Section III.B, logos policy arguments are generally stronger than the other forms of policy arguments because they are more than just an appeal to the decision-maker's values; they involve a judge applying an express policy mandate to the issue at hand. Thus, the first step for a legal advocate who wants to make a policy argument on an issue is to determine if the rule that governs the issue has an accompanying express statement of policy. If an express statement of the rule's policy does exist, the advocate should endeavor to frame his or her policy argument in terms of the express policy. More specifically, the advocate should explain fully and clearly how a result in his or her favor would advance one or more of the policies specifically mentioned in the rule's policy statement.

ii.   *In the Absence of Available Logos Policy Arguments, Opt for Quasi-Logos Policy Arguments*

If an advocate finds that a logos policy argument is not possible for an issue (either because there is no express statement of the applicable rule's policy or because the rule's express policy is detrimental to the advocate's position), then the advocate should, as a second option, endeavor to make a quasi-logos policy argument. Although a quasi-logos policy argument is not as strong as a logos policy argument, it is stronger than the last option, a pathos policy argument. As we saw earlier, a pathos policy argument is based only on an advocate's assertion of the importance of the policies implicated by the present matter. A quasi-logos policy argument, on the other hand, is at least based on some authoritative recognition of the importance of the implicated policies.

In an effort to develop a quasi-logos policy argument, a legal advocate should engage in the reverse engineering process briefly described in Section III.B above. First, the advocate should identify the potential policy implications of the matter at hand. Next, the advocate should search for legal authority, unconnected to the governing rule, that recognizes the importance of the policy consequences implicated by the present matter.[29] There are many potential sources for such authority. The best sources include the following: (1) a legislative policy statement in the same jurisdiction but on a different rule of law; (2) a judicial policy statement on a different rule of law by a binding court or by the same court hearing the current matter; (3) a judicial policy statement from a nonbinding court in the same jurisdiction (such as a sister court of appeal) on the same rule that is at issue in the present matter; or (4) a legislative or judicial policy statement from another jurisdiction on the same rule that is at issue in the present matter. Other less effective potential sources include the following: (1) a judicial policy statement from a nonbinding court in the same jurisdiction (such as a sister court of appeal) on a different rule of law; or (2) a legislative or judicial policy statement from another jurisdiction on a different rule of law.

If the advocate is able to find any such authority, the advocate should cite that authority in his or her policy argument and fully and clearly explain the implications of the policy for the matter at hand. Furthermore, to the extent that the advocate determines that it would be helpful and appropriate, the advocate should frame the policy argument in terms of the language used in the cited authority.

iii. In the Absence of Available Logos and Quasi-Logos Policy Arguments, Make Pathos Policy Arguments

If an advocate sees policy implications for his or her issue but is unable to make a logos policy argument or a quasi-logos policy argument, the advocate should make a pathos policy argument. A pathos policy argument, as we have discussed earlier, entails a legal writer telling the decision-maker how a decision in the advocate's favor would serve the public good. Pathos policy arguments are not based on any legal authority; rather they are based only on the advocate's explanation of the potential precedential impact of the case at hand. Because pathos policy arguments are not based on legal authority, they tend to be weaker than the other two forms of policy arguments. This does not mean, however, that they cannot be effective persuasive strategies.

The strength of a pathos policy argument is directly related to how clearly and convincingly the advocate explains the potential precedential consequences of the matter at hand and the values implicated by those consequences. In short, a compelling pathos policy argument contains the following components:

1. **The precedent:** A clear explanation of the potential precedential rule that the decision in the current matter could establish.
2. **The consequences:** A clear explanation of the potential consequences of the precedential rule (good or bad, depending on whether the advocate is making a positive policy argument or a negative policy argument[30]).

29. The search is for authority "unconnected" to the governing rule because if the rule itself had an associated express policy statement, the policy argument would be a logos policy argument, not a quasi-logos policy argument.

30. See Section II.B for a discussion of the difference between positive policy arguments and negative policy arguments.

3. **The values:** A clear explanation of the values implicated by the potential consequences.
4. **The decision:** A clear explanation of the how a decision in the advocate's favor would advance the implicated values, either by leading to desirable consequences or avoiding undesirable consequences.

iv. Cite Non-Legal Sources for Support

In her article, *Beyond Brandeis: Exploring the Uses of Non-Legal Materials in Appellate Briefs*,[31] Ellie Margolis explains how legal advocates can add strength to their policy arguments by citing non-legal sources such as scientific studies, medical reports, social psychology articles, and the like. According to Professor Margolis, non-legal sources such as these strengthen policy arguments by providing the decision-maker with proof of certain social or scientific phenomena that often underlie the policy arguments. Professor Margolis offers this example:

> [I]n a case in which the court is asked to impose tort liability on a mother for injury to a child caused by the mother's negligent conduct during pregnancy, the mother may argue that a duty to a fetus would be unduly intrusive because it would affect every moment of a woman's life, even before pregnancy (the policy argument). As support, she may provide medical information . . . about the many ways a woman's conduct before and during pregnancy, such as diet, physical activity and choice of work, could affect the health of a fetus. If medical information supports the contention that the mother's health even before pregnancy can affect the health of the fetus, the policy argument will be much more persuasive than the same assertion without any factual support.[32]

While non-legal sources are less important for logos policy arguments (because such arguments are based on express statements of policy), they can definitely add strength to pathos policy arguments and quasi-logos policy arguments. A full discussion of the role of non-legal sources in policy arguments, however, is beyond the scope of this text. For those who would like to learn more, I encourage you to read Professor Margolis's article.

v. Explain the Policy Implications Clearly and Fully

A consistent theme in the discussions of policy in this chapter is that legal advocates should fully and clearly explain their policy arguments. This point cannot be overemphasized. In another article by Ellie Margolis, *Closing the Floodgates: Making Persuasive Policy Arguments in Appellate Briefs*,[33] she notes that policy arguments are often unpersuasive in court briefs because they "rarely identify which 'public policy' is being asserted or discuss specifically how the proposed rule will advance that policy." Legal advocates should avoid this tendency of underexplaining policy arguments and should clearly and completely explain

---

31. 34 U.S.F. L. Rev. 197 (2000).
32. *Id.* at 213-14.
33. 62 Mont. L. Rev. 59, 59 (2001).

how a decision in their client's favor would promote important public policy goals. The discussions in this chapter were designed to assist advocates in this process. To supplement the suggestions made here, readers of this book are encouraged to read Professor Margolis's article.

Exercise 17-3   Maximizing Pathos Strategies

1. Find a judicial opinion that contains (or at least lends itself to) both fact-based persuasion and policy-based persuasion.
2. Employing the guidelines discussed in Section 17.C.6 above, rewrite the opinion to maximize these pathos processes.
3. Write an essay analyzing both the original writer's efforts and your efforts to maximize fact-based persuasion and policy-based persuasion in the opinion.
4. Turn in (a) a copy of the original opinion; (b) your revised version of the opinion; and (c) your essay.

CHAPTER
18

Dealing with Adverse Authority and Your Opponent's Arguments

A. ACCOUNTING FOR YOUR OPPONENT'S ARGUMENTS

Legal advocacy has both offensive and defensive aspects. Not only must you convince the court of the merits of your argument; you also must deflect your opponent's arguments. Thus, an important step in developing your argument is to take stock of your opponent's arguments.

Often this entails anticipating your opponent's argument, for instance, when your memorandum is the first to be written. Ask yourself: What would I argue if I were counsel for my client's opponent? If I were the judge analyzing this case, what are the assertions that I would discuss that would lead me to hold in favor of my client's opponent?

Next, compare your opponent's probable or actual arguments to your own. You very probably will discern both points of concurrence and points of clash. Points of concurrence are propositions on which you and your opponent agree; points of clash are propositions on which you and your opponent disagree. Both may involve various matters:

- You may agree or disagree as to what the governing legal rule is on a topic, how (or whether) to fuse a given set of cases, how to interpret a statute.
- You may agree or disagree about what the relevant facts are, especially inferences to be drawn from the facts.
- You may agree or disagree about how the rule applies to the facts, how policy analysis plays out, or whether a leading case is analogous or distinguishable.

You should take care to discern the points of concurrence and clash with precision because your memorandum should be focused accordingly. Your memorandum should focus on the points of clash, providing the court with compelling reasons to resolve them in your client's favor. Although your memorandum should cover the points of concurrence enough to provide context for your discussion of the points of clash, you should not allocate much space to those points.

B.   STRESSING STRENGTHS AND WORKING AROUND WEAKNESSES

1.   *Discerning Strengths and Weaknesses*

Once you have sorted through the assertions, both legal and factual, that you want to make and thought through your opponent's arguments, you should assess the overall strengths and weaknesses of your case. Every case in litigation has its strengths and weaknesses; truly one-sided cases generally are resolved before litigation by the parties or their lawyers. Of course, one side's strength is usually the other side's weakness.

Some cases are said to be "strong on the law," while others are "strong on the facts" or "strong on policy." A case is strong on the law when the rule is well established, clearly addresses the client's situation, and calls for the client's desired outcome. A case is strong on the facts, or equities, when a reasonable observer easily empathizes with the client and sees the client's desired outcome as sensible and fair. A case is strong on policy when the client's goals reflect an important societal interest.

If the case raises multiple issues, the strengths and weaknesses may vary across issues. For example, the plaintiff may have the stronger legal position as to one claim, while the defendant has the stronger position as to another. Or the plaintiff's case may be strong on facts as to liability but weak on facts as to damages. Moreover, one party may have the advantage on the substantive law, while the other may have the advantage on the procedural law.

In the HomeElderCare case, the two sides have interesting mixes of strengths and weaknesses. Generally, the rule on temporary injunctions favors the party opposing the motion, although the State can counter with the authorization of injunctions in the unauthorized practice statute. The State has a strong legal-document argument, while HomeElderCare has a strong argument under the difficult-or-doubtful-legal-question test. Mr. Nelson's situation is a strength for the State, especially because it illustrates the public policy behind the unauthorized practice statute. However, HomeElderCare has a strong record of client service (apart from Mr. Nelson) in an area of articulated client need and legislative concern.

2.   *Stressing Your Strengths*

As you draft your memorandum, you should, of course, stress the strengths highlighted in your theory of the case. The tools for doing so depend on the nature of your strong-suit material. If your case is strong on the law, overall or in part, emphasize the legal rule by presenting the strongest authority possible and developing it fully:

- If the rule emanates from a statute, quote and paraphrase the statute, discuss its underlying policy, and provide an illustrative case.
- If the rule emanates from case law, present the rule itself, and also describe one or two cases in some depth. You could cite an early case to underscore the rule's long standing, and you could cite a recent case to underscore its continued authority.

If your case is strong on the facts, overall or in part, emphasize the facts:

- Quote from the record.
- Stack evidence on a key fact by showing that it appears in multiple sources.
- Note not only what the evidence shows, but also what it does not show.
- If possible, develop an extended comparison to a decided case, or present several case comparisons, but not so many that the reader loses sight of your client's case.

If your case is strong on policy, overall or in part:

- Quote from cases, a statutory purpose section, or commentary that states the policy clearly.
- Show how the policy plays out in the facts of your case.
- Refute any opposing policy statements by your opponent by citing authority that downplays that policy, showing its inconsistency with your policy, or demonstrating its irrelevance to the case.

These methods may be used in various parts of your memorandum. You likely will seek to emphasize favorable law or policy in the introduction or summary, issues, and argument. In all of these areas, and also in the fact statement, you will seek to emphasize favorable facts.

In the sample HomeElderCare memorandum, you will note an essential contrast in the State's reliance on the law versus HomeElderCare's emphasis on the facts and equities. This contrast is apparent in the parties' discussion of the equities element of the injunction rule: HomeElderCare leading with two versions of the harm factor (starting at pages 372 and 373), the State presenting a short discussion of this factor well into the argument (starting at page 366).

3. Working Around Your Weaknesses

You cannot simply wish that the weaknesses in your client's case will go away and ignore them; they certainly will appear in your opponent's memorandum. On the other hand, you should not dwell on the weaknesses, lest the court also do so. Rather, dispel the weaknesses, even as you make the points you want to make. How to do so depends on the nature of the weakness.

Some weaknesses may be matters of law. If the authority is not mandatory, you should downplay it as merely persuasive and non-binding; you also should criticize any weaknesses in its reasoning or policy. If the authority is mandatory case law, you have a range of options:

- Distinguish the case by showing that the facts or issues differ from your case.
- Narrow the scope of the case by confining its holding to facts not present in your case.
- Show that the adverse statement is dictum, not a holding.
- Demonstrate that the case is inconsistent with other binding precedent and should be discounted.
- If needed, argue that the case should be overruled because it relies on weak reasoning, the trend of the law is against it, or the holding is contrary to public policy.

If the adverse mandatory authority is a statute or procedural rule or regulation, you have several options:

- Argue that your case falls outside its scope, based on definitions or other scope sections.
- Focus on cases interpreting the statute if they afford more favorable material.
- Demonstrate that the law is ambiguous given the facts of your case; then provide a favorable interpretation based on legislative history or intent, canons of construction, or policy.
- The most difficult option is to establish that the law is unconstitutional or outside the power of the lawmaking body; a less radical form of this option is to argue for a limiting interpretation that would avoid unconstitutionality and favor the client.

What Happens When You Try to Ignore the Weaknesses of Your Case?

Northwestern National Insurance Co. v. Guthrie,
No. 90 C 4050, 1990 WL 205945 (N.D. Ill. Dec. 3, 1990).

[Northwestern National sought a declaratory judgment that it had no duty to defend or indemnify Guthrie. The parties contested whether the court could look to matters outside the complaint against Guthrie.]

[T]he Court is deeply troubled by the manner in which [Guthrie's] counsel argued this motion. . . . Counsel's memorandum in support of the motion faithfully recites the *Maryland Casualty Co. v. Peppers* line of cases explicating the general rule. Counsel neglects, however, to discuss the exception to that general rule that is directly on point here—a failure that strikes us as something more than mere oversight. For example, counsel quotes a lengthy passage from *State Farm Fire & Casualty Co.,* Defendants' Memorandum at 5, that sets forth the general rule that the court may not look beyond the allegations of the complaint. *State Farm Fire & Casualty Co.,* 176 Ill. App.3d at 866–67, 531 N.E.2d at 919. The *very next sentence,* explaining the exception to the rule in the declaratory judgment context, is not disclosed by counsel. Nor does counsel mention anywhere in the memorandum that such an exception exists. This failure to disclose relevant legal authority borders perilously close to a violation of the legal profession's ethical canons. *See* Illinois Rules of Professional Conduct 3.3(a)(3) ("In appearing in a professional capacity before a tribunal, a lawyer shall not: . . . (3) fail to disclose to the tribunal legal authority in the controlling jurisdiction known to the lawyer to be directly adverse to the position of the client and not disclosed by opposing counsel"). We will assume that counsel's glaring omission is the result of sloppy research and writing, and not an intentional effort to mislead or misdirect this Court. We request that the head of the Litigation Department of [Guthrie's] law firm write to the Court in response to this concern.

Some weaknesses may be matters of fact, as to which you may have several options:

- If there is conflicting evidence on the fact, emphasize the helpful evidence.
- Discuss other facts that put the unfavorable fact into context, without altering the unfavorable fact. For example, if the client acted unwisely, show why the client did so.
- Show that the record does not present an even worse scenario.

Some weaknesses may be matters of policy; again, you have several options:

- Show that your case does not truly implicate the policy.
- Show that the policy is outdated or needs re-evaluation.
- Shift the focus to a competing policy that is well served by the outcome your client seeks.
- If the law is clear and favors your client, point out that the law must be followed even if the court would favor a different policy.

These methods for handling weaknesses may be used as follows: the law and policy methods in the introduction or summary, issues, and argument; the fact methods in all those components of the memorandum and additionally in the fact statement.

Of the two sample memoranda, HomeElderCare's memorandum better illustrates how to deal with adverse law. The memorandum downplays the unauthorized practice statute by focusing on case law; pointing out ambiguities in its connection to the living will statute; and distinguishing *Gardner,* the leading case, which has a favorable rule but adverse outcome (at page 374). HomeElderCare's memorandum deals with the adverse facts regarding Mr. Nelson's situation by subtly suggesting he may have been at fault and pointing out that no real harm occurred (at page 372-73). The State's memorandum deals with the adverse policy of encouraging living wills by showing how this policy is undercut by incompetent assistance by social workers (at page 365-66).

C.   HOW TO HANDLE ADVERSE AUTHORITY AND ARGUMENTS

Adverse authority will not go away just because you ignore it: if the court does not find it, opposing counsel probably will. There are, in fact, a number of reasons for you to address adverse authority. First, as you have just read, the ethical rules require it. Second, a lawyer who ignores adverse authority is seen by courts as unreliable and unpersuasive, while a lawyer who speaks with candor is more easily trusted and respected by the bench. Third, a lawyer who ignores adverse authority throws away the opportunity—often the only opportunity—to give the court reasons for not following it. The first reason applies only to authority within "the controlling jurisdiction," but the others apply to any adverse authority that can be predicted to influence the court, even precedent from other jurisdictions.

If the authority is a statute, court rule, or administrative regulation, you must show that the provision was not intended to govern the controversy, or that it was intended to govern it but without harm to your client. Although it may seem tempting to argue that a statute you do not like is unconstitutional, courts rarely sustain such attacks. In fact, if a statute or similar provision is susceptible to more than one meaning, courts are obliged to choose one that would not violate a controlling constitution. You should frontally attack a statute only if there is significant doubt—shared by respected lawyers—about its validity.

If the adverse authority is precedent, consider distinguishing it, focusing on significant—and not merely coincidental—differences between the precedent and your case. Be careful. The differences on which you rely should be important enough to impress a skeptical judge. Hypertechnical discrepancies and minor factual variations will not persuade because they seem arbitrary rather than a basis for a just decision. Another approach might be to reconcile the precedent with your case, showing that—although the precedent seems superficially adverse—its underlying policy would actually be furthered by the ruling you want from the court. Still another approach is to attack the precedent head-on, challenging its validity on the grounds that it is poorly reasoned or that changes in society or in public policy have made it unworkable. Although the doctrine of stare decisis does not absolutely forbid the overruling of precedent, a frontal attack on mandatory case law is nearly always an uphill fight, to be attempted only when there is very serious doubt—again shared by at least some respected lawyers—about the precedent's viability. In general, do not ask a court to overrule mandatory authority if you can win through distinguishing, reconciliation, or some other skill of precedent analysis. Judges simply prefer distinguishing and reconciling precedent to overruling it. But things are different where local law has a gap and where the challenged authority is not mandatory: if a judge must choose between competing out-of-state rules, he or she will not be able to decide without rejecting at least some precedent as ill-founded.

With both precedent and statutes, you might consider taking more than one approach, arguing in the alternative—but only if neither alternative would weaken the persuasive force of the other. It is not illogical, for example, to argue, first, that a statute was not intended to govern the facts before the court and, alternatively, that, if the statute is interpreted otherwise, it should be held unconstitutional. (For an example, see the brief in Appendix G [Richard K.

Neumann, Jr., Legal Reasoning and Legal Writing: Structure, Strategy, and Style, 6th ed., (2009)].) It is illogical, however, to argue, first, that the statute was not intended to govern the facts and, alternatively, that it should be construed to provide a benefit to the client.

Attack an opposing argument if it has been made by your adversary, or if there is a reasonable possibility that the court might think of it and be persuaded by it: Otherwise, the court will assume that you have no defense to such an argument. But make your own arguments first. You will win more easily if the court's dominant impression is that you deserve to win, rather than that your adversary deserves to lose. A defensive tone can undermine an otherwise worthwhile argument. And your theory will be more easily understood if you argue it before you attack opposing arguments.

If you are responding to a memorandum or brief that your adversary has already propounded,[1] you know most of the arguments that threaten you because they will appear in the document to which you are responding. The court might itself think up other arguments not mentioned by your adversary. Even if an argument has not been mentioned by your adversary, attack it if it has a reasonable chance of occurring to and persuading the court. (In nonresponsive writing, where you will not see your adversary's writing before submitting your own, use this criterion for all opposing arguments.)

How much emphasis should you give to an attack on an adverse argument or authority? Give it as much emphasis as necessary to convince the judge not to rule against you. Little treatment is necessary if the point is minor and if the argument or authority is easily rebutted. You will, of course, need to say more if the point is more significant or if your counter-analysis is more complex. You cannot reduce the force of adverse arguments and authorities by giving them minimal treatment in your own writing: they have lives and voices of their own.

Beginners often have difficulty writing the transition and thesis sentences that introduce attacks on opposing arguments. In responsive writing, it is enough to refer to what opposing counsel has said and then to get on with the counter-argument. Here are some examples:

> The plaintiff misconstrues §401(d)(1). Four other circuits have already decided that §401(d)(1) provides for X and not, as the plaintiff contends, for Y. [*Follow with an analysis of the circuit cases.*]

> No appellate court has held to the contrary, and the few district court decisions cited to by the plaintiff are all distinguishable. [*Follow with an analysis of the district court cases.*]

> The legislative history also demonstrates that Congress intended to provide for X and not for Y. [*Follow with an analysis of the legislative history.*]

These opening sentences are written so that opposing counsel's contention is surrounded by the writer's counter-contention and the beginning of the

---

1. The attorney going forward—the movant in a trial court or the appellant on appeal—submits a memorandum or brief. Then the opposing attorney submits an answering memorandum or brief. The first attorney may complete the exchange with a reply memorandum or brief. This is called *responsive* writing. In some situations—usually in trial courts—the attorneys submit their documents simultaneously each without having seen the other's writing. Most law school persuasive writing assignments are *non*responsive.

counter-contention's proof. The effect is to argue affirmatively and not defensively. This is much weaker:

> The plaintiff has argued that §401(d)(1) provides for Y, but . . .

In nonresponsive situations—where you suspect but do not actually know which arguments your adversary will make—begin simply by denying the contention while emphasizing your counter-contention:

> Section 401(d)(1) provides for X and not for Y.

The following sounds defensive and almost silly:

> Opposing counsel might argue that §401(d)(1) provides for Y, but . . .

Opposing counsel might never argue it, but it may occur to the judge or to the judge's law clerk.

Both in responsive and in nonresponsive writing, a dependent clause can be useful in thesis and transition sentences:

> Although the House Judiciary Committee report states that its bill would have provided for Y, §401(d)(1) more closely tracks the bill drafted in the Senate Judiciary Committee. Both that committee's report and the conference committee report flatly state that §401(d)(1) provides for X.

Be careful, however, not to use a dependent clause to make a relatively minor problem look like a major one. For example, compare

> Although a few district courts have held that §401(d)(1) provides for Y, every circuit that has faced the question has held the contrary.

with

> Every circuit that has faced the question has held that §401(d)(1) provides for X. [*Analysis of circuit cases.*] The few district court cases to the contrary are distinguishable.

Exercise I.   *The Shoelaces*

Go back to the shoelace arguments on page 222. Imagine that you are a member of Congress and will have to vote on this matter soon. You have to choose between these two sets of arguments. Does one of them persuade you? Why? Does one (or both) leave holes that bother you—and therefore make you hesitate? If the answer to that question is yes, why? What could fill the gap? Why does the gap exist?

Exercise II.   The Painter and the Preschool

Remember that a judge begins to take sides if she or he can visualize real people doing real things to each other. In the memorandum in Appendix F [Richard K. Neumann, Jr., Legal Reasoning and Legal Writing: Structure, Strategy, and Style, 6th ed., (2009)], how and where are the mental images created? Find the passages that put them into your mind. What did the writer do to help you see them?

D. ESTABLISHING LEGAL PLAUSIBILITY

In Chapter 5 [Michael R. Smith, Advanced Legal Writing: Theories and Strategies in Persuasive Writing, 2nd ed., (2008)], we explored the inverse relationship between logos and pathos. In that discussion, we saw an important limitation on the power of pathos as a process of persuasion: If the law on an issue is clear, a judge will generally not consider the emotional facts of the case or any policy arguments, no matter how compelling they may be. The importance of this limitation, however, is not that it tells advocates when to give up on pathos; rather, it tells advocates when they must work harder to achieve it.

If an advocate has strong emotional facts or strong policy arguments but is faced with apparently binding adverse authority, the advocate's first goal must be to find a way around the adverse authority. In this situation, the legal advocate must offer the decision-maker at least a legally plausible argument for why the adverse authority does not control the issue. Without at least a legally plausible strategy for dealing with the adverse authority, the decision-maker is forced to follow that authority and ignore pathos altogether.

Many metaphors have been used to describe this relationship between pathos and adverse legal authority.

- An advocate must get his or her *foot in the door* with a plausible legal argument before the decision-maker will consider the policy implications and emotional facts.
- An advocate must give the decision-maker a *legal hook* on which to hang the policy implications and emotional facts.
- Offering a plausible legal argument for dealing with adverse authority is a *threshold requirement* for arguing policy and emotional facts.

What is particularly interesting about this foot-in-the-door advocacy strategy is its bootstrapping nature (yet another metaphor). If a legal advocate is able to offer a legally plausible argument for dealing with apparently binding adverse authority, the decision-maker will then be able to take into account the emotional facts and policy implications of the case. The more the decision-maker is able to consider the emotional facts and policy, the more motivated the decision-maker will be to favor the advocate's position. And the more motivated the decision-maker is to favor the advocate's position, the more viable and legitimate the advocate's legal arguments appear. Thus, what may start off as merely a legally plausible argument for dealing with adverse authority can end up looking like the preferable interpretation of the adverse authority because the decision-maker will be motivated by pathos to want to interpret the law that way. In other words, the weaker legal position can prevail because the pathos implications of the case motivate the decision-maker to want that position to prevail. And the whole process begins with a legally plausible foot—or should I say boot—in the door.

1. An Example of the Failure to Establish Legal Plausibility

In the case of *United States v. Johnson,*[2] Robert Johnson was prosecuted in federal court for possession of cocaine with the intent to distribute. Johnson had been arrested following a routine traffic stop of his van. During the traffic stop, without Johnson's consent and without suspicion that Johnson possessed drugs, the police officer walked a drug-detection dog around Johnson's vehicle. From outside the van, the dog detected cocaine, and Johnson was arrested.

During Johnson's trial, his attorney filed a motion to suppress the evidence found in the traffic stop, arguing that the search of Johnson's van was unconstitutional. The motion was denied, and Johnson was subsequently convicted. His attorney appealed to the Seventh Circuit Court of Appeal.

On appeal, Johnson's attorney was confronted with the U. S. Supreme Court case of *Illinois v. Caballes,*[3] decided only two months earlier. In *Caballes,* the Court held under very similar facts that, "A dog sniff conducted during a concededly lawful traffic stop that reveals no information other than the location of a substance that no individual has the right to possess does not violate the Fourth Amendment."[4] Unable to distinguish *Caballes,* Johnson's attorney focused instead on policy arguments criticizing the overly aggressive crime detection methods used by the police. This strategy of Johnson's attorney is reflected in the following transcript of the oral argument before the Seventh Circuit. To say that the attorney had a difficult time before the court would be an understatement. (An audio recording of this oral argument can be heard on the Seventh Circuit's website, Oral Argument Case Number 04-2732.)

———————————

Judge #1:   Our third case for argument this morning is United States against Johnson. . . .

Defense Counsel: Your honors. May it please the court. I think I reserved two minutes for rebuttal.

Judge #2:   Yup, you have.

Defense Counsel: Thank you.

Judge #2:   Now go ahead.

Defense Counsel: I'll be honest with this court. I don't think that the position that we have is one that this court has honored, has found to be a very strong one. But I think that we have a problem with police taking advantage of interrogations situations, of hoping that they will find evidence, of making

2. 123 Fed. Appx. 240 (7th Circuit 2005).
3. 543 U.S. 405 (2005).
4. *Id.* at 410.

pretextual stops and using the situation by saying "yes, this gentleman was speeding" and then ultimately finding cocaine and being happy when they make the arrest and ultimately make the conviction.

Judge #3:   Counsel is there anything left of your argument after the Supreme Court's decision in January in the *Caballes* case?

Defense Counsel: I understand. I mean, I'm here because I feel very strongly about this. I mean, my words are probably not being heard by very many people. But I feel it necessary that some people need to listen. There are . . .

Judge #3:   Any way to distinguish it? I mean I understand you object to the premise that . . .

Defense Counsel: I hope *you* can find one.

Judge #2:   Well, what you want us to do is overrule the Supreme Court.

Defense Counsel: I want you to find how we distinguish this Judge. I just, I'm very disturbed.

Judge #2:   Well you can be disturbed on your own time. Why are you intruding in mine?

Defense Counsel: Well because I . . .

Judge #2:   I can't reverse the Supreme Court.

Defense Counsel: . . . because I want you to be disturbed, too.

Judge #2:   Well, if I am disturbed, it's for arguments that have nothing to do with reality.

Defense Counsel: I understand, and I don't want to argue. I want to help effect a change that is positive to this country.

Judge #2:   Is there anything in your argument that is different than your brief, or have you expended your spleen on the brief itself?

Defense Counsel: The only thing I would tell you at this point, that is not in here, is that the government talks about how the consent is, we have to look at the issue of consent. There obviously is no . . .

Judge #2:   Consent isn't necessary on the facts in this case.

Defense Counsel: Based on the dog.

Judge #2:   Based on the Supreme Court.

Defense Counsel: I know, I know. Well I have nothing else to say. Good luck.

Judge #1:   Thank you, counsel. Mr. Brookman

U. S. Counsel: May it please the court, my name is Matt Brookman. I am an assistant U.S. Attorney from the . . .

Judge #2:   I assume you don't want us to overrule the Supreme Court.

U. S. Counsel: I don't.

Judge #2:   That's good.

U.S. Counsel: Thank you very much. I appreciate your time.

Judge #1:   Thank you very much. The case is taken under advisement.

As this transcript demonstrates, the defense attorney's primary strategy before the Seventh Circuit was to argue policy about the chilling nature of the police tactics used in the case.[5] Not surprisingly, however, the judges were not

5. The defense attorney might have argued along the lines of Justice Ginsburg's dissent in *Caballes*: "Today's decision . . . clears the way for suspicionless, dog-accompanied drug sweeps of parked cars along sidewalks and in parking lots. . . . Nor would motorists have constitutional grounds for complaint should police with dogs, stationed at long traffic lights, circle cars waiting for the red signal to turn green." *Id.* at 422 (Ginsburg, J., dissenting).

willing to entertain the attorney's policy arguments unless he could first offer some way of dealing with the *Caballes* case. Because the attorney could not offer a legally plausible theory for dealing with *Caballes*, he was prevented from making his policy arguments. In fact, his attempts to argue policy in the face of *Caballes* appeared to annoy the judges. The Seventh Circuit ultimately affirmed Johnson's conviction, stating the following at the end of its very brief opinion: "At argument, Johnson could not distinguish his case from *Caballes*, and neither can we."[6]

Johnson's attorney was obviously passionate about the policy implications of his case. But, as the court's decision demonstrates, passion and policy alone are often not enough.

2.   *An Example of Dealing with Adverse Authority Prior to Arguing Policy*

In contrast to the previous example, the case of *GECAL v. Violante*[7] illustrates how an attorney can successfully argue policy in the face of adverse authority. In *GECAL*, General Electric Capital Auto Lease (GECAL), operating in New Jersey, leased an automobile to Alfonso Violante. Under the terms of the lease, the lessee (Violante) was required to maintain and repair the car at his own expense.

One day the car was vandalized, and Violante engaged David's Towing Service (DTS) to retrieve and repair the car. DTS towed the car to its lot and awaited insurance authorization to begin the repairs. Before the repairs were begun, GECAL sued Violante for breach of the lease and sued DTS for possession of the car. DTS turned the car over to GECAL, but counterclaimed in the suit, arguing that it had a lien on the car under New Jersey's Garage Keeper's Lien Act for the amount it was owed for the retrieval and storage of the car.

The Lien Act provided in relevant part that "A garage keeper who shall store, maintain, keep or repair a motor vehicle . . . *at the request or with the consent of the owner or his representative*, shall have a lien upon the motor vehicle or any part thereof for the sum due for such storing, maintaining, keeping or repairing of such motor vehicle."[8] GECAL filed a motion for summary judgment against DTS's counterclaim, and the trial court granted it. DTS appealed.

On appeal to the intermediate appellate court, GECAL's attorney argued that the Lien Act did not apply because neither GECAL (as owner) nor its representative "requested" or "consented to" DTS's services as required by the statute. The attorney for DTS countered by arguing that the provision in the lease requiring the lessee to maintain and repair the car amounted to "consent" on the part of GECAL to Violante's request for DTS's services. DTS also argued that the issue was one of first impression in New Jersey and set forth several policy arguments for its position.

The appellate court, however, disagreed with DTS's contention that the issue was one of first impression. To the contrary, the court felt bound by prior decisions by New Jersey's highest court and by the New Jersey intermediate appellate court, *Stern v. Ward*[9] and *Auto Security Co. v. Stewart*,[10] respectively, which

---

6. *Johnson*, 123 Fed. Appx. at 240.
7. 817 A.2d 376 (N.J. Super. App. Div. 2003), *rev'd*, 848 A.2d 732 (N.J. 2004).
8. *Id.* at 379-80 (quoting N.J.S.A. 2A:44-21) (emphasis added).
9. 109 A. 566 (N.J. 1920).
10. 135 A. 92 (N.J. Sup. Ct. 1926).

held that "the lessee of an automobile was not, by reason of that status alone, the representative of the owner for the purpose of incurring the charges at the root of the lien claim."[11] The appellate court thus felt compelled to rule against DTS even though it found DTS's policy arguments persuasive:

> In the face of these decisions, we cannot accept the characterization of this case offered by [DTS], that it is one of first impression. Were we writing on a clean slate, the arguments urged by [DTS] might be seen as persuasive. One position is that the lessor in such a situation is in a better position to protect its interests than the garage keeper is to protect its interests. Another is that, to the extent the services provided preserved and protected the property, a benefit was ultimately conferred on the owner thereof, the lessor. But the power *vel non* of these arguments is beside the point. We are bound by the ruling of the Court of Errors and Appeals in *Stern v. Ward;* and the holdings in cases as venerable as *Auto Security* . . . should not be lightly disregarded.[12]

Undaunted, DTS appealed to the New Jersey Supreme Court.[13] This time around, however, DTS's attorney changed his strategy. Because the intermediate appellate court viewed *Ward* and *Auto Security* as controlling of the issue, the attorney first focused his attention on distinguishing those cases. After dealing with the apparent adverse authority, DTS's attorney then argued why policy supported his interpretation of the Lien Act.

Ultimately, the New Jersey Supreme Court reversed the lower courts' decisions and held that DTS did acquire a lien on the car under the Lien Act. Following DTS's position, the New Jersey Supreme Court explained as follows how it reconciled its holding with *Ward* and *Auto Security* and how policy supported its ultimate decision:

> [T]he Appellate Division primarily relied on *Ward* and *Auto Security Co.* in finding no enforceable lien to exist under the Act. A close reading of those cases, however, reveals that they are distinguishable from the facts presented by this appeal. *Ward* involved a lease agreement, governed by Pennsylvania law, that expressly forbade the lessee from having the vehicle repaired without first obtaining the lessor's consent. Moreover, at that time, Pennsylvania law did not consider a lessee to be an owner's "representative" under such an agreement. Based on the terms of the agreement and the applicable law, the Court of Errors and Appeals concluded that the lessee was not the lessor's "representative" and, thus, did not have the power to incur a garage keeper's lien on the lessor's vehicle. In *Auto Security Co.*, the court found *Ward* controlling because the lease agreement contained similar contractual terms and also was subject to Pennsylvania law. . . .
>
> This case presents a very different lease agreement, one that expressly requires the lessee to repair and maintain the vehicle. That fact alone distinguishes *Ward* and *Auto Security Co.* . . . .
>
> The primary purpose of the statute is to ensure that garage keepers receive payment for storage, maintenance, supplies, repairs, and other services furnished to a motor vehicle. Despite its focus on the garage keeper, the Act affords owners with protection from unauthorized liens through the consent requirement. But by contractually compelling a lessee to maintain the vehicle in good repair, an owner gives its assent to and approval for those services that are necessary for preservation of the vehicle's value. In such circumstances, the owner must be considered

11. *GECAL*, 817 A.2d at 380 (summarizing *Stern v. Ward* and *Auto Security Co.*).
12. *Id.*
13. *GECAL v. Violante*, 848 A.2d 732 (N.J. 2004).

to have "consented" to repairs ordered by the lessee, who similarly must be viewed as the owner's "representative" under the statutory scheme. Although the terms of a lease may allocate financial responsibility for repairs to the lessee, that language is not determinative of the relative rights of the lessor and a third-party garage keeper for expenses related to servicing the vehicle. Because the lessor receives an undeniable benefit from the garage keeper's labor and services, denying the validity of a lien would unfairly prejudice the garage keeper and thereby undermine the statute's central purpose. . . .

Applying the above principles to the facts in this case, we hold that the lessee had the authority to act as GECAL's "representative," as that term is used in the Act, when he requested [DTS's] services.[14]

The *GECAL* case is a compelling example of an advocate effectively combining legal arguments with policy arguments. DTS's attorney was faced with two hurdles as he appealed to the New Jersey Supreme Court. First, he had to somehow distinguish *Ward* and *Auto Security Co.*, which the intermediate appellate court found controlling. Second, even if he was able to distinguish those cases, at best he would be left with an issue of first impression. Thus, he then had to argue convincingly that the policy implications of the case supported his interpretation of the Lien Act. As we can see from the Supreme Court's opinion, the attorney succeeded on both counts.

---

14. *Id.* at 737-38, 738-39 (citations omitted).

CHAPTER

19

Final Steps

A.   PROFESSIONALISM: FOLLOWING FORMAT RULES

Although fulfilling your brief's format requirements is a much less intellectually demanding task than writing the argument, it is nonetheless important. Rightly or wrongly, many readers form an impression of your credibility based on whether you conform to the minutiae of court rules. Your willingness to learn and follow rules about document format and filing guidelines tells the court that you are a professional, and that you take court requirements seriously. More significantly, you may suffer sanctions—from having to fix offending portions of the brief to having your case dismissed—for failure to follow certain rules.[1]

Most state and federal courts in the United States are governed by at least two sets of rules. The more significant rules are the rules of procedure that govern all of the courts within a certain jurisdiction, for example, the Federal Rules of Civil Procedure, the Federal Rules of Appellate Procedure, or the Ohio Rules of Appellate Procedure.

Most courts also have so-called local rules that may deal with requirements such as filing requirements, page length, certificates of service, service on opposing parties, citations, and the like. In 2002, the Ninth Circuit dismissed an appeal for failure to comply with certain Federal Rules of Appellate Procedure (FRAP) and with circuit rules.[2] The court noted that "[a]n enormous amount of time is wasted when attorneys fail to provide proper briefs and excerpts of record that should have supplied the court with the materials relevant to the appeal. The FRAP and Ninth Circuit rules are not optional suggestions . . . but *rules* that . . . are entitled to respect, and command compliance."[3]

In addition to expecting counsel to follow local rules, some courts expect counsel to be aware of local practices, the customs and behaviors that are unwritten but practiced by experienced local lawyers. Appellate courts that allow electronic filing may prefer to have counsel file an additional hard copy if

---

1. Judith D. Fischer, *Bareheaded and Barefaced Counsel: Courts React to Unprofessionalism in Lawyers' Papers*, 31 Suffolk U. L. Rev. 1, 31 et seq. (1997) (this article also contains several examples of courts' reactions to misstatements of law and facts and other failings). *See also* Judith D. Fischer, *Pleasing the Court: Writing Ethical and Effective Briefs* (Carolina Academic Press 2005).

2. *In re O'Brien*, 312 F.3d 1135, 1136 (9th Cir. 2002).

3. *Id.* at 1137 (citation omitted; emphasis in original).

the document is lengthy. Trial judges may have "standing orders" that lay out rules for counsel to follow in all trials in front of that particular judge. Taking the time to read a judge's standing order (often posted on the judge's Web site) may provide you with valuable information that will save you time and trouble and help you to make a good impression on the court. Whenever you have to file a brief, make sure that you have copies of all of the written rules that apply to documents submitted to that court, and try to find out the local practices and customs by consulting court Web sites, more experienced colleagues, or both.

This chapter explains the format requirements that are common to appellate briefs and motion briefs. For appellate brief requirements, it usually refers to Supreme Court rules; however, most of the requirements listed are common in other appellate courts. For motion brief requirements, it usually refers to federal court rules. Samples of a motion brief and of appellate briefs appear in Appendix C [Mary Beth Beazley, A Practical Guide to Appellate Advocacy, 3rd ed., (2010)]. Of course, you should follow the rules of the court to which you are writing or of your professor.

1. Length Requirements

Probably the most significant format mistake that lawyers make is to fail to follow required length limits. Unfortunately, some lawyers see an imposed length limit as a sort of challenge, and they turn the limit into a goal. Most courts design their limits to accommodate even complex cases that require lengthy analysis of each issue. Your goal as a writer should be to write enough about each issue to answer the question that issue presents and to give the reader confidence that your answer is correct. Lawyers do not win any points from judges for padding simple arguments, making the same point in two or three different point heading sections, or describing five cases where one would make the point. On the contrary, most judges are grateful to read a brief that makes its points effectively and then stops.[4]

All of this is not to say that you should give the court only a cursory description of your arguments. Presume that your readers are intelligent, but that they are ignorant of the particulars of the case currently before the court. Your brief should give enough details about your case, and about the cases and other authorities that you cite, for the members of the court to understand your analysis without having to resort to other documents. Of course, they might understand things more deeply if they read all of the cases or reviewed the entire record, but your job is not to give them the same in-depth knowledge of the case that you have. Rather, you should perform a cost-benefit analysis vis-à-vis the information that you provide. For example, a brief case description will give the court a reasonable understanding of the authority and will take two or three sentences. A lengthy case description may take two or three paragraphs, but in most situations, it will not provide any more needed insight than a two-or-three sentence description.

Courts may express a length limit as a page limit, a word limit, or both. The Local Rules of King County, Washington, for example, limit motions for summary judgment and supporting memoranda to 24 pages; Rule 32(a)(7) of the

---

4. *See generally* Fischer, *Bareheaded and Barefaced Counsel, supra* note 1, at 27.

Federal Rules of Appellate Procedure limits a principal appellate brief to 30 pages (with certain typeface restrictions) or 14,000 words. Rule 32(a)(7)(C) specifically allows counsel to rely on the "word or line count of the word-processing system used to prepare the brief." The page limits on briefs may vary depending on what category a brief falls into. Briefs on dispositive motions generally have higher page limits; for example, Rule 3.113(d) of the 2010 California Rules of Court specify that a supporting memorandum for a summary judgment or summary adjudication motion is limited to 20 pages, while memoranda for all other motions are limited to 15 pages.

2. Typefaces and Margins

Many courts have imposed font size and margin requirements in reaction to lawyers who try to evade length requirements by using smaller margins, smaller fonts, or other techniques. Note that courts may sanction counsel who violate length requirements.[5] In addition to font and length *requirements*, some courts have issued suggestions to help counsel make their briefs easier to read. The Seventh Circuit, for example, has published a "Guideline for Briefs and Other Papers" on its Web site, and it recommends that counsel read a law review article to help improve the typography of documents submitted to the court.[6] If the court to which you are submitting your brief does not specify anything beyond page limits, presume standard margins (one-inch all around) and a standard font size (12-point, nonproportional spacing).

3. Filing Requirements and Number of Copies

Courts impose very specific filing requirements on brief-writers, listing specifics for everything from the method of service to the number of copies filed. Although some requirements may seem overly detailed, following them helps both the readers and the users of the brief to do their jobs more easily and efficiently. This section explains some categories of common requirements, but be sure to consult jurisdictional rules, local rules, and local practices before filing a brief in a new court.

In the past, all documents were filed in hard copy at the courthouse, and counsel attached a paper certificate of service (discussed below) to certify that he or she had served opposing counsel as appropriate. These days, more and more courts are allowing or even requiring the electronic filing of documents as a substitute for hard-copy delivery. Most courts that do so provide very precise instructions as to method. If you file a brief electronically, make sure that your document survived the trip through cyberspace. The court may provide an electronic receipt that allows you to open your document to check it. Be sure to do so. Do not rely on the receipt itself: Open the document and make sure that the document transmission was successful. Further, the first time you use an electronic filing system for a particular court, plan to file your brief at least 24 hours

---

5. *See* Fischer, *Bareheaded and Barefaced Counsel, supra* note 1, at 31-32.

6. *Requirements and Suggestions for Typography in Briefs and Other Papers* 4, http://www.ca7.uscourts.gov/Rules/type.pdf (last accessed May 7, 2010) (citing Ruth Anne Robbins, *Painting with Print: Incorporating Concepts of Typographic and Layout Design into the Text of Legal Writing Documents*, 2 J. Assn. Leg. Writing Dirs. 108 (2004)).

in advance. Many courts now have midnight filing deadlines. If you put off filing your brief until shortly before the deadline, you will have no one to ask for help if things go wrong. On the other hand, if you file early and have trouble, you will be able to seek help during normal business hours.

As for number of copies, United States Supreme Court Rule 33.1(f) requires that 40 copies of the brief should be filed with the court in most circumstances. It is common for appellate courts to require a large number of copies because a panel of judges and their clerks will all need to review the brief. Local Appellate Rule 31.1 of the Third Circuit Local Appellate Rules requires that "each party must file ten (10) paper copies (i.e., an original and nine copies) of each brief with the clerk for the convenience of the court" and serve one paper copy on opposing counsel unless counsel has agreed to electronic filing. Of course, if you are filing a motion brief, you are submitting the brief to a single judge rather than to a panel, so a smaller number of copies may be required.

As noted previously, in some courts, local practice dictates that when attorneys file either appellate or motion briefs, they must file "courtesy copies," "working copies," or "judges' copies" with the court. If a document is filed in hard copy, the "official version" of the document cannot be marked up by a judge or the judge's clerk. Thus, counsel may provide one or more extra copies to speed the court's consideration of the brief. Even when briefs are filed electronically, some courts may require either electronic or hard-copy "working copies."[7]

Court rules may also specify particular typefaces or font sizes (to ease reading), the method of binding (to prevent staple injuries), the color of the brief cover (to allow easy retrieval of a particular brief), and the method of service on opposing counsel. Whenever you file a document with a court, make sure that you are following all needed filing requirements. Doing so will impress the court with your professionalism, will avoid sanctions, and may help speed a decision in your case.

B. FORMATTING THE BRIEF

Now it is time to decide what other sections the brief will include. Refer to the instructions you received with your assignment, to section III [Linda H. Edwards, Legal Writing: Process, Analysis, and Organization, 5th ed., (2010)] of Chapter 3 for a description of the various sections, and to the sample briefs in Appendices D and E [Linda H. Edwards, Legal Writing: Process, Analysis, and Organization, 5th ed., (2010)]. Draft all of the components your finished brief will contain except the Statement of Facts. For formatting information, follow first the applicable court rules and your law firm's or teacher's instructions. To whatever extent they do not contradict your other instructions, follow these guidelines:

1. Caption. The court's name, the parties' names, and the document title should appear in all capital letters (all caps). The parties' procedural titles (for

---

7. For example, the court Web site for King County, Washington, notes that electronic filing "does not satisfy any requirement [of] parties to submit working copies," and provides detailed instructions for filing electronic working copies: http://www.kingcounty.gov/courts/Clerk/E-Working%20Copies.aspx (last accessed May 7, 2010).

example, Plaintiff, Appellant, Defendant, Appellee) should appear in initial caps.

2. Components of the brief. The titles of the components of the brief (for example, Question Presented, Statement of the Case, Argument, Conclusion) should be centered and underlined and should appear in all caps. Some court rules require the Question Presented to appear on a page by itself.

3. Point headings. The point headings (those marked by roman numerals) should appear in all caps, single-spaced but not underlined. Some writers center them, but this can make a long point heading even harder to read. A better choice might be to use the full width of the line so the reader isn't confronted with a block of capital letters resembling a ten-story building.

4. Subheadings. Subheadings should be indented one tab space, underlined, and single-spaced. They should use capitalization as if they were a normal sentence of text.

5. Table of Contents. The section titles for the components of the brief (such as Question Presented, Statement of the Case, Argument, Conclusion) should appear in initial caps in the Table of Contents, using Rule 8 of the Bluebook as a guide for determining which words to capitalize.

Point headings should appear in the Table of Contents in the same typeface as they appear in the text of the Argument, that is, all caps, single-spaced, not underlined. Some writers make the typeface for subheadings in the Table of Contents consistent with the typeface in the text as well. However, underlining the subheadings in the Table of Contents, where they appear together, makes them hard to read. Consider omitting the underlining for subheadings.

6. Text. Briefs should be double-spaced except where otherwise indicated. Insert two spaces between sentences. Do not justify the right margin. Page numbers should be centered at the bottom of the page.

Now all of the brief's components are in place except the Statement of Facts. The next chapter covers drafting a persuasive Statement of Facts.

C. AVOIDING SPELLING, GRAMMATICAL, AND TYPOGRAPHICAL ERRORS

Avoiding mechanical errors does not really present an opportunity for persuasion. Your reader will not particularly notice or remark upon a brief that is free of these problems: Perfection on small things is a minimal expectation. Unfortunately, however, mechanical errors will have a negative effect. Many readers presume that someone who writes a document with mechanical errors cannot be trusted to conduct sound legal analysis. While the logic behind this attitude may be questionable, it's unmistakable that the attitude is there, and it provides one more reason why you should proofread diligently.

Chapter Twelve [Mary Beth Beazley, A Practical Guide to Appellate Advocacy, 3rd ed., (2010)] talks about effective proofreading methods, and Appendix A [Mary Beth Beazley, A Practical Guide to Appellate Advocacy, 3rd ed., (2010)] addresses common punctuation mistakes.

D.   CREDIBILITY THROUGH DOCUMENT DESIGN

The way your document looks also creates an opportunity for persuasion. If it is neat, clean, visually easy to read, and complies with all local rules, you will impress the court with your competence, and your credibility will rise. Courts are beginning to recognize the benefits of effective document design, and to encourage—or require—that counsel keep readability in mind. The Seventh Circuit's Web site, for example, features a link called "Guidelines for Briefs and Other Papers" that links to a document explaining the importance of effective typography. The document notes the importance of effective document design:

> Choosing the best type[face] won't guarantee success, but it is worthwhile to invest some time in improving the quality of the brief's appearance and legibility.
>
> Judges of this court hear six cases on most argument days and nine cases on others. The briefs, opinions of the district courts, essential parts of the appendices, and other required reading add up to about 1,000 pages per argument session. Reading that much is a chore; remembering it is even harder. *You can improve your chances by making your briefs typographically superior. It won't make your arguments better, but it will ensure that judges grasp and maintain your points with less struggle.* That's a valuable advantage, which you should seize.[8]

Many small decisions can affect the ease with which the reader can read your brief. The reader's comfort level with the document itself can affect both your credibility and your chances for success as an advocate.

E.   POLISHING

Unfortunately, many writers lose interest when they read advice about polishing the mechanics of a document because they think that people do not notice mechanics or that their administrative assistants will take care of mechanical problems. First of all, people do notice "the small stuff." Judge Wald, of the D.C. Circuit, has recommended that counsel "proofread with a passion":

> You cannot imagine how disquieting it is to find several spelling or grammatical errors in an otherwise competent brief. It makes the judge go back to square one

8. United States Court of Appeals for the Seventh Circuit, *Requirements and Suggestions for Typography in Briefs and Other Papers* 4, http://www.ca7.uscourts.gov/Rules/type.pdf (last accessed May 13, 2010) (emphasis added).

in evaluating the counsel. It says—worst of all—the author never bothered to read the whole thing through, but she expects us to.[9]

Fairly or unfairly, many readers see mechanical mistakes as a sign of overall incompetence; too many typographical errors may lead the judge to mistrust the validity of the legal analysis. Justice Ginsburg has observed that if a brief is "sloppy" in regard to mechanics, "the judge may suspect its reliability in other respects as well."[10] In a 1994 case, a federal district judge dismissing a complaint ordered a sanctions hearing for the plaintiff's attorney, noting that the attorney's mechanical errors were evidence of a lack of due care:

> [Counsel] continues to submit documents to this Court with grammatical errors and misstatements. . . . Moreover, throughout the Amended Complaint [the attorney] repeatedly refers to his client as "he" instead of "she." These types of errors strongly suggest that Mr. Williams has not taken the appropriate care to avoid errors before submitting documents to this Court.[11]

To take a more practical view, failure to take care with polishing may cost you money. In a case that received wide publicity (including a story in the *New York Times*), an attorney whose courtroom work was praised had his fees for his written work cut in half—from $300 to $150 per hour—due in large part to sloppy proofreading.[12] When he was interviewed about the case, the federal judge who decided on the award of attorneys' fees commented that "no matter how good you are in front of the jury, most of your reputation's going to be built on what you write."[13]

The second reason you must learn polishing skills is that you probably cannot afford an assistant who can do this level of polishing. You must take responsibility for polishing the mechanics of your legal documents because your document reflects on your client and on your competence.

Polishing is hard for the same reason that revision is hard. Most people don't really see their writing when they review it. Instead, they see the document that they meant to write; their short-term memory interferes with their ability to see typographical errors or other problems. For that reason, this chapter identifies some objective methods for polishing that will help you to break up that relationship between your short-term memory and your document, and help you to catch mistakes in both your writing and your analysis.

The best way to proofread effectively is to put your writing away for a while. If you've ever gone back and read a document that you wrote last year, or even last month, you've probably noticed several mistakes or style problems that you missed when you wrote it. If you are trying to polish a document that you wrote this morning, your short-term memory makes it hard for you to see your mistakes. It knows what you wanted to say, and it tends to gloss over the

9. Patricia M. Wald, *19 Tips from 19 Years on the Appellate Bench*, 1 J. App. Prac. & Process 7, 22 (1999).

10. Ruth Bader Ginsburg, *Remarks on Appellate Advocacy*, 50 S.C. L. Rev. 567, 568 (1999).

11. *Styles v. Philadelphia Elec. Co.*, No. CIV. A. 93-4593, 1994 WL 245469, at *3 (E.D. Pa. June 6, 1994) (cited in Judith D. Fischer, *Bareheaded and Barefaced Counsel: Courts React to Unprofessionalism in Lawyers' Papers*, 31 Suffolk U. L. Rev. 1, 27 (1997)).

12. *DeVore v. City of Philadelphia*, 2004 U.S. Dist. LEXIS 3635, at *6 (E.D. Pa. Feb. 20, 2004). The court noted that counsel's lack of care "caused the court, and I am sure, defense counsel, to expend an inordinate amount of time deciphering the arguments." *Id.* at *6-7.

13. *All Things Considered*, "Magistrate Judge Jacob P. Hart Discusses His Fight to Get Lawyers to Clean Up Their Written Work" (NPR Mar. 4, 2004) (radio broadcast).

mistakes.[14] Therefore, if you can get a draft done a week before your deadline, *don't* reread it and edit it every day. Instead, wait three days and do a thorough edit, and then wait three more days and do a final edit.[15] Even a little time can make some difference. In a crunch, that might mean taking a 15-minute walk and then coming back to edit, but taking some time can make a difference.

A second effective polishing technique is to "start in the middle" when reviewing your work. Most writing teachers find that mechanical mistakes and other weaknesses show up more often in the second half of the document than in the first half. That's because many writers get bored with editing or polishing as they get closer to the end of the document; many give up before finishing the job. Even conscientious editors should give fresh eyes to different parts of the document at different times.

Generally, it is ineffective to proofread by reading the entire document very slowly once or twice, trying to catch every type of error. Instead, you should read the document through several times on the computer and several times in hard-copy form. Make surgical strikes, focusing on only one or two aspects of the document at a time. For example, you can review the document once just looking at citation form, another time just looking at topic sentences, and so on. This chapter discusses proofreading techniques for both the electronic and hard copy versions of the document.

1. *Methods to Use on the Computer*

You can do some proofreading while your document is still in electronic form. First, you may want to enlarge the font size while you proofread. Enlarging the font (say, to 20- or 22-point size) can have two benefits. First, you can focus more easily because you will have a smaller number of words on the screen at a time. Second, it will be easier to distance yourself from the text because the font change will significantly change the way the document looks. Proofreading electronically also allows you to use your computer software's Find and Replace feature to your advantage. Although your eyes get tired, the computer never misses on a search, presuming you are searching precisely.

1. Pronoun search. Use the Find and Replace feature to search for *he, she, it, they,* and so on. Stop when you hit a pronoun and scrutinize it to make sure that the reader will have *no doubt* about the noun you are referring to (the antecedent). Also, make sure that you have not mistakenly used *they* in place of *it.* For example, both courts and corporations should be referred to in the singular as *it.*

2. Apostrophe search. If you tend to use too many apostrophes, use the Find and Replace feature to search for *s[apostrophe]* or *[apostrophe]s* so that you can scrutinize whether you've used each apostrophe correctly. If you use too

14. Of course, getting a friend or colleague to review the document can also be helpful, since that person will not have the information in his or her short-term memory. In an academic setting, you should not use this method unless you have *specific* permission from your teacher. In a professional setting, asking a friend to review your work is fine; finding someone who has the time to help you is the hard part.

15. *See also* Judge Stephen J. Dwyer, Leonard J. Feldman & Ryan P. McBride, *How to Write, Edit, and Review Persuasive Briefs: Seven Guidelines from One Judge and Two Lawyers,* 31 Seattle L. Rev. 417, 425 (2008).

few apostrophes, your task is a little harder. You could use the Find and Replace feature to find words that end in *s* by searching for *s[space]* or *s.[space]*. Once you are zeroed in on the potential problem words, consult grammar guidelines to see if you are using apostrophes correctly. Appendix A [Mary Beth Beazley, A Practical Guide to Appellate Advocacy, 3rd ed., (2010)] includes advice about the most common apostrophe problems.

3. Quotation mark search.   The rule in American English is that periods and commas *always* go inside quotation marks, even if you are quoting only one word or one letter:

Bad Example

Judge Wald has noted that finding errors in a brief makes her "go back to square one in evaluating the counsel".

Good Example

Judge Wald has noted that finding errors in a brief makes her "go back to square one in evaluating the counsel."

Bad Example

The word "Aspen", which refers to both trees and a publisher, begins with the letter "A".

Good Example

The word "Aspen," which refers to both trees and a publisher, begins with the letter "A."

To find errors of this type, use the Find and Replace feature to search for quotation marks, and check your punctuation. Also, check to make sure that all quotation marks come in pairs. Too often, when writers block and copy quotations, they place an opening quotation mark, then copy the language into the text, and neglect to insert the closing quotation mark. This is the punctuation equivalent of leaving the refrigerator door open, and it is very annoying to readers. Be sure to proofread specifically for this problem.

4. Citation search.   To review your citations, search *[begin underline]* or *[begin italics]* or even *v.* to help you find citations and scrutinize them in isolation. Three types of errors are particularly common: (1) incorrect volume or page numbers, (2) misspelled party names, and (3) missing pinpoint page numbers. As noted earlier, presume that every citation should have a pinpoint. Even if you are just citing to a general principle from the case, find a page on which that general principle appears, and use it as the pinpoint.

5. Spell-check.   Run the spell-check early and often, but keep a few things in mind. First, keep your hand away from the mouse, or your finger off the button, so that you don't hit Replace or Skip by mistake. Second, don't hit Skip as soon as you see a party name or a case name; make sure that you've spelled each one properly and consistently.

Third, after completing spell-check, use the Find and Replace feature to search for typos that the spell-check function won't catch. In every document, look for *statue* for *statute*, *untied* for *united*, *form* for *from* (and vice versa), *reasonable* for *reasonably* (and vice versa), and *probable for probably* (and vice versa). You might consider setting your Quick Correct feature to change *pubic* to *public* to avoid that potentially embarrassing error. If your document is about *probable cause* or *reasonable doubt*, it is even more important to do this kind of search. I have read several briefs in which students claim that there was no "probably cause" for the defendant's arrest, or that the defense could not establish "reasonably doubt." Because both forms of certain problem words could appear in the text, search for each form separately and make sure each use is proper.

As you can see, the Find and Replace feature can help you to proofread on the computer in many different ways. You may be able to figure out other ways to make the computer's tireless brain work for you.

2.   *Methods to Use on the Hard Copy*

Plan to print out a hard copy several times before you must file the document. Because your brain works differently when you are looking at a computer screen than when you are looking at a hard copy, you will undoubtedly find errors on the hard copy that you missed when reading the document on the computer.

1. Check paragraph length.   You may have created some overlong paragraphs as you revised; they will be evident on the hard copy. Remember that there are two reasons to create a paragraph break: substance and graphics. Even if you have not moved on to a new subject, the reader may need the brief visual rest that a paragraph break provides. A good default is to look for at least two paragraph breaks per page (more is fine). If you have only one paragraph break, you must find a place to insert a hard return. Note that if you create an artificial paragraph break in this way, you may need to add a topic sentence to ensure that the reader can instantly understand how the paragraph is relevant to the point under discussion.

2. Check sentence length.   If you have a problem with overlong sentences, edit for them by looking for periods. Take a pencil and make a slash mark at every period; you can do this without even reading the text. When you're done, review the slash marks. If you see several sentences in a row that are over four lines long, review them and try to shorten at least one. One good way to shorten long sentences is to look for verbs. If you have three verbs in one sentence, try giving each verb a subject and its own sentence. If you see several sentences that are only one line long—and you're not using short sentences for occasional, dramatic effect—try to combine a couple of the short sentences.[16]

3. Review the verbs.   Readers subconsciously pay more attention to information in the verb position. Thus, go through your document and circle all of your verbs, trying not to read the sentences. You should scrutinize all vague verbs, including *is, are, was, were, made, involved, concerned, had,* and the like. Unless you are using them purposefully—e.g., in a persuasive document to deemphasize information, or because you are using passive voice to avoid an unusually long subject—you should look for the better verb hidden in the sentence and revise accordingly.

4. Review the signals to the reader.   The best way to review signals to the reader is to review the "template items" identified in Chapter Ten [Mary Beth Beazley, A Practical Guide to Appellate Advocacy, 3rd ed., (2010)]. Look at the first paragraph (or two) of each heading section for needed legal backstory and roadmap. Look at the last paragraph of each heading section for a concluding statement connecting the analysis to the point being covered within that unit of discourse. Scan the first sentence of each paragraph to see how often your paragraphs begin with main points and include the phrase-that-pays. Scan through the document to make sure there are enough headings. If you go more than three or four pages without a new heading, scrutinize that section. Can you break that section down into two subsections? Have you gone onto a new point without labeling it with a heading? Similarly, review each roadmap and mini-roadmap, and then compare it to your headings. The roadmap should predict precisely the headings that follow.

5. Do a ruler-read.   After you have taken these steps, read a hard copy aloud (as slowly as you can) backwards and forwards *with a ruler under each line as you read it.* Using the ruler helps to separate you from your text, breaking up that cozy relationship between your short-term memory and your document. When doing this ruler-read, include all extraneous materials like cover pages and tables; these sections often get short shrift when it comes to proofreading.

6. Repeat any or all of the above as needed.   If you keep finding new mistakes when using these techniques, you need to keep proofreading. Do not print the final version of the document until you can read it through and find *no* mistakes.

---

16. *See* Mary Barnard Ray & Jill J. Ramsfield, *Legal Writing: Getting It Right and Getting It Written* 371-72 (4th ed., Thomson/West 2005).

3. Proofreading Your Revisions

Word processors have greatly improved the quality of written documents, but they are also responsible for a new type of editing error. In the past, when a writer revised a document, someone had to type the whole thing over again, and so it was fairly easy to substitute the new words and to leave the old words out. Now, with the constant editing that word processors allow, it is not uncommon to see both old and new versions of a phrase within a document: The writer typed the new phrase and forgot to delete the old one. Further, writers who carelessly use the Find and Replace feature frequently find sentences like this in their writing:

Bad Example

On Saturday, the Mr. Johnson returned home.

The best way to avoid these types of errors is, once again, to focus on proofreading. After each round of edits, print out the hard copy and highlight the words, lines, or paragraphs in which edits occurred. Read those sections in isolation, so that you don't get caught up in the meaning of the words. In addition, *never* use the Replace All feature; doing so causes mistakes like the one shown above because it's difficult to envision all of the contexts in which a word or phrase might appear. Instead, look at each use of the word you are replacing to avoid mistakes.

4. The Last Thing to Do with the Document

This section is really about the second-to-the-last thing to do with the document. The last thing you should do is file it with the court. But the last proofreading method you should use with your document is to read it aloud, out of order. Either start in the middle, start on the last page and then read the second-to-the-last page, and so on, or mix up the pages and read them in a random order. Whichever method you use, your goal is to pay attention to individual words and sentences rather than to get swept away by your no doubt fascinating discussion of the law.

5. Summary

In practice, you will often need to write and file documents in a hurry, without time to polish and proofread in a leisurely way. Take the time now to develop an effective polishing process. When you submit documents that demonstrate professionalism in both content and presentation, you enhance your credibility and increase your opportunities for success in law practice.

CHAPTER
20

Oral Argument

A. THREE GOALS AT ORAL ARGUMENT

First, you want to engage the judges' attention by getting them *interested* in your case and *motivated* to rule in your favor. They will hear many other arguments on the same day, and they will read many other briefs in the week they read yours. You want to touch their natural desire to do the right thing.

Second, you want to focus the judges' attention on the *few aspects of your case that are most determinative*—the fundamental one or two issues, the most prominent facts in your story, and the most compelling policy considerations. Judges expect oral argument to help them find the heart of the dispute. Oral argument works best when it concentrates on a few important ideas, while details are best left to the briefs.

Third, you want *access to the judges' thinking*. You want to discover each of their doubts about your theory and any way in which they're confused about your case—so you can dispel their doubts and clear up their confusion. Listening to the judges' questions is the only way you can get access to their thinking. And the most effective thing you can do in oral argument is to answer their questions well. Usually when judges interrupt you with questions, they're not trying to debate with you. They're telling you what troubles them and asking you to help them make the decision. Thus, an experienced oral advocate goes into the courtroom *for the purpose of being interrupted*.

B. STRUCTURE OF AN ORAL ARGUMENT

You will (1) introduce yourself and the case, (2) summarize the client's story and identify the core issue or issues raised by the story, (3) make a legal argument, and (4) conclude.

If you represent the appellant, you will argue first. Begin by introducing your client and yourself and identifying the decision below from which you have appealed. Here are two examples of effective openings:

> Good morning, Your Honors. I am [lawyer's name], representing [client's name], the appellant here and the plaintiff below. A jury verdict in her

favor was overturned when the trial court granted a post-trial motion for judgment as a matter of law.

> May it please the court, representing [client's name], I am [lawyer's name]. The jury returned a verdict in favor of [client's name], but the trial court granted a post-trial motion for judgment as a matter of law—a decision she now asks you to reverse.

Next, summarize the story and identify the core issue or issues. If you will use the issues to introduce the story, identify the issues first. Otherwise, tell the story and identify the issues afterward as a bridge into your legal argument.

Focus on the most essential facts so the judges don't get lost in marginal details. Think carefully beforehand about how you will tell the story and what words you will use. One of the most successful Supreme Court advocates once said that "in an appellate court the statement of the facts is not merely a part of the argument, it is more often than not the argument itself. A case well stated is a case far more than half argued."[1] You must mention the facts that hurt you, but you can minimize their effect through juxtaposition, just as you did when you wrote the Statement of the Case. Some courts study the briefs carefully before argument, and they might consider a fact recitation to be a waste of time. In those courts, lawyers are discouraged—either informally or through the courts' rules—from opening with the facts.

If you represent the appellee, your opening may be similar to the appellant's, except that you should explain how your positions differ from the appellant's. For example, rather than tell your version of the story, you might point out the ways in which the appellant has not given a full or accurate picture. Suppose a group of plaintiffs won a judgment against the owner of a dam that collapsed; the owner has appealed; and the owner's lawyer has opened oral argument by stressing that the plaintiffs had reason to know the dam had weakened. The plaintiffs' lawyer can respond like this:

> The key fact is *not* that slowly rising waters in a creek could have alerted nearby residents that something might be wrong, but that the defendant's dam burst, sending a wall of water seven feet high down the valley where the plaintiffs lived. Slowly rising water cannot be considered a warning of that.

You can begin your legal argument with a statement of the rule or rules most essential to your position. If you're arguing two or more issues, you might have to do this separately for each issue. On each issue, your argument can resemble the CREAC structure. Persuade the judges that they should adopt and enforce the rule you urge, explain how the rule works, and apply it to your facts.

If you represent the appellee, listen carefully to the appellant's oral argument. When your turn comes, you will respond to the appellant's contentions. You may have anticipated most of them when you read the appellant's brief and when you planned your argument. But if the appellant surprises you during oral argument by saying something new that truly might hurt, you will need, on the spot, to find a way of neutralizing it.

---

1. John W. Davis, *The Argument of an Appeal*, 26 A.B.A. J. 895, 896 (1940).

Appellate advocates distinguish between a "hot" bench, which erupts with questions, and a "cold" bench, which listens impassively. If the bench is hot, the judges may ask so many questions that you will be surprised to find that your time is about to run out, or already has. Your time is up when the presiding judge says, in a firm tone, "Thank you, counselor." Then conclude with *one short* sentence in which you specify the relief you seek ("Therefore, the judgment below should be affirmed. . . . "). If you're in the midst of answering a question when your time runs out, ask for permission to finish the answer. If your request is granted, finish quickly. If the judges continue to ask you questions after your time expires, answer them fully: The court has implicitly enlarged your time. If you finish your argument before your time expires, conclude anyway, pause to see whether you will be asked further questions, and, if not, sit down. Whatever the situation, you can signal your intent to finish by using an introductory phrase such as "In conclusion,. . . . "

An appellant's lawyer sometimes reserves a minute or two for rebuttal by saying so after the introductory sentences. The time reserved is subtracted from the time allowed for the appellant's main argument. After the appellee has argued, the appellant can use the reserved time to reply. But a court considers rebuttal time wasted if an appellant uses it to reiterate arguments already made or to raise new arguments for the first time. Use rebuttal only to correct significantly inaccurate or misleadingly incomplete statements made by the appellee, and preferably not more than one or two of those. If the appellee's misstatements are trivial, an appellant looks petty correcting them. If it turns out that there's no need for rebuttal, an appellant makes a confident impression by waiving it.

C.   QUESTIONS FROM THE BENCH

Listen carefully to the question and understand it before answering.
Answer the question when it is asked.
Don't evade.
If you don't know the answer to a question, say so.
If the premise of a question is wrong, politely say so.
If a Justice throws you a life preserver, don't bat it away.
Justices ask hypothetical questions because they are concerned about how the decision in your case may affect other cases. What are the limits of the principle you advocate?

—*North Dakota Supreme Court*
Appellate Practice Tips

Some questions are neutral requests for information. Some are challenges, asking you how you would overcome an adverse case or a policy contrary to your argument. Some are expressed as concerns: the judge asks how a particular problem in the case can be resolved. Some questions are openly friendly, asking you to focus on an aspect of your case that the judge believes to be particularly persuasive. And some questions are prompts, suggesting that whatever you're discussing at the time can be dispensed with in favor of something else the court cares about more. Some questions are asked because the answer is crucial to the judge's thinking. Others grow out of the spontaneity of the moment, and the answer may have little or no impact on the decision.

When you hear a question, listen to it carefully. Don't be afraid to pause for a moment to think before answering. Never interrupt a question. Try to figure out the question's purpose and exactly what's troubling the judge. Then craft your answer to satisfy the skepticism or curiosity implied by the question. In your answer, don't say too little or too much. Don't give a one-sentence reply to a question that a judge plainly considers to be the crux of the case. And don't spend three minutes resolving a straightforward request for simple information.

Don't leap to assumptions about a judge's predispositions from the questions the judge asks. A neutral judge might ask challenging questions just to see whether your theory will hold up. A friendly judge might ask challenging questions to cause you to argue matters that the judge believes might persuade others on the bench. And an adverse judge might ask friendly or neutral questions out of politeness and a sense of fairness.

Answer the question on the spot. Don't promise to get back to it later at a place in your outline where you had already planned to discuss the subject. Other questions might prevent you from getting that far, and your answer will be most persuasive immediately after the question is asked. Even if a question asks you to discuss an entire issue earlier than you had planned, do it and rearrange the order of your presentation to accommodate the judge's needs. Later, when you reach the spot where you had intended to discuss the issue, simply skip what you have already covered.

Answer the question you've been asked, not one you would rather have been asked. You can persuade only by facing the problems raised by the question and by showing the judge why those problems should not prevent a decision in your favor. In every fully litigated case, each side has points of weakness. If your side had none, your adversary would have given up long ago. When a judge has truly identified a point of weakness, face it and give a realistic counterargument. Here are three ways to begin:

> I agree, Your Honor, that in that hypothetical the police would have had probable cause, but the facts of the hypothetical are not the facts of this case. For example,. . . .

> Yes, *Soares* did so hold, but later rulings of this court have impliedly undermined *Soares*. For example, ...

> Certainly, the record does reflect two isolated events that might be construed as evidence of good faith by the defendant, but the record also includes many, many events, stretching over several years, that show exactly the opposite. For example,. . . .

During the answer, build a bridge to the rest of your argument. If you do this smoothly, it may be hard for a listener to tell where your answer has ended and your planned presentation has picked up again. Bridge-building helps you redirect the argument back to your theory of the appeal so you can show the court how your theory, as a coherent whole, satisfies each concern raised from the bench.

If you're asked a question to which you do not know the answer, the best thing to say is exactly that. Judges know you're human, and, unless the point is a big one, you gain credibility by admitting that you can't answer. Moreover, judges are skilled interrogators, and if you try to fake your way through an answer, they will realize what you're doing. If you knew the answer when you prepared but can't remember it now, you might feel a little better saying something like "I'm sorry, Your Honor, but I don't recall." In real appeals (not in law school assignments), a lawyer might offer to file a supplemental brief or memorandum if the lawyer fears that the unanswered question might be crucial to the decision. Courts usually refuse these offers, which may suggest that the point isn't critical after all.

If you're not sure you understand the question, signal that indirectly so the judge can correct you, if necessary:

> If your Honor is asking about the possibility that the issue has not been pre-served for review—and please correct me if I've misunderstood—trial counsel objected to the evidence and moved for . . .

Or do it directly:

> I'm sorry, Your Honor. Are you asking whether the order appealed from is final?

Except for the kinds of examples above, it's not a good idea to ask the judges questions.

In many legal writing courses, students are assigned to coauthor briefs, usually in teams of two, and to split the oral argument between them. If you're working with another student, you may be asked questions about material that your colleague intends to argue. Don't respond by saying that your colleague will answer the question. That can disconcert judges because they expect you to know enough of the other student's material that you can give at least a summary answer. If you're arguing first, your colleague can elaborate on your summary later.

D.   AFFECT, DELIVERY, AND STYLE

The most effective way to present arguments is in a tone of what has been called "respectful intellectual equality."[2]

> [I]f the lawyer approaches a court with . . . awe, perhaps verging on fear, he will not be able effectively to stand up to the court's questioning. . . . It is just as important, however, not to talk down to a court. . . . The only proper attitude is that of a respectful intellectual equality. The "respectful" part approximates the quantum and type of respect that a younger [person] should show when speaking to an older one. . . . Counsel must stand up to the judges quite as he would stand up to the senior members of his own

2. Frederick Bernays Wiener, *Oral Advocacy*, 62 Harv. L. Rev. 56, 72-74 (1948).

firm. If he permits himself to be overawed . . . then he—and his case—are well on their way to being lost.[3]

Although the judges have the power to decide your case, their *need* to decide the case causes them to look to you for intellectual leadership.

What works best in this situation is not a speech, but a *conversation* in which you take the initiative, talking *with* the judges—not at them. It's an unusual kind of conversation, limited by the formalities of the occasion and by a focus on the decision the bench must make, but it is a conversation nonetheless. Try to create for yourself a *persuasive presence* that helps you reach and engage the bench.

Think of nervousness as a fact of life. Even the most experienced lawyer is nervous before making an oral argument. But that anxiety tends to disappear once the lawyer becomes engaged in the conversation. For beginners, the *moment of engagement*—when you're so caught up in the work that you forget to be nervous—might not come for several minutes into the argument. But with each succeeding performance that moment will move closer and closer toward the opening, until eventually it coincides with the words "May it please the court" or "Good morning, Your Honors."

Look straight at the judges throughout the argument, preferably making eye contact. Look at your notes only to remind yourself of the next subject for discussion and, even then, get your eyes off your notes and back to the bench as fast as possible. Whenever you look away from the judges, their attention can wander to other thoughts, partially tuning you out. And judges can become impatient with lawyers who read their arguments to the court.[4]

Speak loudly enough that the judges do not have to strain to hear you. If you're soft-spoken by nature, breathe in deeply before you begin and exhale while speaking your first words. Do this again whenever your voice falters. Make your lungs do the work, not your throat muscles. You will be surprised at how well your voice can carry. But if you already have a powerful voice, don't get carried away. A loud voice can make the bench uncomfortable.

Use the tone and volume of your voice to emphasize the more important things you say. Pause before or after your most important remarks.

Communicate tenacity with what one judge has called "disciplined earnestness": "a communicated sense of conviction that pushes a case to the limits of its strength but not beyond," using "words and body language, facial expression and eye contact, to radiate a sense of conviction without making every point a life-and-death issue."[5]

Avoid multitudes of detail when discussing cases and statutes. Focus on the big ideas. If your case is built on a synthesis of authority, describe it generally ("the majority of jurisdictions," "the recent trend of cases in other states," "seven of the federal circuits," "this court has previously held"). If you must quote—as you might with a crucial statute or holding—limit yourself to the half-dozen or so essential words that the court must interpret. Concentrate on the few most determinative facts. But you can also mention along the way a few facts that most bring the story to life. Some facts have little legal significance but help the judges "see" the story and put the case into a realistic perspective.

3. *Id.*
4. *See* U.S. Sup. Ct. R. 28.1 ("Oral argument read from a prepared text is not favored") and Fed. R. App. P. 34(c) ("Counsel must not read at length from briefs, records, or authorities").
5. Frank Morey Coffin, *The Ways of a Judge* 132 (Houghton Mifflin 1980).

Don't distract the court with restless or anxious movement. Stand up straight. Don't play with a pen, shuffle your papers around frequently, put your hands in your pockets, or sway forward and back. Limit your gestures to those that naturally punctuate your argument. A visually busy lawyer radiates nervousness, rather than the confidence needed to establish psychological leadership. Stand at the lectern throughout your argument. Don't stroll out from behind it unless you need to find something in your briefcase to answer a question. And try not to let that happen. Wear conservative clothing that communicates professionalism.

E. FORMALITIES AND CUSTOMS OF THE COURTROOM

While a courtroom is in session, lawyers do not speak to each other. They speak only to the bench and—when the bench gives permission—to witnesses and juries. But because there are no witnesses or juries in appellate courts, you will speak only to the judges.

The dignity of the occasion will be demeaned if you speak in slang, in emotional rhetoric, or in terms that unnecessarily personalize the lawyers or judges. Even when discussing your adversary's arguments, refer to them as the party's, rather than as the lawyer's. There's a world of difference between "The plaintiff mistakenly relies . . . " and "Mr. Maggione mistakenly told you. . . . " Similarly, do not speak to the bench in flattering language. Judges are satisfied with respect. Obsequiousness makes them uncomfortable.

While your adversary argues, listen attentively and without facial expressions that could convey your opinion of what is transpiring. Write down whatever notes you will need to help you respond in your own argument (if you represent the appellee) or in rebuttal (if you represent the appellant). Don't interrupt your adversary's argument.

F. PREPARATION FOR ORAL ARGUMENT

Prepare two versions of the same presentation. One version would include the material that you *must* argue—the absolute core of your case. When delivered without interruption, it should fill no more than 30% or 35% of the time you're allowed. The other version would be an expanded development of the first. It would include the first version, as well as supplemental material that makes the core of your case more persuasive. If delivered without interruption, it should fill about 80% or 90% of the available time. You will know within the first two or three minutes of the argument whether the bench is hot or cold. If it's hot, you can deliver the core presentation and try to work the supplemental material into your answers. If the bench is cold, you can deliver the expanded argument.

There are many ways to prepare notes to use at the lectern. After you have argued several times, you will figure out which type and style of notes work best for you. But the consensus of experienced advocates is that you're better off with the fewest notes possible because you need them only to remind yourself of the subjects you intend to cover as well as a few key phrases that you intend to use.

If you're well prepared, you will know your case so well that a single page on a legal-size pad might be sufficient. If, in preparing the argument, you come up with an excellent phrasing for a difficult concept, you might write down those few words to remind yourself to use them. Otherwise, your notes should be only a list of subjects to cover. You can outline both versions of your argument on a single page divided by a vertical line, the core version on one side of the vertical line and the expanded version on the other side. Or you could take two pads to the podium, one for each version. But try to use only the top page on a pad. If you go to the second page, you might have too many notes. Some advocates take to the lectern notecards with synopses of the record and of the major relevant cases. You might or might not find that helpful. If you already know your case thoroughly, the cards might only get in your way.

Take the record and both briefs to the podium as well, in case you're asked about them.

Make a list of every weakness in your case and every question that you might ask if you were a judge. Prepare ways of overcoming the weaknesses and answering the questions. If you can't imagine hard questions a judge might ask, study your adversary's brief and the precedents that are contrary to your position.

Try also to predict any concessions you might be asked to make. Figure out which concessions you cannot afford to give up and which you might have to make to protect the reasonableness of the rest of your case. If you need to think about this for the first time at the podium when a judge asks you a question, you could make a serious and costly mistake.

Practice making your argument to a person who will ask you tough questions but who knows little about your theory of the appeal. If the person mooting you knows too much about your theory, the experience will be unrealistic.

Finally, update your research the day before you argue. The time between submission of the brief and oral argument might equal up to a month in law school and perhaps several months in the practice of law. Check to see whether controlling statutes have been amended or repealed, whether one of the key cases has been overruled, and whether any of the recent precedents has been reversed or affirmed. You don't need to check every citation in your brief, but it can be devastating to discover in the courtroom that some important texture of the law has changed.

G. ORAL ARGUMENT

Supreme Court Rule 28.1 provides that oral argument "should emphasize and clarify the written arguments in the briefs on the merits. Counsel should assume that all Justices have read the briefs before oral argument. Oral argument read from a prepared text is not favored."

Although most law students think of the oral argument first when they think of appellate advocacy and motions, most judges agree that the brief is more important than the oral argument. Justice Ginsburg has observed that "[a]s between briefing and argument, there is near-universal agreement among federal appellate judges that the brief is more important."[6] In many federal courts, most cases are decided without oral argument. Justice Ginsburg noted that the Fourth, Tenth, and Eleventh Circuits dispense with oral argument in about 70 percent of cases, and Judge Wiener pointed out that almost two-thirds of the appeals filed in the Fifth Circuit are decided without oral argument.[7] In many trial courts, oral argument is not presumed unless counsel requests it when a motion is filed; even then, the judge may not grant the request. Even in cases in which oral argument occurs, the brief usually has more to do with the outcome of the case. A 1986 article conducted a limited study of three appellate judges and noted that oral arguments changed the views they held before the oral argument in 31 percent, 17 percent, and 13 percent of the cases heard.[8]

This is not to say that oral argument is unimportant. After reading the briefs and relevant authorities, many judges form a sort of rebuttable presumption about how the case should be decided. The oral argument usually convinces them that their presumption was correct, but an ill-prepared attorney may convince them that they were wrong. As one judge observed, "if the court intends to rule in your favor, the easiest way to change the panel's mind is to be utterly unprepared or ineffective at oral argument."[9] The late Justice Brennan once observed, "I have had too many occasions when my judgment of a decision has turned on what happened in oral argument, not to be terribly concerned for myself were I to be denied oral argument."[10] Judge Bright, of the Eighth Circuit, has commented that "oral argument is an essential component of the decisionmaking process."[11] It is certainly responsible for generating more adrenalin.

1. Purpose of Oral Argument

The purpose of the oral argument is not to give an impressive speech. Rather, your goal as an oral advocate is simply to highlight your best arguments and to answer any questions that the judges have about the case. Judge Pierce has explained that oral arguments give judges "the opportunity to discuss . . . the issues they consider dispositive or particularly troublesome—issues that may not have been briefed or at least not briefed fully."[12] Justice Ginsburg has observed that questions during oral argument "give counsel a chance to satisfy the court on matters the judges think significant, issues the judges might puzzle over in chambers, and resolve less satisfactorily without counsel's aid."[13]

6. See, e.g., Ruth Bader Ginsburg, Remarks on Appellate Advocacy, 50 S.C. L. Rev. 567, 567 (1999).
7. Id. at 568. See also Jacques L. Wiener, Jr., Ruminations from the Bench: Brief Writing and Oral Argument in the Fifth Circuit, 70 Tul. L. Rev. 187, 189 (1995).
8. See Myron H. Bright, The Power of the Spoken Word: In Defense of Oral Argument, 72 Iowa L. Rev. 35, 40 nn.32-33 (1986).
9. Judge Stephen J. Dwyer, Leonard J. Feldman & Robert G. Nylander, Effective Oral Argument: Six Pitches, Five Do's, and Five Don'ts from One Judge and Two Lawyers, 33 Seattle U. L. Rev. 347, 347 (2010).
10. Commission on Revision of the Fed. Court Appellate Sys., Structure and Internal Procedures: Recommendations for Change, 67 F.R.D. 195, 254 (1975) (quoting Justice Brennan's comments at the 1972 Third Circuit Judicial Conference) (quoted in Lawrence W. Pierce, Appellate Advocacy: Some Reflections from the Bench, 61 Fordham L. Rev. 829, 833 (1993)).
11. Bright, supra note 3, at 36.
12. Pierce, supra note 5, at 833-34.
13. Ginsburg, supra note 1, at 569. See also Wiener, supra note 2, at 199 (noting that oral argument "further crystallize[s] the issues [and enhances the court's] understanding of the factual and legal details, subtleties, and nuances of the case").

Judges use oral argument to test their presumptions about the case and to probe the case's limits, strengths, and weaknesses by asking counsel to clarify difficult issues or to speculate on the impact of a decision on future cases. Because of their intimate knowledge of the facts of the case and the relevant law, counsel for the parties are uniquely qualified to help the judges as they wrestle with the issues presented by the case.

2.   *Format*

In appellate arguments, the petitioner (or appellant) argues first, standing at a podium or lectern, and facing a panel of judges. Petitioner may reserve some of the allotted time for rebuttal. Counsel for respondent (or appellee) follows, after which counsel for petitioner may present a rebuttal. Time allotted to each side for argument varies from 10 to 30 minutes; in many courts, each side is allotted 15 minutes, and counsel for petitioner may reserve one, two, or three of those 15 minutes for rebuttal. Counsel for respondent does not have the opportunity for rebuttal.

In a motion argument, the party who has brought the motion argues first. Motions to dismiss are almost always brought by the defendant, but motions for summary judgment may be brought by either party. The formal requirements for motion oral arguments vary from court to court. Some courts have a "motion docket," where all motions are heard by the same judge, who may not be the judge that the case is assigned to for trial. Other courts may use a "motion day," once a week or on some other schedule. The typical method for oral argument is for a judge or judges to question an attorney standing at a podium, to use strict timekeeping methods, and to allow only the first speaker to present a rebuttal. Some trial judges, however, may dispense with some of these formalities. Because it is usually easier to move from more formal requirements to less formal requirements, this chapter presumes a more formal motion argument. In practice, of course, you should follow local rules and local customs.

3.   *Intellectual Preparation: What do You Need to Know?*

You complete the most important preparation for the oral argument when you write the brief, for it is in writing the brief that you gain an understanding of the facts, issues, and authorities that control the case. Nevertheless, there are two practical things that you must do in specific preparation for the oral argument. First, you must decide what points to argue and then prepare your argument. Second, you must gather the information that the court will expect you to know—to have at your mental fingertips—when you are at the podium.

a.   Deciding What Points to Argue

Your job on oral argument is not to present a summary of your brief.[14] Your short time at the podium will not be suffcient to discuss all of the issues and

---

14. *See, e.g.,* Karen J. Williams, *Help Us Help You: A Fourth Circuit Primer on Effective Appellate Oral Arguments,* 50 S.C. L. Rev. 591, 595 (1999).

arguments that you raised in the brief. When planning your oral argument, identify the two or three points that are most necessary to convince the court of the justice of the result you seek. Frequently, these points will be those that could be resolved in favor of either party,[15] and thus, spending time on these points in oral argument will be particularly important. When deciding what points to argue, you may ignore points that you included for completeness but that are not crucial for your argument. For example, most statutory interpretation arguments include at least a short discussion of the statute's plain language, even if counsel believes that the plain language argument is a sure loser. In that situation, some unfortunate attorneys will begin an oral argument with what they plan to be a short discussion of plain language, thinking they will get past it and move to their more important arguments. Unfortunately, the court is not always in on the plan. As Florida Appeals Judge David Gersten warns, attorneys who try to address too many points may "get bogged down on questions on [their] weaker points and never get to the crux of [the] case."[16]

As you take notes on the points you will present to the court, write down citations to cases and statutes that support your assertions. Although you will not be reading from your notes, the act of writing down the points and their supporting authorities will help cement them in your mind.[17]

In your brief, you may have followed a CREXAC (Conclusion, Rule, Explanation, Application, Connection-Conclusion) model of analysis. When planning your oral argument, a pared-down version of that model can be useful. That is, first, you should state the point—or the conclusion—that you want the court to agree with. Then support that conclusion by stating the rule that governs the issue. If a case or statute is significant to your argument, you may mention it, but in oral argument, the rule is frequently more important than the citation to authority for that rule. On the other hand, you must be thoroughly familiar with all of the relevant authorities so that you may answer any questions about them. In addition, in some cases the relevant authorities become an important part of the argument.

Generally, the explanation part of the formula that was so important in the brief may be all but eliminated in the oral argument. The judges' eyes may glaze over during any lengthy recitation of authority case facts and holdings unless it is given in response to a specific question. How much support you should give for the rule varies from issue to issue. If the meaning of a rule, or which rule to apply, is at issue, you may need to spend more time talking about relevant authorities. In contrast, if you are arguing about how an established rule applies to the facts in your case, you should plan to go into more detail about your client's facts. Of course, you must still be prepared to discuss the relevant authorities if the court asks you questions about those authorities or about how they might apply to hypothetical situations.

After you have stated the rule and supported it (if needed), apply the rule to the facts by naming the particular facts that mandate the result that you seek. Remember that the meaning of the word *facts* in this context may vary from issue to issue. If the meaning of statutory language is at issue, for example, the facts may consist of the words from the statute. While the explanation section of the formula may be shorter (or for some issues, nonexistent) in an oral

15. *Id.*
16. Judge David M. Gersten, *Effective Brief Writing and Oral Argument: Gaining the Inside Track*, 81 Fla. B.J. 26, 29 (Apr. 2007).
17. *See, e.g.*, Williams, *supra* note 9, at 594.

argument, do not skimp on the application of law to facts. The judges will be particularly interested in why the facts of the case mandate the application of the rule in the manner that you suggest. Similarly, they will benefit from a detailed discussion of the result that occurs when the rule is applied to your facts.

Although planning your argument is useful, realize that you will rarely be permitted to proceed through the argument of an entire point without interruption.[18] Nonetheless, you should outline a full discussion of each of the points you plan to make during the argument. Doing so teaches you more about your case as you prepare to face the panel.

b.   Gathering Information

After you have planned your argument, make sure that you know the case, the issues, and the relevant authorities well enough to answer the court's questions. Although you should limit your prepared presentation to only two or three points, the court will probably ask you about other issues. You must be prepared for all relevant—and some irrelevant—questions from the bench.

First, renew your acquaintance with the facts and procedure of the case. You should be able to answer the court's questions about the details of any relevant facts and be able to tell the court where in the complaint, the record, the decisions below, or the joint appendix certain facts have been recorded. Make sure that you understand all of the details surrounding the legally significant facts; very often, these factual details can make a legal difference. In *Bentsen v. Coors*, for example, counsel for the Coors Brewing Company spent a bit of time at oral argument discussing the difference between beer and ale.[19] Judge Wald has remarked that counsel's familiarity with the record can play a crucial role in the argument:

> The more arcane the subject matter . . . the more intimate with the record the advocate needs to be. All the questions of fact . . . that the brief may have raised in the judges' minds will surface at argument, and nothing frustrates a bench more than an advocate who does not know the answers. Your credibility as a legal maven spurts as soon as you show familiarity with the facts of the underlying dispute.[20]

Similarly, make sure you know the procedural details of the case. The judges may rely on you to clear up momentary confusion about what happened in the courts below.

Second, familiarize yourself with all filed briefs and the authorities cited in those briefs. You should be able to tell the court the facts, holding, or reasoning of any significant authority cases, and you should be able to explain how your case is similar to or distinguishable from those cases. Obviously, it is particularly important to be familiar with any mandatory authorities that are on point or that may be relevant. Furthermore, if you are asking the court to apply a multipart test, make sure that you understand all of the parts of the test, even those that are not controversial.[21]

18. *See, e.g., id.* at 598.
19. *See* 1994 U.S. Tr. Lexis 163 at *45-46 (Nov. 30, 1994) (U.S. Sup. Ct. Oral Argument Tr.).
20. Patricia M. Wald, *19 Tips from 19 Years on the Appellate Bench*, 1 J. App. Prac. & Process 7, 19-20 (1999).
21. Williams, *supra* note 9, at 597.

Finally, and perhaps most importantly, figure out what you are asking for. What rule are you asking the court to create or apply? What will be the impact of that rule on future cases? (Knowing the impact of a decision in your favor will enable you to respond effectively to hypotheticals posed by the court.) On a related note, try to anticipate what concessions you may be asked to make. For example, you may be asked to concede that the rule in the case applies to a certain type of plaintiff or defendant, or that your client has or has not met all or part of the standard your opponent espouses. You should know which points you would (or should) concede immediately (those that have little or no effect on your argument), which points you can concede if pressed by the court (those that are important to your argument, but that do not determine victory), and which points you can never concede (any point that would cause you to lose the argument).

Not all judges try to force counsel to concede either minor or significant points, but it is wise to be prepared for the ones who do. Justice Ginsburg has pointed out that "questions are sometimes designed to nail down a concession that will show up in an opinion, perhaps in a footnote that reads: 'At argument, counsel conceded thus and so.' That doesn't mean lawyers should avoid concessions as inevitably damaging. As Judge Wald has observed, a concession once in a while can enhance a lawyer's credibility."[22]

Judge Karen Williams, of the Fourth Circuit, has also cautioned that judges may ask questions that try to get attorneys to "concede away [their] case[s]," stating that counsel should listen carefully to questions that seek concessions, to ensure that "the judge has accurately restated your argument. The judge may be leading you down the slippery slope to an absurd result. At the same time, nothing hurts an advocate's credibility with the court more than the failure to concede an obvious point."[23]

To sum up, at the end of your intellectual preparation for the argument, you should have a command of the issues you plan to discuss, the boundaries of the rule you are advocating, the facts of your case, and the cases and other authorities relevant to your argument—and your opponent's.

4.   Preparation of Written Materials: What Should You Bring to the Courtroom?

At a minimum, the well-prepared oral advocate should bring two things to the courtroom: the briefs that have been filed in the current hearing of the case, and the joint appendix or other record materials that are before the court. In the unusual (but not unheard of) event that the court should ask you to consider information on a particular page in the record or a brief, you want to have the materials there with you. If there is not enough room at the podium, you may leave them at counsel table so you can retrieve them if needed.

It is also appropriate to bring an outline or some form of notes up to the podium, but you should plan to make these materials succinct. Judge Wiener, of the Fifth Circuit, has advised that counsel should not "bring lots of documents to the lectern—shuffling books and papers and reading from them

---

22. Ginsburg, *supra* note 1, at 569.
23. Williams, *supra* note 9, at 599.

interrupts the flow of your presentation and paints a picture of an unprepared or bumbling advocate."[24]

It is the tradition at many law schools for students to use a manila folder for their notes; the students either write their notes on the four sides of the folder, or prepare them on a word processor and tape or staple them in place. The advantage of a manila folder is that it gives the advocate four pages that stay in order even if dropped. Also, four pages is about the maximum number that the oral advocate should try to look at. Many students use the interior of the folder for their main outline and store information about facts and cases, to be referred to if needed, on the outside.

If you want a more professional look, it is fine to use a *slim* three-ring binder instead of a manila folder. A binder will look better on the way to and from the podium, although the pages may be more difficult to turn. Furthermore, having a binder that allows multiple pages may tempt the advocate to write a more detailed outline, or even to write out the text of the argument. If you do use a binder, consider adding tabs to make turning the pages easier, and strive to include no more than four pages of notes.

Although the anxious advocate may believe that writing out a prepared speech will be a tonic to the nerves, reading from a prepared text is certain to antagonize the court. Supreme Court Rule 28.1 notes, delicately, that "[o]ral argument read from a prepared text is not favored." Judge Williams has made the point more directly, suggesting that reading the argument hurts both its style and its substance:

> The worst thing you can do is deliver a stiff presentation by attempting to read your argument verbatim. Such a presentation style is tedious and makes it difficult for you to answer questions from the bench. If you spend your time looking down at the podium reading your argument, you are likely to miss signals from the bench, and you cannot engage in a dialogue with the judges. Try to argue extemporaneously, or at least leave us with the impression that you are.[25]

Thus, when preparing materials to bring up to the podium, think in terms of words, phrases, and lists, rather than sentences, paragraphs, or pages. If you write full sentences, you will be tempted to read them because you will presume that a prefabricated sentence will sound better than an off-the-top-of-your-head remark. Remember, however, that the judges expect the oral argument to be, to some extent, a spontaneous dialogue. Most judges would rather hear an imperfect sentence from an advocate who is engaged in conversation with the court than perfect prose from a reader. Watch a few oral arguments on court websites, or read the transcripts, and you will see that many effective oral arguments are full of half-finished sentences and apparent lapses in grammar. This is because an oral argument is a conversation, not a speech.

Write your outline on full-sized paper rather than index cards, and use felt-tipped markers or large, boldfaced fonts to make your points easy to read. List your points in the order in which you plan to address them, and list supporting authorities under each point. You may want to write key words, or even the main phrases-that-pay, in boldfaced type across the top of the outline—or on

---

24. Wiener, *supra* note 2, at 204.
25. Williams, *supra* note 9, at 598.

every page of your materials—so that you have only to glance down at the podium to see words that will remind you of your main contentions.

Some advocates create both a case list and a fact list. On the case list, they list the name, citation, and relevant information (facts, reasoning, etc.) about each case. On the fact list, they list the legally significant facts and relevant background facts that either side might mention, noting where in the record each fact can be found. Creating these lists can be helpful, even if you never consult them during the argument. Both creating and studying them provides excellent opportunities to help you to commit important information to memory.

5.   Presenting the Argument

When planning your argument, think in terms of three parts: the Introduction, the Argument itself, and the Conclusion. You will spend most of your time at the podium on the Argument, but be sure to spend the needed time planning the Introduction and the Conclusion.

a.   Introduction

Although your introductory material should be short (often less than a minute, and always less than two minutes), the introduction fulfills several important functions. A good introduction tells the court what is happening procedurally—who you are, who your client is, and what your client wants; it provides sufficient factual context, it outlines the argument and tells the court why you are asking for the result that you seek, and it grabs the court's attention by focusing the court on your theme.

As always, you must be aware of local rules and local practice. In some courts, you may be asked to "enter an appearance on the record" before either party begins the oral argument. If so, you will stand (as you should whenever you address the court), and state your name, your law firm, and the party you represent. The party speaking first may be asked if he or she is reserving rebuttal time. If you enter an appearance in this way, you may or may not be expected to take time in your formal presentation to restate your name and your client and to reserve rebuttal time.

Traditionally, advocates begin their arguments by saying, "May it please the court," although "Good afternoon, your honors" or any other respectful greeting will probably be acceptable to most judges.[26] Of course, you should review local rules to see if they require any particular opening, and, whenever possible, observe some arguments in that court before your debut so that you can learn the court's customs. In the United States Supreme Court, for example, advocates never introduce themselves, and they traditionally begin their arguments by addressing the Chief Justice directly, saying, "Mr. Chief Justice, and may it please the Court."[27]

---

26. Wiener, *supra* note 2, at 203.
27. Because the United States Supreme Court has never had a Chief Justice who is a woman, the Court has no protocol for addressing a female Chief Justice. Some students who are faced with a female Chief Justice in a Moot Court setting address her as "Madame Chief Justice." While this may be acceptable, resorting to a foreign language strikes me as odd. Alternatives could include addressing the Chief by name, or by the title without the gender designator. Thus, either say,

However you begin your argument, you should never start without having the attention of the Judge, or the Chief Judge or Justice, on a multi-judge panel. This requirement may mean that you have to wait a moment while the judge finishes with note-taking from a previous advocate, but the benefit it provides in professionalism is well worth any cost in time. Just stand at the podium and wait in silence for the judge to nod at you or to give you some other signal telling you to begin. Do not take notes or review your notes while waiting, because you want to be able to pick up on either verbal or nonverbal signals as soon as the judge is ready.

If you are the petitioner or the party supporting the motion, you may need to reserve rebuttal time at this point. The manner for reserving rebuttal varies from court to court. In the United States Supreme Court, for example, you do not set aside rebuttal time; you simply make your best effort to end your argument while you still have time remaining. In other courts, you may reserve time by speaking directly to the bailiff. In some courts, you may need to both request time from the bailiff and make the request orally from the podium.

Your next task is to introduce yourself and your case. Judge Wiener has recommended opening with "a short, simple introduction: tell the panel your name, the name of your client, your client's role in the appeal . . . and in the trial . . . but refrain from blowing a lot of 'smoke' at the court . . . [b]egin your presentation with a short, attention-getting 'simple and direct' introduction of the points you plan to make."[28] Judge Williams has warned that the only uninterrupted time most oral advocates will have is at the beginning of the argument, and that they must use this time "to succinctly present the issue and explain to the court the most important reason why [they] should prevail. [They] may wish to use this time to give an outline of the points" to be covered during the argument.[29]

Many advocates spend too much time providing factual context. An oral argument does not have a formal statement of the case the way a brief does. You can presume that the court has read your brief and the relevant record materials. The Internal Operating Procedures of the United States Court of Appeals for the Third Circuit, for example, require that briefs and appendices be "distributed sufficiently in advance to afford at least four (4) full weeks' study in chambers prior to the panel sitting.[30] Rule 1.2 lays out the "Responsibility of Panel Prior to Scheduled Sitting," noting that "[t]his court has the tradition of carefully reading briefs and reviewing appendices prior to oral argument or conference."[31]

Most advocates can give enough factual context simply by articulating the issue. In the rare situation where more factual background is necessary, try to spend no more than one or two sentences on these facts. Ideally, the court should not even realize that you are laying out facts; if it does, it should do so only at the moment you move to your argument. Of course,

---

"Chief Justice (with a nod to the Chief), and may it please the Court," or "Chief Justice So to may or, and may it please the Court."

28. Wiener, *supra* note 2, at 201, 203.

29. Williams, *supra* note 9, at 598.

30. Internal Operating Procedures, U.S. Court of Appeals for the Third Circuit 1.1 (Effective July 1, 2002); available at http://www.ca3.uscourts.gov/Rules/IOP-Final.pdf (last accessed May 16, 2010).

31. *Id.*

later in the argument, you should discuss facts in detail as they relate to your points or in answering questions; in the introduction, however, you must be succinct.

Presenting a roadmap of the points you plan to cover has two advantages. First, it gives you at least one opportunity to make those points. With some "hot" courts, that opportunity may be the only one. Second, a roadmap provides the obvious benefit of telling the court the points you plan to address and the order in which you plan to address them. Some courts will let you proceed with your argument if you have named the points that the court is interested in; if you do not provide a roadmap, on the other hand, the judges may interrupt quickly to make sure that you discuss an issue that has provoked their interest. You should not state the points in your roadmap objectively (e.g., don't say, "First, I will address whether the statute passes the heightened scrutiny test"). Instead, state your points argumentatively, and use the roadmap to explain why you are asking for the result you seek.

If you are the first speaker, you may wish to grab the court's attention in the manner in which you describe the case or in your roadmap. Although you should not be overdramatic, you can be argumentative. If you are the respondent or the party opposing the motion, you may wish to grab the court's attention by referring specifically to a question that one of the judges asked of your opponent and explaining its significance to the case. There is no formula for what you should say to grab the court's attention. You must review your case and decide what aspect of the facts, the law, or your argument epitomizes the injustice you seek to have corrected. This is the time to exploit your argument's theme. Identify the commonsense reason why the court should decide the case in your favor.

If you must provide information about your name, your client, and a request for rebuttal, you may believe that the opportunity for an attention-getting opening is lost, but that is not necessarily true. Once you finish this logistical step, simply pause for a brief moment. Just as white space provides a position of emphasis in a written presentation, a pause provides one in an oral presentation. You should use the pause sparingly, but it can be an effective way to separate mundane identification information from the substance of your argument. If you believe that the issue is complex, and that the court needs some legal, factual, or procedural context before it can grasp the crucial point of your argument, move the dramatic statement of your thesis—and the pause—accordingly. That is, identify yourself (if needed), provide needed context, and then pause before stating your thesis in a dramatic way.

The sample introduction below is from a petitioner's argument in *Miller v. Albright*, 523 U.S. 420 (1998). Note that the advocate introduces herself, asks for rebuttal time, tells the court what she is asking it to do, pauses before describing the case in practical terms, and outlines the points that she will address in the argument:

> May it please the Court, I am Glenda de Guzman, and I represent the petitioner, Ms. Lorelyn Penero Miller. At this time I would like to reserve three minutes for rebuttal. Ms. Miller, who was the plaintiff below, is asking this Court to reverse the decision of the United States Court of Appeals for the District of Columbia Circuit. That court upheld the constitutionality of 8 U.S.C. Section 1409(a), which governs the citizenship of children born outside the United States to unmarried parents when only one of the parents has U.S. citizenship. Section 1409(a)

distinguishes among these children based solely on the gender of the child's citizen parent. [Pause.]

Section 1409(a) wrongly uses an irrebuttable gender stereotype to put a time limit on the relationship between a father and his children. This Court should find Section 1409(a) unconstitutional and reverse the decision below for two reasons. First, Section 1409's requirement that only fathers prove a close, personal relationship before their children can be declared citizens is premised on overbroad generalizations abut the relative capabilities of men and women, and thus violates the standard that this Court laid down in the VMI case just last year. Second, even if this Court should apply a less stringent test, Section 1409(a) is still unconstitutional because its concern with unreliable proof of paternity is neither facially legitimate nor rational in 1997.

In the second paragraph, the writer identified her broad themes: The statute should not use irrebuttable gender stereotypes, and it should not impose an arbitrary time limit. Before making this point, she identified the issue that the court is being asked to decide, and provided legal, procedural, and factual context. After stating her themes somewhat dramatically, she provided a roadmap that laid out the legal support behind these themes and told the Court the order in which she plans to proceed.

The respondent need not ask for rebuttal time and can spend much less time introducing the case. The Court should have any needed context thanks to the first speaker's argument.

The respondent should, however, strive to grab the court's attention by showing that he or she is "responsive" to the court's concerns. For example, a respondent representing the other side in the case of *Miller v. Albright* might begin the argument as follows:

> May it please the Court, I am Bradley Walent, and I am counsel for the Respondent, Secretary of State Madeline Albright. [Pause.] A moment ago, Justice Vargo asked counsel for Petitioner whether Section 1409(a) is or is not an immigration statute. Your honors, that question is at the very heart of this argument. This Court has consistently refused to interfere in Congress's decisions about immigration law, and this case is not the time to start. This Court should affirm the decision of the District of Columbia Court of Appeals precisely because Section 1409(a) is an immigration statute, and this Court has traditionally applied a deferential standard when reviewing federal immigration legislation.
>
> Furthermore, under that deferential standard, Section 1409(a) is facially legitimate, and it is rationally related to Congress's goal of promoting close, early family ties with U.S. relatives.

Using the Theme of Your Argument

Trial courts and intermediate appellate courts must follow the mandatory authorities of the Court(s) above them, if any on-point authority governs the case. Courts of last resort, however, and other courts deciding cases of first impression, are more likely to consider the impact that their decision will have on real-world situations.

Accordingly, you must know the commonsense reason behind what you are asking the court to do. Why would a decision in your favor be fair or just? In the case of *Miller v. Albright*, counsel for the young woman seeking citizenship could focus on the inherent unfairness of gender stereotypes or on the problems with imposing an arbitrary time limit on father-daughter relationships. Counsel for the government, on the other hand, might focus on Congress and the importance of respecting Congress's decisions in certain limited areas of law.

The theme is particularly important in oral argument. Having a theme in mind can help you keep the court focused on the reason for a decision in your favor. Frequently, when questions have led you away from the point of your argument, you can recover by returning to your theme. This does not mean that you can avoid answering a question. Instead, answer the question, and then remind the court of your theme. For example, if counsel for the government were asked about the irrebuttable gender stereotype in the statute, he or she could provide a substantive answer, but then say, e.g., "this Court has never examined this type of claim in an immigration statute, because the Court defers to Congress in this area."

In other words, a good theme is a statement that is true even in the face of your opponent's best point. A theme is not a statement of how a legal rule applies, because the court may accept or reject a statement of this type. Instead, it is based on why the court should apply the rule in a certain way. In the *Miller v. Albright* example, both themes are true: the Supreme Court has traditionally deferred to Congress in the area of immigration law, and gender stereotypes are inherently unfair.

Identifying and using a good theme gives you somewhere to "run" when you must concede the existence of a negative fact or legal precedent, and helps you to refocus the court's attention on the equities of your case.

Although the respondent's attorney above did not use a traditional "first, second, third" roadmap, his introduction revealed his theme (deference to Congress), the two points that he planned to make, and the order in which he planned to make them: First, he planned to address the requirement that the Court use a deferential standard; second ("furthermore"), he planned to explain what happens when that deferential standard is applied.

The introduction will take up only a small percentage of your argument time, but you should plan it carefully so that you can obtain optimal benefits.

b.   The Argument Itself

We have already discussed substantive and organizational information regarding the argument itself; Section 20.G.6 and Section 20.I below address how to handle questions during the argument. The transition point from the introduction to the argument is simple. After you have finished the introduction, simply move to your first point. Do not wait for the court to tell you to go on. Although many advocates provide a full sentence of transition between introductory material and the argument, rarely is such a formal shift necessary. Instead of saying, "Now that I have laid out the issues, I will address the first of the three points of my outline," it is usually more effective tobebriefer, e.g., "turning to the first issue . . . " or even "First, . . . " A shorter transition saves both time and the court's patience. If you have prepared effectively, you can proceed to your first point, the rule governing it, the support for that rule (if needed), and the discussion of how that rule applies to the facts. Handling questions from the bench is discussed in Section 20.G.6 and Section 20.I.

c.   The Conclusion

Although the court will often control the amount of time you spend talking about particular points, the good advocate is aware of the passage of time and tries to provide an effective conclusion to his or her argument. In many courts, a podium light system is used: A green light is displayed throughout most of the argument; a yellow light signals that time is running short (how short varies from court to court—e.g., there may be two to five minutes remaining when the light turns on); and a red light signals that time is up. Counsel should never stop the court from asking questions in order to conclude. However, if the court is quiet, and the yellow light is on, counsel may decide to conclude rather than to launch into his or her final (and presumably weakest) point. If you are arguing before the United States Supreme Court, or another court that requires you to preserve your time for rebuttal, you might look for a way to conclude early.

Like the conclusion to a brief, the conclusion to an oral argument should be short and sweet. At a minimum, it should tell the court what you want it to do. In an appellate argument, you will typically be asking the court to affirm, reverse, or reverse and remand a decision; in a motion argument, you will be asking the court to grant or deny the motion. If more time is available, counsel may want to recap the main reasons that support his or her conclusion, as in the following conclusion that might be appropriate for the petitioner in *Miller v. Albright*:

> Even in the area of immigration, Congress does not have the authority to pass a law that violates the Equal Protection Clause of the Constitution. Section 1409(a) denies equal protection to children of men who are U.S. citizens. Rather than promoting family ties between a father and a child, Section 1409(a) prevents those ties from developing further. For all of these reasons, this Court should reverse the decision of the District of Columbia Court of Appeals. Thank you.

If you are still in conversation with the court when your time elapses, you must acknowledge that time has run out and ask for permission to continue. If the court is asking you a question when your time elapses, pay careful attention to the question and plan your answer. Before answering, however, inform the court that time is up and ask if you may have time to answer the question. Most courts will give you permission. Unless you are asked still more questions, segue from your answer into your conclusion. Even if you have a strong, dramatic conclusion planned, do not use it if time has already elapsed, even if the court has given you permission to continue. This is the time to move to a one-sentence conclusion, e.g., "Therefore, because Section 1409(a) makes unconstitutional distinctions based on gender stereotypes, this Court should affirm the decision below. Thank you."[32]

32. For more information on making your conclusion effective, see Section 14.5.3 [Mary Beth Beazley, A Practical Guide to Appellate Advocacy, 3rd ed., (2010)].

6.   *Handling Questions from the Bench*

All of the hard work that you have completed to prepare you for the argument should have one purpose: enabling you to answer the court's questions.[33] Some questions may be answered by your argument itself—that is, you will have anticipated the court's concerns—but many others will come up the old-fashioned way: The court will interrupt your presentation and demand your attention. How you handle these interruptions says everything about your skill as an oral advocate and may even determine whether you win or lose your case.

The first thing you must do is let the court interrupt you. As Justice Ginsburg has noted, some attorneys—foolishly—try to squelch the court's questions by talking louder and more quickly when a judge tries to speak:

> A race the lawyer is bound to lose is the press-straight-on run when a judge attempts to interject a question. More than occasionally, I have repeated a lawyer's name three times before he gives way to my inquiry. Despite his strong desire to continue orating, the lawyer should stop talking when the judge starts.[34]

Remember that your job is not to "get through your stuff." Instead, you are there to find out what the judges are interested in, and so you should stop talking immediately when one of them tries to reveal an area of interest by asking a question. As one judge has noted, "questions are your friends."[35] Judge Williams has suggested that "[q]uestions are not interruptions, they are opportunities. The questions from the bench are the only indication of what issues are bothering the judges[,] and [the questions] may clue you in on what is preventing them from seeing the case your way."[36]

Thus, maintain eye contact so that you can see any nonverbal signals that one of the judges has a question. Speak slowly enough to allow the judges time to interject. If one of the judges makes the slightest noise or attempts to interrupt, you should stop speaking to give the judge a moment to ask a question. Use every technique possible to let the court know that you welcome its questions.

Do not presume that all questions will be hostile. On multi-judge panels, judges frequently use counsel to advance an argument that they already agree with, in hopes of gathering more votes. Justice Ginsburg has admitted that "[s]ometimes we ask questions with persuasion of our colleagues in mind, in an effort to assist counsel to strengthen a position."[37] Judge Williams has advised that "you may encounter a judge who is in favor of your position and spends time asking you easy questions that lead you to an even stronger version of your position."[38]

Second, you must listen to the question. Do not rush to give an answer. Oral argument is not a quiz show in which you must beat your opponent to the buzzer. Instead, listen carefully to make sure that you understand what the court is trying to do.[39] Some questions ask for a concession. At other times, as noted

---

33. *See* Richard H. Seamon, *Preparing for Oral Argument in the United States Supreme Court*, 50 S.C. L. Rev. 603 (1999), for advice on preparing for oral argument primarily by anticipating and planning answers for the court's questions.

34. Ginsburg, *supra* note 1, at 569.

35. Judge Bruce D. Willis, *Suggestions from the Bench: Things Judges Wish That Appellate Lawyers Would Do Differently*, 35 Wm. Mitchell L. Rev. 1281, 1285 (2009).

36. Williams, *supra* note 9, at 599.

37. Ginsburg, *supra* note 1, at 569.

38. Williams, *supra* note 9, at 599.

39. *See* Gersten, *supra* note 11, at 28 (noting that one of the two most common oral argument mistakes is "not listening to the judges' questions and the tenor of the discourse); *see also* Dwyer,

previously, a judge may try to advance your point of view by asking a question designed to reveal your best arguments. Some questions ask you to identify or explain a policy supporting your thesis or seek information about a case or other authority. Some questions focus on the point you are addressing, while others show that the court has moved on to a new issue. Listen to the question and assess what the court is asking before you try to answer.

If you do not understand the question, you may seek clarification. Ideally, you should try to articulate what you think the court has asked, e.g., "I'm not sure that I understand your question, Judge Lowe. I believe that you are asking whether this Court has ever invalidated an immigration statute." This statement does not demand an answer from a court, but it allows the court to correct you if you are mistaken. Tone is important here; do not emphasize the word "believe" in any way, lest you imply that you are struggling to understand a poorly-worded question. Admittedly, the question may have been poorly worded (which is not surprising, since the judge may be figuring out the question while asking it), but you do not want to point this out to the court. After you signal that you may need clarification, pause very briefly to give the court an opportunity to correct you if needed. If no correction comes, simply answer the question as you have stated it. Few judges will take offense at an attempt for clarification, as long as counsel does so in a respectful way.

Third, you should answer the question directly. Judge Williams has recommended that advocates "[r]espond immediately to a question with a 'yes,' 'no,' 'it depends,' or 'I don't know.'"[40] Some advocates, perhaps fearful that a direct answer will reveal a weakness in the case, try to launch into an explanation of the significance of the answer before they give the answer itself.[41] This tactic is a mistake because the court doesn't hear the explanation; it hears only that counsel has refused to answer a direct question with a direct answer.[42] Furthermore, you risk forgetting to answer the question directly or, more commonly, being interrupted before you can do so. The court will be much better able to listen to your explanation if you first satisfy the court's need for an answer to its question. Of course, it is very important that you *give* the explanation. Many attorneys refer to this kind of exchange as a "yes, but" answer. You must agree with the fact or legal rule that the court has laid before you, but you disagree as to its significance. It is perfectly appropriate to make a concession and then explain why that concession does not affect your argument.

Fourth, you should tie your answer to your argument. Judge Williams has advised, "Follow your short answer with a concise explanation and citation to the record or precedent as necessary."[43] This technique is just as important with friendly questions as it is with more challenging questions. If a judge asks you a question that advances your argument, you should use the opportunity to advance that point to its end. If you must answer a difficult question with a "yes, but" answer, you should answer a friendly question with a "yes, and" answer, as in "yes, and here's why." The judge who asks you a friendly question may well

Feldman & Nylander, *supra* note 4, at 348-51 (identifying common categories of questions and describing how to deal with them effectively).

40. Williams, *supra* note 9, at 599.

41. *See also* Gersten, *supra* note 11, at 29 ("Answer the question honestly, even if you are afraid this might hurt your case. There is nothing worse than losing credibility with the court.").

42. *See also id.* ("If you do not answer the question directly, or if you become evasive, the judge will find it difficult to listen to your argument because he or she will still be thinking about the unanswered question.").

43. Williams, *supra* note 9, at 599.

be disappointed if you do not do so. As one judge has noted, "a judge might ask you whether there is sufficient evidence in the record to support a jury's find-ing[.] [S]he is not asking because she thinks the evidence is insufficient, but because she wants you to describe that evidence in detail for the benefit of the other judges."[44]

After you have finished answering the question and explaining your answer, it is time to move back to your argument. Do not wait to be told to go on. If the Court is not asking you a question, you have the floor, and you set the agenda. At this juncture, you must decide whether to return to the point you were mak-ing, or continue on to another point.

If the court has asked a question that moves you to your second issue while you were still addressing your first, for example, you may be wise to continue with other support for that second point. The court may have been signaling you that it is not interested in the first issue, either because it already agrees with you or because there is no way that it will ever agree with you. In either circum-stance, time is better spent on an issue in which the court has shown its interest.

If the court has asked you about an issue that you believe is irrelevant to the case, you must still answer the question, if you are able. You may let the court know that you think the question is irrelevant by respectfully pointing out the fact, legal rule, or other information that shows that the resolution of your case does not require resolution of the issue that it asked about, e.g., "Yes, your honor, that is true. However, in this case, Officer O'Donnell testified that he had no reason to believe that Mr. Richardson was violating any laws when he conducted the search."

Similarly, do not dismiss hypothetical questions without an answer. Justice Ginsburg has expressed dismay over advocates' repeated dismissals of hypothet-ical questions with the pat answer, "That is not this case, your honor": "[The judge] knows, of course, that her hypothetical is not this case, but she also knows the opinion she writes generally will affect more than this case. The precedent set may reach her hypothetical."[45] When judges pose hypotheticals, they are testing the boundaries of the rule you suggest. The good advocate knows the boundaries of the rule he or she recommends, and so is able to explain how the proposed rule would govern the hypotheticals posed by the court.

7.   Rebuttal

Counsel for the petitioner or moving party should not reserve important *arguments* for rebuttal. Supreme Court Rule 28.5 provides that "counsel making the opening argument shall present the case fairly and completely and not reserve points of substance for rebuttal." In many courts, including the United States Supreme Court, counsel may not set aside time for rebuttal; counsel can preserve time for rebuttal only by stemming the tide of the justices' questions before his or her allotted time has elapsed. You may wish to reserve time strate-gically, depending on local custom. For example, some courts allow counsel to reserve time for rebuttal, and give counsel only the time reserved. Other courts, in contrast, give counsel the reserved time along with any argument time that

---

44. Dwyer, Feldman & Nylander, *supra* note 4, at 350.
45. Ginsburg, *supra* note 1, at 569-70.

was unused. If the court limits rebuttal to the time reserved, you should reserve a more generous amount of time; if the court adds unused argument time to the rebuttal, you can reserve less time. Be sure you understand your own local rules as to rebuttal before the day of your argument.

Although final decisions about what to say in rebuttal must be made on the spot, there are some guidelines you can follow to make your rebuttal more effective. First, remember that rebuttal is for rebuttal only.[46] Any point you make on rebuttal should be a response to a point made during your opponent's argument. Some courts will interrupt counsel who try to use rebuttal to "finish up" the main argument, saying, "Counselor, do you have any rebuttal to offer?"

Second, even though you must use rebuttal to respond to statements that opposing counsel has made during the argument, you should prepare for rebuttal while you prepare your argument. You can reasonably anticipate many of the points that your opponent will make. In a moot court argument, you might identify the points to which you have a "clean" response—that is, a response that will not draw painful questions from the bench. In real life, of course, you should identify the points that are most crucial to your argument, for you must address those points even if they result in painful questions.

Plan ahead, even make an outline, and then, during the argument, note which points your opponent actually makes. You might even jot down a word or phrase from your opponent's presentation to make your point more effective, e.g., "Your honors, counsel for Respondent stated that Ms. Miller's attempts to establish a relationship with her father were 'too little, too late.' This time limit on family relationships is precisely what is wrong with Section 1409(a)."

Third, don't sweat the small stuff. Unless an otherwise small error has legal significance in your case, rebuttal is not the time to point out that your opponent has given the wrong year in a case citation, confused the parties' names, or made some other picayune error. This kind of fussiness hurts you more than it helps you.

Finally, make your points and then sit down. Although this advice holds true at all stages in the argument, it is particularly important on rebuttal. When you stand up to give your rebuttal, address the court and then tell it how many points you plan to make, e.g., "Your honors, I have two points on rebuttal. First, counsel for Respondent stated. . . . This is irrelevant because . . . . Second, counsel cited. . . . That case does not apply here because. . . . Thank you."

Be aware that many courts do not listen passively to a rebuttal. Thus, you must be as prepared to answer questions during the rebuttal as you were during your main argument. It can be helpful, therefore, to let the court know how many points you intend to make; courts that have this knowledge may allow you to make all of your points, even if they have used up your time with questions.

H.   PREPARATION

1. The Record.   Thoroughly know the facts in the Record. For the important facts, be able to cite the page on which they appear. Do not overstate the facts, and do not state as facts the inferences you ask the court to draw from the facts.

---

46. *See, e.g.,* Wiener, *supra* note 2, at 199, 202.

If you misstate facts, you will have lost credibility with the Court, and if you misstate facts intentionally, you will have acted unethically.[47]

2. Outline your argument.   Usually the outline of your argument should mirror the large-scale organization of your brief, as described in Chapters 19 [Linda H. Edwards, Legal Writing: Process, Analysis, and Organization, 5th ed., (2010)] and 15. The first level of headings should articulate your position on each relevant element of the governing rule. Under each heading, place as subheadings each argument you will make on that element, and under that subheading, place each point you will make in that part of the argument.

3. Prepare your folder.   Prepare a folder with your notes for oral argument. You can use a file folder and small index cards. Open the folder and use both sides for your opening and closing language (in case you panic), for important factual information to which you might need to refer (for example, dates and relevant numbers you might not remember), and for the outline of your argument.

Consider including two outlines, one for a cold bench (a bench that asks few questions) and one for a hot bench (a bench that leaves you little time for your scripted material). The outline for the cold bench is your expanded outline—the one you will use if the judges are quiet and you have time to present most of your prepared material. The outline for the hot bench is compressed into just the main points you want to make in case you have only a few minutes. You can start with the expanded outline but shift to the compressed outline as necessary during the argument.

Reserve one area of the folder for the index cards. For each important case, statute, or regulation, summarize on a card the important information from that source and quote any key language. Tape the cards on top of each other with the bottom of each card protruding a quarter of an inch from beneath the card on top of it. Tape the cards to the folder along the card's top edge, so the cards can be flipped up like an address file. In the visible space on the bottom of each card, write the name or the case, statute, or regulation. Practice finding the information on the cards and in the other parts of the folder quickly and easily.

4. Script the entire opening, the conclusion, and your prepared rebuttal. While you cannot and should not try to script the body of the argument, the opening and closing should be scripted, essentially memorized, delivered with full eye contact, and spoken as if they were not memorized. This preparation will guarantee that you say what you want to say and that you say it smoothly and effectively. Although your extemporaneous responses might not always be smooth, your beginnings and endings can and should achieve a high level of poise and persuasion.

5. Practice.   Practice delivering your argument to friends. Have the friends question you just as they would if they were the judges before whom you will argue. Practice at least five or six times, and more if possible. Go through the whole argument each time, and then ask for feedback. Use these practice

---

47. *See* Chapter 3.

benches to improve both your knowledge of the case and the smoothness of your delivery.

6. Visit the courtroom.   Familiarize yourself with the room where you will argue. Imagine yourself delivering your argument there, and remind yourself that you belong there, advocating for your client. Psychologically claim the space.

I.   HANDLING QUESTIONS FROM THE BENCH

Because a primary purpose of oral argument is to answer the judges' questions, a big part of your preparation should consist of getting ready to provide those answers. Here are some important points to guide your preparation.

1. Anticipate questions.   Ask yourself what you would want to know if you were a judge hearing the case. What parts of the argument would be hard to accept and why? What will your opponent argue? What key cases or statutes will the court be most concerned about? Also, pay close attention to the questions you receive in your practice rounds. Prepare answers for all of these questions.

2. Attitude.   The judges will ask you questions and they will often interrupt you to do it. This is part of the role of a judge. It is efficient and it saves you precious time. When a judge interrupts you, stop talking *immediately* and listen to what the judge is saying. Then answer the judge's question as best you can. Treat the question for what it is—a valuable opportunity to clarify a point about which the judge is concerned. Do not appear to be rushing through the answer so you can get back into your prepared argument. The judge's question is more important than your prepared argument.
The right to interrupt belongs only to the judge, however. Never interrupt a judge. No matter how badly you want to speak, wait patiently until the judge has finished speaking before you utter a sound.

3. Recognize types of questions.   You will encounter three basic kinds of questions: friendly questions; questions genuinely seeking clarification of information; and adversarial questions.
A friendly question is designed to help you present your argument or make an additional point. A judge might want you to make a certain point primarily for the benefit of another judge, or a judge might simply be pleased to have thought of another point and might want to share it. Be sure to recognize a friendly question and to make use of the opportunity it gives you to agree with a judge and to articulate and validate the judge's point.
A question genuinely seeking information is an opportunity to be helpful to a judge who needs a point clarified. Do so willingly. Then, if you have a point to make about the subject of the inquiry, you can use this chance to make it, but only after you have answered the judge's question.
You might find that most of the questions you receive are adversarial, designed to test your arguments. Despite their threatening nature, these are the questions you should welcome most because these are the questions that

allow you to resolve the concerns that could stand in the way of achieving the result you seek. Often these questions will be politely phrased, but sometimes a judge will deliver the question in an intimidating, angry, or even rude manner. Your job is to answer politely but firmly, ignoring the packaging of the question and responding only to its content. Do not respond in anger, even if you are feeling angry. Remain calm, at least outwardly, and answer the question as best you can.

> Your Honor, I must respectfully disagree. In the *Jones* case, the Supreme Court did not hold that. . . . Rather,. . . . And this is precisely why. . . .

4. Listen carefully to the question. You might find that your nervousness impedes your ability to listen carefully to the question. After you hear the first part of the question, you might assume that you know what the judge will be asking, and your nervousness could cause you to begin scrambling to formulate an answer. Yet you cannot answer a question that you have misunderstood. When a judge begins to speak, remember to listen carefully to the whole question before you answer.

5. Clarify the question. Sometimes you will not understand a question even when you have listened carefully. This could happen because you are nervous or because the judge has not articulated the question clearly. Simply admit that you did not understand the question, apologize, and ask the judge to repeat it. If you think that you might have understood it but you are not sure, you can clarify your understanding: "Is Your Honor asking whether . . . ?"

6. Begin with a clear, direct answer. Usually you will want to say a number of things in response to a question. However, you should always begin with a very short, direct answer to the question in the form in which the judge posed it: "Yes, Your Honor," or "No, Your Honor, I must respectfully disagree," or "Your Honor, that has sometimes been the case, but not always." After you have responded directly, you can go on to explain your answer, but the judge should know within roughly your first ten words what your answer to the question will be.

7. Returning to your prepared presentation. When you have finished answering a question, return immediately to your prepared presentation. Do not wait for the judge to respond or to give you permission to return to your prepared material. Try to find a way to connect the ending of your answer to an entry point into your argument so that the answer seamlessly weaves you right back into your prepared material. However, if you cannot think of a connection on the spot, simply return to your argument.

8. Handling questions on your co-counsel's issue. Sometimes a judge will ask you a question about the issue your co-counsel has already argued or will shortly argue. Try to answer it if you can, but qualify your answer by admitting that your co-counsel might be able to provide a better answer. This should minimize the chance that the judge will pursue the matter further.

Your Honor, since *Home Finders* dealt with the issue of sufficiency of money damages, my co-counsel may be the best person to assist the Court on this question. However, I believe that the court there held that. . . .

9. Handling a question for which you do not have an answer.   Your your hard work should prepare you for most questions, but you might be asked a question for which you do not have an answer. A judge might ask you about a case or a statute with which you are not familiar, about how your issue compares to the comparable issue in some other area of law, or about how some particular procedural practice would affect your position. Even experienced appellate attorneys do not know all aspects of the law. If you do not know the answer to a judge's question, admit it. You can offer to find the answer and provide it to the court promptly after the argument concludes:

Your Honor, I regret that I am not familiar with *Hatcher v. Norman.* However, if the Court allows, I will provide the Court with an answer to this question within twenty-four hours after today's argument concludes.

10. Agreeing when you can.   Remember that you will probably receive a friendly question here and there, so don't automatically disagree each time the judge engages you. You can even agree partially with the concerns underlying some adversary questions as well, but go on to show why that valid concern does not defeat your position:

Yes, your Honor, I agree that this is a legitimate concern. However,. . . .

11. Referring to earlier questions or comments from the bench.   Remember the questions directed to you or to your opponent; you can refer to them when appropriate in your argument. If a judge has asked you a friendly question or made a friendly comment, you can refer to it later in the argument. You can refer also to the adversarial questions or comments directed to opposing counsel.

As Justice Bailey pointed out,. . . .

Use this technique sparingly, however. Some judges might be irritated to hear their own words used in this manner more than once or, at most, twice during an argument.

J.   PRESENTATION

1. Dress.   Wear a conservative suit.

2. Body, hands, and eyes.   Stand straight, with your weight equally placed on both feet, and remain behind the podium. Maintain eye contact with the judges, and include the whole bench in that eye contact. Do not read your argument. Rather, speak to the judges conversationally, looking down at your notes now and then. Lay your hands on the podium, and use them only moderately for occasional small gestures. Don't grip the podium. Don't put your hands in your pockets or clasp them behind your back.

3. Voice.   Speak at a moderate pace. Don't allow your nervousness to cause you to speak too quickly, but do speak with a degree of energy appropriate for discussion of an important matter about which you and your client care deeply. Speak firmly and loudly enough to be heard.

4. References.   Refer to the bench as "Your Honors" or "the Court." Refer to individual judges as "Your Honor" or "Justice [last name]." Refer to clients by their last name preceded by "Mr." or "Ms." or by other appropriate titles, such as "Dr." Refer to other lawyers as "counsel for Appellant/Appellee" or as "opposing counsel."

5. Nervousness.   Oral argument will probably make you a little nervous, but remember that judges are human beings. Like you, they are trying to do a hard job well, and they will sometimes fall short. Although they have more experience than you do at this point in your legal career, they probably remember when they did not. All they ask of you, and all you need ask of yourself, is to do your best.

___

COFFEE SYSTEM OF ATLANTA v. FOX
226 Ga. 593, 176 S.E.2d 71 (1970)

Supreme Court of Georgia

HAWES, Justice.

The appeal here is from the final judgment and order dismissing the complaint for failure to state a claim upon which relief can be granted. Coffee System of Atlanta sued Fox and Intercontinental Coffee Service Plan seeking damages and a temporary and permanent injunction against the continued violation of a restrictive covenant entered into between Fox and the plaintiff as[1] a part of an employment contract. Under the contract, Fox was employed by Coffee System, Inc., as a senior sales representative "to offer, on its behalf, its 'Coffee System' service, and to sell its replacement kits, within" the territory of Fulton, DeKalb, Cobb and ten other named counties in the State of Georgia. The trial court issued a temporary ex parte restraining order on the 7th day of January, 1970. On January 26, 1970, the matter came on for a hearing on the question of whether the temporary injunction should be granted, and at that time the defendant Fox filed a written motion to dismiss the complaint for failure to state a claim. The judge, before whom the matter was heard, passed an order, which, insofar as is pertinent, reads: "After hearing argument of counsel for defendant and plaintiff, . . . it appearing that the restrictions in the contract under consideration . . . are uncertain, indefinite, unreasonable, and impose upon the employee greater limitations than are necessary for the protection of the employer, they are therefore illegal, unenforceable, null and void. . . . Therefore, it is hereby ordered, adjudged and decreed that the complaint be, and it is hereby, dismissed for failure to state a claim upon which relief can be granted."

The material and relevant parts of the contract sued on provide that Fox "agrees to use his best efforts to the exclusion of all other employment, in order to promote and solicit sales of the company's coffee system service in the aforesaid territory, and to perform any and all other services reasonably required by company in connection with the merchandising of such service . . . [He] agrees that, for the term of this agreement and for one (1) year following the

___

1. [Citations and footnotes within the cases reprinted here have been deleted without indication. Where footnotes are included, the original footnote numbers have been retained.]

termination hereof, he will not, directly or indirectly in any capacity, solicit or accept orders of business located within the area assigned to [him] during any part of the two (2) year period immediately preceding the termination of his employment for any program, service, equipment or product similar to or competitive with the business of the company from any organization or individual which or who has been a customer of the company during any part of the two (2) year period immediately preceding termination of his employment, or who or which was actively solicited as a customer by company during the period of this agreement. . . . That he will not, during the term of his employment, and for a period of one year thereafter divulge to anyone other than an authorized employee of employer, and after the term of his employment will not use any information or knowledge relating to sales prospects, business methods and/or techniques which were acquired by him during the term of his employment."

1. Among those contracts which are against public policy and which cannot be enforced are contracts in general restraint of trade. Code § 20-504. However, "a contract only in partial restraint may be upheld, 'provided the restraint be reasonable,' and the contract be valid in other essentials. A contract concerning a lawful and useful business in partial restraint of trade and reasonably limited as to time and territory, and otherwise reasonable, is not void."

2. An examination of the decided cases on restrictive covenants reveals that this court has customarily considered three separate elements of such contracts in determining whether they are reasonable or not. These three elements may be categorized as (1) the restraint in the activity of the employee, or former employee, imposed by the contract; (2) the territorial or geographic restraint; and (3) the length of time during which the covenant seeks to impose the restraint. It has been said that no better test can be applied to the question of whether a restrictive covenant is reasonable or not than by considering whether the restraint "is such only as to afford a fair protection to the interest of the party in favor of whom it is given, and not so large as to interfere with the interest of the public. Whatever restraint is larger than the necessary protection of the party can be of no benefit to either; it can only be oppressive, and if oppressive, it is in the eye of the law unreasonable. . . . There can be no doubt that an agreement that during the term of the service, and for a reasonable period thereafter, the employee shall not become interested in or engage in a rival business, is reasonable and valid, the contract being otherwise legal and not in general restraint of trade. This is the rule followed by a majority of the American Courts and is supported by reason. . . . This court seems to be committed to the rule that the contract must be limited both as to time and territory, and not otherwise unreasonable. If limited as to both time and territory, the contract is illegal if it be unreasonable in other respects. And, with respect to restrictive agreements ancillary to a contract of employment, the mere fact that the contract is unlimited as to either time or territory is sufficient to condemn it as unreasonable." Shirk v. Loftis Bros. & Co., 148 Ga. 500, 504, 97 S.E. 66.

3. Two of the elements referred to in the preceding division lend themselves to more or less exact comparison with the yardstick laid down by previous cases. The proscription against competition by the defendant embodied in the restrictive covenant in this case extends to 13 named counties in the State of Georgia. Insofar as geographic area is concerned, this is undoubtedly a reasonable restriction to be upheld by the courts if the contract is otherwise reasonable and not oppressive. The limitation as to the time within which the defendant may not engage in a competitive employment or enterprise, being one year

from the termination of his employment with the plaintiff, is reasonable and not such a restriction as would render the contract void.

4. We now turn to the question of the reasonableness of the restriction against the activities of the defendant as contained in the covenant. The defendant Fox was employed by the defendant as a sales representative to offer on behalf of the plaintiff its " 'Coffee System' service, and to sell its replacement kits." He agreed that he would not, directly or indirectly, in any capacity, solicit or accept orders of business located within the area assigned to him (that is, the 13 named counties) during his employment with the plaintiff and for one year thereafter "for any program, service, equipment or product similar to or competitive with the business of" the plaintiff, and that he would refrain from doing this with respect to any organization which, or individual who, had been a customer or had been solicited as a customer of plaintiff during that term. It must be noted that the contract does not restrict the plaintiff from accepting *employment* with a competitor, so long as such employment does not involve the direct or indirect solicitation and acceptance of orders from customers or those solicited as customers of the plaintiff. Even if the enforcement of the broad language forbidding the use by the defendant of business methods and techniques acquired during his employment with the plaintiff should, if enforced, effectively prevent the defendant from accepting employment with any other competitor of the plaintiff within the limited area and time of the operation of the contract, it would not render the contract void as a matter of law. See Shirk v. Loftis Bros. & Co., supra, where a contract in which the employee covenanted that he would "not directly or indirectly, under any circumstances or conditions whatsoever, for himself [or] for any other person, firm, or corporation, engage in or be or become interested or be employed, directly or indirectly . . . as an individual, partner, stockholder, director, officer, clerk, salesman, buyer, principal, agent, employee, trustee, or in any relation or capacity whatsoever, in the line of business carried on by" the plaintiff. That contract was upheld by this court as not imposing too broad a restriction on the defendant since the proscription of the contract only related to Fulton County and was limited as to time to four years. As a general rule, this court seems to have established the principle in cases of this kind that, where the restraint as to time and territory is reasonably limited, a general prohibition against soliciting customers and accounts of the employer will be upheld. We need hold no more than that in this case.

With respect to the definition or description of the business engaged in by the plaintiff and which the defendant was employed by the plaintiff to conduct, the contract only refers to it as a "Coffee System Service," but we think this is enough. This court has upheld restrictive covenants where the description of the business was no more specific. The restraint imposed by the contract in this case is no more than is reasonably necessary to afford fair protection to the interests of the employer and is not unduly oppressive of the employee. It is not void for any reason urged by the appellee.

5. It follows that the trial court erred in sustaining the motion to dismiss and in dismissing the complaint. It should be kept in mind that this case was brought under the Civil Practice Act, and that the former rules of strict pleading no longer apply. We have looked only to the contract, as it is apparent the trial court did, in reaching the conclusion we have reached. The complaint, itself, sufficiently sets forth the existence of the contract and a breach thereof and it was not subject to being dismissed for failure to state a claim. From the

language of the order appealed from, it is clear that the trial judge did not reach the question of whether to grant or deny a temporary injunction. Therefore, no question in that regard is presented for our decision on this appeal.

Judgment reversed.

All the Justices concur.

CLEIN v. KAPILOFF
213 Ga. 369, 98 S.E.2d 897 (1957)

Supreme Court of Georgia

ALMAND, Justice.

The bill of exceptions assigns error on orders overruling general demurrers to an equitable petition, and granting an interlocutory injunction.

The petition of Harry Kapiloff and Sam Turetsky sought to restrain the defendant Sidney A. Clein from engaging in the retail clothing business in violation of a restrictive covenant entered into by the defendant Clein and other named defendants with the plaintiffs. In substance, the petition alleged: that the plaintiffs, prior to August 28, 1950, owned and controlled Macey's, Inc., a corporation engaged in the retail jewelry business at 110 Whitehall Street in the City of Atlanta; that the plaintiffs sold said business to Sterling Jewelry Company, a corporation owned and controlled by the named defendants; that the written contract of sale, signed by both corporations through the plaintiff Kapiloff as president of Macey's, Inc., and the defendant Clein as vice-president of Sterling Jewelry Company, Inc., contained the following covenant: "4. *Restrictive covenants.* Seller covenants and agrees that it will not, throughout the term of the lease assigned hereunder [July 31, 1959], engage in the retail jewelry business, or in the sale of any items normally sold by a retail jewelry company, other than television sets, within a radius of one mile from the premises herein described, and *buyer covenants that it will not engage in the operation of a retail clothing business on the premises, nor will it engage in the sale of items normally sold in a retail clothing store on the premises or within a radius of one-half mile of the premises, throughout the term of the lease* [July 31, 1959] *herein assigned.*" (Italics and brackets supplied.) Following the corporate signatures in the contract of sale, all of the named plaintiffs and defendants agreed in writing that the "restrictive covenants mentioned in paragraph 4 of the within agreement are hereby adopted and agreed to by us individually, and any one acting for us, or any firm, corporation, or partnership in which any of us may have an interest." The seller conveyed to the buyer all of his accounts receivable, the plaintiff Kapiloff agreed to assign the lease in 110 Whitehall Street to the buyer, and the defendant Clein agreed to endorse the purchase money notes. At the time of the sale, the plaintiffs were engaged in the retail clothing business at 114 Whitehall Street under the name of Hollywood Credit Clothiers. It was alleged that, at the time of the sale, the defendants "knew that the accounts of customers of said jewelry business were in a great part the same as the accounts of the petitioners' retail credit clothing business and petitions as a consideration of said sale and agreement insisted that defendants covenant not to engage in the clothing business because a great number of the accounts of the two said stores were of the same customers. Petitioners show that defendants knew that if they were allowed to sell clothing to petitioners' jewelry accounts after said jewelry business was sold to them, that they would be dealing with many of the customers of petitioners' said credit clothing business, as aforesaid, and they knew that petitioners insisted upon said covenant to protect themselves from that situation." It was further alleged that the defendant Clein is now engaged in the business of selling clothing at retail at 132 Whitehall Street, which is within one-half mile of the premises at 110 Whitehall Street, in violation of this covenant, and that the defendant Clein, by engaging in the retail clothing business in competition with the plaintiffs, will cause them irreparable damage and injury.

1. As a general rule, a contract in general restraint of trade is void, but a contract only in partial restraint may be upheld provided the restraint is reasonable and the contract is valid in the other essentials. In determining the reasonableness of a restrictive covenant, a greater latitude is allowed when the covenant relates to the sale of a business than in cases where the covenant is ancillary to a contract of employment. The agreement must be considered with reference to the situation, business and objects of the parties in light of all of the surrounding circumstances. The restrictive covenant in the instant case is reasonable as to time and territory, its area of operation being within a radius of one-half mile, and its time being limited to July 31, 1959. The true test of the validity of the contract is whether it is supported by a sufficient consideration and whether the restraint is reasonable. In determining whether the covenant is "otherwise reasonable," the covenant must be reasonably necessary to protect the interests of the party is whose favor it is imposed, and must not unduly prejudice the interests of the public, and must not impose greater restrictions than are necessary for the protection of the promisee.

In this case, the plaintiffs bound themselves not to compete with the defendants in the retail jewelry business within one mile of 110 Whitehall Street during a period ending July 31, 1959, and the defendants, knowing that the plaintiffs were then engaged in the retail clothing business at 114 Whitehall Street, agreed that, within a like period of time, they would not engage in the retail clothing business within one-half mile of 110 Whitehall Street. The covenant is reasonable in all respects, and there are no allegations in the petition which indicate that the public would suffer in having one less retail clothing store in this limited area for the time specified. We have here simply a case where the sellers and the buyers of a business have entered into a valid contract containing mutual obligations, and one party has chosen to ignore his obligation. In such a case, equity will exercise its restraining arm and require him to abide by his promise.

The petition sets forth a cause of action for the relief prayed, and the court did not err in overruling the general demurrers of Clein.

2. On the interlocutory hearing, the case was submitted upon an agreed stipulation of facts. Under the evidence submitted, the court did not err in granting an interlocutory injunction.

Judgment affirmed.

All the Justices concur.

INDEX